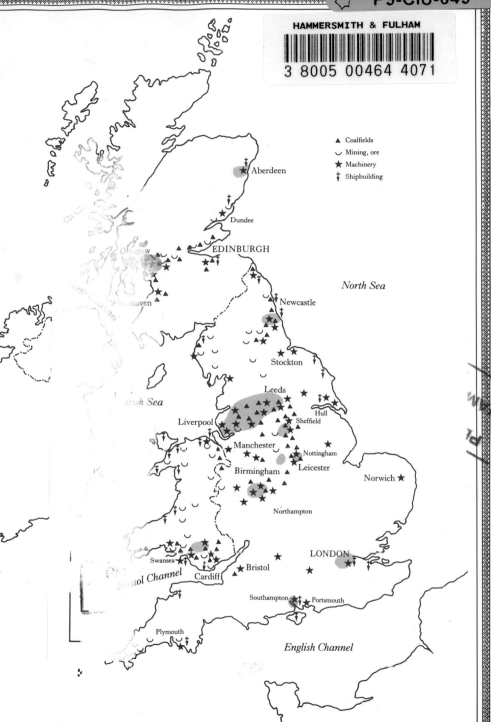

▲ Coalfields
⌣ Mining, ore
★ Machinery
‡ Shipbuilding

North Sea

Aberdeen

Dundee

Glasgow

EDINBURGH

Whitehaven

Newcastle

Stockton

Irish Sea

Leeds

Liverpool

Hull

Sheffield

Manchester

Nottingham

Birmingham

Leicester

Norwich ★

Northampton

LONDON

Swansea

Bristol

Cardiff

Bristol Channel

Southampton

Portsmouth

Plymouth

English Channel

THE SEARCH FOR JUSTICE

A HISTORY OF BRITAIN
AND THE BRITISH PEOPLE

VOLUME III

THE SEARCH
FOR JUSTICE

Arthur Bryant

'Ring out a slowly dying cause,
  And ancient forms of party strife;
  Ring in the nobler modes of life,
With sweeter manners, purer laws.

'Ring out false pride in place and blood,
  The civic slander and the spite;
  Ring in the love of truth and right,
Ring in the common love of good.

'Ring out old shapes of foul disease;
  Ring out the narrowing lust of gold;
  Ring out the thousand wars of old,
Ring in the thousand years of peace.'

Tennyson

COLLINS
London w1
1990

William Collins Sons & Co. Ltd
London · Glasgow · Sydney · Auckland
Toronto · Johannesburg

A CIP catalogue record for this book is available from the
British Library.

ISBN 0 00 217412 X

Some of the material in this book was first published in 1940,
1943, 1957, 1959, 1967

Picture research by Sara Waters
Maps by Leslie Robinson

Photoset in Linotron Imprint by
Rowland Phototypesetting Ltd
Bury St Edmunds, Suffolk
Printed and bound in Great Britain by
William Collins Sons & Co. Ltd, Glasgow

CONTENTS

ILLUSTRATIONS

PUBLISHER'S NOTE

When Sir Arthur Bryant died, this book, like its predecessor *Freedom's Own Island*, was found to be substantially complete. The small number of gaps left by Sir
Arthur have been filled by incorporating material he
had published during his lifetime. The publishers are
grateful to Mr J. M. Thomas for his invaluable help
in preparing the final typescript for publication.

They would also like to thank Lady Bryant, Mrs
Pamela McCormick, Mrs Alwynne Bardsley, Mr
Christopher Falkus and Mr Alan Macfadyen for their
continuing encouragement and advice.

CHAPTER ONE

Triumphant Island

'For States, as for individuals, true
prosperity consists, not in acquiring or
invading the domains of others, but in
making the best of one's own.'
Talleyrand

'There lives not form nor feeling in my soul
Unborrowed from my country'
Coleridge

'ENGLAND HAS SAVED HERSELF by her exertions,' Pitt declared at the
Lord Mayor's Banquet after Trafalgar, 'and will, I trust, save Europe
by her example'. Ten years later all he predicted had come to pass. In
the closing months of the war, Britain had crowned her victorious
campaigns on sea and land by subsidizing the entire Grand Alliance.

Her strength and prosperity were the wonder of mankind. And,
while withstanding and defeating tyranny abroad, she had preserved
liberty at home. Cohesion without coercion, wealth without slavery,
empire without militarism, such was the spectacle Britain presented.
Was the reality beneath the splendid façade, the nation behind those
proud white cliffs as strong and healthful as it seemed? The good
manners of the country folk who greeted the Allied sovereigns on their
way to London in the victory summer of 1814, their open friendly
faces, the curtseys of the children on the roads and the raised hats of
their elders, all bespoke a society against which the waves of egalitarian
revolution had beaten in vain. The great mass of her people seemed
happier and more respectable than any other he knew, thought Louis
Simond, a French American observer, who had spent the last two years
of the war travelling England and studying her institutions.

The English plainly loved their country and found inspiration in
serving it. They were free as individuals to rule themselves, which
made them self-reliant, resourceful and morally, as well as physically,

courageous. They had a religion, deeply personal, which enabled them to set a course by conscience and common standards of belief and behaviour.

Their belief in freedom was a passion, almost a religion. 'Tis liberty alone,' proclaimed their favourite poet,

> 'that gives us the flower
> Of fleeting life, its lustre and perfume,
> And we are weeds without it. All constraint,
> Except what wisdom lays on evil men,
> Is evil.'

For the abstract liberty of the mass acclaimed by revolutionary France, the English had little use. The fabric of their law had been woven in the course of centuries to sustain that of the individual. The legal protection of his person and property against all comers, particularly against the King's officers, was, even more than Parliament, England's distinguishing institution. Parliament itself had been created to ensure it.

For this pragmatic race, hatred of power was an obsession. The British Constitution was an intricate balance of rights and functions in which it was impossible to say precisely where power resided. The King having in the past tried to monopolize it, his powers had been drastically shorn. Though he still possessed influence and could be a source of grave embarrassment to the Ministers whom he appointed, in all major matters he could act only through them. His right even to a private secretary was questioned. Yet the Ministers who exercised his powers were themselves dependent on the good will of Parliament. Without the support of a majority of its members, they could not carry on the business of the country.

Nor did power reside in the people – that question-begging abstraction, so dear to the rationalizing philosophers of the century, in whose name the French had drenched the world in blood. The House of Commons, like the House of Lords, so far as it represented anything definable, represented the interests and property of the country, though not as they were in 1815 but as they had been centuries before when the parliamentary system began. Little more than 400,000 out of the English and Welsh population of ten and a half millions enjoyed a parliamentary vote, and only 4000 out of two million Scots. Nor did the electorate even possess an absolute right to vote. It could be deprived of it by Parliament, which if the Crown consented might, as it had done in the past, prolong its own existence. For the English left every Parliament free to change the laws as it chose. They would not be bound even by a Constitution.

Only one thing could be said for certain of English politics. No power could be openly exercised without provoking a reaction. The greater the power, the greater the reaction. Even the mob was subject to this law of diminishing returns, since, whenever it went too far, it automatically created an alliance of law-abiding persons against it. England might canonize admirals – their sway was too distant to threaten anyone's liberty – but she never worshipped long at the shrine of any living statesman. Popularity with one faction was certain to arouse the enmity of another; vilification of William Pitt, the national saviour during the war, became the *credo* of Whigs and radicals for a generation after his death. It was symptomatic of this jealousy of power that the office of Prime Minister had no recognition in law, and that the Cabinet – the inner council of supreme office-holders, who were at once the Government and the managers of the parliamentary majority – was unknown to the Constitution. Its members modestly called themselves 'his Majesty's confidential servants.' They did not even possess an office or a secretary.

As for bureaucracy, what there was possessed no political power. The Civil Service was purely clerical and was nominated by the statesmen for whom it devilled. These viewed it chiefly as a means of rewarding supporters and providing for younger sons. Walter Scott praised Croker, the Secretary of the Admiralty, for never scrupling to stretch his powers to serve a friend. Such patronage, though valuable for securing party discipline, was no foundation for a strong executive. Ninety-nine Englishmen out of a hundred viewed with sturdy contempt a bureaucracy recruited by jobbery. Any attempt to increase its size and powers was certain to be assailed. Even the Foreign Office had a staff of only twenty-eight, including the two Under-Secretaries and a Turkish interpreter. The Home Office consisted of twenty clerks. As every document had to be copied by hand, such administrators had no time for regulating other people's lives.

It was a source of amazement to foreigners that a country so governed, without a regular police and with so small an army, should be so orderly. At Brighton, a town in 1811 of 14,000 people, there were neither justices nor municipality, yet crime was almost unknown and the doors left unbarred at night. The capital, the world's largest city, was patrolled by a handful of law officers and a few hundred elderly

3

night-watchmen. Little Mr Townsend, the Bow Street 'runner', with his flaxen wig and handful of top-hatted tipstaffs, constituted almost the sole force for executing the Government's will. Everything else was left to the justices and parish constables.

Yet the British were not a submissive people. English schoolboys rose against their masters and had to be driven back to their class-rooms by the military; an attempt to raise the prices of the London theatres provoked the galleries to shout down every play for months. The common people enjoyed a licence known in no other country. Nor, for all the deference paid to rank, did they respect persons. The Chancellor of the Exchequer, when he attended divine service at the Millbank Penitentiary, was bombarded with stale bread by the aggrieved lady inmates. Appalling crimes of violence passed unpunished for lack of police. Lonely turnpike-keepers were robbed and beaten to death; gangs of smugglers and poachers fought pitched battles with keepers and revenue officers. Pickpockets surrounded the doors of the coaching inns for 'Johnny Raws' from the country, and during fairs and public processions packs of thieves swept through the crowds emptying pockets, snatching purses and even stripping men and women of their clothes. Dusk around London was called footpad hour. Yet the nimbleness and courage of its pickpockets was almost a matter of pride to Londoners. 'A man who saunters about the capital with pockets on the outside of his coat,' a guide-book warned its readers, 'deserves no pity.'

A little rough-and-tumble seemed a small price to the English for avoiding the ills of arbitrary power. 'They have an admirable police at Paris,' wrote Lord Dudley, 'but they pay for it dear enough. I had rather half a dozen people's throats were cut every few years in the Ratcliff Highway than be subject to domiciliary visit, spies and the rest of Fouché's contrivances.' The British attitude towards the agents of executive power was instinctively hostile; Stendhal on a visit to London was amazed to see soldiers jeered at in the streets. The Life Guards, who carried printed orders to avoid giving offence to civilians and repeatedly showed the most exemplary restraint under showers of stones, were known in the capital as the 'Piccadilly butchers.' Even the Prime Minister who reaped the glories of Vittoria and Waterloo viewed General Graham's proposal for a club for military officers as a threat to the Constitution.

As there was no adequate standing Army, police force or bureaucracy to secure property and privilege, the gentry had to preserve these themselves. Having no professional deputies as in more regimented lands to stand between them and those they ruled, they learnt to command respect by force of character, courage and good sense. Instinctive, unreflecting and fearless leadership was a by-product of the country's libertarian laws. It began in boyhood, when future legislators and magistrates took part with the sturdy ragamuffins of the countryside in running, swimming and bird-nesting, riding the wild ponies of the commons, making midnight expeditions and climbing trees, rocks and steeples. They learnt to endure knocks and hardships, to face risks, conceal fear, be quick, bold and adaptable. They acquired, before they inherited wealth and luxury, habits of hardihood such as early rising and cold bathing; John Mytton, with his £20,000 a year, dressed in winter in a thin jacket and linen trousers without drawers, and once stalked wild-fowl all night on the ice stark naked.

From their earliest years Britain's rulers indulged with passionate intensity in field sports. It gave them, as Walter Scott wrote, a strong and muscular character, saving them from all sorts of causeless fears and flutterings of the heart. Men who rode straight to hounds, shot duck on wintry marshes with breech-loaders, learnt as boys to snare and kill wild-fowl, snakes, hares, rabbits, badgers and all forms of game and vermin, and continued to do so, whenever they had a chance, so long as they could walk or stride a horse, were not likely to fail for lack of courage. Their versatility in sport was amazing. The great Master of the Quorn, George Osbaldeston – 'little Ossey' or, as he was called later, the 'squire of England' – a shrivelled-up, bantam-cock of a man with short legs, a limp, a gorilla chest and a face like a fox cub, excelled at every sport he touched, boxing, pigeon-shooting, steeplechasing, billiards, was one of the six best amateur cricketers in the country, rowed for the Arrow club – forerunner of Leander – beat the famous professional, Barre, at tennis, and kept harriers, gamecocks and fighting mastiffs.

The hunting field played a big part in such education. Under the famous East Midlands masters a new form of foxhunting was superseding the slower and less specialized sport of the past. Its pioneers, establishing a new convention and discipline, were almost as much leaders in their kind as Nelson and Wellington. Their hounds ran from scent to view; 'neck or nothing,' 'a blazing hour,' 'the pace was too good to inquire,' were their watch-words. Their followers – for no man who wished to be respected spared either person or fortune in this pursuit – went like a scarlet streak across the green, enclosed

shires. 'Throw your heart over and your horse will follow!' the great
Assheton Smith used to say. It was a rule gentlemen instinctively
applied in time of danger, and to which the people responded.

All Britons admired what they called 'bottom.' 'God don't love
those,' they were told, 'who won't strike out for themselves!' Little
John Keats, affronted by boy or master, put himself 'in a posture of
defence'; even the gentle Shelley fought a mill at Eton. Byron used to
thrash a pacifically-minded Harrow friend to make him thrash others
'when necessary as a point of honour and stature'; he himself fought
his way out of the ridicule attached to a club foot by winning six out
of seven successive battles. No one but a 'game chick' could thrive in
this land.

Boxing was the national nursery of manliness. A gentleman was
expected to be a 'proper man with his fists' and know how 'to clear a
lane of men' with his 'morleys.' Thomas Assheton Smith, when Master
of the Quorn, after a set-to in a Leicester street with a six-foot coal-
heaver, clamped a raw steak on both eyes and sent his prostrated
opponent a five-pound note for being the best man that ever stood up
to him. Some foreigners landing at Dover were amazed to see a
Lord of the Treasury, dispossessed of his ministerial box by officious
Customs men, put himself in a sparring attitude to regain it. Young
noblemen took boxing lessons in Gentleman Jackson's rooms in Bond
Street or walked proudly arm in arm with the bash-nosed champions
of the 'Fancy'; an engraving of Tom Cribb was part of the normal
furniture of an undergraduate's rooms.

A contest between two 'milling coves' was the most popular spectacle
in the country. Its finer points were debated, not only by draymen and
coal-heavers, but by men of culture. Keats, describing the match
between Randall and Turner, illustrated its ups and downs by rapping
with his fingers on the window. All England followed the fortunes of
its 'men of science,' those prize specimens of the race who met in the
green ring by the river at Mousley Hurst or sparred before the 'Fancy'
in the Fives Court. The heroes of the ring – Tom Hickman the
Gas-Light man, Sutton 'the tremendous man of colour,' the 'Flaming
Tinman,' 'Big Ben Brain,' the 'Game Chicken,' Mendoza the Jew,
Belcher 'the yeoman,' and Tom Cribb, for ten years unchallenged
champion of England, were as great men in their way as the Duke of
Wellington. What, asked Borrow, were the gladiators of Rome or the
bull-fighters of Spain in its palmiest days compared to England's
bruisers? With the ring formed, the seconds and bottle-holders in

readiness, the combatants face to face, the English were in a kind of heaven. The gladiators, stripped to the waist, walking round each other with their fine, interlaced muscles and graceful strength, the naked fists, the short chopping blows delivered with the swiftness of lightning, the dislodged ivories, the noses beaten flat, the pause between rounds when the 'pinky heroes,' poised on their seconds' knees, were revived with brandy and water, the crashing blows delivered in the jugular with the full force of the arm shot horizontally from the shoulder, and the game, battered faces under punishment impressed themselves on the memory of the islanders more than all their country's martial victories. 'Prize fighting,' wrote Pierce Egan, 'teaches men to admire true courage, to applaud generosity, to acquire notions of honour, nobleness of disposition and greatness of mind; to bear hardships without murmur, fortitude in reverse of fortune, and invincibility of soul.'

Within the framework of law and property the English rule was that a man should look after himself and have freedom to do so. If he failed no one pitied him. It was his own fault; he had had his chance. The islanders had not yet thought out the full implications of this rule; they were to have opportunities for doing so later. But at the time it seemed fair enough; it had the warrant of nature and the law of things. 'Fear God,' said Isobel Berners to the Romany Rye, 'and take your own part. There's Bible in that, young man; see how Moses feared God and how he took his own part against everybody who meddled with him. So fear God, young man, and never give in!' From the time they could stand Englishmen were expected to fend for themselves. There was nothing they valued like spunk. In men, indeed, they respected nothing without it.

The religion of a people so libertarian was fundamentally Protestant. The font of English Protestantism was the Authorized Version of the Bible. With the growth of literacy this great book had become the daily mentor of millions. In country districts its words, heard week by week in church or chapel, formed the mould of men's minds. Its phrases strayed into their every-day speech; when Samuel Bamford returned from sea, his father, the weaver, greeted him with the words, 'My son was dead and is alive again, he was lost and is found.'

Looking back on his experience of the politics of anarchical India and revolutionary Europe, Wellington declared that it was England's religion that had made her what she was, a nation of honest men. By this he meant one in which a majority of men could trust one another and whom others could trust. 'I would rather sacrifice Gwalior and every other portion of India ten times over,' he once wrote, 'to preserve our credit for scrupulous good faith.'

This insistence on truth and frank dealing had a profound influence on the country's overseas empire and trade. It caused peoples on whom the expansion of the British impinged, if not to like, to trust them. A Bordeaux merchant, on whom a penniless British officer was billeted, offered, unasked, to lend him any sum without security; he had complete faith, he said, in the word of an Englishman. Richard Hotham, the hatter, made it a rule only to sell the best so that every new customer became an old. Though cheats and knaves abounded as in every society, a bright skein of honesty ran through the nation; a poor Lancashire weaver almost starved on the road from Manchester to London sooner than risk not being in court when his bail was called.

The ruling principle of English society was the conception of a gentleman. A gentleman did not tell a lie, for that was cowardice; he did not cheat, go back on his word or flinch from the consequences of his actions. A man's reputation as a gentleman was looked on as his most valuable possession. Any action, or even association, incompatible with it was regarded as a stain which must be immediately expunged. This accounted for the extreme sensitivity with which public men reacted to any slight on their honour, vindicating it, if necessary, in some dawn encounter with pistols on suburban common or foreign beach. Pitt, Castlereagh, Canning, Wellington and Peel all risked their lives in this way while holding high office. 'Throughout the whole of his career,' Gronow wrote of Wellington, 'he always placed first and foremost, far above his military and social honours, his position as an English gentleman.' The founders of Sandhurst laid it down that the professional education of British officers ought to aim at producing, not corporals, but gentlemen. So long as it did so, they knew it would produce the kind of leaders Englishmen would follow.

The ideal of equality which had so intoxicated the French, had as yet made little impression on the British mind. Whenever Squire Lambton, with his £40,000 a year, visited his northern home, the Durham colliers turned out in thousands to draw his carriage. It was injustice and tyranny that this pugnacious people resented, not privilege. 'Gentleman are, or ought to be, the pride and glory of every civilized country,' wrote Thomas Bewick, himself of humble origin; 'without their countenance arts and sciences must languish, industry be paralysed and barbarism rear its stupid head.' The radical Bamford, for all his life of rebellion, wrote with nostalgia of the freedom that had existed in his youth between the gentry and their tenants. 'There were no grinding bailiffs and land-stewards in those days to stand betwixt the gentleman and his labourer. There was no racking up of old tenants; no rooting out of old cottiers; no screwing down of servants' or labourers' wages; no cutting off of allowances, either of the beggar at the door or the visitor at his servants' hall; no grabbing at waste candle-ends or musty cheese parings.' For the English liked the rich to be splendid, ostentatious and free with their money. It was what, in their view, the rich were for.

They liked them, too, to share and excel in their pastimes. 'Nothing,' the Duke of Wellington declared, 'the people of this country like so much as to see their great men take part in their amusements; the aristocracy will commit a great error if ever they fail to mix freely with their neighbours.' Sport in England was a wonderful solvent of class distinction. Even foxhunting, with all its expense and showy competitiveness, had something of a rough democracy about it, at once exclusive and classless, of master and huntsman, groom and whipper-in, dog-stopper and stable boy, meeting day after day on the level of a common love. The coloured prints depicting its scarlet coats and glossy horses hung in village alehouses as well as manor houses; when the Manchester weavers, true to their country past and oblivious of their proletarian future, went out hunting on the Cheshire hills, Sam Stott, the huntsman, used to treat them to a warm ale and ginger. On the cricket field, too, the conventions of rank were forgotten; the best man was 'the hardest *swipe*, the most active *field*, the stoutest *bowler*.' 'Who that has been at Eton,' asked the author of the *English Spy*, 'has not repeatedly heard Jem Powell in terms of exultation cry, "Only see me *liver this here* ball, my young master"?' The game was played at Brighton by the Prince Regent – before he let down his belly – and by the aristocracy who liked to gamble over it, and by the young farmers and labourers of almost every south country village.

For the English, as Hazlitt said, were a sort of grown children. They loved Punch and Judy and games like skittles and shove-halfpenny, leap frog, blind man's buff, hunt-the-slipper, hot cockles and snapdragon. When Nelson went round the *Victory*'s gun-decks before Trafalgar, the men were jumping over one another's heads to amuse themselves until they were near enough to fire. 'Cudgel-playing, quarterstaff, bull and badger-baiting, cock-fighting,' Hazlitt wrote, 'are almost the peculiar diversions of this island . . . There is no place where trap-ball, fives, prison-base, football, quoits, bowls are better understood or more successfully practised, and the very names of a cricket bat and ball make English fingers tingle.' Nothing would deflect them from their sport; when 'Long Robinson,' had two of his fingers struck off, he had a screw fastened to one hand to hold the bat and with the other still sent the ball thundering against the boards that bounded old Lord's cricket-ground.

They liked, and honoured above all, what they called 'game, bone and blood.' It was because their rulers possessed these qualities that, despite all their unimaginativeness and selfishness, they had so little difficulty in ruling them. Most Englishmen were far more interested in dog-fighting, coursing, hunting vermin, fishing and fowling, boxing and wrestling, than in the pursuit of equality or the class war. The man of the age was not the Benthamite philosopher, the radical martyr or the wage-hungry cotton spinner – however important in retrospect – but the sporting type. Jem Flowers, the Eton boys sang of a local 'cad,'

> ' baits a badger well
> For a bullhank or a tyke, sir,
> And as an out-and-out bred swell
> Was never seen his like, sir!'

One common denominator linked Englishmen of all classes – the horse. The friend who called Charles Lamb the one man who had never worn boots or sat in a saddle was only exaggerating. Almost every Englishman born within sight of a highroad or a field thought it the height of felicity to be 'well mounted on a spunky horse who would be well in front.' The English loved horses; O'Kelly, owner of Eclipse, declared that all Bedford Level could not buy him. 'When you have got such a horse to be proud of,' the ostler told the Romany Rye, 'wherever you go, swear there a'n't another to match it in the country, and if anybody gives you the lie, take him by the nose and tweak it off, just as you would do if anybody were to speak ill of your lady!'

'Something slap', a 'bit of blood', 'an elegant tit', were the phrases with which the English expressed this love. A smart or 'spanking' turn-out was, more than anything else, the symbol of national pride; there was no comparison, a visitor to Paris in 1815 reckoned, between French and English equipages; neatness, beauty, finish, lightness, quality, all were on the side of the islanders. 'The exercise which I do dearly love,' wrote Mary Mitford, 'is to be whirled along fast, fast by a blood horse in a gig.' During the first years of the nineteenth century the great coachbuilders of London and the provincial capitals turned out a succession of equipages perfectly adapted for their purposes, from the fashionable landau and deep-hung, capacious barouche to the dashing curricle, tilbury, buggy and gig, and the phaeton 'highflyer' with its towering wheels and yellow wings. The most wonderful of all were the mail-coaches built for speed on the new metalled highways, with their blood horses, bright brass harness, blazoned colours, horn-blowing guards, and coachman with squared shoulders, vast capes, multiple coats and nosegays. Young aristocrats prided themselves on mastering the accomplishments of these professional knights of the road, even to filing and spitting through their teeth; to handle the 'ribbons' and be a first-rate 'fiddler' was passport to any company.

Supporting the noble institution of the horse was an immense community of grooms and ostlers, of sharp-eyed, wiry little men with bow legs and high-lows and many a string dangling from the knees of their breeches, and lads in dirty pepper-and-salt coats and low-crowned hats with turn-up ears. They were members of an *alma mater* of which almost every English lad aspired to be a graduate. Under its splendid clothes and yellow varnished equipages Regency England stank of the stable and was proud of it. The fraternity of the curry-comb – that knowing under-world of inn tap-rooms and raffish-looking parties with hats on one side and straws in their mouths – stretched from Dover to Galway. From it sprang the English poet whose mastery of sensuous imagery has only been surpassed by the offspring of the Stratford-on-Avon glover and corn factor. John Keats was the son of an ostler who married his master's daughter and succeeded him as keeper of a livery stable in Moorfields.

The itch for horse-dealing and betting created, like everything English, its institutions. Weatherby's was to the Turf what the Bank of England was to the City, and Tattersall's, 'that hoarse and multifarious miscellany of men' below Hyde Park Corner, with its circular counter – a kind of temple to the goddess of chance – and its painting of Eclipse over the fireplace, was the Stock Exchange of the equine world. A little Newmarket quizzing or hocussing was reckoned an essential part of a young gentleman's education for a rough, wicked world. It taught him, in the cant of the day, to keep his peepers open. It helped to give him and his race that strong practical sense – horse sense, they called it – which made them, wherever they went, the lords of the earth.

*   *   *

At the time of Waterloo three-quarters of the English people still lived in villages and small market-towns. Though a new industrial population was growing up in the North and Midlands, it was as yet an insignificant fraction of the national community, hidden out of sight in lonely Pennine valleys and remote heaths. Set against rural 'Britain's calm felicity and power,' the helot settlements beside the Irk and Swayle seemed accidental and unimportant. Only a prophet could have foreseen that the England of the future lay there and not in the pastoral and feudal south.

Here, Washington Irving wrote, everything was the growth of ages, of regular and peaceful existence, conveying an impression of 'calm and settled security, an hereditary transmission of home-bred virtues and attachments which spoke deeply and touchingly for the moral character of the nation.' That traditional life could be seen on Sunday in the villages: the well-dressed family groups converging through the fields and lanes as the church bells pealed – a continuous chain of sound at that hour across the country – the spacious pews of the gentry, the old peasants in the aisle, the choir with their strings, clarinets and serpents in the gallery, the old men and girls in white gowns on either side of the chancel, the dignified high-church rector and parish clerk intoning 'England's sublime liturgy,' the happy neighbours meeting afterwards in the churchyard that Harry Smith and his fellow Riflemen recalled with such nostalgia on a Sabbath morning in the Peninsula. One saw it in the market towns with their beautiful houses – Georgian, Queen Anne, Tudor and Gothic – the broad high streets with driven cattle and umbrellaed market tables, the fine trees casting their shade over garden walls, the pillared market-halls. Such towns crowned nearly a thousand years of unbroken civilization. From their upper windows one looked across gardens to fields, woods and clear rivers whose waters carried trout and crayfish. 'One of those pretty, clean, unstenched and unconfined places,' Cobbett called Huntingdon, 'that tend to lengthen life and make it happy.' At Winchester, when Keats stayed there in 1819, nothing ever seemed to be happening in the still, cobbled streets; nothing but the sound of birds in the gardens, the echoing, unhurrying footsteps of passers-by, the roll of market carts flooding in or out of the city with the tides of the encircling shire.

Everywhere, as one travelled this rich, ancient land, one saw the continuity and natural growth of a community that had never known invasion and where the new, not confined as on the continent by fortifications, had been free to develop without destroying the old. At Norwich, capital like York and Exeter not of a shire but of a province, the city was grouped round an episcopal tower, a Norman castle and a vast market square from whose stalls poured that abundance of foodstuffs which so astonished the German, Meidinger. 'The most curious specimen at present extant of the genuine old English town,' Borrow called it, 'with its venerable houses, its numerous gardens, its thrice twelve churches, its mighty mound.'

England still preserved a pageantry, beautiful and impressive though homely, that educated men in the meaning of society. The mayor with his laced cloak, sword-bearer, maces and aldermen, the gentlemen of the shire dining together in lieutenancy uniform, the humble beadles and criers in their cocked hats, flaxen wigs and silver lace, the very postmen in red and gold were unconsciously teaching history. At assizes the judges drove into the country towns in scarlet and ermine, with outriders, javelin men and halberdiers, while the bells pealed and the streets were thronged with gentlemen in dark-blue coats, glossy hats and shining boots, and misses in white muslin and their prettiest bonnets. In Edinburgh the Lord Justice Clerk and judges passed through the city to their daily tasks in robes of red and white satin; in the grey streets of university and cathedral cities there was usually a flutter of gowns and a glimmer of wands and maces. The sense of history had not yet been dulled by the impersonal segregation and ugliness of an industrial society; men understood something of the march of their country through time, of its traditions and culture. When the Guards' band played the old martial airs of England outside the palace, a visitor noted that many in the crowd had tears in their eyes. It was not, Paley wrote, by what the Lord Mayor felt in his coach that the public was served, but by what the apprentice felt who gazed on it.

Though by 1815 all this pageantry was beginning to wear a little thin, it still served its purpose of enriching the imagination of successive generations. Men felt at one with their native place, loved its beauty and took pride in its history. Old castles and monastic ruins were sources not only of intellectual interest to the few but of wonder and poetry to the many. So were the rude signs in bright colours swinging over the tavern doors, of Admiral Keppel or Vernon braving the battle and the breeze, the Marquis of Granby in scarlet coat, or St George busy, with plumed helm and shield, slaying dragons. Unlettered lads from Tyneside colliers stood 'beneath the wondrous dome of St Paul's with almost awful surprise,' and Bewick's neighbours, the Northumbrian peasants, spent their winter evenings listening to the tales and ballads of the Border. The earliest rhymes that Thomas Cooper, the Chartist leader, remembered were those of Chevy Chase. He used to repeat them until they made him feel as warlike as the sight of Matthew Goy riding into the town with news of a victory in the Peninsula or the scarlet-coated volunteers marching through Gainsborough on exercise days to the sound of fife and drum. 'As I came down here to-day,' wrote Lady Bessborough, 'I met a procession that I thought quite affecting – numbers of men without an arm or leg or variously wounded, with bunches of laurel in their hats, and women and children mingling with them. I inquired what it was and found it to be the anniversary of the battle of Talavera.'

So, too, the English commemorated their faith and the seasons of the pastoral year. Before Christmas the weavers of south Lancashire sang all night at their looms to keep themselves awake as they prepared for the holiday. In the West the yule-log was brought home and tales told over posset and frumenty, and the carolers and string-choirs went their frosty rounds. With the farmhouses and cottages full of greenery and the kissing-bush hanging from the rafters, the traditional roast beef, plum pudding, mince-pie and roasted crab were eaten, while the mummers in painted paper and floral headgear – King George, the Doctor and the Turkey Snipe – banged one another with their wooden swords. On New Year's Eve the wassailers came round with garlanded bowls, cleaving the wintry skies with their song:

> 'Here's to our horse and to his right ear,
> God send our master a happy New Year;
> A happy New Year as e'er he did see,
> With my wassailing bowl I drink to thee!'

and neighbours, made kindly by the season, sat in one another's houses, 'fadging' over cakes and wine.

There were occasions, too, when the poor had a right to largesse and the hungry were filled with good things. There were rituals which marked the course of the farm year; the Whitsun Ale and the sheep-shearing festival, the Holy Night at Brough, when a burning ash was carried in front of the town band with everyone dancing and firing squibs behind, the hiring fairs when the markets were full of toys and ginger-bread stalls and young men and women stood in the streets wearing the emblems of their craft to sell their services for the next year. The greatest of all the farm feasts was Harvest Home when the Kern Dolly or Ivy girl, fashioned from the corn, was set upon a pole and borne home in the last cart, with music playing and the farmer and his men shouting in procession while the good wife dished up the supper that was to crown the rustic year. There, at the long wooden tables, the reapers – 'with sunburnt hands and ale-enlivened face' – rejoiced over their beef, beer and pipes, singing familiar songs and tossing down sconces with double forfeits for every drop spilt, until the time-honoured chorus was reached:

'Here's a health unto our master, the founder of this feast!
I hope to God with all my heart his soul in Heaven may rest,
And all his works may prosper that ere he takes in hand,
For we are all his servants and all at his command –
So drink, boys, drink, and see you do not spill,
For if you do, you shall drink too, for 'tis our master's will!'

After which those able wound their way home, and those who could not slept where they lay, well content, in barn or stable.

Other dates in the calendar linked craft or calling to the Christian faith: the Spinners' Feast at Peterborough when workhouse children in white dresses and scarlet ribbons marched through the streets singing the spinning song; the processions of wool-combers on St Blase's Day in the cloth towns of Yorkshire and East Anglia, with their heralds, banners and bands; before the Lancashire wakes, proclaimed by the bellmen in the churchyards on successive Sundays, every fold and hamlet vied in preparing the rush cart, decking its ornamental sheet with ribbons, streamers and silver ornaments. With lanes resounding with fife, drum and fiddle, the girls all flounces and frills in new kirtles and bonnets, the lads in jingling horse-collars and bright with ribbon and tinsel, the whole community followed the cart to the parish church, while the morris dancers leaped and spun before:

'My new shoon they are so good,
I cou'd doance morrice if I wou'd,
An' if hat an' sark be drest
I will doance morrice w' the best.'

When Keats, in his *Ode on a Grecian Urn*, asked

'What little town by river or sea-shore . . .
Is emptied of its folk, this pious morn?'

15

he may have recalled the customary rites – doomed by the advance of an iron economy – of the Lancashire villages through which he had recently passed on his way to Scotland.

The English poor loved to voice their patriotism in a song. Bob Johnson, the jockey, after his victories on the turf, would climb on the table and strike up his favourite:

> 'If ye ax wheer oi comes fra,
> I'll say the Fell side;
> Where fayther and mither
> And honest folk bide.'

Having to make their own music, many Englishmen knew how to perform vocally and instrumentally; at a homecoming, a wedding, a gathering of neighbours, a man would take down his fiddle or send for his neighbour's. Bamford's weaver father could read from the book and play both fiddle and flute, and even compose. The yeomen of Cranborne Chase gathered weekly at an inn on Salisbury Plain for instrumental music and part singing; the artisans of Lincoln formed a choral society to render Handel's Oratorios.

This love of singing came out in the folk songs which, despite enclosure, lingered on in the villages like the string choirs and morris dancers. In the alehouse or the fields over the midday cheese and ale, countrymen would sing of their craft and skill, prizing them the more for the singing:

> '"Hold, gard'ner," says the ploughman, "my calling don't
> despise,
> Since each man for his living upon his trade relies,
> Were it not for the ploughman both rich and poor would rue,
> For we are all dependent upon the painful plough."'

The seamen, roughest and hardest-used of men, had their traditional songs and shanties, whose rhythm served their work and whose poetry sprang from the element they sailed:

> 'Then a-weigh our anchor, my jolly, jolly tars,
> For the winter star I see.'

Deep down a vein of poetry, simple, sensuous and strangely delicate, ran through this healthy, courageous, cohesive people. There were songs that kept England's history bright; of ships with names like poems, of pastoral duties transformed by imagination into acts of significance and beauty; of courtship, tender, tragic or bawdy, but always shot with the haunting loveliness of the green, peaceful land that gave them birth; of wild rovers and the misfortunes which befall poor men when passion sounds and the reckless heart tries to transcend the iron bars of destiny; of indignation against cruel laws and injustice and foul play; and, underlying all, the moral sense of a great people and their perception of the sweetness of love, courage and loyalty to wife and home, and of the unchanging goodness of laughter and comradeship, striking, as the pewter pots beat time on the dark, dented, malt-stained alehouse table, chords that rose from the very depths of the English heart.

Because of these things humble men respected learning and culture. It was still natural for English artisans to admire the best: to distinguish civilization from barbarism. Good taste was widespread; it was no coincidence that both the artisan radical leaders to whose autobiographies we owe much of our knowledge of working-class outlook in the transitional stages of the Industrial Revolution, acquired in youth a love and knowledge of engraving. The unspoilt countryside of Britain, its songs and folklore created a natural instinct for poetry; more than one of the rustic giants whose mechanical and scientific genius charted the course of mankind's industrial future wanted in youth to become poets. Burns was no isolated phenomenon; he sprang from the conditions of his age. So did Hogg and Clare, both peasants, Keats the liveryman's son, Lamb the serving man's, Wordsworth the petty yeoman's, Blake the poor artificer. Such a man as Bamford the weaver might lack their literary gifts, but he was cast in the same mould. Such simple folk thought there was no country like theirs; they felt, as Lord Dudley put it, that 'abroad was a poor place compared with England.' A Wiltshire peasant, sitting at his door on a summer's evening, recalled how, having heard the parson preach of Paradise, he had made up his mind that 'if there was but a good trout-stream running down Chicken Grove Bottom, Fernditch Lodge would beat it out and out.' Even where the dark mists of industrialism were settling on the northern fells and moors, the love of England's beauty remained strong; the young lovers in Manchester in the early years of the century would seek out and walk together in Tinker's Garden, 'then a sweet bowery place.'

*   *   *

The first thing that struck every visitor to England was the beauty of the landscape. It derived from her exquisite turf and foliage and soft, aqueous atmosphere: what Leigh Hunt, pining among the Apennines for the buttercup meadows and elms of the vale of Hampstead, called the grassy balm of his native fields. Everywhere was the sense of peace, wealth and security: the avenues of huge elms, the leafy Middlesex landscape, the great trees on Hampstead's airy height, the blue horizons, the farmhouses of beautifully fashioned brick and stone, the pastoral Thames still set, as Horace Walpole had pictured it, amid enamelled meadows and filigree hedges, with brightly-painted barges, solemn as Exchequer barons, moving slowly up to Richmond or down to Syon, the sculptured, classical bridges, the wayside alehouses with placid drinkers under their spreading oaks and chestnuts, the old grey churches and barns, the ghostly trees in the evening twilight, the drinking cattle and homing rooks, the mystery and the mist.

Though England's forests had long been shorn to feed her fleets and furnaces, the sense of fine trees was all-pervading. She was still, as Constable painted her, carpeted with her native hard-woods, which gave moisture to her soil, shade to her cattle and depth and mystery to every horizon. From the terrace at Richmond, or from Harrow hill, one looked across a vast plain from which trees rose in endless waves of blue. Every commentator dwelt on the same phenomenon: the great oaks, the hedgerows of elm and ash, the forest trees scattered about the meadows. Cobbett, stumbling for the first time on the Hampshire hangars, sat motionless on his horse, gazing down on that mighty flood spilling into every valley. In Sherwood Forest avenues stretched for miles in every direction, the solitude broken only by the whirring of partridges and pheasants. Cranborne Chase in Dorset had still nearly ten thousand deer; Windsor Forest, Burnham Beeches and Epping, close to the capital, almost as many. In the Berkshire woodlands south of Reading, Mary Mitford described the forest-like closeness – a labyrinth of woody lanes, crossroads and cartways leading up and down hill to farmhouses buried in leaves and wreathed to their clustered chimneys with vines, and little enclosures so closely set with growing timber as to resemble forest glades. One could scarcely peep, she wrote, through the leaves.

Probably at no period was England so beautiful. Man had everywhere civilized nature without over-exploiting and spoiling it. The great landscape-painters and water-colourists – Gainsborough, Morland, de Wint, Cozens, Rowlandson, Crome, Cotman, Girtin, Turner, Bonington and Constable, the Suffolk miller's son who revolutionized European painting – were the human products of that countryside.

Like the poets they were not isolated phenomena but men inheriting, though in expression they transcended, the common feelings of their countrymen. Cobbett, who prided himself on being a plain man with no nonsense about him, travelling from Redbourne to Chesham described how in every field the haymakers had left a closely-mown strip between the hedgerow and the corn; 'this,' he wrote, 'is most beautiful. The hedges are full of shepherd's rose, honeysuckles and all sorts of wild flowers, so that you are upon a grass walk with this most beautiful of all flower-gardens and shrubberies on your one hand and with the corn on the other. And thus you go on from field to field, the sort of corn, the sort of underwood and timber, the shape and size of the fields, the height of the hedgerows, the height of the trees, all continually varying. Talk of pleasure-grounds, indeed! What that man ever invented under the name of pleasure-grounds can equal these fields in Hertfordshire?'

This landscape was constantly being enriched. It was ditched, hoed and hedged to an extent elsewhere unknown. Stacks over forty feet high, meticulously finished and roofed with straw, barns built to outlast the centuries, outhouses, windmills and watermills which were miracles of fine workmanship, sturdy gates and fences made by men who were masters of their craft, were the commonplaces of the English scene. The thrifty and loving use of nature's resources and the spirit of active and methodical enterprise seemed almost universal. 'The white farms, . . . the well-stocked rickyards behind,' wrote Mary Mitford, 'tell of comfort and order.'

Yet every shire, every parish, differed in its farming methods, being cultivated in the way which soil, climate and immemorial experience had proved best. Every district had its particular abundance, the bleak lands as well as the fine. From sandy Norfolk came the enormous turkeys – 'the grand Norfolkian holocaust' that at Christmas smoked round Elia's nostrils from a thousand firesides. The stony fields round Bridport were blue with hemp and flax. Salisbury Plain and the Dorset uplands were cropped and fertilized by immense flocks of sheep: 'it is the extensive downs in its vicinage,' explained the Weymouth guidebook, 'which produces the sweetest herbage and gives a peculiarly fine flavour to the mutton.' And all over England the folded sheep, fed from the turnip-root, made it possible to grow good crops on marginal lands otherwise too light to bear them: on the Wiltshire downs Cobbett counted four thousand hurdled on a single acre.

The golden creed of 'Hoof and Horn,' use and return, was the firm and, as it seemed, unalterable base of the country's wealth. The meadows that fed the suckling ewes and lambs in spring yielded hay by midsummer; and, when the corn was cut, the stubble kept the pigs. A Yorkshire squarson – for the very priests were farmers – recorded as the crown of a holiday tour the spectacle of a hundred and twenty shorthorns tethered and fed where they stood in open sheds on successive crops of vetch, mown grass, clover and tares from fields manured by the straw they had soiled. The yields of such rotational agriculture, judged by the standards of other lands, were amazing. The Isle of Wight, with its fine wheat crops, pastures stocked with Alderneys and downs bearing vast flocks of sheep, grew seven times more than its inhabitants consumed. At Milton in the Vale of Pewsey, where three thousand five hundred acres produced annually three thousand quarters of wheat and six thousand of barley and the wool of seven thousand sheep, as well as eggs, milk and poultry, Cobbett reckoned that every labourer raised enough food to support from fifty to a hundred persons.

Necessity acted as a spur. A fast-rising population, which for a generation had been cut off by war from foreign supplies, needed ever more grain, meat and ale and was prepared to pay for it. Landlords and farmers, sowing root crops and clovers, liming, marling and draining, carrying the plough and hurdled sheep to the hills, reclaiming moor and marsh, breeding ever fatter livestock, and pursuing husbandry as a high science, had obtained from the soil the utmost output of which it was capable. The productivity of Norfolk doubled in two decades, largely through the genius of one of its squires, Coke of Holkham, who, working in a smock-frock like a labourer, first taught himself to farm and then taught his tenants. The heaths to the west of London, the haunt from time immemorial of highwaymen, were turned into the finest market gardens. New methods were constantly being tried; horses superseded oxen in the plough, threshing machines the flail, and drills broadcast-sowing, turnips and swedes eliminated the bare fallow of the past and fed the livestock in winter. 'Everyone,' wrote a foreigner, 'has planted or is planting his thousands or millions of timber trees, has his flocks, talks of turnips, clover and lucerne, drains and enclosures.' Scott took greater pride in his compositions for manure than in his literary ones and boasted that his oaks would outlast his laurels.

This wonderful performance was achieved by organic farming without injury to the permanent capital of the soil. Its object was not to seize the maximum profit from sales against costs in the minimum

Probably at no period was England so beautiful. Man had everywhere civilized nature without over-exploiting and spoiling it. The great landscape painters and water-colourists – Gainsborough, Morland, de Wint, Cozens, Rowlandson, Crome, Cotman, Girtin, Turner, Bonington and Constable, the Suffolk miller's son who revolutionized European painting – were the human products of that countryside. Like the poets they were not isolated phenomena but men inheriting, though in expression they transcended, the common feelings of their countrymen.' *The Valley of the Stour with Dedham in the distance* by John Constable.

'The most wonderful of all were the mail-coaches built for speed on the new metalled highways, with their blood horses, bright brass harness, blazoned colours, horn-blowing guards, and coachmen with squared shoulders, vast capes, multiple coats and nosegays.' *The* 'Comet' *London to Brighton Stage and Mail Coach* by James Pollard.

'In Manchester and the surrounding cotton towns, children, sent to the looms at seven years of age, worked from five in the morning until six at night', *c.* 1835.

'By the end of the Napoleonic War the new coke furnaces of the North and Midlands were turning out between a quarter and half a million tons more iron than at its beginning.' The steam-hammer at James Naysmyth's foundry, *c.* 1832.

time, but to secure over the years the highest possible increase from soil, plant and beast. The goal was the productive fertility of the land rather than the immediate saleability of particular crops in relation to costs: output per acre instead of output per wage-earner. The farming was multi-, never mono-cultural, and much of the all-pervading plenty arose from by-products like the snow-white ducks of the Vale of Aylesbury. 'Whenever cows are kept, so must pigs,' wrote a country gentleman, 'or the profit of buttermilk and whey will be lost.' The finely thatched roofs of the cottages and barns were made from the combed straw left over by the threshers. When timber was cut, a temporary shed was erected round it so that every piece could be worked for the exact purpose for which it was suited, without leaving a splinter on the ground.

The value of farm land soared with its use. No class had ever enjoyed such riches as the English landed gentry. The greatest of all commanded revenues larger than those of reigning continental princes. The Duke of Northumberland's annual rental was over £150,000; the owner of Berkeley Castle's £180,000. Four-fifths of the House of Commons and almost the entire hereditary personnel of the House of Lords were landowners. Such was the respect for landed wealth that Englishmen felt reluctance in entrusting political power to any man without it.

As one travelled the country one saw that illimitable wealth; 'farm-houses in sight everywhere, . . . large fields fresh ploughed, black and smooth, others ploughing, always with horses, never with oxen; farmers riding among their workmen, great flocks of sheep confined by net-fences in turnip fields, meadows . . . of the most brilliant green.' At the autumnal sheep fair at Weyhill more than a quarter of a million pounds changed hands annually, to be borne home by plaided shepherds or their top-booted, blue-coated masters who gathered over the 'ordinary' in the White Hart. At Falkirk Fair a tenant of Lord Egremont's bought 12,000 head of cattle with £30,000 Bank of England bills carried in his pockets. A man who could raise prize bullocks or grow outsize turnips did not need a pedigree; in their passion for agricultural improvement the English even forgot to be snobs. After local ploughing competitions and cart-horse trials the worthies of a whole county, gentle and common, would dine together to discuss over roast beef and October ale the methods they had successfully pursued. The Duke of Bedford's or Coke of Norfolk's annual sheep-shearing were events as important as the Derby or a meeting of Parliament.

Coke's rustic palace, Holkham, became a place of pilgrimage that rivalled Walsingham in the age of faith: the interminable drive, the triumphal arch, the lakes, the woods, the obelisk, the distant view of the sea, the overawed Norfolk church peering through its modest cluster of trees, the exquisite changes of autumnal leaf as the shooting parties, in green and buff and brown, moved like regiments across the landscape, the coverts with never-ending partridges rising out of wastes of sand bearded with stunted corn, and, all around, the wilderness flowering like a garden.

All this abundance, though directed by landlords and farmers applying the knowledge gleaned from the great agricultural experiments of the past three generations, was founded on the plentiful labour of an hereditary race of husbandmen bred in the cumulative lore of centuries. In a single field in East Lothian a traveller counted forty-eight reapers; near Bury St Edmunds he saw ten ploughs turning at the same hedge. In haymaking time squads of labourers moved from tract to tract, leaving the fields cleared behind them, the mowers going before with their scythes, the haymakers following. There were gangs of boys to pull the charlock and keep the land clean, and women to pick stones, weed, reap and glean.

These skilful, simple and generous-hearted men, with the gaunt bony frames, slow gait and stolid, patient eyes, followed husbandry in all its branches, including wood-cutting, hurdling, thatching and sheep-shearing. Their industry was prodigious. They worked from first light till dusk; in a day a good dibbler would sow a bushel and a peck, and a mower cover two acres. They wasted little or nothing; a reaper with his sickle would cut the ears of corn with so short a straw that scarcely a weed found its way into the sheaf. In their spare time – often only achieved after a walk of several miles home – they kept pigs and bees and cultivated their gardens, those long irregular slips with gooseberry bushes, neatly tended vegetables and flowers, which Cobbett thought distinguished England from the rest of the world; 'we have only to look at these gardens to know what sort of people English labourers are.'

While their husbands and fathers toiled in the fields, the wives and children at home added their own contribution to England's wealth. They worked at the loom, made lace, buttons, string, netting, packthread and gloves, and plaited straw into a thousand useful and beautiful shapes. In season they tramped into the woods or orchards to gather fuel, nuts and fruit, or worked in gangs in the hay and harvest fields.

In the pasture lands the unmarried women watched and milked cows, going out in traditional fashion with cans balanced on their heads and wooden milking-stools in their hands. Their younger brothers, in patched round smocks, took service on the farms at eight or nine years of age, learning their father's lore and working as long as their elders. For all their hard usage they seemed healthy and happy – 'wild, nimble, gleesome beings,' as Bamford, looking back, remembered: the 'open, spirited, good-humoured race' of Mary Mitford's village, with brown and ruddy cheeks and merry eyes, always ready for a bird's nesting or a game of cricket, 'batting, bowling and fielding as if for life' at the end of twelve or fourteen hours' field labour. They grew up to be farmers' boys or 'chaw-bacons' – bucolic, round-faced, hardy – the 'clods' of whom the county regiments were made which held the ridge at Waterloo. With their grey slouch hats, bright neck-cloths and ribbons and proverbial pitchforks, they could be seen in the aggregate at the hiring fairs in the county towns or at the traditional farm feasts of harvest and sheep-shearing.

The farm labourer's work was supplemented by a host of rustic craftsmen. The drover with his lacquer-back curry-comb, the swearing carter, the shepherd with his dog and crook and eye watchful for tick, foot-rot or blow-fly, the wood-cutters, sawyers, hurdlers, spoke-choppers, faggoters, rake and ladder-makers of the forest lands; the village blacksmiths, saddlers, tailors, wheelwrights, masons, carpenters, glaziers, millwrights, carriers, shoemakers and pedlars who kept the rustic economy self-sufficient, were part of an army many times larger than Wellington's and without which his could neither have been recruited nor maintained. Many were craftsmen of exquisite quality, like Miss Mitford's humble neighbour, 'famed ten miles round and worthy all his fame,' whom few cabinet-makers, even in London, surpassed. England's wealth rested on the fact that they were able and willing in their lifetime of unresting work to do so much in return for the food, clothing, shelter and modest comfort which in all ages, whatever the nominal money-level of wages and prices, remains the highest reward of manual labour. The nation which employed them received for their keep a *per capita* return in skill and industry probably greater than that enjoyed by any other in history.

* * *

23

On this lowly, but strong, foundation – and that of the chawbacon's working-kin, the tarpaulins of the coastal ports and estuaries – rested, in the last resort, the wealth, elegance, culture and civilization of victorious Britain. Together they supported the sober merchant grace of Georgian London with its streets of uniform, proportioned red or grey brick and its skyline of parapet, tile and chimney-stack, broken only by the white stone of Wren's belfries and, far above, the domes of his vast cathedral, with its remote ball and cross; and the fashionable aristocratic West End with its mile after mile of splendid mansions, wonderful clothes and horses, liveried servants and gleaming barouches and landaus. It comprised the new Edinburgh, Britain's 'northern Athens' – a paradise, it seemed to contemporaries, of order, light and neatness – which had risen near Calton Hill, away from the crooked closes and stench of Auld Reekie; the provincial cities and country towns with their elegant crescents and railed squares aping Mayfair and St James's; the seaside and inland watering-places with their Grecian and Pompeian terraces of white stucco with raised and green-painted jalousies, and exquisitely windowed shops and lending libraries and assembly rooms; the turnpike roads traversed by beautiful equipages in all the pride of the loriner's art, with silver trappings and coloured housings and outriders in yellow and scarlet facings. And everywhere, in shire and county – flanking the highways and lanes, the park walls, crested gates and castellated lodges, with their noble parks and avenues, commemorative obelisks and Corinthian arches – the country houses which were England's crowning glory. They ranged from palaces like Blenheim, Petworth and Castle Howard to unassuming residences of pillared stone, brick or white stucco, little bigger than the houses of the professional classes in the county towns, but set among the common denominator of park, plantation, lawn and drive. They were, above everything else, the distinguishing feature of the landscape. A gentleman stranded on the road could be sure of shelter under the roof of one of his own kind, where he would find, though with infinite variations, the same classical, Tudor or Gothic architecture, the same fine furniture of mahogany, walnut or rosewood, the same oriental carpets and china and their English ceramic counterparts, the same ancestral worthies in gilded frames flanked by masterpieces or pseudo masterpieces from Italy and Holland, the same libraries of leather-bound books, containing the solid culture of three centuries. And outside would be the cedars, the close-mown lawns, the flower-beds, conservatories and ice-houses, the vistas cunningly blending the artificial with the natural, lawns, plantations, park and water merging into the landscape which they commanded and to which they belonged.

Though during the London season the enchanted groves and flowers were often left to waste their sweetness on the uninhabited air, their owners always returned to them and with delight. 'Tixhall is in radiant beauty,' wrote Harriet Leveson Gower 'all over rain, sunshine and a few fireplace in the hall. I really do love it beyond expression.' 'After having been at a ball until three o'clock,' Lady Shelley concluded her journal of a metropolitan July, 'Shelley, Mr Jenkinson and I drove down to Sutton in the barouche, and at nine o'clock we mounted our horses and galloped over that delightful turf . . . As I breathed this pure air my jaded spirits were restored. We rode across country to Maresfield which "in all its blueth and greeneth" reproached us for our absence. Thank God! I can leave the vanities of London without a sigh and return to my dear home with every good feeling unimpaired!' An English squire, wintering in Rome in the first year of peace, told a friend that he had seen nothing among its southern profusion equal to Cowesfield House. 'Never mind the climate – stay where you are; all their tinsel and show can never be put in comparison with the solids and substantials of England.'

CHAPTER TWO

Dark Satanic Mills

'An inventive Age . . . I have lived to mark
A new and unforeseen creation rise
From out the labours of a peaceful land
Wielding her potent enginery to frame
And to produce . . . From the germ
Of some poor hamlet, rapidly produced
Here a huge town, continuous and compact,
Hiding the face of earth for leagues – and there
Where not a habitation stood before,
Abodes of men irregularly massed
Like trees in forests – spread through spacious tracts
O'er which the smoke of unremitting fires
Hangs permanent . . .'

William Wordsworth

'And was Jerusalem builded here
Among these dark Satanic mills.'

William Blake

IN DEFEATING NAPOLEON and the Revolution in arms Britain had grown richer than ever before. Her twenty-two years' struggle, though it had cost her seven hundred million pounds, had doubled her export trade and trebled her revenue. Her merchant tonnage had risen from a million to two and a half million tons; the carrying trade of the world was in her hands. Her commerce with the Spanish and Portuguese colonies in South America alone had increased fourteenfold. By her conquests in India, her occupation of the Cape, Ceylon and Malta, and her voyages of trade and discovery in southern and eastern seas, she had extended her tentacles into every shore of earth and raised the population of her empire from twenty to seventy millions.

Year in, year out, the ships of maritime Britain carried her trade abroad, sailing from her estuaries under great wings of white canvas, with manufactured cottons, woollens, hardware and cutlery, guns, wrought copper and brass, linens, lace and silks, saddlery and tanned leather, pottery, china clay, ironware, coal and rock salt, and returning with raw cotton from the United States, timber from the Baltic, wine from France, Sicily, Portugal and the Atlantic islands, sugar, rum and mahogany from the Caribbean, tea and spices from the East Indies, cod from the Newfoundland fisheries. Nor did Britain only enjoy unrivalled elegance and comfort; she exported it. From Wedgwood's famous factory at Etruria in Staffordshire went out the wares – 'neat, strong and beautiful' – which were famed all over Europe. In every good inn from Paris to St Petersburg, it was said, travellers were served on English ware. The workmanship, durability, ingenuity and variety of British goods were the wonder of the age.

During the war the annual value of Britain's imports rose from nineteen to thirty-two million pounds, of exports from twenty-seven to fifty-eight millions. The principal article exported was manufactured cotton. This industry – trifling when the war began – had outdistanced even the cloth trade, for centuries the country's premier commercial interest, though this, too, under the impact of war and machinery, was also fast expanding. Spinning had now become almost entirely a machine and factory activity. In Glasgow alone there were more than forty mills employing over two hundred work people apiece; Dale and Owen of the great New Lanark Mills employed as many as sixteen hundred. Flax and worsted spinning were following the example of cotton, though weaving in all branches of the textile trade was still mainly done 'out'. But the steam-power loom, first set up in Manchester in 1806 as the rival of the handloom, was already proving a godsend to manufacturers trying to capture the markets which Britain's naval victories had opened. Three years after Waterloo two thousand power-looms were in operation; thereafter their numbers doubled every other year.

It was the blast furnaces which had made the armanents that broke Napoleon. With the growing demand for iron – the main sinew of war – and the exhaustion of the south country forests which had fed the old charcoal furnaces and built the nation's wooden ships, steam-power – the invention of a succession of native geniuses – had been applied to the new coke furnaces of the North and Midlands. By the end of the war these were turning out between a quarter and half a million tons more than at its beginning. To feed the furnaces and the steam-power engines which could do with one man's labour what it had needed a dozen to do before, landowners and contractors prospected eagerly for coal and, finding it in abundance, made power-pumps and machinery

27

to mine it, and iron-grooved or railed tracks to carry it to their customers.

A vast working population had been called into being to supply every manner of article to countries too busied in mutual slaughter and destruction to be able to make it for themselves. No one could gainsay the tireless energy with which the British worked to supply them. The operatives who combed and sheared the cloth of the West Riding worked from four in the morning till eight at night; at Birmingham, a foreigner reported, no one spoke or thought of anything but labour. The London shops closed their shutters at midnight and opened again at dawn. When the first edition of Scott's *Fortunes of Nigel* reached London from Edinburgh on a Sunday – the one day of rest observed by this nation of toilers – the bales were cleared from the wharves by one o'clock on Monday morning and 7,000 copies distributed before ten.

Punctuality and dispatch were universal attributes. 'With habits of early rising,' Cobbett asked, 'who ever wanted time for any business?' 'Sharp's the word and sharp's the action,' was the motto of the great carrier, William Deacon. The founder of W. H. Smith's built up his firm's fortunes by galloping the morning newspapers to catch the out-going mails. There was something heroic about the energy of the English, Scots and Welsh in their struggle for existence. A penniless widow in a little Lincolnshire town made and hawked pasteboard boxes for sixteen hours a day to feed and educate her son; her only respite was an occasional pipe with a neighbour who kept her children by sewing sacks for a factory; whereupon, her son wrote, 'the two brave women would go again to work after cheering each other to go stoutly through the battle of life.'

They wasted little. The refuse of the capital was sold to the Essex and Hertfordshire farmers; the scourings of the streets were shipped to Russia to mix with clay for rebuilding Moscow. Frugality was the handmaid of industry; the possession of property, saved or inherited, was viewed as the only way in which a man could become master of his fate and independent. For in all they did the English fended, and expected to fend, for themselves. With energy and frugality went a sense of enterprise and adventure. A nine-year-old Gainsborough boy, having raised fourpence by selling old bits of iron salvaged from the Trent, turned it into a half-crown by begging a lift to Hull, fifty miles away, and returning with a bag of cockles for sale in his native inland town.

At this time Britain was the most ingenious and inventive national society on earth. The first suspension bridge was built over the Tagus in 1812 by a major of the Royal Staff Corps to ensure swift communication between the two wings of Wellington's army. A society which venerated freedom of thought and action, peopled by an hereditary race of skilful mechanics, had proved a seed-plot for invention. For man in England was not only a tool-using, but a tool-making, animal. The country's educational system – based on Latin grammar school and craft apprenticeship – like most British institutions at the beginning of the nineteenth century, was overgrown with antiquity and in need of reform. But it threw up that wonderful company of country lads who, building on the foundations laid by the great artificer inventors of the eighteenth century, were to transform in the next fifty years the face, not only of Britain, but of the entire civilized world. Smiles's *Lives of the Engineers* is a saga of miraculous achievement wrought out of the native genius and character of a succession of Scottish and English country lads: Rennie, the millwright's apprentice who drained the Lincolnshire Fens and built docks and iron bridges; weavers and machinists like Samuel Crompton and Thomas Johnson, who, backed by their employers, made lonely Lancashire the economic corner-stone of the world; the engineers, Bramah – a village carpenter's boy – Roberts and Whitworth, Trevithick the Cornish giant, and George Stephenson the Northumberland collier's son who laid the foundations of the railway age. Steampower to raise water and coal and drive engines, ships and vehicles; gas to light streets, shops and houses; safety lamps to prevent explosions in mines; water-closets instead of foul-smelling privies; wooden legs with elastic springs to reproduce the motions of nature, umbrellas and waterproof hats, chairs which sprang out of walking-sticks, even braces to keep up trousers, were all, in their different ways, manifestations of the tireless British will to tame nature for use, amenity and social betterment, and grow rich in the process.

So were the ingenuities of the scientists who, voyaging ahead of the practical possibilities of their ages, were laboriously charting new courses for the future. Young Michael Faraday, the Newington Butts blacksmith's son, at his work on electricity; John Dalton studying the combination of the elements and determining atomic weights while teaching mathematics at half a crown an hour; Sir Humphrey Davy, who invented the safety lamp for miners in the year of Waterloo and thrilled fashionable London audiences with his chemical discourses at the Royal Institution in Albemarle Street. It was part of the same revolutionary urge that threw up in philosophy a Rousseau, in politics a Robespierre, and in war a Napoleon. Being a practical people, the English and Scots made their contribution to it in a utilitarian form. By doing so they did more to transform the material world and man's life in it than any of the other aspirants of the age.

Improved transport was a first condition of this revolution. The unlettered Derbyshire millwright, James Brindley – who with James Watt, the Greenock-born contriver of the expansive use of steam, was, in his humdrum, practical way, the British counterpart of Rousseau – conceived the revolutionary idea of making canals independent of rivers on a nation-wide scale. He and his fellow engineers created man-made inland waterways, straight and easily navigable, to take the place of God's, controlling water-levels, tunnelling mountains and bridging valleys with aqueducts. Before and during the war, more than 3000 miles of canal were built, enabling coal, iron, timber, pottery and heavy goods to be carried to any part of the country as easily and as cheaply as by sea.

At the same time the character of road travel was transformed. Before the war, even on the main trunk roads, postilions had to quarter ceaselessly from side to side to avoid huge pools of water and ruts deep enough to break a horse's leg; as late as the winter of 1797-8 the highway from Tyburn to Oxford was from a foot to eighteen inches deep in mud. The genius of two Lowland Scots, Thomas Telford, a Dumfriesshire shepherd's son, and John McAdam, provided the country, during the first quarter of the nineteenth century, with smooth-metalled highways built on Roman lines. Their engineered gradients, culverts and bridges raised the speed of post-chaises and coaches from four or five miles an hour to ten or even twelve. The mail-coaches, with their chocolate-coloured panels, scarlet wheels and melodious horns, became the national time-pieces. Such was their regularity that all along the roads men set their clocks by 'Nimrod', 'Regulator' or 'Tally-ho.'

* * *

Thanks to Adam Smith and his great germinative bible of commercial liberty, *The Wealth of Nations*, few administrative swathes impeded this process. While Bumble and the squire still governed by ancient lights in the village, the winding road to the smoky towns in the Northern dales and Midland heaths was open to every man of enterprise. Activity followed opportunity, and wealth and power activity. The whirling wheels of Brummagem and Manchester set the patterns of a new world.

Yet the underlying stresses and strains on Britain's polity were enormous. Taking place in the midst of a great war, it involved an immense dislocation of social life. Absorbed in the struggle for national survival and European liberation, the country's rulers had had neither time nor thought for the regulation of a new kind of society. Their eyes were riveted on southern horizons where their fleets and expeditions were containing the immense explosive force of continental revolution. They could spare only a hasty glance northwards when some riot in hungry Lancashire or Staffordshire sent the yeomanry clattering over the cobblestones. Trade and men alike had had to find their own level in the rough Britain of endurance which stood the long siege of the revolution militant and Napoleon.

Most of the steam-factory towns were situated on wild heaths and moors in scantily populated neighbourhoods little influenced by gentry or clergy. In these settlements, almost doubling in population during the war, with their filth, noise and perpetual inflow of new inhabitants, the old framework of society round church, manor-court and the ancient village democracy of constable, way-warden and overseer, broke down completely. Here only the law of the jungle operated. Success in discovering new forms of livelihood was uprooting growing numbers from the county's traditional life. While many thrived in that freer society, many more, the old props gone, went to the wall. Those swept into the slums of the squatters' towns round the steam factories could transmit to their children only a memory of the Christian traditions and influences among which their parents had grown up. A generation after Trafalgar and Waterloo only a third of Manchester's children attended church, chapel or school.

To the few with perception and conscience who visited the new towns it seemed as though the nation was selling its soul to Mammon. Under the double impact of war and the new price-cutting economics, men, women and children were being subjected to influences which endangered the future morality and physique of the race. At a moment when British patriotism had been invoked as never before to defeat the French, the conception of patriotism was being discarded in economic matters for the creed of a bagman. Ancient pieties and ways of life were being uprooted by the action of machinery and cut-throat competition; liberty for the thrustful to grow rich was held to justify every abuse. Thousands were being driven from their homes and traditional crafts

31

by enclosure and unemployment and herded like slaves into the new mills without the leaders of national opinion uttering a word in protest or even seeming aware of their plight. In Manchester and the surrounding cotton towns, children, set to the looms at seven years of age, worked from five in the morning till six at night, while the adult population, ceaselessly multiplying in numbers, was crowded into narrow, airless, sunless streets and underground cellars. Little girls of ten, naked and black with coal dust, dragged trucks on all fours down the tunnels of Northumbrian mines, and in Birmingham men went about with thumbs crushed into formless lumps by unfenced machinery. Stench and darkness, hellish din and ignorance were becoming the lot of an ever-growing proportion of the race. And this in a Christian country whose social happiness and freedom was the envy of the world!

For here in the industrial North and Midlands was revolution – one more permanent and, to those who could comprehend its effect, more terrifying than any wrought by mob or guillotine. A whole society was being transformed by the impact of whirling wheels and grinding machines, while the nation's constitutional rulers, far removed from the wild moors, mosses and lonely valleys where the revolution was taking place, stood aside and let it take its course. Though this transformation of the nation's life was still only in its infancy and affected as yet only a small part of the total population, in the industrial districts the whole appearance of the countryside was changing. In south Lancashire and north-east Cheshire, in the West Riding, on Tyneside and Clyde, on the Warwickshire and Staffordshire heaths, the landscape was growing black, the villages were turning into towns and the towns were running into one another. The trout streams were poisoned by dye-vats and the valleys studded with smoke-stacks; the willows and the hazels of the Irk blackened and laid waste, the groves of birch, wild rose and rowan and the green hills with the classical names and haunting rustic deities – Babylon Brow and Stony Knows – desecrated by money-grinders.

* * *

The character of economic relationships was changing with the appearance of the countryside. The weaver, spinner, or stockinger of the past, working in his own cottage with the help of his family and, perhaps, a single apprentice, owning or hiring his own tools and selling the finished article to a capitalist wholesaler in the nearest town, from whom he also obtained the raw materials of his trade, was being superseded by the proletarian factory worker operating expensive power-machines owned by others and owning nothing himself but his labour. With every advance of the technological revolution the control of the capitalist over the conditions of work tightened. Before the end of the war the East Midland hosiers were letting out frames to stockingers in the Leicestershire and Nottinghamshire villages at thirty per cent per annum of their capital cost. Workmen who, rather than pay such rentals, tried to buy their own machines, found themselves shut out from both raw materials and markets. If they could not sell their wares promptly, their families starved. The decent hosier's standards were constantly forced down by the price and wage-cutting of his less scrupulous rivals. So were the good craftsman's.

It was a tragedy that, at the moment when the introduction of labour-saving machinery effected this social revolution, the prevailing economic philosophy should have been so fanatically opposed to any protective regulation of conditions of employment. There were many regulations on the statute book dating from Stuart, Tudor and even medieval times, but the political economists, who since the time of Adam Smith had monopolized the ear of Parliament, held them in contempt. The idea of regulating men's economic actions for their own good ran counter to the whole spirit of the age. Jeremy Bentham, father of utilitarian radicalism – the creed of every progressive for a quarter of a century after Waterloo – maintained that all law was an evil, since it involved a restraint of liberty. To him, as to the great seventeenth-century Whig merchant, Josiah Child, the laws of England were 'a heap of nonsense compiled by a few ignorant country gentlemen.' Most educated men at this time subscribed to Burke's dictum that the chief inlet by which oppression entered the world was by one man pretending to determine the happiness of another. 'The right of the State to interfere to prevent a man from injuring himself,' wrote the economist, Nassau Senior, 'supposes that the legislator knows better how to manage the affairs of an individual than the man does himself.'

The effects of this theory could be best observed in places where the new industrial workers lived. In the first two decades of the nineteenth century the population of Manchester increased from 94,000 to 160,000, of Bolton from 29,000 to 50,000 and of Lancashire from 672,000 to 1,052,000. The houses sheltering this growing multitude were put up by jerry-builders as cheaply as possible, without water-pipes or drains, with roofs and floors supported by planks, and bricks so thin that neighbours could hear one another speaking. In the sinister, sunless city beside the filthy Sheaf – whose forges, set against the bleak Derbyshire hills, made the world's finest cutlery – Samuel Bamford, the handloom weaver, and his wife were driven from their inn by the bugs which swarmed on the dirty walls and bedding. Fever caused more deaths in the industrial towns every year than Wellington's armies suffered in the Peninsular War. Thousands sheltered in foetid cellars and airless courts side by side with Irish 'bog-trotters' in search of a subsistence their own country could not afford them. Within a few months of Bamford's migration from a moorland village to Manchester, his entire family was struck down by typhus.

The early cotton-spinning mills, driven by water power, were mainly operated by pauper child-apprentices hired from poor-law over-seers. Situated in the lonely upper reaches of Pennine rivers, there was no other way of staffing them. When steam-power transferred the mills to large centres of population – generally in the neighbourhood of coal mines – pauper indentured labour was reinforced by a plentiful supply of women and children from the families of skilled artisans who, being thrown out of work by machine competition, were of necessity forced to let them enter the factories in their place. For their need was exploited with ruthless realism. 'When a manufacturer,' wrote Walter Scott, 'wishes to do a particular job he gathers one or two hundred weavers from lanes, streets and garrets without the slightest attention to character or circumstances or to anything but that they have ten fingers and can drive a shuttle. These men are employed perhaps for a fortnight and then turned off, the employer knowing no more or caring no more than if they were so many old pins or shuttles.'

In the great cotton manufactory at Lanark, employing 2,500 hands, mostly children who had started work at the age of seven or eight, the hours were from 6 a.m. till 7 p.m. followed by evening school from 8 p.m. to 10 p.m. These long hours – sometimes more than fifteen a day for six days a week – were regarded by employers and economists as essential to enable manufacturers to compete against undercutting and secure the markets without which their employees might be thrown out of work and starve. Viewed in this sense, the labour that crippled children's limbs, rotted their lungs and stunted their minds, was seen as a blessing, a means of preserving them from famine.

Every year machines exerted a greater tyranny over men's lives, forcing them to work yoked to automata which neither wearied nor rested. For, though multiplying and cheapening consumer goods, the effect of machinery was disastrous for man considered as a producer.

No longer was his work adapted to his nature – to his physical needs, pride, skill and affections. Instead he was forced into the unnatural mould of forms of labour dictated by the capacity of machines and the figures of machine-made accountancy. He was deprived of the control of his tools and of his familiar home, of access to the fields and the fresh fruits of the earth. Herded into factories like prisons and towns like pig-sties, he saw his children grow up to a life utterly unlike that in which he and his forebears had lived.

*　　*　　*

A breach within the nation was allowed to develop and widen because the ruling class had been taught by the new economists that the pursuit of self-interest was the key to national well-being. To buy at the cheapest and sell at the dearest was the new Commandment which in economic matters was taking the place of the original Ten. Any restriction on what was called 'free' bargaining was repugnant to 'enlightened' opinion. Kindly employers – whose hearts were touched by the sufferings of children in their mills and in those of their harsher competitors – who sought restrictive legislation to render humanity compatible with solvency, were able to do little or nothing against such a combination of doctrinal theory and self-interest.

This determinist philosophy – the precursor of Marxism – accorded perfectly with the requirements of landowners and manufacturers, who, needing ever-larger sums for a competitive and showy society or for the enlargement of their businesses, accepted the undernourishment, disease and degrading surroundings of their fellow countrymen as an inevitable dispensation of Providence. It received an intellectual justification from the works of a clergyman named Thomas Malthus, who, living from 1766 to 1834, contended that population automatically outran subsistence, nature's law being to preserve the economy of the world by eliminating surplus mouths and hands through starvation. 'We are bound in justice and honour,' he wrote, 'formally to disclaim the *right* of the poor to support. To this end I should propose a regulation to be made declaring that no child born from any marriage taking place after the expiration of a year from the date of the law should ever be entitled to parish assistance . . . If he cannot get subsistence from his parents on whom he has a just demand, and if the society does not want his labour, he has no claim or right to the smallest portion of food, and in fact has no business to be where he is. At nature's mighty feast there is no vacant cover for him.' It was a proof of the extent to which educated and humane Englishmen were bewildered by the rise in population and the corresponding cost of poor relief, that they accepted, and even with a kind of melancholy enthusiasm, this monstrous doctrine from a pastor of the Christian church – himself a kindly and reasonable man.

In the international sphere Britain's rulers had resisted the revolutionary claim that, in the sacred name of freedom, the strong had a natural right to override the mutual obligations of law. Yet in the economic sphere the same rulers, in disregard of their country's historical traditions, accepted the revolutionary thesis that the strong had a right to enrich themselves without regard to social obligations and the continuing claims of the community. In England the legatees of the supremacy of natural right – the untrammelled liberty of superior energy and brain – was not the soldier of fortune, but the thrusting, broad-shouldered *condottieri* of commerce and finance. They, too, like Napoleon, regarded the world as their oyster and ravaged and exploited as they conquered. Like him, they made themselves rich but uprooted millions of their fellow countrymen in the process. And, in accordance with the revolutionary economic doctrine that the pursuit of private gain must automatically enrich the community, they were allowed almost unfettered control of the ordinary Englishman's home, environment, food, health and conditions of labour.

*   *   *

It was not only in the towns that the poor suffered on a cross of supposed economic necessity. The British revolution, unlike that of France, did not spring from the corruption and inefficiency of an outworn society but from the country's very vigour and success, of which its fortitude and valour in its twenty-two years' struggle against the armed Jacobin and Napoleon were witness. With population rising by at least fifteen per cent in every decade, and grain imports stopped by the war, increased corn-growing had become an urgent national priority as well as a means of vast private profit to those who farmed and, above all, owned the land. To overcome the opposition of the less well-educated peasantry and the wasteful overcropping of the soil under the old communal system of open farming, and apply the new methods of stock breeding and root-cultivation on a nation-wide scale, the landowning class, having boldly invested enormous sums to increase agricultural production, had used its monopoly of political power to secure private acts of Parliament redistributing the arable fields and commons. Between 1796 and 1815 more than 1800 enclosure Bills were passed, 400 more than in the previous forty years. In no other way could the supply of home-grown food – and none other was available – have kept pace with the rise in population.

The social, as opposed to the economic, consequences of this agrarian revolution were, however, disastrous. Growing numbers of husbandmen who had enjoyed a small but vital stake in the land – a strip or two in the parish arable fields, pasture on the common for a few ragged cattle, pigs and geese, the right to gather manure and fuel – found themselves deprived of them. Unable to face the initial costs of legislation, fencing and drainage involved in enclosure, they were forced to sell their compensatory allotments to their richer neighbours. Those who possessed only squatters' rights on the manorial commons or waste received no compensation at all. Men with an hereditary talent for dealing with soil and beasts were requited with payment in a medium in whose use they had neither skill nor experience. As often as not, they spent it in the alehouse. Henceforward they and their children had no resource but that of the wages they earned. They ceased to be peasants and became proletarians, without security and therefore without liberty.

The rich welcomed the changed status of the rural poor because it made them easier to discipline. The more profitable farming became and the more eager the rich to buy, the greater became the temptation of the poor to sell. Every year the amount of land in well-to-do hands increased. It was leased from them at high rents by a new race of tenant farmers who, operating under almost ideal conditions, with expanding markets, rising war prices, and cheap and abundant labour, could afford to operate on a far bigger scale than their fathers. Capital was found to drain, improve and compost the soil, experiment in new root and grass crops, and raise the herds and flocks of fine cattle, pigs and sheep that were the wonder of the world.

For the farm labourer on the other hand, these improvements meant a fatal deprivation of amenities. He lost with the open field and common his milk, butter, poultry, eggs and cooking fuel. Having no stake in what he raised, he gained nothing from its increased price. On the contrary, having now to buy most of his own and his family's food, he was doubly the loser. Though his wages rose during the war, they did not rise as quickly as prices. The inflationary rise began for him at the wrong end, with the proceeds of labour instead of its reward. It was aggravated by the growing tendency of farmers, producing no longer for sustenance but for profit, to sell to middlemen whose profits had to be added to the price of the farm labourer's bread and ale. At the same time his family's supplementary earnings from domestic handicrafts were being reduced or eliminated by the growing competition of machines. The farmhouse where the young unmarried labourer had formerly boarded with the homely family of his yeoman employer became the residence of a finer kind of farmer, whose sons hunted and whose daughters played the piano and who could not be bothered with the board of farm domestics. Many of the smaller farmhouses disappeared altogether in the engrossment of farms which followed the enclosures. The landlords and their new tenants, Cobbett wrote in 1821, stripped the land of all shelter for the poor. Simond earlier noted the same phenomenon; the countryside swarmed with gentlemen's houses and opulent farms, but the dwellings of the real poor were hard to discover. Among the roofless ruins of Valle Crucis Abbey he saw peasants and their children squatting with pigs and poultry. 'The poor are swept out of the way,' he wrote, 'as the dust out of the walks of the rich.'

Before enclosure the chief source of hired agricultural labour had been the small holder or commoner, who devoted two or three days a week to looking after his own land and worked on that of a richer neighbour for the remainder. Though the latter was now becoming the peasant's sole support, the farmer who employed him, being in an advantageous bargaining position – for a man with a hungry family cannot stand on terms – was slow to raise his wages. As early as 1795 the rapidity with which prices rocketed under the stimulus of war and a bad harvest, threatened the landless labourer with famine. In the face of this threat the Berkshire magistrates at their meeting at Speenhamland had taken a fateful decision. Instead of enforcing a minimum wage – a measure which they shirked out of deference to the new economic teaching – they fixed a basic rate of subsistence, based on the fluctuating price of corn and the size of the family, and authorized a grant in aid to all who were being paid less than this by their employers. By thus subsidizing wages out of rates, they pauperized the labourer.

Magistrates in many parts of the country followed their well-intentioned example. Not only were farmers countenanced in their reluctance to pay an economic wage, but poor-rates rocketed out of all proportion to the incomes of the smaller rate-payers, who thus became saddled with part of the working costs of their richer neighbours. The decent employer was taxed to subsidize his unfair competitor and – since no man with savings could qualify for relief – the thrifty husbandman to maintain the unthrifty. By 1818 the annual national contribution to poor-rates, little more than £700,000 before the War, had risen to nearly eight millions. More than a fifth of the rural population of England and Wales – Scotland had no poor law – was in receipt of some form of parochial relief. Thousands of small husbandmen, faced by rate demands beyond their means, were also driven into the ranks of the landless workers and became themselves a charge on the rates. The poor laws, wrote Malthus, had created the poor they assisted.

The effect on the labourer was even more disastrous, for he was robbed of his self-respect. Having lost his proprietary rights, he found himself a member of a pariah class; a labour reserve from which landlords and farmers drew when it suited them without regard to human rights and feelings. In many places the overseers – generally farmers little in birth and education above those they administered – insisted that the grant of parish relief entitled them to complete control over the lives of those whose wages they subsidized.

This accumulation of evil circumstances had fallen on the rural poor so rapidly, first in one locality and then in another, that few who were not directly affected were even aware of what was occurring. In most places its effect was not felt until the great agricultural depression set in after the war. But wherever it struck, it left the English peasantry – the traditional backbone of the country – suffering from a feeling of bewildered helplessness. Old England was tightening into neat-hedged and gated fields and high-walled parks; the sense of property was running mad and cruel, and there seemed no place in it save a serf's for the poor countryman whose ill-requited labour had wrought the transformation. Though many landlords and farmers maintained the old kindly, paternal relations with those who worked on their own farms and gardens or lived in their immediate vicinity, others, in their absorption in fashionable and sporting pleasures, increasingly left the management of their estates to professional intermediaries. The way in which bailiffs and land-stewards whittled away or ignored ancient rights was bitterly resented.

The labourer's suffering was aggravated by the increasing rigour with which the game laws were enforced by landowners obsessed with the new mania for vast battues and game-bags. A Parliament of game-preservers, in the south of England at least, was banishing the peasant

39

from the sports of his fathers. Men whose families were hungry, and who saw pheasants, hares and partridges in every wood around them, could not resist the temptation of going out at night with gun and net to fill the pot or reap the rewards – far higher than their wages – offered by the agents of the London poulterers. When caught, they received short shrift from magistrates, who in this matter, so close to their hearts, could be utterly ruthless. By a savage act of 1816 a man caught at night in an enclosure with instruments for trapping game could be sentenced to transportation by two magistrates, one of whom might be the injured property owner, while a blow, struck or even threatened in a poaching fray, could be punished by the gallows. The war between poachers and gamekeepers reached a terrible crescendo in the agricultural depression after the Napoleonic wars. Hundreds were killed or maimed in pitched battles in the woods or by the spring-guns and man-traps with which the more ignoble landlords protected their property and pleasures. Not all was grim, however. Walter Scott wrote to a friend, in 1825: 'Nothing would induce me to put up boards threatening prosecution or cautioning one's fellow-creatures to beware of man-traps and spring-guns.'

Because of these things the peasant's unquestioning patriotism and respect for his feudal superiors were being replaced by a growing sense of injustice. At the time of Waterloo the social cataclysm which befell him was still far from universal. In the north, where the competition of the industrial towns for labour kept up wages, its effects had been comparatively little felt. And everywhere the sufferings of the poor, in this tremendous and little understood revolution, were modified by the decency and kindliness of thousands of worthy men and women, whose sense of duty to their fellow-beings remained unaffected by opportunities of self-enrichment or by the new philosophy of *laissez-faire*. Yet taking a broad view, while the horizon had lifted for the rich and strong, for the poor, it was fast darkening. The rulers of Christian England, and those who by their writings helped to form educated opinion, were blind to the changes which new opportunities of enrichment for the rich had brought to their poorer countrymen. They failed to see the hopelessness and hunger of the peasant deprived of his stake in the land and of the produce that had sustained his family. They failed to comprehend the agony of once independent countrymen imprisoned in the discipline of the factory and surrounded by the hideous squalor of the industrial town, or the mentality of children who grew up among these gloomy phenomena knowing no other. There was some excuse for their incapacity to realize the social consequences of the Industrial Revolution, since this, in the year 1815, was still in its lusty infancy and cradled in the most remote and unfrequented parts of the island. There was far less for their failure to understand the tragic social transformation wrought by the agricultural revolution at their park gates. They knew that by its means more food was obtained for their country and more rent for themselves. They turned a blind eye to its inability to produce the free and contented men and women who for so long had been the main source of England's wealth.

CHAPTER THREE

Years Of Disillusion

'Men of England, wherefore plough
For the lords who lay ye low,
Wherefore weave with toil and care
The rich robes your tyrants wear.'
Percy Bysshe Shelley (1819)

IT COULD BE SAID in excuse of the rich that, while the war continued and prosperity with it, many working men shared in that prosperity, and that when the war ended and the full force of depression fell on the poor, it was no longer in the rich's power, struggling with lapsing leases and tumbling rentals, to help them. And, contrary to all expectation, prices fell even before the war ended. The cessation of Government buying to feed the armies and the opening of the American and European grain ports brought down agricultural profits with a run. The magnificent English harvests of 1813 and 1815, and that of 1814 in France, flooded the markets. Few farmers had saved money, for, unable to visualize anything but rising prices, they had re-invested everything in their land. The poorer soils that they had ploughed to satisfy wartime demand became economically unworkable with wheat prices dropping from 120s. a quarter – the 1813 level – to 76s. in 1815 and 53s. 6d. in the spring of 1816. The value of farm stock fell fifty per cent.

Having undertaken leases on terms compatible only with wartime profits, farmers found themselves unable to pay their rents or to meet the interests on their loans and mortgages. The banks, fearful for the capital they had advanced, called in their money. Hundreds of tenants defaulted, and thousands sought rent remission. Rentals everywhere shrank, though to a level much higher than that of a generation before. The doors of the landed gentry were still guarded by armies of liveried retainers, their woods abounded with game, their wonderful horses shook the earth. But they were thrown into a flurry of anxiety and spoke of ruin, both national and personal.

Their representatives in Parliament tried to bolster up prices by legislation. For twenty years the Corn Laws, which from time immemorial had prevented the export of corn in domestic shortages and protected the home-grower during foreign gluts, had been abrogated by war and blockade. Now they had suddenly become a necessity if the farmer was to pay his rent, taxes, tithes and mortgage interest. On both sides of the House it was contended that the rising number of mouths to be fed necessitated more home-grown corn, even if it involved uneconomic tillage. To rely for part of the nation's food on foreign supplies was too risky; more than once during the war England had nearly starved. It seemed better that the people should pay more for their corn in fat years to be sure of it in lean. It was in their interest, too, it was argued, that prices should be stabilized – a traditional aim of the Corn Laws.

But the landless labourers of England, both rural and industrial, dreaming, after all that they had suffered in war, of the traditional first-fruits of peace – a cheap loaf – viewed these landowners' arguments with suspicion. So did the northern manufacturers, seeking to effect cheap sales abroad through reduced wages at home – a policy impossible to enforce while food prices remained at their wartime level. The House of Commons was flooded with petitions: one from Leeds bore 24,000 signatures, another from Bristol 40,000, others from Liverpool and Manchester 50,000 apiece. Despite, however, their being referred to a select committee, a Bill excluding foreign corn until the price of native corn reached 80s. a quarter passed both Houses in March 1815.

Legislators were left with no illusions about the measure's unpopularity. The degree to which the landed interest had been weakened by the destruction of an independent peasantry now became apparent. Outside Parliament landowners and farmers found themselves almost alone; the agricultural labourer, having nothing left to gain from high food prices, was either apathetic or against them. Crowds surrounded Parliament, holding up halters and shouting, 'No starvation!' 'No landlords!'; the house of the minister who had introduced the Bill was sacked by the mob.

Industry was also in trouble. The Government, which had been spending fifty million pounds a year supplying the Fleet and Army and almost as much in subsidizing foreign States to buy British munitions and uniforms, went out of business. The bottom fell out of the armament market. The price of iron dropped from £20 to £8 a ton and of copper from £180 to £80. Other commodities fell in proportion. Exports, after a brief hectic rise, declined by seven million pounds, those of foreign and colonial produce from twenty millions to scarcely ten. After so long and destructive a war the European nations were too poor to buy.

This recession was turned into a disaster by the reckless way in which British exporters poured their wares into war-ravaged or under-developed countries that lacked the buying-power to absorb them. The Spanish colonies – now in revolt against the mother country – were deluged with improbable wares. The multiplying power of Britain's machines was not yet matched by the capacity of her merchants to forecast markets or of her customers to absorb goods. From the moment the war ended a mounting shortage of purchasing-power developed in every department of national life. By 1816 two-thirds of the Shropshire blast furnaces had shut down. Steam-engine manufacturers, unable to meet their wage bills, either reduced wages or discharged hands. Needing not skilled men so much as machine-minders, of which the towns at their factory gates offered an inexhaustible supply, they felt under no obligation, economic or moral, to maintain their employees. Simultaneously the labour market was flooded by thousands of ex-soldiers and sailors who, being without any income whatever, contributed no consumer-demand but, by their competition for employment, forced down wages further.

Finding itself short of money, the country turned on the Government and demanded reduction of taxation. If landowners, farmers and manufacturers could no longer enjoy war prices, they could no longer stomach war charges. So long as the war lasted, Britons had borne their burdens with patience. In 1815 a population of fourteen millions was contributing £72,000,000 per annum in taxes, or a fifth of the national income, as compared with the £19,000,000 paid in 1792 by one of ten millions.

The charge fell on almost every commodity. It was said that the Government owned one wheel of every coach on the road. The price of glory, wrote Sydney Smith, was 'taxes on the ermine which decorates the judge and the rope which hangs the criminal – on the poor man's salt and the rich man's spices – on the brass nails of the coffin and the ribands of the bride . . . The schoolboy whips his taxed top, the beardless youth manages his taxed horse with a taxed bridle on a taxed road, and the dying Englishman, pouring his medicine which has paid seven per cent into a spoon that has paid fifteen per cent, flings himself back upon his chintz bed, which has paid twenty-two per cent, and expires into the arms of an apothecary who has paid a licence of a hundred pounds for the privilege of putting him to death.'

Every year in his budget the Chancellor of the Exchequer rang the changes on these omnipresent imposts. The result was always the same: the poor, having no reserve after satisfying their bare needs, paid relatively most of all. Beer – their chief drink – contributed a sixth of the revenue; Cobbett, on a hot day, reckoned that, in their exchange of beer for sweat, the haymakers in the Middlesex alehouses along the road were contributing threepence-halfpenny on every fivepenny pot. The hardships suffered by poor workers at the time are described in Cooper's memoirs; 'of poor widows conspiring to outwit tax-collectors, who, knowing their straits, pursued them with indecent solicitations: of midnight removals of household goods to prevent distraint; the curse upon taxes and the tax-gatherer was in the mouths of thousands.' At St Ives the populace celebrated the first Christmas of the peace by throwing a tax-collector out of the window.

Among those with the power to show resentment the most hated impost was the ten-per-cent income tax which Pitt had instituted in an hour of national peril. He had undertaken that this inquisitorial measure, as it was deemed by those who paid it, should be repealed as soon as the war ended. But the Government, faced with the charge, first of the American War and then of Napoleon's escape from Elba, struggled for more than a year before abandoning it. The Opposition was furious; so were the Government's supporters. The young Whig, Lord John Russell, declared that the tax's continuance would erase the last vestiges of British freedom. Why, it was asked, should the country's military establishment be six times greater than in 1792, especially as France was disarmed and Britain now allied to all Europe. Brougham accused Ministers of plotting to alter the character of the Constitution and make it a military state. The Foreign Secretary, Castlereagh, set on preserving the Grand Alliance which had won the war and guaranteed the peace, and regarded by his insular countrymen as the villain of the piece, was charged with having imbibed so many Continental customs as to have forgotten England was an island.

On August 11th, less than two months after Waterloo, the Prime Minister wrote to warn him that the financial situation was too grave for the nation to be able to shoulder further foreign commitments. The Navy and Army were the first to be pared. Within eighteen months

300,000 soldiers and sailors were turned adrift. A naval officer in charge of a Sussex coastguard station received sudden orders to discharge his men in the dead of winter, though they were on a hilltop miles from anywhere. The men who had fought their way from Torres Vedras to Toulouse were given neither pension nor medal; the finest army England had ever had was dismissed without regret or gratitude.

*   *   *

Other wartime obligations were less easy to evade. Those who had fought England's battles could be relegated to a life of selling trinkets on the highways or sweeping the London streets, but not those who had lent the State cash to pay them. It was the essence of the system of financing war by borrowing that faith must be kept with the public creditor; that is, with the rich investor. The war had raised the National Debt from £252,000,000 to £861,000,000: a 'poisoned dart,' Napoleon boasted, left in England's vitals. The annual interest was £32,645,618, or five times more than the poor rates about which so much fuss was made.

This borrowing, added to every year, and the punctual discharge of interest, was regarded as a triumph of national strength and good faith. It profoundly impressed foreigners. So did the maintenance of 'a paper currency not convertible into gold and therefore not liable to be withdrawn, and yet issued in such moderate quantities as satisfied the wants of man without exceeding them.' Since Pitt's government, by suspending cash payments, had given the privately-owned Bank of England – the principal proprietor of the National Debt – the right to issue paper currency unbacked by gold, there had been a huge increase in circulation. Yet it had been matched by the expansion in real wealth brought about by the machinery and improved farming which an enlarged currency had helped to buy into existence. Without it Britain, under her free system, could not have defeated Napoleon.

Yet though, on the whole, the Bank had exercised its privilege with patriotism and restraint, its directors, and the provincial bankers whose private note-issues had been rendered more valuable, would have been less than human had they not pursued their delegated monopoly of creating money to a point where the increase in note-circulation exceeded the creation of real wealth. In 1810, when the House of Commons set up a Bullion Committee to investigate, £100 of paper currency was selling on 'Change for £86.10s. Yet even this modest inflationary depreciation, as the event proved, was due more to the drain of bullion to feed Wellington's army than to internal inflation. Though speculators did a roaring trade smuggling guineas abroad, and at one time a premium of nearly thirty per cent was paid for gold, the latter started to flow back to England as soon as the war ended. Considering the Bank's opportunity, the degree of permanent inflation was extraordinarily small – a tribute both to the integrity of British bankers and the increase in national production.

In a great nation – the first industrial and trading power in the world – a paper currency based on public credit had been successfully substituted in wartime for one based on precious metals. It had proved capable not only of financing the war but of stimulating a vast creation of real wealth. The increased production of farm and factory Britain had needed for victory had not been retarded by any financial inability of the home consumer to buy it into existence. What was physically possible had been made financially possible. But, realizing neither the character of the transformation through which the country was passing nor the permanent need under it for an elastic system of creating purchasing-power, the British repudiated their wartime financial expedient as soon as the war ended. Anxious at the drain of bullion abroad, bewildered by economic disasters caused by the transition from war to peace, and resentful of the immense fortunes made by bankers, they mistakenly saw in their unorthodox, revolutionary currency the cause of their troubles. The English had a sober respect, almost veneration, for gold; they despised paper. Since the latter was the creation of a Tory Government, the first demand for a resumption of cash payments came from the Whigs, one of whose leaders, Francis Horner, had presided over the Bullion Committee of 1810. It was resisted by the Government on grounds of expediency, but gradually yielded to by ministers as the country's troubles deepened.

The clamour for a return to gold was naturally supported by the fund-holding class. The moderate inflation of the past few years had constituted a concealed tax on the fund-holder, which observers like Simond thought just, partly because the sums lent to the State during the war had been borrowed on terms highly favourable to the lender, and partly because the 'funds' were unburdened by charges like those on land and farm produce. But this modest depreciation of the investor's capital in favour of the owner and producer of real wealth had constituted an intolerable charge on the propertyless labourer, whose wages had failed to rise as quickly as prices. The new proletariat, both rural and industrial, shared neither in the enhanced profits of farmers and manufacturers nor in the fund-holder's discount and interest. Now, by artificially enhancing through a return to gold the value of the latter's claims on the taxpayer – the producer of real wealth on whom the burden of taxation ultimately fell – the Government increased the mortgage on the nation's productive capacity. For, though the payment of the annual debt charge – approximately half the revenue raised by taxation – was only in theory a transfer of money from one pocket of the nation to another, the fund-holders or 'tax-eaters' were not necessarily the same people as the taxpayers. The new policy of deflation increasingly handicapped the latter in their struggle to produce. 'There,' wrote Cobbett six years after Waterloo, 'is the Debt pulling the nation down like as a stone pulls a dog under the water.'

In deference to the Government's plea that so early a return to gold was impracticable, the change-over was fixed for the summer of 1818. The decision, however, caused an immediate restriction in circulation. Commercial paper under discount at the Bank of England – more than £20 million a few years earlier – sank to £11½ million in 1816 and to less than £4 million in the following year. The circulation of country banknotes dropped in proportion. The restriction coincided with a phenomenal reduction in the world's supply of precious metals and a consequent fall in global prices. Civil war in South America had dried up the chief source of bullion at the moment that Britain, with her steam-power machines and improved agriculture, had evolved a new means of multiplying real wealth. In 1816, the quantity of gold and silver raised in the Spanish colonies was only a third of what it had been.

*　　*　　*

Mass production – Britain's gift to the world – necessitated mass consumption. This could only be achieved through an expansive financial policy. The indispensable means in a free society to set the wheels of the new machines turning was buying-power in the pockets of those who needed their products. If, through a restriction of currency, this was lacking, the increased wealth which mechanical science offered could not be brought into existence. Those who had been drawn by the demands of war into the service of the machines, and had become dependent on them, were left workless and, having no alternative means of employment, deprived of the power of buying bread. This in turn halted an expanding agricultural economy and left farmers unable to sell their produce at a time when the industrial population was starving.

In their noble belief in the validity of human freedom, Adam Smith and the early economists had failed to foresee this. Nor had they reckoned on the disturbing passions, destruction and economic dislocation of a generation of global war financed by State borrowing. They had supposed that, through the operation of a just and divinely inspired law of supply and demand, profits, prices and wages must invariably find their true level; that it was only necessary to remove artificial restrictions on freedom of trade and contract to ensure a beneficial and progressive equilibrium. If under free conditions, they held, for any reason wages fell, prices would automatically fall too; and employers, enabled thereby to sell a correspondingly greater quantity of goods, would be able and anxious – seeing it was to their interest to increase production – to pay out, not less, but more in wages. If a labour-saving machine threw men out of work, it would soon, by reducing the price of the goods they and others needed, recall them to the same or other work through the greater demand it created. But it was now found on trial that men who were thrown out of work by new machinery, or whose wages were reduced below a certain level, could buy nothing at all and starved or grew demoralized before the operation of the laws of supply and demand had time to restore things to their proper balance. So did their children.

These monetary laws did not, therefore, appear to be so providential as Adam Smith had supposed. They were merely inevitable. Even though machinery offered man a swifter means of satisfying his needs, their operation involved impoverishment, hunger and degradation. The less sanguine successors of Adam Smith explained this by Malthus's melancholy theory of population and by a new law which that kindly and ingenious clergyman expounded to the world for the first time in 1814 and 1815. By an inescapable dispensation of arithmetic, he explained, there existed at any given moment a fixed sum or fund out of which wages – and taxes – could alone be paid. It was useless for workmen to agitate for, or for employers to wish to pay, more, since the only result of their succeeding must be to diminish the amount available for wages elsewhere. This thesis, explaining and vindicating the terrible economic phenomena of post-war Britain, was expanded by the economist, David Ricardo, who, in a work published in 1817 which became the capitalist's Bible, concluded, by a process of un-

49

answerable deduction from false premises, that wages invariably depended on a ratio between population and capital. Any rise in wages, by automatically stimulating an increase in population, must not only defeat its own end but lead to a general decline of the wage-level.

What manufacturers who accepted this theory overlooked was that on this seemingly insufficient wage-fund depended, not only the livelihood of the starving weaver and sweated mill-hand, but the purchasing-power which could alone keep their own factories in full operation. It was its inadequacy to feed, house and clothe workers who were also buyers that damped down their furnaces, stopped their revolving wheels, emptied their order-books, and threatened them with periodic bankruptcy and the nation with social misery and unrest. For out of this rigid wage-fund had to come, too, the capital needed to install new machinery, or the interest on it, which, while increasing future productive potential, diminished still further the existing purchasing-power that could alone, in the wage-earners' hands, afford an effective and continuous demand for maximum current production. It was because the workers did not receive a proper share of the wealth they helped to create that such wealth did not increase to the extent that the means for creating it admitted. By using their ever-growing bargaining-power to keep the wages of their employees below the maximum level production justified, manufacturers, without realizing what they were doing, put a brake on their own production.

The Government was responsible in that it took no steps to restrain such greed and enforce a reasonable standard of social justice. However understandably, it failed to perceive that, with the novel means afforded by machinery for increasing real wealth, the credit of the State might be used simultaneously to reduce taxation and enlarge consuming-power to a point which would equate it with the power to produce. With agricultural and industrial production lagging behind both capacity and demand, an expansive financial policy might have changed the whole course of nineteenth-century history. By using direct taxation to check inflation in boom periods and judiciously expanding the currency to facilitate reduction of taxation in a depression, a far-seeing Government might have raised the workers' standards of living step by step with the rising wealth of the capitalists. Britain might then have emerged from the Industrial Revolution one nation instead of two.

But both the economic experience and administrative machinery for doing anything so revolutionary were wholly lacking. The nation's only resort in the impasse in which it so unexpectedly found itself was

usury. Like a private subject in straitened circumstances, it resorted
to the pawnbroker and the banker. The era of the Regency, under all
its glittering brilliance, was the age *par excellence* of the moneylender;
almost everyone was borrowing or lending. 'This declining age,' Mary
Mitford called it, 'when too many worthy members of the community
seem to have an alacrity in sinking.' Across rich, victorious England
stalked a shadow: that of the seedy individual pinched for 'the needful',
whom Charles Lamb called 'the deep insolvent'. It was no accident
that to this deflationary era – that of the young Dickens's martyrdom
in the blacking factory – belongs the genesis of Micawber. The shadows
behind countless humble English homes were the dun, the tipstaff and
the debtors' prison. They menaced the socially privileged too; Rawdon
Crawley's fate was not uncommon. Any man might be 'blown up at
Point Non-Plus': John Doe, Richard Roe and the 'leary Bum-trap' were
waiting at the end of many an avenue of promise. Even Lord Byron,
who inherited an estate worth £140,000 and married an heiress, had
an execution in his house. There were bailiffs discreetly disguised as
footmen in ducal, spendthrift Blenheim; the Horsemonger Lane jailor
remarked to Leigh Hunt of the royal brothers: 'They knows me very
well, mister, and, mister, I knows them!'

It was the age of the great bankers – the Barings, Hopes, Coutts,
Hoares and higher Smiths, negotiating loan after loan and mortgaging
and buying up everything around them. The greatest phenomenon of
the age after Napoleon were the Rothschild brothers. Meyer Amschel
Rothschild, who started his career in 'the filthy Judengasse' of Frankfurt, trading old coins and making himself useful to the rich Elector of
Hesse by his money-lending transactions, set up his five sons, born in
the 1770s, in the commercial capitals of war-divided Europe. Lacking
the graces of the aristocratic societies they served, and contending
against constant humiliations, these astonishing brothers possessed
courage, energy, resource and a profound knowledge of human nature.
Never missing any opportunity of profit or of what they valued more
than profit – a new connection – they made themselves indispensable
to those with wealth and power, discounting bills, collecting interest,
making advances, acting as intermediaries between court and court,
and spiriting bullion through the blockade and armies. Their greatest
service, and their own chief source of profit, was the transmission from
capital to capital, and from currency to currency, of the loans and
subsidies with which Britain armed her allies. Ingratiating themselves
with everyone, for they could afford neither friends nor foes, they

used their family network, transcending frontiers, as an unofficial international clearing-house. With governments tumbling about their ears and armies crashing through their gossamer webs of borrowing, they never failed to fulfil, exactly and punctually, every obligation. In a time of universal impecuniosity the House of Rothschild, whose trading profits when the war began were only a few hundred pounds a year, raised themselves to a position of dominating credit in almost every capital of Europe.

The English representative of the family, Nathan, started business at Manchester in his early twenties, with a few thousand pounds and without a word of English. In just over twelve years he built up a vast fortune by the skill with which he used the balances sent him for investment in England by his father's European clients, by conveying bullion through the heart of France to Wellington's armies, and by transmitting to the Continent the subsidies which armed the Grand Alliance. Acting as agent for the paymasters of Europe, he was able to help his brothers establish themselves in similar positions at the courts of Austria, Prussia and Bourbon France. In keeping with the family tradition, he made it his business to offer private accommodation on easy terms to all in high place who needed it, including, it was believed, both the Regent and the principal Permanent Secretary of the Treasury. It was Nathan's courier, outdistancing Wellington's dispatches, who brought the first news of Waterloo to London. Within a few years of the battle he was said to control the national rate of exchange.

What this great man achieved on an international stage, others did on a humbler. They did not succeed without arousing resentment and envy. Cobbett in his blind rage at the debt system – IT, as he called it – which he believed was changing the values of the England he loved, wrote of 'dark, dirty-faced, half-whiskered vermin' to whose expenditure he attributed the alarming expansion of London, Brighton, Cheltenham and other 'odious wens'. He did not confine his venom to Jews; Scotsmen in his view were as bad or worse. Instead of a resident, native gentry attached to the soil, known to every farmer and labourer from childhood, practising hospitality without ceremony, he complained, there was a tribe of fund-lords, contractors, loan-jobbers, brokers and bankers, who were buying up the entire countryside near the capital – 'a gentry only now-and-then residing, having no relish for country delights, foreign in their manners, distant and haughty in their behaviour, looking to the soil only for its rents, viewing it as a mere object of speculation, unacquainted with its cultivators, despising them

Above left: 'From Wedgwood's famous factory in Etruria in Staffordshire went out the wares – "neat, strong and beautiful" – which were famed all over Europe. In every good inn from Paris to St Petersburg, it was said, travellers were served on English ware.' Cream coloured Wedgwood teapot with print and enamel 'Agricultural Implements' pattern.

Above right: James Watt, 'the Grenock-born contriver of the expansive use of steam'. A wax medallion by Peter Rouw.

Below: 'Little girls of ten, naked and black with coal dust, dragged trucks on all fours down the tunnels of Northumbrian mines. Stench and darkness, hellish din and ignorance were becoming the lot of an ever-increasing proportion of the race.' Illustration from the First Royal Report on Mines, 1842.

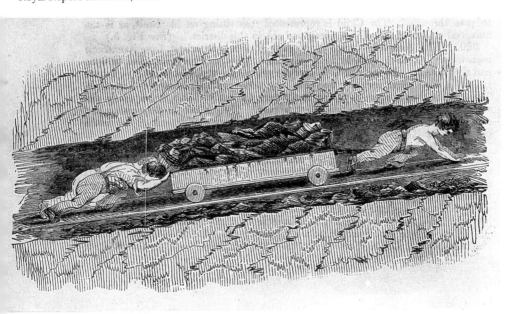

'On the outskirts of Manchester in 1842 there were still sloping wooded valleys with girls keeping sheep a stone's throw from the flat slate roofs and tall smoking chimneys' From the *Illustrated London News*, 1842.

Peterloo, August 1819: 'As soon as Hunt began to speak the alarmed magistrates instructed their police officers to arrest him and ordered a detachment of yeomanry to force a way to the hustings. Jostled by the crowd, the yeomanry lost their heads and started slashing with their sabres. In the panic nine men and two women were killed, and several hundreds wounded.'

and their pursuits, and relying for influence, not upon the good will of the vicinage but the dread of their power.' It was from this class that the great economist, David Ricardo, came – a most kindly, amiable man, inheriting a younger son's portion from his Dutch-Jewish father, starting life in a stock-jobber's office at fourteen and making a fortune before he was forty, when he purchased the estate of Gatcombe Park in Gloucestershire. Later, buying an Irish rotten borough, he entered Parliament where, despite his painful lack of oratory, he became immensely respected, his economic views being treated by all parties almost as holy writ.

*   *   *

'According to the best information I can obtain,' wrote a correspondent in the October after Waterloo, 'the landlords will fall short of their Michaelmas receipts upon an average one half.' All over the country, banks were calling in their money; some, like that in which Jane Austen's brother was a partner, had already closed their doors and stopped payment. As 1815 gave place to 1816 the situation grew worse. With bankers unwilling to advance or discount, no one, not even the rich, seemed to have any money to spare; by the spring ten thousand livery servants were said to be out of place. Among those who went down in the general ruin was the Prince Regent's friend, Beau Brummell, the great dandy, who decamped for Calais with a few pounds. Art prices fell to a level unknown in the history of the sale rooms; even the fashionable portrait-painter, Sir William Beechey, was forced to beg for a settlement of his account with the royal household, 'the unexpected alteration of the times making a shocking impression on the arts.' The only things which seemed to sell in the universal ruin were Scott's novels.

The summer of 1816 proved the worst in memory, though in a brief spell of fine weather at the end of May young Keats, after a day in the Hampstead meadows, wrote his sonnet, 'I stood tiptoe upon a little hill.' Six weeks later, in a torrential July, Jane Austen among the sodden Hampshire fields finished her last and greatest book. 'Oh! It rains again! it beats against the window,' she told a friend. Such a summer, her fellow writer, Mary Mitford, thought, was enough to make one wish for winter all the year round.

It was the same all over western Europe. The English visitors who flocked to the Continent that summer – the first without war in fourteen years – found sullen, pitiless clouds, and the crops destroyed by snow and hailstones. Such stupid mists, fogs and perpetual density suggested to Byron that Castlereagh must have taken over the Foreign Affairs of the Kingdom of Heaven. Meanwhile, in every port British goods were piling up or selling below cost. During one week that year not a single entry for export or import was made at the London Custom-House – an event without parallel in its history. The whole of the manufacturing districts seemed to be out of work.

With the corn sprouting in October, wheat touched 103 shillings in December. In Ireland, where the potato crop failed, the poor were reduced to stalks and nettles. Bamford saw an unemployed calico weaver's wife drop dead from hunger, with her babe at her breast, as she begged before the Middleton overseers for relief. A Scotsman travelling across England at the year's end found half the houses along the road with placards announcing the sale of farming stock; everywhere farmers were ruined, bankers failing. The odious cotton and worsted mills, Dorothy Wordsworth wrote from Halifax, had become mere encumbrances on the ground. 'Few get more than half work – great numbers none at all . . . For a time whole streets – men, women and children – may be kept alive by public charity, but the consequences will be awful if nothing can be manufactured in these places where such numbers of people have been gathered together. . . . If there be not a revival of trade in a smaller way, people and things cannot go on as they are.' The national debt, it was rumoured, was to be wiped out, and Parliament reformed.

Humbler men, no more able to understand what ailed their country than their rulers, took their own remedy. Throughout 1816 a savage anger, unknown in England since the Civil War, spread through the labouring classes. It began in the early summer among the population of the enclosed villages. In Suffolk, Essex, Norfolk, and Cambridge-shire ricks and barns were burnt, some by night and others openly by day, while crowds surrounded mills and bakeries shouting for price reductions. The worst outbreak was at Littleport, where the cellars were broken into and the town subjected to a sack. Anxious Justices were sent galloping Londonwards for help, and cavalry was dispatched to the shires. At Cambridge, where the arrival of the angry fenmen was hourly expected, three hundred special constables were enrolled and the Vice-Chancellor prepared to arm the undergraduates.

Despite resort by a Special Commission to the gallows – Govern-ment's sovereign remedy for all ills – the rioting spread first to the south-west and then to the manufacturing districts. The pitmen of Tyneside and Staffordshire, the Irish slum-dwellers of Glasgow, who, nestling in crowds about the Calton, Bridgeton and Gorbals, were always ripe for mischief, the housewives of Sunderland, the Preston weavers and Welsh iron-moulders all attacked shops and factories. In October the employees of the Tredegar ironworks, faced by further wage reductions and rising prices, marched on Merthyr Tydfil to stop the blast furnaces. Later, 12,000 strong, they crossed the mountains to call out the colliers of Crundin, Newbridge and Abercarne. Only the arrival of the military prevented worse.

The most alarming outbreak of all came at the year's end. Throughout the autumn the radicals of the capital had been gathering strength. At a charitable meeting for the relief of the manufacturing poor organised by Wilberforce and presided over by the Duke of York, they shouted down the royal chairman and forced him to leave amid storms of booing. All over the country Hampden Clubs – revived from an earlier period of republican agitation and thrown open to workers by penny-a-week subscriptions – met in alehouses and dissenting chapels to debate electoral reform, manhood suffrage and annual parliaments. Their proceedings were kept at fever heat by Cobbett, who, evading the stamp duty on cheap newspapers by issuing his *Political Register* as a twopenny pamphlet, sold nearly 50,000 copies of a single number. Thereafter he repeated his defiance weekly. Mass meetings occurred in all the principal industrial towns; at Manchester, Glasgow and Paisley over a hundred thousand were reported to have attended. In the middle of November a still larger gathering took place in Spa Fields, London, where the orator, Henry Hunt, supported by the tricolour and a cap of liberty on a pike, told an excited crowd that their all was being taxed to pension the bastards of the Tory aristocracy. He ended by promising to carry their petition – 'the last resort before physical force' – to the Prince Regent. A few days later Shelley, writing to Byron in Italy, predicted either radical reform when Parliament met in January or the triumph of anarchy and illiterate demagogues.

On 2 December 1816 a further mass meeting was called in Spa Fields. It was preceded by a distribution of handbills proclaiming that death would be a relief to millions. Yet just as Hunt had stolen the earlier meeting from the parliamentary demagogue, Sir Francis Burdett, so Hunt's limelight was now stolen by a wagon-load of fanatics supported by a gang of seamen with revolutionary tricolours. A rabble-rouser named Watson, after an inflammatory oration, asked who would follow him. Thereupon, before Hunt had even arrived, the sailors and a portion of the crowd set off for a gunsmith's shop and, after killing a merchant, marched on the City. They were opposed at the Royal Exchange by the Lord Mayor with a small detachment of police officers, whereupon they made off with a great hullabaloo for the Minories, where they broke into two more gunsmiths' shops and acquired two small cannon. Later, after a futile summons to the Tower and a skirmish with the Life Guards in Aldgate High Street, they dispersed in small groups, whooping, breaking windows and robbing passers-by.

*   *   *

The English poor were not weaklings; they were suffering almost beyond endurance. They were passionate, easily swayed by rumour, and uneducated. Behind the stubborn, rather bewildered, law-abiding artisan, marching with banners to demand bread or debating the Constitution in his penny Hampden Club, lurked a more menacing figure. The slums of London and the industrial towns swarmed with criminal types who, led by demagogues, were as capable of a massacre as their Paris prototypes. During that winter even the prisoners in Newgate rioted and attacked their jailors. The roughness of that outcast populace was a constant menace to a rich society. Such folk could not be ruled by milksops. Their blood was up; when Cashman, the man who committed the Spa Fields murder, was hanged, he shouted from the cart, 'Hurrah! my boys, I'll die like a man; give me three cheers when I trip!' and then to the hangman as the mob yelled encouragement, 'Come, Jack, you——, let go the jib-boom!'

The rulers of England faced their peril with courage. Though unimaginative and narrow – 'Mouldy & Co.,' as their opponents called Liverpool's Tory Government – they had strong nerves. They had not fought Napoleon and the Revolution in-arms to shrink from Orator Hunt and a pack of weavers. Even 'goody' Sidmouth – 'Britain's guardian gander' of invasion days – declared that no man was fit to be minister to whom it was not a matter of indifference whether he died in bed or on the scaffold. Resolved to maintain public order, he and his colleagues made no concessions to popularity. Confronting committees of both Houses with widespread evidence of an intended insurrection, they suspended *habeas corpus*, stopped the unemployed 'blanketeers' who tried to march on London, and sent Bow Street runners to Lancashire to arrest the ringleaders. They enrolled special constables, strengthened the law against attempts to seduce soldiers from their duty, and took measures to put down Cobbett, whose 'twopenny trash' threatened to turn every working man who could read into an agitator. Fearful of arrest for debt, the great journalist fled to America.

Yet though England's rulers, in their fear of Jacobinism, closed down on the political aspirations of the workers, they showed little vindictiveness. Despite their lack of imagination and understanding they still behaved, even when scared, as members of a Christian society. Though ministers, magistrates and manufacturers were all convinced of the hopelessness of interfering with economic law, the Staffordshire gentleman who put himself and his family on short rations to feed the unemployed was characteristic of thousands. It was still unnatural for Englishmen of different classes to hate one another. When the St Albans justices stopped the Bilston colliers' march to Carlton House, pointing out that their action might result in a breach of the peace, the hungry, angry men listened with attention, admitted they had been ill-advised, and expressed their readiness to return home, and were helped to do so by a subscription. Bamford and his fellow radicals, though wrongly charged, were treated with courtesy and consideration by the Privy Council who examined them. The number brought to trial for treasonable conspiracy and libel was comparatively small, and most were acquitted, including Watson, the leader of the Spa Fields Riots, and the bloodthirsty Arthur Thistlewood, who had carried the tricolour in the attack on the Tower. Orator Hunt was not prosecuted at all.

And, after an intense but temporary spell of suffering, trade revived, as the economist Ricardo had always predicted. The prices of manufactures having fallen to rock-bottom, foreign customers began to buy again, and, employment improving as a result, internal purchasing-power became more plentiful. By the autumn, the monthly average of bankruptcies was only a quarter what it had been at the beginning of the year. Agriculture revived, too, while the lovely summer of 1817 and moderate imports of foreign grain under the sliding scale kept the cost of bread within tolerable limits for the urban worker. Consols, which had been down to 63, recovered to 80. England was becoming herself again.

For she was still immensely strong and rich. A gentleman wrote that if he were to shut his eyes and open his ears he would believe the country ruined, but if he were to open his eyes and shut his ears, he would think it the most prosperous in the world. Even in the terrible summer of 1816, when her trade was at a standstill and her harvest ruined, Lord Exmouth with the Mediterranean Fleet had stood in under the guns of the pirate stronghold of Algiers and, in pursuance of an international policy agreed at Vienna, destroyed, in an eight-hour bombardment, forts defended by 40,000 men, so ending the cruel trade in Christian slaves which had terrorized the Mediterranean for centuries. During 1818 every building site on either side of Regent Street was taken, and the great avenue, halted for lack of funds at Piccadilly a year before, resumed its majestic sweep towards the Marylebone fields where Nash was laying out Doric-pillared crescents. In all the environs of London neat, blue-slated terraces were rising on either side of the trunk roads, and pseudo-Grecian edifices of white stucco were replacing the red and grey bricks of the sober Hanoverian past. So were stately West End club houses with wonderful cellars and kitchens, vast docks with attendant slums, and grim prisons built on principles which made escape impossible. Soon, it was rumoured, Oxford Street was to be extended as far as Bayswater brook, making it the longest street in Europe. Gas was twinkling – still a little uncertainly – in shop windows, and steamers, blowing black smoke from high funnels, were appearing in rivers and estuaries; Keats on a walking tour through the Highlands was astonished to see one on Loch Lomond. And all the while the wheels of the north country factories turned ever faster and the smoking chimneys multiplied, and the ships of Britain carried goods to the farthest corners of the earth.

Yet underlying all this prosperity – the glittering streets and great houses where the 'fifteen hundred fillers of hot rooms called the fashionable world' supped nightly on ortolans and champagne, the ever-lengthening chain of mail coaches speeding across the land, the stupendous bridges planned to span the Menai Strait, Tyne estuary and Avon gorge – the foundations of society remained troubled. In vain did architects press forward with the new churches which Parliament had voted and towards which the pious so liberally subscribed, so that, as Arthur Young put it, the poor might learn 'the doctrines of that truly excellent religion which exhorts to content and to submission to the Higher Powers.' Discharged sailors and soldiers still begged, half-naked, in the gutters. Stendhal, visiting the capital, was shocked by the fear of starvation that haunted its outcasts; 'such,' he wrote, 'was the fruits of England's victory.'

The boom of 1818 which followed the post-war slump was short-lived. In the summer of 1819 the same phenomena recurred – glutted foreign markets, slashed wages, shrinking purchasing-power and men and women unable to buy the goods whose sale would have given them the wherewithal to live. With their reappearance vanished the belief that the disaster and misery out of which Britain had so painfully climbed was something exceptional, attributable solely to the transition from war to peace. The storm had returned, and without explanation. Yet the Government's attitude to it remained one of invincible helplessness. 'Mr Bamford,' said Lord Sidmouth, when that honest weaver was discharged by the Privy Council, 'I would have you to impress seriously on your mind that the present system of distress of the country arises from unavoidable circumstances.' Convinced of this, ministers and the ruling classes were bewildered by the growing bitterness of the poor; the kindly magistrate who visited Bamford in prison remarked that it was a pity that men should be so deluded. Yet, as the latter pointed out to Sidmouth, had the gentry investigated the conditions of their humbler countrymen, they would have seen that they were intolerable. It was England's tragedy that in the social revolution that followed the war those who had led their country so well in battle should have felt so little call to give them leadership in peace and have confined themselves to the negative task of repressing the disorder caused by the ensuing economic anarchy. Their only remedy – one instituted more as a safeguard for property than as a cure for poverty – was to hasten the return to gold.

*　　*　　*

By the middle of 1819, the plight of the textile operatives had again become desperate. The wages of the Glasgow handloom weavers, once twenty-five shillings a week, shrank that autumn to five shillings, or half what they had even been in 1816. In some places they were worse; at Maybole they fell to half a crown. The streets of the manufacturing towns and villages were silent and deserted, except where strikes brought thousands of sullen spectres clattering on to the cobblestones to stop the wheels and damp down the furnaces. To all thoughtful men, and many thoughtless ones, too, an explosion seemed imminent.

It was a summer of intense heat. The *Annual Register* reported that political agitators, taking advantage of the general misery went about disseminating their doctrine through the great centres of manufacture. Hundreds of field meetings were held to hear harangues on the iniquities of Government and the necessity of radical reform. At one, accompanied by all the outward symbols of Jacobin revolution – inflammatory banners, caps of liberty and tricolours – 50,000 Birmingham artisans acclaimed a local radical landowner as their 'législatorial attorney.' Leeds and Manchester attempted to follow suit.

All this could only end in one of two ways – revolution or repression. Most folk with property to lose were resolved to defend it. The Duke of Wellington, who had seen many popular ferments, remarked that the reformers' object was 'neither more nor less than the plunder of the rich towns and houses which fell in their way.' A peer declared that public meetings ought to be dispersed by grapeshot, the liberal John Ward thought that the first day of reform would be the first day of English revolution, and strikes were denounced as illegal combinations of foolish and 'refractory work-people' misled by Jacobin agitators – coercive attempts to dictate the wages paid by employers and, therefore, gross interference with private freedom. 'I cannot,' wrote Walter Scott, 'read in history of any free state which has been brought to slavery until the rascal and uninstructed populace has had their short hour of anarchical government.'

As throughout the industrial North companies of workmen assembled to drill with bludgeons and pikes, sometimes under the tuition of Peninsular War veterans – Harry Smith, on strike duty in Glasgow, reported that the weavers were organized in sixteen battalions based on streets – the Government urged magistrates to stand firm and marched its scanty Army into the manufacturing districts. And, as in the invasion years, it fell back on the spontaneous enthusiasm of those who felt their security at stake. A year or two earlier Wordsworth, in a letter to his patron, Lord Lonsdale, had urged the creation of an equestrian order of armed yeomanry; 'if the whole island was covered with a force of this kind, the Press properly curbed, the Poor Laws gradually reformed, provision made for new churches to keep pace with the population, order may yet be preserved and the people remain free and happy.' Walter Scott, always to the fore when either volunteering or repression of Jacobinism was in question, busied himself in raising a company of sharpshooters from Ettrick and Teviotdale to march on the Tyne.

To those whose homes and factories were imperilled by a servile war such well-to-do volunteers, flooding into the shabby industrial towns with their bright yeomanry uniforms and handsome horses, were saviours, to be cheered and feasted for their patriotic self-sacrifice.

To the workers they seemed heartless upstarts – young farmers or millowners' sons who, having risen in the world, treated their poorer neighbours like dirt and rode over them. Bewick wrote of 'the pride and folly which took possession of their empty or fume-charged heads when they got dressed in scarlet.' To themselves, as they sharpened their swords in the village smithy and bade farewell to wife and sweetheart, they seemed heroes, ready to die for God, King and country.

On August 16th 1819 the clash came. On that day, the culmination of weeks of drilling on the moors, from fifty to eighty thousand reformers – a force as large as Napoleon's at Waterloo – converged from all directions on St Peter's Field, Manchester, to listen to Orator Hunt and demand reform. They marched, unarmed, behind revolutionary banners, in columns of five and locked-step, to the sound of bugles and drums, followed by dense crowds of stragglers of both sexes. Their menacing looks and numbers terrified the sober and respectable. As they poured into the town they were received with wild enthusiasm by the poor, particularly the Irish weavers, who flocked after them to St Peter's Field.

As soon as Hunt began to speak the alarmed magistrates, watching from a neighbouring house, instructed their police officers to arrest him and ordered a detachment of yeomanry to force a way to the hustings. Jostled by the crowd, the yeomanry lost their heads and started slashing with their sabres. There was a panic, the hustings were overturned and the people began to run, a few stalwarts fighting back. In the panic nine men and two women were killed, and several hundreds wounded. 'The field,' wrote the leader of the Rochdale column, 'was left an open and deserted space. The sun looked down through a sultry and motionless air. The curtains and blinds of the windows within view were all closed . . . Over the whole field were strewed caps, bonnets, shawls and shoes, trampled, torn and bloody. The yeomanry had dismounted – some were easing their horses' girths, others adjusting their accoutrements, and some were wiping their sabres. Several mounds of human beings still remained where they had fallen, crushed down and smothered. Some of these were still groaning . . . all was silent save those low sounds, and the occasional snorting and pawing of steeds.'

The country's immediate response was confused. It did not strictly follow class lines. Before the sabres flashed there appeared to be two Englands, both preparing to resort to force. The effect on the industrial workers was one of stunned shock, followed by intense indignation. The response of the other England was divided. The Tory party, the local magistracy which had precipitated the events, and the advocates of firm action everywhere, regarded the affray as the timely dispersal of a dangerous demonstration by a gallant handful. When Walter Scott heard the news he wrote that the yeomanry had behaved well, upsetting the most immense crowd that was ever seen and, despite the lies in the newspapers, without needless violence. There had been a blunder, it was true, in using yeomanry instead of regulars. But the meeting had itself been illegal, an organized conspiracy to intimidate for political purposes.

Yet the Government had spilt blood, and the English did not like blood to be spilt. Military massacre was no part of their recipe for government. Because of this it became apparent that, instead of there being two Englands pursuing an unappeasable quarrel to its logical conclusion, there were three. The third consisted of an indeterminate majority which reacted against any resort to force, regarding, like the great seventeenth-century Lord Halifax, 'all violence as a kind of foul play'. It even included many employers, who, though they hated strikes and rioting, inherited their forebears' liberal instincts. This feeling was expressed by a large and by no means purely radical section of the Press, by the Common Council of London, who protested at the Regent's official message of congratulation to the Manchester magistrates, and by meetings up and down the country, one of which was attended by the great Whig magnate, Earl Fitzwilliam, Lord Lieutenant of the West Riding. Other Whig aristocrats, like the Duke of Hamilton and Earl Grosvenor, interested themselves in befriending the victims and the arrested organizers of the Manchester meeting.

The reformers' leaders, who were nothing if not histrionic, did all they could to exploit the anger of the people and the sympathy of the middle class. The printing presses poured out a stream of wildly exaggerated accounts of what became known as the Peterloo massacre. When Orator Hunt returned to London in September, after his release on bail, an enormous crowd, running it was said to over a hundred thousand, met him at Islington. Among those who watched it with sympathy was Keats.

But, like the Government before them, the radicals overplayed their hand. Lacking all sense of responsibility and constructive statesmanship, they toyed with fire. The men they led were passionately angry, and everyone who lived near the manufacturing districts felt the hot breath of that anger and knew what it portended. For weeks after Peterloo the youth of industrial Lancashire was surreptitiously engaged in making pikes, grinding scythes and converting hatchets, old swords and mop-nails into weapons; 'anything,' wrote Bamford, 'which could be made to cut or stab was pronounced fit for service.' At Manchester a special constable was stoned to death. At Newcastle keelmen assaulted the magistrates with showers of brickbats and cries of 'Blood for blood!' By inciting and advertising such activities the radicals, most of whom were men of boundless vanity, frightened the very middle-class allies who, by co-operating with them against the Government's rigid conservatism, might have made some measure of parliamentary reform possible.

*   *   *

The Government's remedy was to strengthen the laws. Before Christmas it introduced six Bills prohibiting private drilling, the bearing of arms and certain kinds of out-of-door meeting, and virtually muzzling the cheap press. Even the street ballad singers were temporarily suppressed by anxious magistrates. The feeling for strong measures was reinforced by the return to England of Wellington with the withdrawal of the occupying armies from France and his accession to the Cabinet at the end of the year as Master General of the Ordnance. Like a soldier, he saw the situation in terms of force, and knew that in such matters resolute decision was everything – a knowledge of which the Government's vain and noisy adversaries were devoid.

The sense of imminent doom was heightened in January 1820 by a change on the throne. Two years earlier, the Regent's only child, Princess Charlotte, had died in childbed. Her death left the English without hope of a crown they could respect. A year later passed, with the Queen's death, the last royal symbol that enshrined the moral feeling of the nation; the weight had gone, wrote Scott, that slammed the Palace door on whores. At the beginning of 1820 the old mad King drew himself up in his bedclothes, said, 'Tom's a cold!' and turned his face to the wall. His only son with surviving legitimate offspring, the Duke of Kent, preceded him to the grave by a few days. At that moment the succession turned on five middle-aged brothers, every one of whom seemed either a bad life or a bad hat, and on the Duke of Kent's eight months' old child, Victoria. When King George IV was proclaimed and the officers of State and Judges dutifully waved their hats, the people, accustomed only to hiss and pelt him, stood silent and still.

As the bell of St Paul's tolled through the fog for George III's funeral, the news reached London that the ultimate heir to the French throne had been assassinated. It seemed like the signal for a renewal of Jacobin revolution in Europe. At that moment a fanatic gang led by Arthur Thistlewood, a ruined gamester who had tried to capture the Tower during the Spa Fields riots, was preparing the assassination of the British Cabinet. Their plan was to break in on them as they dined together in Grosvenor Square and, with a bomb and hand-grenades, to massacre the lot, including the Prime Minister, Liverpool, Castlereagh, Sidmouth and Wellington. One of the assassins, a butcher named Ings, was equipped with a sack for the ministerial heads which were to be exhibited to the mob and borne on pikes to the Mansion House, where Thistlewood was to be proclaimed President of a Provisional Government. But for the unreliability of two of the broken men to whom he entrusted his plan, the entire Administration might have perished over the walnuts and wine. As it was, the conspirators were surprised by police officers and a platoon of the Coldstream Guards just as they were about to sally forth from the hay-loft off the Edgware Road where they had secreted their bombs and cutlasses. Though the leader of the police was killed and Thistlewood himself and most of his gang escaped in the mêlée, they were quickly rounded up. Five of them suffered the fate they had prepared for the Cabinet, the executioner displaying their dripping heads to a groaning crowd. They died maintaining that high treason had been committed against the people of England.

*   *   *

It was the almost complete absence of affection for the throne – that recurrent but unifying *motif* in our history – which accounts for the extreme bitterness of those five divisive years after Waterloo. For though its underlying cause was the total inadequacy of purchasing-power available under the country's peacetime financial system to call into being enough of the productive potential of Britain's new machines and cultivated farms to feed and employ her people, the latter's hunger, misery and frustration were greatly aggravated by the spectacle at the national summit of an old blind King, irrevocably mad and immured with his medical attendants in Windsor Castle, while the eldest of his sons – all deep in debt and ludicrous scandals – the vast, bandy-legged, dropsical Prince Regent was afraid to show himself in the streets, while his equally disreputable and separated wife, the Princess of Wales, a pantomime source of ribaldry and indecorum, spent her time gallivanting round the Mediterranean with an amorous Italian courier and a court of rogues and buffoons. The country was now treated to the spectacle of its new King seeking a divorce in a public trial of his Queen before the House of Lords for her adultery with her Italian lover, whom the London mob, her enthusiastic champions, persisted in calling 'King' Bergami. The scenes of public uproar and tumult which throughout the summer of 1820 attended the trial and the twice-daily spectacle of the defiant Queen driving to and from Kensington Palace to Westminster Hall followed by a cheering rabble of pickpockets and prostitutes, ultimately caused a reaction in the King's favour. With trade starting to pick up after its long post-war eclipse, the coronation in the summer of 1821 was attended, not only with traditional splendour, but even by a degree of transient enthusiastic loyalty.

For in its unaccountable way, the country had once again gone about. It had had a debauch and was now sober. Trade was doing well, food prices were low and the North was back at its looms and spindles. The more dangerous radicals were safe under lock and key; the harmless ones like Bamford, were released and allowed to return to their employment.

*　　*　　*

The eroding bitterness and division of the post-war Britain had sprung from the inability of whose who ruled to cope with change. Being able to think only in patterns of thought which they had defended so long against foreign violence, they regarded with abhorrence all who found those patterns outworn, and were in turn anathema to them. Those who, suffering or perceiving injustice, demanded a reform of the country's laws and institutions, they denounced as Jacobins and potential assassins, and were themselves denounced by them as tyrants. By their defiant, but pathetic conservatism, they made Crown, Church and Constitution suspect to millions. They not only failed to find a common denominator for readjusting British society after the war; they failed even to realize one was needed. They could not reconcile, they could only denounce; they could not lead, but only repress.

Because of this, in the hour of victory, with as noble a material and spiritual heritage as any nation had ever had, Britain faltered and almost failed. With the means, physical and intellectual, of solving all her problems – which were not in reality very great – she staggered like a blind man from distress to distress. Yet she was not only immensely rich, but more advanced in real civilization than any other country. There was no land in Europe where so many were so free, and none anywhere where some had a freedom so complete and satisfying. There was none where men had such mastery over material phenomena and enjoyed opportunities for such comfort, elegance and happiness. There was none where man had done so much – in home-making, the shaping of landscape and the manufacture of amenities – to adapt his environment to his nature.

But the dispossessed peasants starving in the midst of plenty, the pallid machine-minders at the closed factory gates, the poachers in the county lock-ups awaiting transportation, felt that they had no longer any part in that inheritance. 'Suppose,' the flash coves sang in Salford gaol after Peterloo,

> 'the Duke be short of men?
> What would old England say?
> They'd wish they had those lads again
> They sent to Botany Bay!'

For when the war, which had united men in sacrifice, was over, society was seen to assume a new face. The rich man in time of trouble withdrew to his castle and left the poor to fend for themselves against bewildering economic forces which ultimately made the rich still richer but engulfed the ancient communities of the humble like a flood. And the officers of the realm – princes, peers, legislators, judges, parsons, lawyers, lifeguards, bumbles – instead of endeavouring to rescue the poor from their unmerited plight, behaved as though the only purpose of the State was to preserve the wealth and property of the rich.

Yet the rich were not the oppressors the champions of the poor made out. They were seldom sadists or robbers or even tyrants. They were, for the most part, cultivated and kindly Englishmen, brought up in a Christian tradition and with a sense of personal responsibility and honour. Yet, intoxicated by their good fortune – the riches, luxury, elegance and power heaped on them by the nation's triumphs – the gentlemen of England had unconsciously come to think of these as the end of their country's existence. They regretted that the poor must suffer, but when their economists told them that the wealth of the nation

– that is, their own wealth – depended on the periodic unemployment, starvation and degradation of their humbler countrymen, they accepted it as an inevitable dispensation of Providence and did their best, not unsuccessfully, to banish it from their minds.

Yet Wellington and his fellow officers had not applied the criterion of *laissez faire* on the battlefields of the Peninsula. Nor had they shrunk from any duty demanded of them. In war they had been ready to suffer and sacrifice everything that their country might live. Throughout its struggle against Napoleon Britain had found its leaders equal to every need. All she now needed in peace was a reform of her financial system to harness and canalize the productive forces unloosed by her inventors, and a restatement of her ancient laws and institutions to give renewed effect to the moral principles in which ninety-nine out of a hundred of her people believed. Those principles, founded on Christian religion, were that a man should be free to live as he chose in his own home and follow his craft without the interference of arbitrary tyranny. They comprised a belief in the moral right of the individual to liberty, self-respect and the ownership of property. A system of society in which so many were deprived of their traditional livelihood, of their customary standards of living and of any real freedom of choice by the action of remote economic forces over which they had no control, in which they were forced to work under conditions which robbed them of health and pride in their labour and to live in habitations which deprived them of self-respect, was one which stood in urgent need of reform. It wanted the first essential of a society that could content Englishmen: it was unjust. For the broad framework of justice in which real liberty could operate was lacking.

CHAPTER FOUR

Economist's Curse

'We have game laws, corn laws, cotton
factories, Spitalfields, the tillers of the land
paid by poor rates, and the remainder of the
population mechanized into engines for the
manufactory of new rich men; yea the machinery
of the wealth of the nation made up of the
wretchedness, disease and depravity of those
who should constitute the strength of the nation.'
Samuel Taylor Coleridge

THE DECADE FOLLOWING the coronation of George IV saw the
beginning of administrative, legal and political changes which were to
give nineteenth-century Britain the 'other heart and other pulses' of the
poet's prophetic phrase. They began after the death in 1822 by his own
hand of the great Foreign Secretary, Lord Castlereagh – worn down
by endeavours to reconcile his countrymen to the maintenance of
the Grand Alliance which, in Pitt's footsteps, he had used to break the
power of Napoleon. This, after victory, had increasingly taken the
form of a league of reactionary Continental despots – the crowned
rulers of Russia, Austria, Prussia, with the restored Bourbons of France
and Spain, banded together in a so-called Holy, or, as it seemed to most
Englishmen, unholy, Alliance to suppress revolutionary or popular
movements, or even expressions of liberal opinion, which might
threaten the sacred principle of hereditary monarchical 'legitimacy'
restored.

Castlereagh's successor as Foreign Secretary, George Canning, had
also been Pitt's disciple, but of the younger pre-war Pitt, who, at the
age of twenty-four, called by George III to restore Britain's ruined
finances after the disastrous American War of Independence, was
the parent of more practical reforms in administration and political
economy than almost any other English statesman: free trade, the

68

Sinking Fund, income tax, national insurance and family allowances, the abolition of slavery and an end of religious disability can all in part trace their ancestry to him. Until tragically interrupted by the French Revolution's fanatic leaders' resolve to subject the whole world by war to their ideological dictation, his policy of reform and reconstruction might have ante-dated by three decades Britain's long Victorian era of peaceful progress. For five years, until Canning's untimely death in the autumn of 1827 – only a few months after he succeeded the ailing Liverpool as Prime Minister – the country's foreign policy was dictated by this brilliant and imaginative pupil of Pitt's who once, in earlier days, had fought a duel against his colleague and rival, Castlereagh. In place of the latter's reliance on a succession of backward-looking European Congresses as a means of ensuring international concord, the keynote of Canning's more publicly conducted foreign policy was epitomized in his phrase that 'for Europe' he would sometimes like to substitute the word 'England'. This struck an answering chord in the hearts of a mercantile society seeking oceanic markets for English manufactured goods, particularly in the Iberian colonies in South and Central America, where, following the restoration of Bourbon rule, the rigid Spanish protectionism – against which English traders and seamen had contended ever since the days of Hawkins and Drake – precipitated a spontaneous rebellion of colonials long cut off by the naval blockade from their authoritarian mother countries. Within a decade of Waterloo, with the help of British volunteers and sympathizers – including an outstanding radically-minded, 42-year-old Scottish naval captain, Lord Cochrane, who, rivalling Drake's exploits on the Pacific coast, became the naval liberator of Chile and Peru – their independence was finally achieved after Canning, who refused to intervene in the anti-Bourbon rising in Spain itself, had made it clear that the Navy would allow no intervention by the European Powers in South America. In 1824, following President Monroe's and the United States' lead, he recognized the independence of the new republics of South and Central America, delighting his more liberal-minded countrymen in a speech claiming that he had 'called the new world into existence to redress the balance of the old.'

Nor was it only beyond the Atlantic that Canning offered encouragement to liberty and nationhood. He did so also in the Aegean, where Byron's death in 1824 in besieged Missolonghi had awoken an echo in the heart of every Englishman brought up on the history of ancient Greece and Rome. The poet's prophetic lines –

'The mountains look on Marathon
And Marathon looks on the sea;
And musing there an hour alone,
I dream'd that Greece might still be free,
For standing on the Persian's grave
I could not deem myself a slave.' –

formed the background to Canning's patient diplomatic endeavours to create a setting for international intervention by the Christian powers to end the horrors of the barbarous struggle of Greek peasants and fishermen against Turkish despotism. A few weeks after Canning's death in 1827, one of Nelson's Trafalgar captains, Sir Edward Codrington, commanding a watching British, French and Russian fleet in Navarino Bay, gave orders which, following a chance shot, sent a Turkish-Egyptian invasion fleet to the bottom, and led, indirectly, to the recognition of Greek independence.

Meanwhile at home the more liberal members of Lord Liverpool's Tory government had embarked on a series of long-delayed measures to bring the administration of Hogarth's England into line with the needs and conscience of the nineteenth century. The most important were concerned with finance and commerce where the war, having quadrupled the National Debt, had caused the interest on it at one time to absorb half the annual budget. But, with the manufacturing wealth and trade of the country steadily expanding, particularly after the commercial crisis of 1825, the monetary size of the debt, with the aid of the Sinking Fund, grew year by year relatively less as the real wealth of the country increased. Under the President of the Board of Trade, William Huskisson, more than a thousand antiquated laws restricting the free flow of trade were removed from the statute book to conform to the fashionable new economic philosophy of *laissez-faire*. So, too – as a result of the labours of a Glasgow tailor, Francis Place, and a Radical MP Joseph Hume, who organized the collection and presentation to Parliament of hundreds of thousands of signatures – the wartime Combination Acts, which had made the actions of trade unions illegal, were modified or repealed. Even more significant for the future was the work of a young Home Secretary, Robert Peel – the Harrow and Oxford son of a Lancashire mill-owner – who in 1822 had succeeded the reactionary Lord Sidmouth. Though more conservative in his sympathies than either Canning or Huskisson and an ally of the Government's two diehards, Wellington and old Lord Chancellor Eldon, he brought an end to the system of spying and repression practised by his predecessor. Reforming the antiquated criminal law, he abolished the death penalty for a hundred petty crimes, and in 1829 introduced a civilian Metropolitan police force to take the place of the old and grossly inadequate Bow Street runners. Nicknamed 'Bobbies' or 'Peelers' after him, dressed in stout top-hats and belted overcoats and armed with truncheons, Peel's police rendered unnecessary the use of the military in repressing rioting in a population which had doubled since the beginning of the Revolutionary and Napoleonic Wars.

All this was accompanied by a growing demand by those outside it for reform of the antiquated parliamentary constitution, with its intolerant religious disabilities against Catholics and Non-conformists and its numerous 'rotten' or 'pocket' boroughs. These, a species of transferable private property collected or inherited by aristocratic magnates or purchased by rich East India or West Indian 'carpet-baggers', gave to the owners of long depopulated or even totally uninhabited medieval parliamentary boroughs, like Old Sarum, a right of returning members to Parliament which was denied to the great manufacturing cities and towns which had grown up in formerly uninhabited northern moors and heaths. But the first assault on this absurdly outdated system came from Ireland, where seven million ragged barefoot Catholic peasants, denied all representation of their religion in Parliament, were governed – so far as they were governed at all – by a Protestant bureaucracy in Dublin Castle and the votes of an imperial Parliament at Westminster where representation of the Irish was confined to the landowning Protestant 'ascendancy' of the South and a million thrifty and thriving Protestant settlers, mainly Presbyterian, of Anglo-Scottish descent, who had been planted during the seventeenth century in Ireland's turbulent north-eastern province of Ulster. Outside it lived a race entirely different from the sober law-abiding English and thrifty, tenacious Scots. The difference was partly one of religion, economics and history, and partly of diet. The English lived on meat, beer and wheaten bread, the Irish on potatoes and whisky. They were at once a tragic, reckless, kind-hearted, superstitious and, by English standards, lawless and unreliable people, always doing wild things in so gay and absurd a manner that their irresponsibility was a jest rather than a reproach. Their only point in common with the English, apart from their courage and love of fighting, was their passion for horses. Ireland's vivid green Atlantic landscape, with its mournful bogs and misty mountains, its stinking hovels, and elegant, filthy, drunken capital seemed almost to belong to a foreign country. Here, women, half-naked, with matted hair hanging over their bosoms, sat at cabin doors smoking pipes and staring at melancholy horizons, and men in blue cloaks and slouching hats, carrying shillelaghs, stood jesting at street corners in sinister-looking groups. In this John Bull's other island the most savage crimes were constantly being committed for religious, patriotic or agrarian reasons by a peasantry whom Harry Smith, serving with them in the Peninsular War, found the lightest-hearted, kindest, most generous creatures he had ever known.

Subjected after the victory of the Boyne in 1690 by a then bigoted Protestant England to a monstrous repression of their religion and trade, though most of these wrongs had since been righted by more tolerant English rulers, the Irish Catholics, given by Pitt the right to vote but not to sit in Parliament, combined during the 1820s in a national crusade for religious and civic equality, under the leadership of a dynamic Catholic orator and lawyer, Daniel O'Connell, and their parish priests, returning to Westminster in defiance of the law, in election after election, ineligible Catholic candidates. Faced by the fanatic unity of O'Connell's Catholic Association, and unwilling to face civil war – the evil which, with his memories of an anarchic India and Spain, he dreaded above all others for his native land – Wellington, who, a year after Canning's death had formed, with Peel as his lieutenant, a new Conservative administration dedicated to opposing Catholic Emancipation, suddenly surrendered to O'Connell's demands. In 1829 he granted to both Ireland and England the Catholic Emancipation which forty years before, Pitt had promised the Irish as the price of parliamentary union with England, but which had been denied them by George III's Hanoverian scruples over his coronation oath.

This sudden and unexpected triumph of the Irish peasantry over religious obscurantism opened the floodgates of the long dammed-up demand for constitutional reform in Britain's larger Protestant island and emotionally 'distressful country'. In June 1830 the worn out and reactionary debauchee, George IV, was succeeded by his brother, William IV – a bluff, breezy ex-sailor of mildly liberal sympathies – who, interpreting the prevailing popular mood, sent for Lord Grey. A lifelong advocate of parliamentary reform who, though leader of the Whig Opposition, in Parliament, had spent much of the long years of Tory rule in semi-retirement on his Northumbrian estates, Grey invited the more liberal members of the late Government to join him in a broad-based reforming ministry, including Graham, Stanley and Huskisson (who, unhappily, was run over soon after by a train at the opening of the new Manchester-Liverpool railway). To the delight of the country and the horror of the borough mongers and the Tory defenders of proprietary rights, he introduced a sweeping bill abolishing every close and rotten borough in the country and conferring the borough franchise on £10 householders. Bitterly opposed by Wellington and the Opposition, the measure was carried in March 1831 by one vote in the Commons, but was subsequently defeated in committee.

A general election followed which gave the reforming Whigs and their Canningite allies a substantial majority in the Commons. But the reintroduced Bill was defeated in the Lords. The excitement in the country was by now intense. The demand for immediate reform was universal, and in middle-class and working-class circles alike the cry was for 'the Bill, the whole Bill and nothing but the Bill'. In Bristol the mob rose and burnt the Mansion House; in Birmingham, still without the franchise, a Political Union, copied by every major industrial city in England, was formed which threatened a mass march on London. But a second and a third Reform Bill were both rejected by the Lords, and in the spring of 1832 Lord Grey resigned, and the anxious king sent for Wellington who, in the teeth of public opinion, and in defiance of the noisy attentions of a riotous mob, persisted in maintaining that, as the old unreformed constitution had enabled England to achieve such great things, it was incapable of improvement. In the end, as the Duke proved unable to form an administration, to avert civil war the King promised Grey and his radical Chancellor, Lord Brougham, that he would create enough peers, if necessary, to ensure the passage of the Bill through the Lords. Accordingly, in June 1832 it became law, and Britain embarked on the rest of the nineteenth century with a new constitution, in which power lay with the predominantly middle-class electorate, yet continued, for the time being, to be exercised on its behalf mainly by members of the politically conscious land-owning – but no longer borough-owning – class which had hitherto monopolized it.

Lord Grey's Whig Coalition Government, which had achieved this great thing, remained in power for the next nine years, with one brief interlude when a reconstituted and newly named 'Conservative' Party under Peel took office temporarily in 1834. In addition to Lord Melbourne, who succeeded Grey as Prime Minister, when it resumed power in 1835, it included two other future Prime Ministers, Lord John Russell and Palmerston. It put the seal on its work by the Burgh Act of 1833, giving Scotland for the first time popularly elected representative municipalities, and, two years later, the Municipal Corporation Act which replaced England's 'rotten' municipal boroughs by elected ones in the larger towns and cities, in which all ratepayers, and not only £10 householders, were entitled to vote. Twice in 1833 it passed a great liberating measure – Lord Althorp's Factory Act, limiting the hours of apprentice and other children in factories and creating for the first time government inspectors to enforce it; and, to crown Wilberforce's life's work against the slave trade, the abolition of slavery throughout the British Empire, anticipating its abolition in the United States by more than thirty years. A more controversial reforming measure was the Whig Government's Poor Law Act of 1834, abolishing the well-meaning, but socially disastrous, Speenhamland system of subsidizing agricultural wages out of rates, which for forty years had been pauperizing the rural wage-earner.

But though of the 961,000 families engaged in agriculture in 1831, 686,000 now worked the land for others, having been robbed by enclosures of prescriptive rights of grazing and fuel-gathering and by cruel and selfish game laws of their wonted share in the dwindling wild food supply of the open countryside, at the time of the Reform Bill one countryman in three still possessed a stake in the land, while one in seven worked his own land without hiring labour. Everywhere the English peasant still clung to his hereditary standards and virtues. An intense confidence in his skill and capacity for work sustained him through a life of hardship – that and love of the land he tended. And though outside the grinding poverty of the south-western shires, where the machines of the North were depriving the farm-worker and his family of a market for their domestic handicrafts, the old cottage folk of England were very tenacious of the good things of life they had been brought up by their forebears to honour. They loved to keep a bright fire in the hearth, choice old china on spotless shelves, smoked flitches of bacon and ham hanging from the ceiling, and home-brewed wine to offer their neighbours. They took pride in their mastery of oven and vat, in their skill in keeping a garden, in raising poultry and bees. Above all, they valued the Christian virtues of decent living and good neighbourhood – honesty, truth, and purity of word and life.

Though in the Lancashire cotton-mills and the London slums a proletarian labouring class had emerged, its significance was hidden from contemporaries by the multitude of domestic skilled craftsmen who still constituted the rank and file of British industry – one rooted in its rural past and an, as yet, unravished country environment. Except for cotton, no textile trade had been radically affected by machinery before 1830; wool combing was still governed by skill of hand as was the hardware industry of the Midlands and the cutlery of Sheffield. The old trades were still more extensive than the new: at the time of the Reform Bill, there were more shoemakers in England than coalminers. The unit of industry was small: apprentices frequently lived with their employers over their own workshop, and every craftsman might aspire to be a master. The Spitalfields weavers of London, who on summer evenings could be seen seated in the porticoes of their houses enjoying their pipes or digging their allotments in Saunderson's Gardens; the 200,000 bricklayers, masons, carpenters, house-painters, slaters, plumbers, plasterers and glaziers who made up the close corporation of the building trade; the serge and cloth workers of the West Country, Gloucestershire and East Anglia; the bootmakers of Northampton, the blanketers of Witney, the chair-turners of the southern Chilterns, and the cabinet-makers and clock-makers of almost every country town – for all the threat of the new machines to their employment and standards of living – were men with a status in the country based on personal skill and character.

So were the rural handicraftsmen – blacksmiths, wheelwrights, carpenters, millers, cobblers – the fishermen and sailors of the coastal towns, and the engineers who were coming into existence to make and tend the new machines of steel and iron. North of the border in Lanarkshire, a French traveller found the Scottish craftsmen the best educated in Europe, 'well-informed, appreciating with sagacity the practice of their trade and judging rationally of the power of their tools and the efficiency of their machinery.' Such men – even the Durham miners whose working conditions so distressed Cobbett – enjoyed solid houses, substantial fare and fine sturdy furniture made by craftsmen worthy of themselves. Pride in their domestic establishment was the hallmark of the British artisan and his wife: the Handloom Weavers' Commissioners' Reports of 1838 speak of the Midland weavers' cottages as good and comfortable and much superior to those of the surrounding agricultural labourers, with a solid dower of nice clocks, beds and drawers and ornamented with prints. Within was cleanliness, good order and fine frugal cooking.

Such was the old English system. It was based on the home, and home spelt contentment. Here was the seat of man's love – of his birth and continuance. Here, too, he did his work. For the cottage, so long as the old economy persisted, was both home and factory. Yarn was spun and woven under a single roof: 'the wife and daughter spun the yarn and the father wove.' Cottage labour for the womenfolk, such as the beautiful lace industry of Buckinghamshire, supplemented the household income and gave additional pride and interest to family life. In his leisure hours the good man, home from farm or smithy, cultivated his own little piece of land. 'He was no proletarian, he had a stake in the country, he was permanently settled and stood one step higher in society than the English workman of today.' Such men, as Engels wrote in the changed world of 1844, 'did not need to overwork; they did no more than they chose to do, and yet earned what they needed'.

*   *   *

For those fortunate enough to inherit a share in that still unvanished rural England – for all not imprisoned in the great industrial towns or disinherited by the poverty that followed the enclosures – there was a sober joy in it. It came from healthy living, from quietude begotten of continuity, from the perceiving eye and undulled sense. In the mid-century letters of Edward Fitzgerald one sees green England sunning herself in her immemorial peace – 'the same level meadow with geese upon it . . . the same pollard oaks, with now and then the butcher or the washerwomen trundling their carts.' 'I read of mornings the same old books over and over again,' he wrote, 'walk with my great dog of an afternoon and at evening sit with open window, up to which China roses climb, with my pipe, while the blackbirds and thrushes begin to rustle bedwards in the garden.' 'We have had,' he recorded on another occasion, 'glorious weather, new pease and young potatoes, fresh milk (how good!) and a cool library to sit in of mornings.' Down in his native Suffolk this gentle patriot found the heart of England beating healthily: whenever he returned from sophisticated London he was amazed at 'the humour and worth and noble feeling in the country.' Fishing in 'the land of old Bunyan . . . and the perennial Ouse, making a fantastic winding . . . to fertilize and adorn,' he stayed at an inn, 'the cleanest, the sweetest, the civillest, the quietest, the liveliest and the cheapest that was ever built or conducted . . . On one side it has a garden, then the meadows through which winds the Ouse: on the other the public road, with its coaches hurrying on to London, its market people halting to drink, its farmers, horsemen and foot travellers. So, as one's humour is, one can have whichever phase of life one pleases: quietude or bustle; solitude or the busy hum of men: one can sit in the principal room with a tankard and a pipe and see both these phases at once through the windows that open upon either. To such a one the changing seasons only brought new contentment but, he wrote, 'England cannot expect long such a reign of inward quiet as to suffer men to dwell so easily to themselves'. For he knew that it could not last. The portents of change were already blazing in the Northern and Midland sky.

In the summer of 1842, the summer in which Fitzgerald was writing, four men had published a document which profoundly troubled the conscience of England. It was called the First Report of the Children's Employment Commission. It dealt with the conditions of labour of children and young persons working in coal mines. The Commission had been set up two years before by Lord Melbourne's Whig Government, largely through the pertinacity of Lord Ashley – the Earl of Shaftesbury's heir – an inconveniently well-connected young Tory of strong evangelical tendencies who had taken up the cause of the north-country factory operatives with an enthusiasm which seemed to some of his contemporaries to border on the hysterical.

Everybody by now knew that the conditions of life and labour in the new factory towns of the North and Midlands were rough and primitive. There had always been rough and primitive Englishmen, and in these smoky and unsavoury districts they were on the increase. It was part of the price that had to be paid for the nation's growing wealth. But the revelations of the Commissioners took the country by surprise.

From this document it appeared that the employment of children of seven or eight years in coal mines was general. In some pits they began work at a still earlier age. A case was even recorded of a child of three. Some were employed as 'trappers,' others for pushing or drawing coal trucks along the pit tunnels. A trapper, who operated the ventilation doors on which the safety of the mines depended, would often spend as many as sixteen hours a day crouching in solitude in a small dark hole. 'Although this employment scarcely deserves the name of labour,' ran the Commission's report, 'yet as the children engaged in it are commonly excluded from light and are always without companions, it would, were it not for the passing and repassing of the coal carriages, amount to solitary confinement of the worst order.'

Those who drew the trucks were 'harnessed like dogs in a go-cart' and crawled on all-fours down passages in some places only eighteen inches high. Other children worked at the pumps in the under-bottom of the pits, standing ankle deep in water for twelve hours. One who was cited, only six years of age, carried or dragged half a hundred-weight every day up a distance equivalent to the height of St Paul's Cathedral.

What struck the conscience of early Victorian England with especial horror was the fact that girls as well as boys were employed in these tasks. Naked to the waist, and with chains drawn between their legs, the future mothers of Englishmen crawled on all-fours down tunnels under the earth drawing Egyptian burdens. Women by the age of 30 were old and infirm cripples. Such labour, degrading all who engaged in it, was often accompanied by debauchery and sickening cruelty: one witness before the Commission described how he had seen a boy beaten with a pick-axe. Lord Ashley in a speech in the Commons mentioned another whose master was in the habit of thrashing him with a stick through which a nail had been driven: the child's back and loins were beaten to a jelly, his arm was broken and his head covered with the marks of old wounds.

Here was something never contemplated by Church and State. 'We in England,' wrote a leading journal, 'have put ourselves forward in every possible way that could savour of ostentation as champions of the whole human race; and we are now, on our own showing, exhibited to the world as empty braggarts and shallow pretenders to virtues which we do not possess . . . We have listened to the cries of the slave afar off, but we have shut our ears to the moaning of the slave at our feet.' When Ashley, striking while the iron was hot, rose in the Commons a month later to introduce a Bill excluding all women and girls from the pits and boys under 13, he found himself almost a national hero.

Yet there was nothing new in what the Report revealed or Ashley described: these things had been going on for years. They had been defended, as they were defended on this occasion, by honourable men with all conscientiousness on the grounds that they were the unavoidable result of the laws of supply and demand. The more the population increased and the greater the consequent suffering of the poor, the more incumbent it became on those who governed to refrain from any interference with economic processes. For it could only end in calamity. The most one could hope for, in the view of the professors of 'the dismal science,' was that the poor should be fed at all. Hardships suffered by them in the course of obtaining food were in reality blessings in disguise, since without them they and all mankind would starve.

Expounded for more than half a century by a rich and respectable philanthropist of genius, the promotion of 'the greatest happiness of the greatest number' had become the faith of most 'enlightened' English reformers. It was Jeremy Bentham's belief that happiness could most readily be realized by the free exercise on the part of every individual of enlightened self-interest. Freedom of contract was the necessary pre-requisite of the utilitarian creed.

This belief was widely held by humane and enlightened reformers who were passionately anxious to eradicate ancient abuses, and to mitigate human suffering. The English individualists who subscribed with such uncritical zeal to the doctrine of *laissez-faire* in economic matters, were among the world's greatest humanitarians. They had led a reluctant mankind in every philanthropic crusade; by their unflagging efforts they had abolished slavery in the British dominions, removed from the statute book the barbarous laws which condemned men to the pillory and women to the lash, reduced from more than a hundred and fifty to six the crimes punishable by death and rendered illegal the cruel sports of cock-fighting and bull-baiting. These humanitarians rigidly opposed the infliction of all needless pain except in the factories and mines of their own country. For here, in their view, it could not be avoided.

A theory, running counter to the whole course of English social history, was thus employed both by members of the government and by manufacturers, as well as by academic economists, to justify almost any suffering or inhumanity. Employers and employed must be left free to make whatever bargains they chose: legislative interference could only make confusion worse confounded. Nine years before the Report of 1842, when Ashley had been struggling to get a Bill through Parliament limiting the hours of children in textile mills to ten a day, he was opposed on the ground that the measure would hamstring one-sixth of the nation's producing power and, by weakening British industry in competition abroad, react fatally on the wages and employ-ment of the adult worker. Even so humane a man as Lord Althorp, the Whig Leader of the Commons, argued it would make famine inevitable. Cobbett's common-sense remark that the House had discovered that the stay and bulwark of England lay, not as was hitherto supposed in her Navy, maritime commerce or colonies, but in the labour of 30,000 little factory girls, was regarded as perverse nonsense.

The early factory reformers, a little minority of humane men, several of them millowners like the first Sir Robert Peel – father of the Canning's and Wellington's Home Secretary who, on the fall of the

Whig Administration in 1841 became Conservative Prime Minister – concentrated their efforts on regulating the worst abuses of indentured child labour in the cotton mills. Later they were able to extend their tentative reforms to what was ironically termed 'free' child labour and to other branches of manufacture. But the only reforms they could smuggle on to the statute book were of the most rudimentary kind, such as the prohibition of the employment of children under nine in cotton mills and the limitation of hours of labour for young persons under sixteen to twelve a day. Even these were avoided in practice. The Factories' Inquiry Commission of 1833 showed that many manufacturers were still employing children of six and seven and that the hours of labour were sometimes as high as sixteen a day. Flogging was regarded as a necessary part of the process of production. Harassed parents, with their eye on the family budget, accepted all this as inevitable and even desirable: many fathers acted as sub-contractors for the employment of their own children. And humane and kindly men regarded as inevitable the spectacle of women with blackened faces and tears coursing down their cheeks as they dragged their loads up pit ladders, of work-dizzy cotton spinners mangled in the shafts of unfenced machinery, of workhouse children rented by frugal-minded overseers to rough north-country millowners who treated them like beasts of burden. They treated them worse, for while only a fool would maltreat his horse, a manufacturer could always replace crippled or prematurely senile human workers by further supplies of cheap labour which cost him nothing but their keep.

Nor did such reforms as there were keep pace with the growth of the system. The victims of the factory – at first only an insignificant fraction of the population – increased by leaps and bounds. Every year new inventions widened the scope of machinery, offered new opportunities for growing rich and forced more hungry craftsmen to seek employment for their wives and children in the factory towns. What had hitherto been a localized evil became a national one.

During this period of transition from cottage to factory labour, the course of nature was reversed. The breadwinner was left idle in the home, the wife and her little ones driven by want to the mill. In 1833 the cotton mills employed about 60,000 adult males, 65,000 adult females, and 84,000 young persons of whom half were boys and girls of under fourteen. By 1844, of 420,000 operatives less than a quarter were men over eighteen and 242,000 were women and girls.

The result was appalling. A wife who worked twelve or thirteen hours a day in a factory had no time to give to her children. Put out to be nursed by some half-savage creature for a few pence a week until old enough to become wage-earners, they learnt nothing from their mothers of the arts of domestic life and little of its charities. The home to which they returned at night after their labours, often too weary even to eat, was an untended hovel. The machines to which they hurried back before dawn never tired as they did. In the country which had abolished slavery and was vigorously opposing the slave trade in every corner of the world, 'strappers' were kept to flog drowsy factory children lest they dropped asleep at their work, and groups of pallid mites could be seen supporting each other home as they dragged their limbs up the dark cobbled lanes of the Lancashire and Yorkshire valleys.

Many were crippled for life: few grew to mature and healthy manhood or womanhood. Long, monotonous and unnatural working positions resulted in permanent curvature of the limbs. Whole families went about with crooked legs or twisted shoulders. Knees bent inwards and backwards, ankles were thickened and deformed and spinal columns pressed forward or to one side. Every street had its company of cripples, of prematurely aged and arthritic youths bent double and limping, of hag-like girls with deformed backs and hips. Constitutions were permanently enfeebled: long hours in hot, damp, crowded rooms and foul and vitiated air left debilitated bodies and listless minds. The factory population of Lancashire and the West Riding was discoloured and stunted and seemed more like some ill-fated race of pygmies than normal human beings. A Leeds surgeon testified that but for the constant new recruits from healthy country stock, the race of mill-hands would soon be wholly degenerate.

*   *   *

When such simple Englishmen, feeling themselves cheated and lost, turned for relief to their rulers they received little comfort. The new Poor Law – enacted in 1834 to remedy the effects of the Speenhamland system of subsidizing wages out of rates – bore the cold impress of the mathematical mind. It was based on the principle that the smaller the burden placed by the relief of poverty on the taxpayer, the greater the country's wealth. Itself a contradiction of the strict letter of that economic law, it adhered as closely to it as was compatible with the traditional English dislike of allowing a man to die of hunger. Outdoor relief, with all its kindly charities, was sternly discouraged: in its place the new workhouse, built with sombre economy by the administrative unions of parishes formed under the new Act, offered to the needy poor the maximum of deterrent with the minimum of subsistence.

If its aim was to reduce or abolish the pauperization induced by the Speenhamland system, its efforts were cruel in their effect. Parents were separated from each other and from their children. Elderly spouses were separated from each other. The life inside what were popularly known as 'Bastilles' was deliberately made harder than life outside the walls, and the food and staff were as bad or worse than Dickens described in *Oliver Twist* in 1838. One assistant commissioner declared that their object was to establish a discipline so severe that workhouses would be a terror to the poor which would prevent them from entering.

For the economists did not see labour as a body of men and women with individual needs and rights, but as a statistical abstraction. Labour was a commodity of value on which the man of capital, with whom all initiative lay, could draw as the state of the market demanded. And as that market – a world-wide one – was at the mercy of accident and fluctuated unpredictably, a 'reserve' of labour was indispensable. In exceptionally good times the whole 'reserve' could be quickly absorbed by productive industry: in normal or bad ones, it remained unemployed and subsisted on poor relief or beggary. 'At the gates of all the London docks,' an East End preacher testified, 'hundreds of the poor appear every morning in winter before daybreak, in the hope of getting a day's work. They await the opening of the gates; and, when the youngest and strongest and best known have been engaged, hundreds, cast down by disappointed hope, go back to their wretched homes. When these people find no work and will not rebel against society, what remains for them but to beg? And surely no one can wonder at the great army of beggars, most of them able-bodied men, with whom the police carries on perpetual war.' Engels, writing in 1844, reckoned the unused labour reserve in England and Wales at a million and a half or about a tenth of the population.

The economic justification of this was that the factories were giving to the country wealth she had never before possessed and bringing within the purchasing-power of the poor articles which had hitherto been available only to princes. The evils inseparable from the system were transitional; the nation had only to be patient, to refrain from palliative and wasteful measures and observe the laws of supply and demand, and all would be well. The general body of the middle class accepted this comforting proposition.

'Our fields,' declared Macaulay, 'are cultivated with a skill unknown elsewhere, with a skill which has extracted rich harvests from moors and morasses. Our houses are filled with conveniences which the kings of former times might have envied. Our bridges, our canals, our roads, our modes of communication fill every stranger with wonder. Nowhere are manufactures carried to such perfection. Nowhere does man exercise such a dominion over matter.' Few heeded Coleridge's warning that the price of neglecting human health, breeding and character for the sake of profits would have to be paid with heavy interest in the future. 'You talk,' he wrote, 'about making this article cheaper by reducing its price in the market from 8d. to 6d. But suppose, in so doing, you have rendered your country weaker against a foreign foe; suppose you have demoralized thousands of your fellow-countrymen and have sown discontent between one class of society and another, your article is tolerably dear, I take it, after all.' The wealth and power of Britain to which the economists and their middle-class disciples loved to draw attention were not merely the result of machinery and the laws of supply and demand. They were based on the skill, discipline, industry and social cohesion of the British people – qualities which they had derived from generations of healthy living and sound social organization. The early Forsytes, for all their integrity and frugality, never comprehended this and, unknowingly, committed waste on the national estate.

The new England they built was housed not so much in towns as in barracks. These were grouped round the new factories, on the least expensive and therefore most congested model attainable. Since the rate of profits was not affected if their inhabitants died prematurely, no consideration was paid to matters of sanitation and health. The dwellings which housed the factory population were run up by small jerry-builders and local carpenters, back to back and on the cheapest available site, in many cases marshes. There was no ventilation and no drainage. The intervals between the houses which passed for streets were unpaved and often followed the line of streams serving a conduit for excrement.

The appearance of such towns was dark and forbidding. Many years had now passed since the first factories appeared among the northern hills. Now the tall chimneys and gaunt mills had been multiplied a hundredfold, and armies of grimy, grey-slated houses were encamped around them. Overhead hung a perpetual pall of smoke so that their inhabitants groped their way to work as in a fog. There were no parks or trees: nothing to remind men of the green fields from which they had come or to break the squalid monotony of the houses and factories. From the open drains and ditches which flowed beneath the shade of sulphurous chimneys and between pestilential hovels arose a foetid smell. The only symbols of normal human society were the gin shops. Here on the rare days of leisure the entire population would repair, men, women and children, to suck themselves into insensibility on 'Cream of the Valley' or Godfrey's Cordial.

In a terrible passage in one of his novels of the 'forties, Disraeli described such a town. 'There were no public buildings of any sort; no churches, chapels, town-hall, institute, theatre; and the principal streets in the heart of the town in which were situated the coarse and grimy shops . . . were equally narrow, and if possible more dirty. At every fourth or fifth house, alleys seldom above a yard wide, and streaming with filth, opened out of the street . . . Here, during the days of business, the sound of the hammer and the file never ceased, amid gutters of abomination, and piles of foulness, and stagnant pools of filth; reservoirs of leprosy and plague, whose exhalations were sufficient to taint the atmosphere of the whole of the kingdom and fill the country with fever and pestilence.'

Reality was more terrible than art. Disraeli did not exaggerate but, out of deference to Victorian proprieties, toned down the horror of his picture. The official Reports of the Royal Health of Towns Commission of 1845 were more graphic, for they were more exact. In 442 dwellings examined in Preston, 2400 people slept in 852 beds. In 84 cases four shared a bed, in 28 five, in 13 six, in 3 seven, and in 1 eight. The cellar populations of Manchester and Liverpool, nearly 18,000 in the former and more in the latter, were without any means of removing night-soil from the habitations. Even for those who lived above ground water-closets were unknown and the privies, shared in common by hundreds, were generally without doors.

In Little Ireland, as it was called from its swarming population of poor Irish immigrants, the German merchant, Frederich Engels – co-author with Karl Marx of the *Communist Manifesto* – seeking material for his great work on the proletariat of south Lancashire, described the standing pools, full of refuse, offal and sickening filth, which poisoned the atmosphere of the densely populated valley of the Medlock. Here 'a horde of ragged women and children swarm about, as filthy as the

Above: 'The mechanical and civil engineering
explosion of the first half of the nineteenth
century arose from the talents of engineers
like Telford . . . some of them unlettered
men, who possessed a natural genius for the
working of iron, steel and stone and who
achieved in their relatively short lives an
international reputation.' Telford by S. Lant,
with one of his great viaducts in the
background.

Above right: 'In 1840 England was still
regional in outlook: by 1850 it was national.'
George Stephenson 'was more than any other
individual' responsible. He is painted here by
John Lucas with his famous 'Rocket' behind
him.

Right: 'Isambard Kingdom Brunel, many of
whose civil engineering works remain in use
150 years after their construction. His breadth
of talent and capacity for design and
engineering detail were extraordinary in an
age which was unique for its innovation; but
he possessed a power of leadership and a
friendship for people at all levels of society
which was unusual for his time.' Brunel
photographed by Robert Howlett against the
chains of the *Great Eastern*, 1857.

Above: 'For five years, until Canning's untimely death in 1827 – only a few months after he had succeeded the ailing Liverpool as Prime Minister – the country's foreign policy was directed by this brilliant and imaginative pupil of Pitt's. It was epitomized in his phrase that for "Europe" he would sometimes like to substitute the word "England".'

Above right: 'For all his Harrow and Oxford gloss of classical learning, the leader of the gentlemen of England in the fatal crisis of their history was a Lancashire mill-owner's son. Sir Robert Peel was a man of splendid talents and industry but, like those from whom he sprang, he was not at home with original ideas.'

Below: Cobden, Bright and the sturdy middle-class interests they championed held that the proper organisation of human society was one in which Britain devoted herself to the production of manufactured goods, and the rest of mankind supplied her with food and raw materials in exchange.' Here Cobden addresses the Anti-Corn Law League in the 1840s.

swine that thrive upon the garbage heaps and in the puddles . . . The race that lives in these ruinous cottages behind broken windows mended with oilskin, sprung doors and rotten door-posts, or in dark wet cellars in measureless filth and stench . . . must really have reached the lowest stage of humanity. . . . In each of these pens, containing at most two rooms, a garret and perhaps a cellar, on the average twenty human beings live . . . For each 120 persons, one usually inaccessible privy is provided; and in spite of all the preachings of the physicians, in spite of the excitement into which the cholera epidemic plunged the sanitary police by reason of the condition of Little Ireland, in spite of everything, in this year of grace, 1844, it is in almost the same state as in 1831.' In this district, where one group of thirty hovels housing 380 people boasted not even a single privy, the joint founder of modern Communism obtained his famous view of the Irk from Ducie Bridge:

'The view from this bridge, mercifully concealed from mortals of small stature by a parapet as high as a man, is characteristic for the whole district. At the bottom flows, or rather stagnates, the Irk, a narrow, coal-black, foul-smelling stream full of debris and refuse which it deposits on the shallower right bank. In dry weather, a long string of the most disgusting, blackish-green slime pools are left standing on this bank, from the depths of which bubbles of miasmatic gas constantly arise and give forth a stench unendurable even on the bridge forty or fifty feet above the surface of the stream. . . . It may be easily imagined, therefore, what sort of residue the stream deposits. Below the bridge you look upon the piles of debris, the refuse, filth and offal from the courts on the steep left bank; here each house is packed close behind its neighbour and a piece of each is visible, all black, smoky, crumbling, ancient, with broken panes and window frames . . . Here the background embraces the pauper burial-ground, the station of the Liverpool and Leeds Railway and, in the rear of this, the Workhouse, the 'Poor-Law Bastille' of Manchester, which, like a citadel, looks threateningly down from behind its high walls and parapets on the hilltop upon the working people's quarter below.'

As Engels asked, how could people compelled to live in such pig-styes, and who were dependent for their water supply on this pestilential stream, live natural and human lives or bring up their children as anything but savages? And what kind of posterity was England, in her feverish search for wealth, breeding to preserve and enjoy that wealth? It was a question to which the economists gave no answer.

*   *   *

If reflection could not teach the intellect that men who inhabited the same country were dependent on one another, germs could. The microbes of infection never acknowledged the economists' law that every man could find and maintain his own separate level. Asiatic cholera in 1831 and typhus in 1837 and 1843 from their strongholds in the industrial towns defied every effort of hastily improvized sanitary police and chloride of lime to dislodge them and threatened to devastate the whole country.

There were other warnings that a nation could not neglect a substantial part of its population without endangering its safety. A sullen and savage proletariat, growing in numbers, was turning against the rest of the community, its symbols and traditions. Carlyle, with his poet's sensitivity, felt from the seclusion of his Chelsea study the imminence of some terrible explosion among the northern workers. 'Black, mutinous discontent devours them . . . English commerce with its world-wide, convulsive fluctuations, with its immeasurable Proteus steam demon, makes all paths uncertain for them, all life a bewilderment; society, steadfastness, peaceable continuance, the first blessings of man are not theirs. This world is for them no home, but a dingy prison-house, of reckless unthrift, rebellion, rancour, indignation against themselves and against all men.'

In such a soil the orator of social revolution could look for speedy returns. In the year after the accession to the throne in 1837 of the eighteen-year-old Princess Victoria, daughter of George III's fourth son, a People's Charter had been put forward by a small group of radical members of Parliament, dissenting ministers and Irish and Cornish orators. It demanded the immediate transfer of electoral power from the middle-class electorate of 1832 to the numerically superior labouring class, through universal franchise, the ballot, annual parliaments, the abolition of the property qualification, payment of members and equal electoral districts.

Agitation for the Charter caught on like wildfire in the industrial towns. Arms were called for by excited Celtic orators, and forests of oak saplings were brandished at mass meetings by grimy sons of toil. Stories were whispered about the country of how the master workmen of Birmingham – the savage 'bishops' of heathen Midland tradition – were manufacturing pikes which, smuggled out in the aprons of Staffordshire chain and nail makers, were being sold to honest revolutionaries at 1s. 8d. a piece or 2s. 6d. polished. Men spoke of kidnapping the wives and children of the aristocracy and carrying them into the northern towns as hostages, of the secret manufacture of shells and hand-grenades and caltrops for strewing in the path of the hated yeomanry. Newcastle was to be reduced to ashes: 'if the magistrates *Peterloo* us,' the cry went round, 'we will *Moscow* England.'

The climax came in 1842, the year which saw the publication of the Report on the employment of children in the coal mines. One of those prolonged and periodic depressions which attended industrialization had culminated in almost unbearable hardship in the Midlands and North: factories were closing and the families of the operatives starving. That year the first illustrated weekly appeared in London and the pages of its earliest issues were full of sombre pictures of distress in the manufacturing districts. At Burnley, where weavers were working for 7½d. a day, the guardians, with a quarter of the population destitute, were forced to appeal to the Government for help. Idlers with faces haggard with famine stood in the streets, their eyes wearing the fierce and uneasy expression of despair. A doctor who visited the town in June found in eighty-three houses, selected at hazard, no furniture but old boxes, stone boulders for chairs and beds of straw and sacking. The whole population was living on oatmeal, water and skimmed milk.

Revolution was in the air. The workers were talking openly of burning down the mills in order to enforce a nation-wide strike. Haggard orators bade starving audiences take cheer, for soon 'Captain Swing' would rule the manufacturing districts. At a Chartist gathering on Enfield moor near Blackburn, a speaker announced that the industrial North would soon be marching on Buckingham Palace; if the Queen refused the Charter, every man would know what to do.

Across St George's Channel, Ireland – the mother of many a factory operative in England – starved and rioted. In Ennis the mob attacked the flour mills; at Cork, wearying of a diet of old cabbage leaves, it stormed the potato markets. Dear corn – popularly believed to be the price of the time-honoured Corn Laws which protected the landowner at the expense of the poor – the new machines and the middle-class franchise were indicted by bitter and angry men as the cause of their sufferings. As the uneasy parliamentary session of the summer of 1842 drew to a close, the authorities reinforced the troops in the industrial areas.

The first rumblings of the storm came from Staffordshire. Here towards the end of July, the colliers, following a reduction of their wages to 2s. 6d. a day, turned out and, marching on every works in the neighbourhood, compelled their comrades to do likewise. Those who refused were flung into the canals, plugs were hammered out of the boilers and furnaces extinguished. The word went round that all labour was to cease until the Charter had become the law of the land. The markets in the towns of the western Midlands were deserted and every workhouse besieged by vast queues of gaunt women and children and idle men.

The explosion came on August 4th at Stalybridge, where the employees of Messrs Bayley's mill had received notice of a further reduction in wages. The strikers, as though acting on prearranged orders, turned out the workers at every factory in Ashton and Oldham. Next morning they marched on Manchester. For a few noisy hours the main body was held up by a small detachment of police and troops at Holt Town. But other rioters swarming out from the streets on either flank, the authorities were forced to fall back, leaving factories and provision shops at their mercy. At Messrs Birley's mill, where momentary resistance was encountered, the roof was stormed, every window broken, and two policemen and an onlooker killed. The great 'turn out,' long threatened by heady orators and whispered among the people, had come at last. On Sunday the 7th the rioting spread to Stockport and other parts of Cheshire. Mills were attacked, bakeries looted and the police pelted with stones. At Preston the mob attacked the military, and several lost their lives. In the Potteries some colliers arrested by the police were rescued by their fellow miners who subsequently stormed the Burslem Town Hall, burnt its records and rate books, and sacked the George Inn and principal shops. Afterwards the town looked as though an invading army had passed through it.

Work throughout the industrial north was now at a complete standstill. In Manchester all the shops were shuttered and the streets thronged with thousands of workmen who besieged the sidewalks demanding money and food from passers-by. Similar scenes were enacted in almost every industrial town from Leicester to Tyneside, and in western Scotland. At Stoke-on-Trent the mob gutted the court of requests, the police station and the larger houses; at Leeds the chief of police was seriously wounded, and fatal casualties occurred at Salford, Blackburn and Halifax. The wildest rumours circulated: that in Manchester the police had been cut to pieces with volleys of brickbats; that the redcoats, welcomed by the hungry populace as brothers, had risen against their officers; that the Queen who had 'set her face against gals working in mills' was ready to grant the Charter and open the ports to cheap corn.

The alarm of the well-to-do classes in the adjacent rural areas was by now intense. In the factory towns of Lancashire 6000 millowners and shopkeepers enrolled as special constables to defend their menaced interests. The Government decided to act with vigour. In every Northern and Midland county the yeomanry were called out, and farmers' sons sharpened sabres on the grindstone at the village smithy before riding off to patrol the grimy streets of a world they did not understand. Tall-hatted magistrates rode beside them ready to mumble through the Riot Act and loose the forces that had triumphed at Peterloo over the urban savagery their own neglect had created.

On Saturday, August 13th, there was fierce rioting in Rochdale, Todmorden, Bury, Macclesfield, Bolton, Stockport, Burslem and Hanley. At the latter place 5000 strikers marched on a neighbouring country mansion and left it blazing. Hordes of rough-looking men in fur caps carrying clubs and faggots patrolled the squalid unpaved roads around the idle mills; others attempted to hold up the mail and tear up the permanent way on the Manchester-Leeds railway. Next morning, though Sunday, the Cabinet met and issued urgent orders to the Guards and the artillery at Woolwich to hold themselves in readiness for Manchester. That evening as the 3rd battalion of the Grenadiers debouched with band playing through the gates of St George's Barracks into Trafalgar Square, vast numbers of working men and boys closed in and tried to obstruct its progress. In Regent Street the crowd became so menacing that the order was given to fix bayonets; all the way to Euston Square station, which was packed with police, hisses and groans continued. The 34th Foot, summoned in haste from Portsmouth, was also continuously hooted on its march across London.

By the evening of the 16th, Manchester was held by three regular infantry battalions, the 1st Royal Dragoons and artillery detachments with howitzers and six-pounders. A few miles away the streets of Bolton were patrolled by companies of the 72nd Highlanders. Other troops poured in by the new railroads with such rapidity that the rebellion quickly began to lose its dangerous appearance. All that week the magistrates and police, protected by the military, were busy arresting ringleaders and detachments of rioters, and every main road and railway was watched by mounted constables and dragoons.

After that the insurrection crumbled. Further resort to force was useless. Hunger did the rest. Anger and hectic excitement gave place to weakness and despair. The shops were guarded and, with the mills closed, even the miserable wages of the past year of want ceased. The poor rates in every Lancashire town soared as pale, famished multitudes besieged the workhouses, and ruined householders, unable to pay their rent, abandoned their homes. In November Engels saw gaunt, listless men at every street corner in Manchester, and whole streets of houses in Stockport standing empty.

Gradually the factories reopened and a defeated people crept back to work. The insurrection had failed. Yet, like the Report on the employment of children in coal mines, it had done something to awaken the conscience of England. It had added to pity, fear, and, as is the way with the English in times of trial, a sober resolve to remove the cause of the evil. So long as the rioting continued, worthy and peace-loving folk set their faces resolutely against the rioters. But when it was over they took counsel of their consciences.

Many, particularly the manufacturers and the new middle-class, who had nothing to gain by the protection of agriculture and much by the cheapening of provisions, laid the blame on the Corn Laws. Others, like the country landowners, condemned the inhumanity of the millowners, who retaliated by pointing to the low wages and neglected hovels of the agricultural workers in the southern counties. As Ashley, the factory reformer, knew to his misery, none were worse than those on the Dorset estate of his father, Lord Shaftesbury. The economists and the statesmen who subscribed to their theories continued to reiterate the importance of non-interference with the laws of supply and demand.

But with the general thinking public the view gained ground that there were limits to the efficacy of *laissez-faire* where public health and the employment of children were concerned. Sanitary reform and factory regulation began for the first time to be taken seriously. Early in 1843 Ashley was able to carry without opposition an address to the Crown for the diffusion of moral and religious education among the working classes. In the following year a new Factory Bill became law limiting the hours of children under sixteen to six and a half a day and establishing further regulations for the fencing of machinery and the inspection of industrial premises. In the same year a commission on the Health of Towns was appointed. Its Report written by Edwin Chadwick revealed that of fifty large towns examined, only six had a good water supply and not one an adequate drainage system.

Public opinion was by now far ahead of parliamentary action. During the 'forties the novels of Dickens, Disraeli, Mrs Gaskell,

Charlotte Bronte and Charles Kingsley, the pamphlets of Carlyle and the poems of Thomas Hood and Elizabeth Barrett Browning educated the reading classes in the Condition of the People question and stimulated their desire for social reform. Intelligent England had become conscious of the new towns and showed it was far from being complacent. The sweated labourer's voice, for instance, could be heard in Hood's *The Song of the Shirt*, its poignant bitterness crying to heaven. Even the young Tennyson turned from his dreams of a remote chivalry to confront the inescapable problems of his age:

'Slowly comes a hungry people, as a lion creeping nigher,
Glares at one that nods and winks behind a slowly dying fire.'

The thought of a new generation was crystallized in Ashley's question, 'Let me ask the House, what was it gave birth to Jack Cade? Was it not that the people were writhing under oppressions which they were not able to bear? It was because the Government refused to redress their grievances that the people took the law into their own hands.'

The urge for social reform was spontaneous and its first fruits were voluntary and unofficial. It took the form of numberless remedial activities of a private or only semi-public nature, from church building and the foundation of industrial schools for the waifs and strays of the urban slums to the 'poor peopling' which became so fashionable an occupation for well-to-do young ladies in the late 'forties: it was in this work that Florence Nightingale began her life of voluntary service. All over England and Scotland isolated individuals began to tackle self-imposed tasks, each striving to cleanse his or her own small local corner of the Augean stable. Such were provincial doctors who faced fever and vested interest in a tireless campaign against insanitary conditions, devoted clergymen and nonconformist ministers, city missionaries and temperance workers, and young men and women of comfortable circumstances — often evangelicals or Quakers — who gave up their leisure hours to teach in ragged schools or to organize clubs, sports and benefit societies for their poorer neighbours.

In 1844, at Toad Lane in Rochdale, twenty-eight working men, many of them trade unionists, opened a little shop, the trading rules of which were based on Robert Owen's ideas of co-operation. There had already been other experiments elsewhere, some more ambitious in size, which had failed, but this one was destined to succeed. The Rochdale Pioneers' formula – that goods be sold at market prices and that profits be returned to members as 'dividends' in proportion to the sums they spent – was to be copied, with variations, eventually throughout a large part of Europe. In England alone some 130 stores existed by the time of the 1851 Great Exhibition.

Then in 1863 the Co-operative Wholesale Society was founded in Manchester by the retail co-operatives to act as their supplier, manufacturer and banker. It was an essential factor in the growing success of the whole movement, a success which, in spite of many difficulties, including boycott by existing shopkeepers, made working people aware of their own potential and worth through the practice of self-help and self-education. The Co-operative movement was their own creation, and one which in time contributed notably to the democratic and non-violent revolution within their nation.

Yet in the 'forties the level of exploitation was deeply rooted, and the remedy, for all the energy and enthusiasm behind it, so ill-co-ordinated and tardy that those who prophesied revolution and social chaos might have been proved right had it not been for one overriding factor. The social maladies which provoked revolt were not destroyed though they were henceforward slowly mitigated. On the other hand, while diminishing in intensity, they continued to grow in extent through further urbanization. Revolution was avoided by extending the area of exploitation. But the very factor which most hastened that process ended the isolation of the industrial areas from the rest of the community. The railways had already been decisive in the suppression of the rebellion: an express train had brought a critical appeal for help from Preston to Manchester, and the Guards had been transferred from London to Lancashire in the course of a single night. Rapid internal communication and a new habit of travel, born of cheap transport, was within a few years to transform England and give her a new unity and orientation.

CHAPTER FIVE

Iron Horse and Free Trade

'Along the iron veins that traverse the frame of our
country beat and flow the fiery pulse of its exertion, hotter
and faster every hour. All vitality is concentrated through
those throbbing arteries into the central cities; the country
is passed over like a green sea by narrow bridges, and we
are thrown back in continually closer crowds on the city
gates.'

John Ruskin: The Seven Lamps of Architecture

TO TURN OVER the pages of the early volumes of the *Illustrated
London News*, founded in 1842, is to experience a social revolution.
The first volume depicts an England that, apart from the capital, is
mainly rural – a land of cathedral spires embowered in trees; fairs and
markets; fat cattle, gaitered farmers and squires and smocked peasants.
Where the manufacturing districts appear they do so as an almost savage
terra incognita, with rough unpaved roads, grim gaol-like factories and
men and women of sullen and brutish appearance. Even here one feels
the country has only been occupied by a horde of nomad invaders: on
the outskirts of the Manchester of 1842 there were still sloping wooded
valleys with girls keeping sheep a stone's throw from the flat slate roofs
and tall smoking chimneys.

Yet before the end of the 'forties the scene has completely changed.
It is an urban England that is engraved on the crowded page. The
stress is now on paved streets, vast Gothic town halls, the latest
machinery, above all the railroad. The iron horse, with its towering,
belching funnel and its long load of roaring coaches plunging through
culverts and riding the viaduct, had spanned the land, eliminating
distance and reducing all men to a common denominator. And the iron
horse did not go from village to village: it went from industrial town
to town. The England of Winchester, Canterbury and Chester was a

thing of the past. The England of smoking Rotherham and Hull and colonial Crewe had arrived.

This revolution in transport came with an extraordinary rapidity. In 1830, and in most places in 1840, a man who wanted to take a journey did so on the roof of a stage coach. Tom Brown went to Rugby of all places in the old Tally-ho! To travel by the London Tantivy Mail to Birmingham along the macadamized turnpike, a distance of 120 miles, took twelve hours; to Liverpool another eleven. One left London shortly before eight in the morning, changed in the course of ten minutes into the Birmingham-Liverpool Mail at the same hour in the evening, and reached one's destination, bleary-eyed and exhausted, at seven next day.

That was the very fastest travel. And what travelling it was! On a cold, damp, raw December morning one waited in the dark at the posting-house for the Highflyer or Old True Blue Independent coach 'coming hup' and, when the muddied, steaming horses drew up in the courtyard, took one's 'preference' seat in the hot, suffocating, straw-strewn box. There one sat in cramped darkness for many hours of creaking, lumbering and jolting until the 'many-coated, brandy-faced, blear-eyed guard let in a whole hurricane of wind' with the glad tidings that the coach had reached another inn 'wot 'oss'd it,' where the company was allowed half an hour's grace to dine. The only alternative was to travel on the roof, in dust and glare in summer, and muffled to the nose in a frozen eternity in winter. It had its romantic side, of course, but no man would undertake such travel lightly. And what with the fare of sixpence a mile for inside accommodation, the cost of meals at the posting-inns, and the tips to ostler, boots, guard, post-boy and waiter, it was beyond the means of all but a small minority.

In what seemed to our ancestors only a few years all this was changed. The first tentative steam railway from Stockton to Darlington had been opened in 1825, and the Liverpool and Manchester line had followed in 1830. A year after Queen Victoria's accession there were only 500 miles of operating railway in the British Isles. The first railway boom in 1838–9, following a run of good harvests and financed mainly by provincial money, added another 5,000 miles of projected track. Of these, 1,900 miles were open by the summer of 1843. They included the lines from London to Birmingham, Manchester, Brighton and Bristol.

Once they had got over the first shock of noise, sulphur and speed,

94

travellers were entranced by the railroad. Greville in 1837 travelled in four and a half hours from Birmingham to Liverpool to the races, sitting in a sort of chariot with two places and finding nothing disagreeable about it but the whiffs of stinking air. His first sensation, he admitted, was one of slight nervousness and of being run away with, but a feeling of security soon supervened and the velocity was delightful. 'Town after town, one park and *chateau* after another are left behind with the rapid variety of a moving panorama.' At every stop all heads appeared at the windows, while the platform resounded with astonished cries of 'How on earth came you here?' The most surprising feature of it all, apart from the speed and smoothness of motion, was the wonderful punctuality. It gave to man something of the precision and power of the machine.

At first, until people got used to the idea, there was a certain amount of opposition. Landowners, corporations and venerable cathedral clergy and dons were at pains to keep the vulgar, snorting intruders away from their domains, thus both impoverishing and inconveniencing their successors. Gentlemen resented their noisy intrusion on their parks and huntsmen on their favourite gorses. Poets like Wordsworth thought them hideous, and farmers complained of frightened horses and cattle; keepers of posting-houses, stage coachmen and canal proprietors naturally hated the puffing billies. 'I thought likewise,' wrote Jasper Petulengro, 'of the danger to which one's family would be exposed of being run over and severely scorched by these same flying fiery vehicles.' Such opponents found a doughty champion in the Tory MP for Lincoln, Colonel Sibthorpe, who 'abominated all railroads soever' and made it his business to oppose every bill for their promotion.

These efforts could not avert the march of progress. The taste for railway travel, once acquired, continued to grow. In 1842 the linking of England by rail was still very incomplete. When a Chartist agitator was arrested in Northumberland for a seditious speech at Birmingham, he was taken by hackney coach to Newcastle, by ferry across the Tyne to Gateshead, by rail to Carlisle, by stage coach over Shap Fell to Preston, and thence, by what was soon to become the London North-Western Railway, to Birmingham. In this fashion a man could travel from Euston to Glasgow in twenty-four hours – by rail to Fleetwood, by steamer to Ardrossan and by rail on to Glasgow. 'What more can any reasonable man want?' asked the *Railway Times*. Yet the reasonable man and the railroad speculators who catered for his needs wanted more.

Of the latter the most famous was George Hudson, the York linen-draper. Under his dynamic and sanguine leadership a railway mania developed which rivalled the South Sea Bubble. During the period of cheaper money after 1843 nearly ten thousand miles of new railway were sanctioned by private parliamentary acts. Much speculative money was lost in the process – the sudden slump of 1847 was a minor social calamity – but amalgamation of the smaller and more hare-brained ventures by the larger resulted in ultimate stabilization.

All this involved a revolution in English life and organization. For years the country was covered by armies of 'navigators' or 'navvies', whom contractors employed to translate the grandiose dreams of the railway projectors and the capital of their shareholders into solid cutting, embankment, tunnel and permanent way. In 1848 nearly 200,000 labourers, many of them Irish, were engaged in this vast task. With their rough habits and speech, high wages – pay day was usually a brutal debauch – and their generous taste in steak, plush waistcoats and whisky, they uprooted ancient ways of living in every place where they encamped. To many of the older skilled workers in the country districts their square-tailed coats of velveteen, their soiled white felt hats and spotted scarlet vests symbolized the 'accursed wages of savagery and sin'. For the younger villagers their sojourn had an exciting, unsettling quality that in after years caused many to follow them to the great cities along the gleaming lines they had laid.

In 1840 England was still regional in outlook: by 1850 it was national. Save in the remoter shires where there was still no puff of smoke in the valleys to mar the soft horizons, it had become the common lot of an Englishman to live near a railroad. And the new travel had been made accessible to the poor. In 1845 Gladstone, then President of the Board of Trade in Sir Robert Peel's Conservative administration, brought in a measure compelling every railway company to run at least one train daily over its system with covered third class accommodation at a penny a mile. Within a few years the receipts of such cheap travel had become almost the most valuable part of the companies' revenue. With the railroad came also cheap coal and cheap food, linking mine, port and countryside to the all-consuming town, and the creation of a vested interest carrying the capital of thousands of shareholders and employing a growing multitude of workers. By 1848 there were 5,000 miles of railway in Britain, an increase of 3,000 miles since 1843. The growth continued throughout the middle years of the century until, by 1886, just under 17,000 miles of track had been laid and the railway network had taken on the general form it retained till the second half of the twentieth century.

This growth represented a prodigious feat of engineering construction. It provided the essential arterial system for the transportation of coal, minerals, iron and steel, and the other heavy and bulky loads on which the expanding economy was based. No less important was the easier and more rapid carriage of people on the iron road which brought a degree of comparative luxury to travel.

The mechanical and civil engineering explosion in the first half of the century arose from the talents of engineers like Telford and George and Robert Stephenson, some of them unlettered men, who possessed a natural genius for the working of iron, steel and stone and who achieved in their relatively short lives an international reputation.

No individual's work was more varied than that of Isambard Kingdom Brunel, many of whose civil engineering works remain in use 150 years after their construction. He created the route, track, tunnels, bridges and locomotives of the Great Western Railway, designed the Clifton suspension bridge and built and designed the Saltash bridge and many others. He was also a pioneering marine engineer who built the mighty steamships *Great Western, Great Britain* and *Great Eastern*. His breadth of talent and capacity for design and engineering detail were extraordinary in an age which was unique for its innovation; but he possessed also a power of leadership and friendship for people at all levels of society which was unusual for his time.

In other ways England had become more closely knit internally, as well as better connected with the outer world. The first electric telegraph was tried in 1838; eight years later the Electric Telegraph Company was formed to exploit it commercially. Within two years there were nearly 2,000 miles of public telegraph with offices open day and night. Meanwhile the Penny Post, introduced by Rowland Hill in 1840, had led to a far-reaching change in social habit: in three years the weekly delivery of letters in the United Kingdom rose from a million and a half to nearly four million. Correspondence, hitherto an activity of the well-to-do classes alone, became common to all who could read and write. The prepaid adhesive stamps, affixed to the new paper bags or envelopes which took the place of folded sheets and wafers, were the symbols of a new conception of life, less local and more universal.

So were the trails of smoke that marked every sea-coast horizon. The first British steamboat had been launched on the Clyde in 1811:

97

in the next thirty years over six hundred were built. In 1838 the first iron sailing vessel crossed the Atlantic. Four years later the *Great Western* steamship arrived one June morning in King's Road, Bristol, from New York, having performed in twelve and a half days a passage which until then had normally taken a month. The world of which industrial Britain was the centre was daily growing smaller.

To grasp it she stretched out eager and vigorous hands. History had never recorded such an expansion of wealth and opportunity as came to island Britain in the first half of the nineteenth century: even the gold and silver Spanish discoveries in the Americas three centuries before paled beside it. Exports of unmanufactured iron soared from under 30,000 tons in 1815 to five times as much in 1830, ten times in 1840, and nearly twenty times in 1850. In the first half of the century coal exports were multiplied fifteen-fold. Between 1839 and 1849 alone the exports of mixed wool and cotton fabrics from the West Riding expanded from 2,400,000 to 42,115,000 yards.

In that torrent of opportunity nothing seemed to matter but getting rich. In Merthyr Tydfil, where an army of iron-workers lived, sleeping sometimes sixteen in a room, there were no drains, the water supply came from the open gutters, and the filthy streets were unpaved. At the palace of Cyfarthfa Castle a few miles away stood, in the Hammonds' phrase, 'the home and monument of the man who had started life on the road to London with all his fortune in his stout arm and his active brain, and had died worth a million and a half.' 'Persons in humble life,' wrote the editor of the *Mechanic's Magazine*, 'should be the last – though, we regret to say, they are the first – to speak disrespectfully of the elevation of individuals of their own class, since in nine cases out of ten the individual is the architect of his own good fortune, and the rise of one man by honest means furnishes a ground of hope to all that they may by a proper exertion of the powers which Nature has given them be equally successful.' It was the model which the early Victorian moralist held out to his countrymen. Self-help seemed almost divine.

*　　*　　*

Of all avenues to individual wealth – as well as to misery, pauperism and degradation – the chief was cotton. In the late eighteen-twenties Britain imported annually an average of 100,000 tons of cotton, ten years later of 200,000 tons, and in 1849 of nearly 350,000 tons. Cotton came to represent nearly a third of the nation's trade. It seemed to many that the national centre of gravity must shift from London to Manchester. The railways underlined the change. What cotton, in other words Lancashire, needed England could no longer deny.

Even in adversity Lancashire was wont to speak out its mind: and Lancashire with brass in its pocket spoke it loud. What Lancashire needed most was to import and export more cotton. Any policy that tended to check its imports of raw cotton was opposed to its interests. For centuries the domestic policy of England had been based on the protection of the industry on which the health, social well-being and safety of the bulk of its people depended – agriculture. But to Lancashire the Corn Laws which afforded that protection were an impediment and an affront. By restricting imports, they restricted the growth of the industries which manufactured for export and blocked the channel of expanding profits for Lancashire.

What Manchester thought to-day, it was said, England would think to-morrow. As the power of Lancashire grew, a nation-wide campaign was begun for the abolition of the Corn Laws. It enlisted the services of two cotton-spinners of genius, both of whom entered Parliament, Richard Cobden and John Bright. They and the sturdy middle-class voters whose interests they championed held that the proper organization of human society was one in which Britain devoted herself to the production of manufactured goods, and the rest of mankind supplied her with food and raw materials in exchange. The cheaper these, the cheaper and therefore the larger the quantity of goods sold. In this view, the maintenance of duties on foreign corn was a form of national insanity. For they restricted the foreign sales of Lancashire cotton. They could only be explained by the power of monopoly possessed by a handful of selfish and reactionary landowners.

The case for the repeal of the Corn Laws received new strength from the misery of the industrial proletariat and the rural worker. Both, confronted by the refusal of the authorities to relieve their sufferings, felt a sense of grievance. The fine gentlemen in Parliament and the landowners on the board of guardians who refused outdoor relief and ignored the promptings of common humanity in the name of *laissez-faire*, themselves enjoyed a protection that was the antithesis of *laissez-faire*. In the shape of a tax on food, protection wore its most odious and therefore most vulnerable form. Wages being low and employment uncertain, the obvious remedy was to remove the impost and cheapen the workers' bread. A Tudor statesman, viewing the interests of the

99

nation as a whole, would have deemed it wiser to seek the same end through minimum wage rates and political action stabilizing markets and trade. But to a student of *laissez-faire* such a course could only seem a flagrant breach of immutable economic law.

The cry for cheap bread, therefore, had a triple force. It respected hallowed and eternal truths. It appealed to the needs of the hungry and the hearts of the charitable. It offered enhanced industrial profits. Instead of having to pay higher wages, the north-country manufacturer could reasonably expect, through a fall in the cost of living, to pay lower wages, and at the same time, by selling more goods, to increase his returns. That this gain would be at the expense of the landed interest did not trouble him. In the view of Manchester the landed interest was composed of stupid and antiquated feudal snobs. The sooner they could be swept away to leave room for the unhampered rule of progressive talent, the better.

But despite the Reform Bill of 1832 the benches of Parliament were still mainly occupied by country gentlemen. The Whig aristocrats who had passed the Reform Bill were landowners like the Tory squires who had opposed it. Neither were yet ready to dispense with a principle on which their own wealth and power and, as they therefore believed, the security of the nation depended. The Conservative majority which supported Sir Robert Peel had pledged itself to maintain the existing agricultural duties. The most the Government of 1841 would concede to the reformers was a modification of the sliding scale of 1828 and the fixing of a maximum duty of 20 shillings a quarter. Even this, to many of its back-bench supporters, seemed too much. A corn-law reformer's motion for total repeal was rejected in 1842 by a majority of more than four to one.

But when Lancashire made up its mind, it took more than a Parliament of squires to stop it. If the House would not see its duty, the electorate would teach it. The power of the vote should be mobilized to destroy the vested interest of the past and, incidentally, to create a new and better one in its place. From its Manchester headquarters, the Anti-Corn Law League had already started on its famous eight-year campaign to arouse the voting middle class against the protective system and the 'Corn Law monopolists.' The agitation was brilliantly successful. In 1841, 'Free Trade' was still a panacea of a minority of radical idealists. In 1846, in the face of ever-growing clamour, it was officially adopted by the Conservative government which had pledged itself to oppose it. By 1850 it had become the classic creed of the country.

There were many reasons for this. The chief were the spirit of the age and the economic dogma which had captured the imagination of the educated classes. Free Trade was the logical application of Benthamite *laissez-faire*. In the past the English had been little given to abstract speculation: the descendants of farmers, peasants and sailors who had tilled the earth and sailed the seas with an adaptable eye forever cocked at their changing island skies, they had tended to distrust logical theories and based their lives on constant and instinctive improvization – an art in which they excelled all others. The Lancashire and West Riding capitalists were particularly susceptible to the beguilements of abstract political theory, provided it was put to them in a simple form and one likely to benefit their pockets. It was England's fate that the leader of her great traditionalist party during the second quarter of the nineteenth century was himself a man of this class. For all his Harrow and Oxford gloss of classical learning, the leader of the gentlemen of England in the fatal crisis of their history was a Lancashire millowner's son. Sir Robert Peel was a man of splendid talents and industry but, like those from whom he sprang, he was not at home with original ideas.

His betrayal of the traditional system he had been elected to defend was as unconscious as it was gradual. Peel never saw the Corn Laws and the protective system of which they were the core as anything but a collection of fiscal instruments. That underlying them might be an enduring principle of government, giving continuity to national life and strength and security to unborn generations, never occurred to him. Like most of his countrymen, he began by accepting the Corn Laws as a matter of course, and ended by swallowing whole the doctrine that destroyed them. The theory of Free Trade was novel, easy to understand and ably and persistently expounded: the ancient principle of state it ignored remained unstated.

Throughout the first half of the nineteenth century the country, largely as a result of the anarchy created by its own feverish pursuit of quick profits in foreign markets, suffered from a series of commercial crises. Various attempts were made to explain them. At one time they were attributed to the unrepresentative nature of the unreformed House of Commons. After the Reform Bill a new scapegoat was sought. It was on the Corn Laws, now assailed by the brilliant oratory and pamphleteering of the League, that the blame was laid. The same simple explanation was held to cover every suffering endured by the industrial masses. Cheap bread was the open sesame which would solve all difficulties. The selfish and stupid landlord with his antiquated Corn Laws alone stood between the nation and perpetual peace and prosperity.

In 1842 Peel, faced by an acute trade slump and the threat of a revolution in the starving north, met the situation by reducing the sliding scale duties on corn. During the trade revival of the next three years he left matters as they were. But all the while the doctrine of the Anti-Corn Law League was gaining on his mind, and though he continued dutifully to regard himself as bound by his electoral pledge to maintain the existing duties and even denounced Cobden as a dangerous agitator, he was already his unconscious disciple. When in the autumn of 1845 – one of the wettest and most miserable in human memory – the Irish potato crop was affected by disease, he was ready to adopt immediate repeal as the only remedy.

For to feed Ireland, England would have to import surplus corn from abroad, and neither the English nor the starving Irish could be expected to pay duty on it. Yet as was pointed out by Stanley – the future Lord Derby and only leading member of Peel's cabinet not to be carried away by him – abolition of the Corn Laws only took from the starving Irish peasant with one hand what it gave with the other. Having by an act of God been robbed of the first of his two staple crops, potatoes, he could only be further injured by a reduction in the price of the second, oats. In the climax of their own industrial revolution the political rulers of Britain, now suddenly and almost wholly obsessed by an urban viewpoint, forgot that the people of Ireland were country, not town, producers. For the remedies they offered were calculated to relieve the latter at the expense of the former.

Like so many of his countrymen, Peel was in the grip of an economic theory. He saw the Corn Laws as a challenge to that theory and wished to remove them. Having given his electoral pledge to maintain them, he had regretfully decided that they would have to stay on the statute book until the election of a new Parliament. But the 'potato cholera,' with its threat to the Irish food supply, gave him, the first public servant of Britain, the chance to effect the great change himself – one which, as he now believed, would set his country and the world on the path to lasting economic prosperity. It gave him not a reason for his action – he needed none – but a pretext. For he was seeking not a mere suspension to meet the emergency of the moment, but permanent repeal. It was not, as the Duke of Wellington thought, 'rotten potatoes' that had put 'Peel in his damned fright!' Peel was not in a fright at all but, having been subjugated, as public men in a democracy are apt to be, by continuous pressure and propaganda, he was able to use the Irish calamity to carry a measure in which he now profoundly believed.

The change in Britain's historic policy came with startling suddenness. Early in November, 1845, Peel proposed in Cabinet that the ports should be opened by immediate Order of Council and that a Bill for the permanent modification of the Corn Laws should be introduced in the new year. Before this decision became public, the leader of the Opposition, Lord John Russell, fearing that the Tories by reversing their policy would steal the electoral tide to power a second time, issued a hasty manifesto to his constituents abandoning the old Whig principle of a fixed duty on corn and declaring for total repeal. This was capped in early December by a Cabinet decision for immediate repeal and an unauthorized announcement in next day's *Times* which precipitated such a crisis in the betrayed Tory ranks that the Government resigned and the Queen sent for Russell. But the latter, prevented from forming an administration by party intrigues centring round the stormy personality of Palmerston, was unable to make use of his opportunity. Instead he 'handed back with courtesy the poisoned chalice to Sir Robert'.

Peel took it gratefully. He was convinced that, as the most experienced administrator in the country and the leader of its strongest party, he was the proper man to carry the measure. That he had been accredited by the electorate and his own followers to pursue a contrary policy did not trouble his conscience. For like many other zealous and over-worked public servants, he had never fully understood the nature of the English constitution. He had forgotten that its essence was that a politician should identify himself with a principle and resign when that principle was defeated. In a speech in which he declared that he would no longer resist the inference that employment, low prices and abundance contributed to the diminution of crime Peel made known his intention to the House when it reassembled in January 1846. His prestige was such, and the popular agitation against the Corn Laws so bitter, that a sufficient number of his own betrayed and shattered party followed him with the Opposition into the lobbies on May 15th, 1846, to secure a majority of 98 for repeal. When two months later rising Tory anger culminated in the fall of his Government, he justified himself in a speech which has gone down to history:

103

'I shall leave a name execrated, I know, by every monopolist
. . . But it may be that I shall be sometimes remembered with
expressions of goodwill in those places which are the abodes of
men whose lot it is to labour and earn their daily bread by the
sweat of their brow; in such places, perhaps, my name may be
remembered with expressions of goodwill when they who inhabit
them recruit their exhausted strength with abundant and untaxed
food, the sweeter because no longer leavened with a sense of
injustice.'

*   *   *

It takes a great man to oppose the tide of his age. Benjamin Disraeli
was a great man. Alone among statesmen of his generation he perceived
the fallacy of the Manchester School and of the departure in national
policy which it had initiated. The immediate interests of the factory
owner, the worker and the investor might be served by a free trade
policy. But in the long run he knew that the policy must ultimately
leave the nation at the mercy of world-wide forces beyond its control.

A back-bencher when the agitation for the repeal of the Corn Laws
began, a Jew with brilliant but flashy literary antecedents and for that
reason denied office in Peel's Government, a parvenu without territorial
or commercial influence, Disraeli nevertheless saw, with the vision of
genius, the flaw in the logic of the Manchester School. The free
traders rightly assumed that it was the present interest of the British
manufacturer and urban worker to sell manufactured goods to a mainly
agricultural world and of the world to purchase them by sending its
primary products untaxed to Britain. They also assumed that such a
favourable situation, once created, would always continue. Disraeli
realized that other nations would not forever acquiesce in a British
monopoly of industry. They might wish to extend their own industrial
markets just as Lancashire had done. If they found their British rivals
could undersell them at home, they would put pressure on their
governments to raise prohibitive and uneconomic tariffs behind which
their growing industries could shelter.

For, as Disraeli reminded his unheeding countrymen, governments
were swayed by considerations other than the economic gain of the
living individual which Adam Smith had enshrined as the wealth of
nations. They might deliberately restrict the course of commerce and
limit profits to increase their country's strategic and military strength,
safeguard its health and social stability or advance some religious or

other ideological conception to which economics were subordinate. Swayed by such reasons, for all Cobden's confident prophecies, they might refuse to follow the British lead and adopt free trade. In place of a world liberated from commercial restrictions and growing ever richer and more peaceable, Britain might one day find herself confronted by 'a species of Berlin decrees, more stringent even than those of Napoleon'.

Disraeli therefore pleaded, though in vain, that his country should hesitate before abandoning, for a system of unrestricted imports, the ancient protective and reciprocal principle under which she had lived and traded for so long. Her aim, he contended, should not be free trade, but fair trade giving a just and stable reward to the producer. 'Protection to native industry', he wrote, 'is a fundamental principle'.

Unlike his machine-struck contemporaries, Disraeli refused to see cotton-spinning as the end of British policy. Agriculture was still the most vital of national industries. To sacrifice it for the sake of profits, however vast, was to mortgage the country's future security. Three years before the repeal of the Corn Laws, he had recalled in the House of Commons the words of a Venetian Doge who, looking out from the windows of his Adriatic palace on the commerce of the world anchored in the lagoons beneath, exclaimed, 'This Venice without *terra firma* is an eagle with one wing!'

To the mind of this half-alien patriot the Corn Laws were no mere plank of fiscal policy but an outwork of an historic system which protected a priceless civilization. That system had based the possession of wealth on the performance of social duty. 'The feudal system may have worn out,' he wrote, 'but its main principle – that the tenure of property should be the fulfilment of duty – is the essence of good government'.

Against the radical and levelling tendencies of his age, Disraeli reacted, not because he was opposed to popular rights and social amelioration, which he wished to extend, but because he wished to base both on something more stable than the despotic will of an all-powerful popularly elected assembly and an attendant bureaucracy. At the back of his mind lay always certain historic English ideals of a united nation and a continuing community of different classes, composed of men and women possessing inalienable privileges and rights secured by a stronger tenure than that of their own lives. His conception of society was essentially religious and humane – an ordered hierarchy based on a universal recognition of human needs and rights. He wished to restore dignity, romance and personal influence to the throne, responsibility to the nobility and gentry, moral authority to the Church; above all, status, pride of craft and security to the peasant and worker.

His contemporaries took the strength, assurance and vital character of England for granted. Disraeli, viewing the land of his adoption with detachment, knew that the virtues which made her people great and prosperous were nourished by institutions and principles whose abandonment might one day bring about a gradual national decay and ultimate ruin. He could not share the easy optimism of reformers who supposed that they had only to rationalize to improve. He distrusted human reason, knew it to be fallible and its conclusions subject to ceaseless and unpredictable change. Like Burke he preferred to rely on the instinctive wisdom and prejudice of the older England. An intellectual himself, he fell back on instinct and precedent: on the accumulated reason of generations tested by experience. 'A precedent,' he once said, 'embalms a principle.'

It was a rational opinion, widely held by economists, that the capacity to make profits was the proper test of all economic activity. It was an ancient national principle and a popular prejudice that every man should receive a fair price for the product of his labour, that he should be protected in his employment, his enjoyment of home and his dignity as a man, however great the potential profits others might make in depriving him of these. In this Disraeli joined vital issue with the Free Traders. For they were not concerned with the social consequences of the system of trade they advocated, believing that those consequences, through the unimpeded operation of economic law, would always look after themselves.

It was Disraeli's lot to see his counsel neglected and his country adopt the policy he deplored. Until the Corn Laws were repealed he was only a back-bencher. On the day that the fatal measure finally passed the Lords, he became a leader of the Tory rump which Peel had betrayed. For twenty years, with two short breaks, he remained in the political wilderness – the derided mentor of 'a fat cattle opposition' which had lost touch with the spirit of the age. Like a wise man who realized the strength of his countryman's infatuation, he accepted their decision and warned his bucolic followers that they must allow a fair chance to the experiment on which Parliament and the nation had resolved. 'You are in the position of a man who has made an improvident marriage,' he told them. 'You have become united to Free Trade, and nothing can divorce you except you can prove the charmer to be false.

Wait, then, till that period has arrived; when you find that you have been betrayed, then will be the time to seek a divorce from that pernicious union. You have become united to the false Duessa, and you must take the consequences; and the consequence, I venture to predict, will be that the House of Commons, after a fair, full and ample trial of this great measure, will be driven to repeal it from absolute necessity, though at the termination of much national suffering; but that that suffering will be compensated for by the bitterness and the profundity of national penitence.'

'It may be idle now,' he said of his deluded countrymen, 'in the springtide of their economic frenzy to warn them that there may be an ebb of trouble. But the dark and inevitable hour will arrive. Then, when their spirits are softened by misfortune, they will return to those principles that made England great and which, in our belief, will only keep England great.'

CHAPTER SIX

The Fighting Fifties

'A lady with a lamp shall stand
In the great history of the land,
A noble type of good
Heroic womanhood.'

Longfellow

THOUGH THE REPEAL of the Corn Laws failed to end the famine in Ireland, whose starving population continued to fall, and, in desperation, to emigrate – dropping in the course of a generation from eight to five millions – Cobden's triumph and Peel's apostasy, as his rank-and-file followers called it, were attended by a gradual return of industrial prosperity. 1847 was a year of violent fluctuations: corn, which touched 124 shillings a quarter in June, had fallen to 49 shillings and sixpence by September. Corn dealers and bill-brokers were ruined; there was a crash in the railway market, and the Bank Act was suspended. But after that things began to look up. Though repeal of the Corn Laws made little difference to the price of wheat, which averaged no less a quarter in the Free Trade 'fifties than it had done in the Protectionist 'forties, the new railways cheapened the price of provisions, clothes and coal. Everyone had a little more to spend, and there was room for expansion. The hungry 'forties were over. The Free-Traders to whom these blessings were attributed were felt to have earned well of their country. Protection, formally abandoned by the repeal of the Navigation Laws in 1849, was a lost cause. Thereafter for the disciples of *laissez-faire* everything seemed to prosper.

Yet the real key to the prosperity of the booming 'fifties after the 'hungry 'forties' was the purely accidental discovery in 1847 of gold in California and the wild rush to the 'diggings' which followed. Four years later even more gold was found in Australia to which scores of thousands emigrated to seek their fortune. Both countries were able to increase their purchase of British goods with gold payments, while at home this entirely fortuitous shot-in-the-arm stimulated a currency based on gold. By 1852 there was more gold in the Bank of England than ever before. With purchasing power expanding and interest rates low, the demand for the products of British machines, mines, mills and factories rocketed. Everyone had more money to spend, and its spending released the country's productive capacity. As new, hitherto unexploited markets opened out in Asia and the underdeveloped Americas, a golden era dawned for south Lancashire, the West Riding, Tyneside, Staffordshire, the Clyde and South Wales. Industrial Britain was becoming the workshop of the world.

As eager capitalist hands seized their chances, and trade began to boom, the lot of the worker improved also. Employment expanded, and the larger firms which wider markets created had no need, with their increased turnover, to resort to such petty economies and merciless conduct as their predecessors. Wages tended to rise, hours of labour to fall, and the worst abuses of truck, sweating and child labour to diminish. Lord Shaftesbury's Ten Hours' Bill, limiting the hours of child labour, and other measures incompatible with the strictest letter of *laissez-faire* found their way on to the statute book. Pleased with its growing prosperity, the country felt at last that it could afford them.

A Britain, growing rich through increasing dependence on other lands, needed a peaceful world to ensure her abundant raw materials and expanding markets. Her difficulty was to control it. Insular England could never fathom the cause of European events: it merely observed their consequences in its export orders. In 1848 they suddenly became exceedingly grave. On Monday, February 22nd, the people of France enjoyed to all appearances the rule of a powerful, peaceful and impregnable monarchy. Two days later her pacific bourgeois king Louis Philippe was a fugitive in England, and the flag of the terrible Republic again flew over barricaded streets. By the summer she was drifting into mob rule and all Europe was following her bloodstained example. Italy and Germany, with their confused, divided petty kingdoms and principalities, were in a blaze from the Baltic to the Tyrrhenian Sea: even Vienna and the aged high priest of the *ancien regime*, Prince Metternich, did not escape. In Dresden, where the King of Saxony fled, the corpses were piled high in the streets. In all Europe, only Britain seemed to ride out the storm. The fact gave Englishmen considerable satisfaction: 'in the midst of the roar of revolutionary waters that are deluging the whole earth,' wrote Greville, 'it is grand to see how we stand erect and unscathed.' *Punch* depicted the proprietor of Mivart's Hotel – forerunner of Claridge's – presenting his humble respects to the crowned heads of the Continent and begged to inform them that his hotel in Brook Street continued the favoured house of call for dethroned potentates.

Not that England in this year of revolutions escaped a little revolution of its own. But though prefaced by a prodigious amount of noise and oratory, it was only a mock one and did no one any harm but the revolutionaries. It was staged by the Chartists who, relying on the hitherto general substratum of poverty, called a monster demonstration on Kennington Common for April 10th to present a petition to Parliament. But the Government, remembering 1842, promptly called in the military, put the defences of London into the hands of the aged victor of Waterloo and swore in City and Whitehall clerks as special constables. Against such preparations the mob was powerless. The day, a fine one, ended in Fergus O'Connor, the Chartist leader, shaking hands effusively with the police inspector who forbade the procession and, after advancing on Westminster in a cab, thanking a rather astonished Home Secretary for his leniency. A rising in wretched Ireland later in the year fared even more ignominiously: here the liberator, Smith O'Brien, was taken prisoner by a railway guard after a broil in the widow McCormack's cabbage patch.

It was not surprising, as the dust of the European arena settled down and a dishevelled continent tried to return to normal, that the English congratulated themselves. In Doyle's *Punch* cartoons of 1849 one can see them doing so – a fat, good-humoured, smiling British working family sitting by its own fireside with a picture of Queen Victoria on the wall and a newspaper on father's knee describing the awful state of Europe; while round the border scowl and grimace a crew of mad, savage foreigners – Spanish peasants chasing priests with knives, licentious and brutal soldiers charging barricades, the artillerymen of tyrants bombarding defenceless capitals, and slavish Frenchmen worshipping a Napoleonic hat and jackboots on bended knees. The liberty enjoyed by a Briton was never so attractive as when contrasted with the slavery of his neighbours.

The truth was that the British working class had tired of revolutionary politics. With the aid of the railways and the 7*d.* loaf it was learning to accept urbanization as its lot. The improvement in trade and the growing attempts of the middle class to ameliorate conditions in the factory towns assisted the change. The first effect of the repeal of the Corn Laws was largely psychological; it took the bitterness out of public life. The mob orator with flashing eyes, a brogue and a leaning to incendiarism was superseded by the earnest student reading in the public library and taking minutes at small meetings of the republican elect under a gas jet. It was the age in which Karl Marx, driven from the continent by the suppression of the German and French workers' revolutions, settled in furnished rooms at Camberwell and started in the fusty calm of the British Museum to evolve his universal but apparently harmless philosophy of hate. Among his innumerable hates were the Christian religion, his parents, his wife's uncle – 'the hound' – his German kinsfolk, his own race – 'Ramsgate is full of fleas and Jews' – the Prussian reactionaries, his Liberal and utopian Socialist allies, the labouring population – 'Lumpenproletariat' or riff-raff – democracy – 'parliamentary cretinism' – and the British royal family – 'the English mooncalf and her princely urchins,' as he called them. His self-imposed task he defined as 'the ruthless criticism of everything that exists.'

Under this sober stimulus Chartism died and was buried, and its place taken by radicalism and academic republicanism. The latter was not so much a practical attempt to overthrow monarchy as a creed. It was not at all blood-thirsty; to cater for its high-tea tastes the title of Harney's 'Red Republican' was changed to 'The Friend of the People.' It met at places like the Discussion Hall in Shoe Lane, the Temple Forum in Fleet Street, the Cogers tavern near St Bride's and the John Street Institution, Bloomsbury, where the chairman sat in a canopied chair with pipe and brandy and water, and the famous Mrs Dexter lectured on, and in, the 'bloomer' costume. Its adherents were eager young artisans who had educated themselves. They were much enamoured of foreign revolutionaries whose doings they followed with intense and quite uncritical enthusiasm: for them they generously subscribed their scanty pennies and when, as destitute fugitives, the latter fled to England, they lionized them in a humble but fervent way. In the eyes of these English radicals Poles, Hungarians, Italians, Germans and other oppressed minorities were all heroes and pioneers of European freedom. Incidentally their foreign friends with the ingratitude of their kind were apt to be a good deal less enthusiastic about them.

For as these interesting exiles found to their annoyance, England was not a revolutionary country at heart. Given a modicum of bread and beer and a little liberty and leisure to enjoy himself, the sweating toiler in the classic island home of the proletariat proved astonishingly good-humoured. Despite the sufferings of the factory operative and the slum-dweller, there was something incorrigibly jolly about England. If it was given the chance to be, it was fundamentally healthy, kept its pores open and its heart kindly and merry. With the passing of the Factory Act in 1850 and the legal enforcement of a Saturday half-holiday, the week-end habit began and, as wages increased, the supply of cheap amusement arose to cater for the demand. It was often of a rather vulgar, garish, sodden kind: there was much drunkenness and a good deal of brutality. But at its core was an invincible love of good fare and of sport. In Lancashire and the West Riding, gala days, wakes and feasts emptied the mine and stopped the wheels of the mill at customary times every year. Excursion trains, packed with pale-faced workers and their families, with bands, banners and bottled beer, descended annually from the cotton towns on Rock Ferry and Black-pool: it was close by the cheap ferry from Liverpool to the Cheshire shore that Nathaniel Hawthorne in 1853 saw a working man pulling from his pockets oyster after oyster 'in interminable succession' and opening them with his pocket-knife. There was whippet-racing and pigeon-flying for miners and scarlet-vested railway navvies, horse-racing of a rough kind on the Yorkshire and Lancashire moors, wrestling, boxing, quoits, bowls, and cricket and football. In London the working-class population affected open-air gardens where in the summer families could eat, drink and be merry at little expense. Vauxhall, sinking rapidly lower in the social scale, lingered on until 1859; Cremorne in Chelsea, founded by a uniformed Prussian baron in 1830, proffered fireworks, cascades, balloon ascents, bad music, rather indecorous dancing, alfresco theatrical entertainments, and polar bears in white cotton trousers; and there were pleasure gardens at Chalk Farm, Hackney, Hoxton, the Eagle, Islington, the Red House, Battersea, and many another suburban resort. In all this, partaking of the village from which it had sprung, the proletariat of urban England showed how little its heart was in a revolutionary ideological abstraction. It was difficult to make it class conscious. It just wanted to be comfortable and have a good time. Its anthem was not the *Marseillaise* but the deathless song whose roaring refrain went:

> 'Damn their eyes
> If ever they tries
> To rob a poor man of his beer!'

*   *   *

It was the Teuton Consort of the Queen, Prince Albert, who demonstrated to the world how harmless and pacific the British proletariat was. In 1849 he and a little group of cultured persons of like mind began to prepare plans for a great Exhibition of Industry in London. All the world was to be invited to contribute exhibits and to view in turn the triumphs of British art and manufacture. Nobody at first took the idea very seriously, but the Prince was persistent, and in the following winter, after 5000 guarantors had been reluctantly enlisted, a Royal Commission was set up. Sixteen acres of land on the southern side of Hyde Park were secured and a design for a monster palace of glass accepted from Joseph Paxton who had built the Duke of Devonshire's conservatories at Chatsworth. At first nobody thought either the money or the glass 'ark as big as a warehouse' would ever be raised, but, as the giant iron columns, some of them over a hundred feet high, appeared in the Park, laughter changed to apprehension. With the vast concourse of visitors whom it would draw to the West End of London from abroad and from the dangerous working-class districts, almost anything might happen. The Park – favourite haunt of beauty and fashion – would be filled with East End rowdies who, with their tobacco smoke, Waterloo crackers and practical jokes, would turn it into another Greenwich Fair, with lousy and potentially murderous foreigners; and, most ominous of all, with savage heathens from the Northern industrial towns. The beds would be trampled on, the flowers picked and finally the great human tide, leaving its scum behind in the devastated Park, would surge out by night to pillage Belgravia and Kensington. The American press, even more alarmist than the English, prophesied general massacre and insurrection.

But Prince Albert was not to be turned from his purpose. Gradually, under the hands of two thousand workmen, the great building, over 600 yards long, containing nearly a million square feet of glass and affording over eight miles of table space for the exhibitors, rose like a dazzling Aladdin's palace of crystal over the grass, the birds and the trees.

On May Day, 1851, the Great Exhibition was formally opened by the Queen. The capital was prudently filled with troops: the Rifle Brigade was moved from Dover to Woolwich, the 1st Royal Dragoons from Nottingham and the 8th Hussars from Brighton to billets in Hampstead and Highgate, and the 4th Light Dragoons from Dublin to Hounslow, while a strong contingent of artillery was quartered in the Tower. The Park itself was protected by three cavalry regiments,

113

seven foot battalions of the Household troops and two regiments of Lancers. In addition over 6,000 police were on duty in the capital. Even before it was light every road leading to the park was thronged. After long rain the sun was shining. At seven o'clock the gates were opened and the great multitude poured in.

Yet it proved astonishingly good-humoured and appreciative. On that lovely May Day it was out, not to stampede the police and sack London, but to enjoy itself. It accepted the rich in their carriages, the great ones driving to their allocated places in the crystal palace, the Queen and the royal family as part of the splendid show provided for its entertainment.

In this great national triumph, the dedication of the 'grandest temple ever raised to the peaceful arts,' there was a supreme moment. After Prince Albert, standing at the head of the Royal Commissioners, had read aloud the report that told of the completion of their labours, and the Queen had replied and the Archbishop prayed, the massed choirs of the Chapel Royal, Westminster Abbey, St Paul's and Windsor Chapel, supported by the members of the Royal Academy of Music and the Sacred Harmonic Society, and accompanied by an organ with 4,700 pipes, broke into Handel's 'Halleluiah Chorus.' Outside, where the waiting crowd covered every available inch of the Park, the artillery beyond the Serpentine sounded welcoming salvoes. Then the Queen with her husband and children about her, and at the head of a procession which included the aged Commander-in-Chief and the Master General of the Ordnance – who thirty-six years before had respectively commanded the British army and cavalry on the field of Waterloo – swept down the west nave, threading their way between lines of statuary, objects of art and the products of industry. The sword wielded by the English brave had been melted into ploughshares: righteousness and peace had kissed each other. For that ecstatic moment the English were really happy.

In the weeks that followed, the humblest in the land came to view the Great Exhibition. Throughout the summer the daily attendance at times exceeded 60,000. After the third week the admission fee was reduced to a shilling on four days a week. The shilling days proved the wonder of the season. Instead of the brutal behaviour and rioting which many had expected, an endless stream of orderly, good-humoured working-class folk, gaping and admiring, passed under the crystal dome. Here were the dreaded working-class people of England and they had come as friends. The great event attracted thousands who perhaps had never seen a train before, people speaking the strange tongues of Lancashire and Durham, and the official reports of their behaviour as they flocked through museums and gardens were full of unconcealed pride. Not a flower was picked, a picture smashed. And ten years before, the Londoners who now welcomed them had stood silent in the streets to watch the guns going north to Lancashire.

To the nation that fairy palace towering over the blossom and foliage of the park symbolized a great social reunion and the dawning of a new era of hope, based on enterprise, freedom of trade and cheapness of production and communication. To innocent eyes – and there were many that saw it – it seemed a palace of light glittering in the summer sun with its central crystal fountain reflecting all the jewels of the world, an Arabian nights' creation 'so graceful, so delicate, so airy that its translucent beauty remains graven on memory as something which must defy all rivalry.' To the simple sons of toil from the industrial North who had saved up their pennies to make the first and only pilgrimage of their lives to visit it, its beauty seemed something that was scarcely of this earth. They saw it, not like a sophisticated posterity as something comic, but as a dream of fairyland and, in a world which contained the slums of Irkside and Little Ireland, and in which all things are comparative, it is not surprising.

*   *   *

The Great Exhibition was expected by its promoters to herald the dawn of perpetual peace. It was a hope shared by every Briton. In the past Britain had won many great prizes in war. But she had done so because she had emerged victorious from her wars and not because she had sought them. Her people, though redoubtable fighters, were deeply impregnated by a desire to live at peace and by a belief that wars were always caused by foreigners.

This had never seemed so true as in 1851. Increasingly dependent on free imports, with a growing export trade, with a vast empire (in which they had almost lost interest), and with a glorious record of victories behind them, the islanders had nothing to gain by war and everything to lose. All that was now necessary was to persuade foreigners who were not in the same state of blessedness to think likewise. The light of reason, the healing gospel of Free Trade and the outward and visible sign afforded by the Crystal Palace would surely convert them. It was to their material advantage.

The weakness of the Englishman's attitude towards foreigners was that he expected them to think and behave exactly like himself. When, true to their own alien natures, they failed to do so, he either laughed at their folly or – if their behaviour outraged his moral code, as it frequently did – became justly indignant. And as, being a free-born Briton, he scorned to conceal his laughter or disapproval, misunderstanding between him and his Continental neighbours was bound to arise.

The ruling principles of Britain's foreign policy were to preserve the balance of European power, protect the Low Countries and the Channel coasts, keep open her trade routes and establish the rule of righteousness on earth. The last object – that of playing St George to the dragon of foreign tyrants – generally coincided with the first, since any ambitious despot with a large army who threatened to overthrow the balance of power inevitably trampled in doing so on the liberties of his own subjects and weaker neighbours. In repelling such threats to her own interests, Britain was thus in the happy position of also fighting the battle of human freedom and morality. As her statesmen and people were always quick to emphasize this point, she was less liked by large nations than by small. And by making herself the unofficial patron of every liberal or subversive movement abroad, as well as by her generous policy of granting refuge to political exiles, she won the sometimes embarrassing goodwill of foreign rebels but the suspicion and resentment of their governments. This policy, alike unaggressive and provocative, was pursued by both political parties – the Whigs because they liked foreign Liberals on principle and the Tories because it was a cheap way of escaping the reproach of being reactionary.

During the forty years of peace which followed the downfall of Napoleon, the Channel shores were secured by the international neutralization of the Low Countries – divided after 1830 into the small pacific kingdoms of Holland and Belgium – and the temporary exhaustion of France. So long as the latter remained quiescent, Britain's jealousy of despots was spasmodically directed towards her three former allies of 1813–15 – Russia, Austria and Prussia. But these states, though governed by despots under very illiberal constitutions and therefore a proper source of contempt to an English patriot, enjoyed the comparative advantage of being a long way away. Only one of them, Russia, which was the possessor of a fair-sized navy, offered any threat to British interests. For Russia was an Asiatic as well as a European

'As the dust of the European arena settled down and a dishevelled continent tried to return to normal, it is not surprising the English congratulated themselves. In Doyle's *Punch* cartoons of 1849 one can see them doing so – a fat, good-humoured, smiling British working family sitting by its own fireside with a picture of Queen Victoria on the wall . . . while round the border scowl and grimace a crew of mad, savage foreigners.'

'In a famous cartoon England's leading comic journal apostrophied Father Thames as a filthy old man dragging up dead rats from a liquid, gaseous mass of black mud and dying fish. The water supply of three million people was polluted.' *Punch*, 1848.

'It was fitting that the chosen leader of such a land should be Lord Palmerston. That familiar figure – the tilted white hat, tight-buttoned coat, cane, dyed whiskers – riding down Piccadilly before breakfast or rising to jest or bluff away an awkward situation in the House, gave the English confidence. It was just so that they liked to think of themselves, boldly confronting a world of which they had somehow become lords.'

'This great national triumph, the dedication of "the grandest temple ever raised to the peaceful arts".' Queen Victoria and Prince Albert opening the Great Exhibition, 1851. Painting by Henry C. Selous.

power, and her steady expansion towards India and Persia caused constant uneasiness in Whitehall. Above all her tendency to intervene in the affairs of the decaying Ottoman empire on behalf of the Christian subjects of the Sultan was regarded with a suspicious eye by statesmen responsible for preserving British communications with India. If Antwerp was a pistol pointed at London, Constantinople was one levelled at India. Britain preferred to keep it in the palsied hand of the Turk.

All this, however, was of much more interest to the serious states-man and student of politics than to the ordinary Briton. Russia was a long way away. And though its Czars were unquestionably tyrants and the knout and Siberian prison camp were horrors that outraged every honest heart, it was hard to present the maintenance of the corrupt and cruel rule of Turkish pashas over Christian subject peoples as a campaign for moral righteousness. And even the protection of vital British interests – especially such distant ones – could not arouse the public without the stimulant of a great moral cause.

In the early years of Victoria's reign the English therefore contented themselves with a good deal of genial abuse of tyrants in their parliamen-tary speeches and newspapers without taking any very active steps to oppose them. The Emperors of Russia and Austria and the King of Prussia were regularly caricatured as a trio of stupid, arrogant, absurd, epauletted, high-collared, tight-breeched, top-booted tyrants, and any act of high-handed dealing by their minions – of which there were plenty – that found its way into the British press was held up to moral obloquy. This national habit of lecturing, combined with so much good fortune and wealth, made the English extremely unpopular in the greater chancelleries of Europe and led to charges being brought against them of hypocrisy, meddling and Machiavellian warmongering. It was particularly resented when, as often happened, it took the form of holding out the British constitution as the model for every other country and intriguing, regardless of local circumstances, against the established authorities on behalf of discontented radical minorities. Behind the convenient cloak of parliamentary forms, British politicians in oppo-sition, and sometimes in office, did a good deal of this.

In his bold, confident and even dashing behaviour towards foreign rulers, one English statesman of the time above all others represented the moral feelings, prejudices and generous if narrow sympathies of his countrymen. Palmerston, who with one brief break was Whig Foreign Secretary from 1830 to 1841, and again from 1846 to 1852, was the pride of Britain and the *enfant terrible* of Europe. In all that he said and did, in which there was much shrewdness and an incontestable love of his country and her institutions, he was animated by a belief that he was exposing the powers of darkness. Except for a few over-travelled and superior persons, every Englishman shared his faith and most of them applauded the steps he took to give it effect. That these were as often as not tactless, impetuous and needlessly provocative did not trouble them. However much they pained the meticulous Prince Albert and Palmerston's own colleagues – it was his rollicking practice to act first and consult afterwards – they well suited the mood of England, rustic, middle-class or proletarian. When in 1850 the honest draymen of Barclay's Brewery chased an Austrian general, who was reputed to have flogged some rebel Hungarian ladies, down Bankside into good Mrs Benfield's bedroom in the George public-house, and bombarded him with mud pies and cries of 'Cut off his beard!' they were only enacting in their own rough way the familiar Palmerstonian technique. They meant no harm but they wished a foreign scoundrel to learn what an Englishman thought of him.

Rebukes and scrapes only enhanced Palmerston's popularity and stimulated him to new outrages on the authoritarian proprieties of Europe. Like a true Englishman he was irresistible in recoil. His famous *Civis Romanus sum* speech in the summer of 1850, after a vote of censure on his high-handed Don Pacifico policy, won round the House in spite of itself and made him, not for the last time, the hero of his country. When eighteen months later he was forced to resign after a further outrage on the royal prerogative and the rights of his colleagues, the London urchins, voicing the universal feeling of the common people, paraded the streets singing:

> 'For he's the people's darling!'

Whatever grave persons and a prosy German Prince Consort might say, 'the Viscount, full of vigour and hilarity and overflowing with diplomatic swagger,' was the man for England.

'Let tyrants tremble!' might have been his motto, and it was certainly his country's. Yet, so long as tyrants kept their distance, neither Palmerston nor England wished to go to war. They merely claimed the right to speak out their mind freely about them. But there was one species of tyrant whom an Englishman not only hated but feared – a French tyrant.

* * *

The Revolution of 1848 made France once more a republic. Before the year was out, worse had happened. In a violent revulsion of popular opinion against disorder and egalitarian excesses, a nephew of the great Napoleon was elected President. The alarm aroused in England coincided with a period of misgiving about the nation's military and naval preparedness. As always after a long peace, the Army seemed quite insufficient for any warlike task: its most serious preoccupations were sartorial such as the new shell jacket and the peculiar-looking shako recently designed for its use by Prince Albert. The aged Duke of Wellington could not sleep at night for thinking of the defenceless state of the coasts. Worse, the Navy itself was growing rusty. The greater part of the battle fleet was laid up in harbour, 'dismantled aloft and disarmed below.' And in the new inventions which had come to revolutionize maritime warfare the volatile and nimble-witted French had stolen a dangerous march. In 1837 they had adopted explosive shells in place of the solid shot that had won Trafalgar and their pioneer efforts with steamers in the early 'forties had been more successful than those of the statelier and more conservative British Admiralty.

All this combined with the events in France to cause a good deal of surface alarm. Yet the sense of England's superiority was so innate and the general complacence and love of peace and comfort so deep-rooted that it quickly died away. *Punch* depicted a number of seasick French colonels and poodles attempting to cross the Channel while a very senile Duke of Wellington in a Field Marshal's cocked hat vainly tried with a quill pen to tickle up a sleeping British lion which only replied, 'All right, old boy, I shall be ready when I'm wanted.' Palmerston confessed to Russell in 1851 that it was 'almost as difficult to persuade the people of this country to provide themselves with the means of defence as it would be for them to defend themselves without those means.'

At the end of that year there came a new alarm. Louis Napoleon, interpreting the will of the rising generation in France, established himself in permanent power as life President by a military *coup d'etat*. A year later he became Emperor of the French in fictitious succession to his famous uncle. This arbitrary act, though accompanied by remarkably little loss of life, aroused the utmost indignation among English radicals, who merely saw it as a brutal attack on their liberal and socialist brethren across the Channel. Faced by the situation, patriotic feeling revived. Cobdenism and Free Trade notwithstanding, the nation began to rearm. A Militia Bill was brought in by a short-lived

Conservative government in the summer of 1852, and a new, almost querulous, note crept into national journalism – of the first rifle clubs, of serious searchings of heart about Navy victualling scandals and the boilers of the new steam warships, of Admiral Napier KCB, of 'Little Billee' fame, and of jolly tars in big straw hats, striped jerseys and bell-bottom trousers getting ready to show the world that peaceful England could still teach a presumptuous foreigner a lesson.

Yet, after all, it was not the French tyrant with whom an awakening England was to test her strength. For it happened that British interests, real or illusory, caused Britain to fight beside the French tyrant instead of against him. The Eastern question cropped up again, and the island victors of Trafalgar and Waterloo, who had dedicated themselves at the shrine of the Crystal Palace to perpetual peace, drifted into a war to safeguard the overland route to India. And in challenging those who threatened their vital communications they challenged tyranny too. No one could deny that Nicholas of Russia was a despot. Though a more remote one, he was both more autocratic and more offensive than Louis Napoleon.

For being an upstart, far from certain of his position and anxious to prevent any revival of the Waterloo coalition against France, Napoleon III sedulously courted England and did his best to soothe her fears and susceptibilities. The despot of all the Russias cared nothing for the English or any other public. In his own remote and barbarous country public opinion did not exist. He was accustomed to dealing only with despots like himself. In pursuit of his imperial interests he had for some time been proposing to British statesmen and diplomats that as the Turkish Empire was obviously dissolving through its own inertia and corruption, Russia and Britain should forestall competitors by anticipating the demise and dividing the carcass between them. Russia should have its long-sought outlet to the Mediterranean, and Britain should have Egypt and Candia.

In two momentous conversations in 1853 with the British Ambassador at St Petersburg this impertinent tyrant outlined his plans for partitioning the possessions of 'the sick man' of the Porte. Had he known anything of the mind and conscience of England, he would never have suggested making her a partner in anything so outrageous. Had he been able to foretell the future he would have known, too, that in another half-century Britain would be honourably installed in Egypt, while the landbound Muscovite would still be as far as ever from his Mediterranean goal and his hope of exercising suzerainty over his fellow

Christians of the Balkans. The British government returned no answer but made it clear that it was without territorial ambitions of any kind.

The Czar of all the Russias was not to be turned from his purpose by the nicety of British scruples. If Britain would not join in his designs, he would execute them by himself. Meanwhile he had become involved in a dispute with Louis Napoleon, whom he persisted in treating as a low upstart, over the protection of the Christian shrines in the Turkish dominions. Consequently when in pursuance of his grand design he moved his troops into the principalities of Wallachia and Moldavia – now Romania – he was confronted with the opposition not only of Britain but of France.

The British government – a talented but uneasy coalition of Peelites, Whigs and Radicals bound together by no other principle but dislike of the Protectionists – was in a difficulty. It had no wish to involve the nation in a war over the ownership of remote Syrian shrines and Balkan villages. On the other hand, a principle of British diplomatic policy was at stake and a foreign despot was openly flouting her Majesty's government. A compromise was therefore sought which recognized both the independence of the Ottoman Porte and the Czar's right to protect the Orthodox Christians in Turkey.

Yet it was one thing to propose a compromise: another to get two despotic orientals to accept it. The Sultan was resolved to keep his Christian provinces and to yield nothing. The Czar was equally resolved to obtain the substance of his ends, though, being anxious to obtain them if possible without war, he was temporarily the more reasonable of the two. But the Turk, seeing an opportunity of fighting a war (which he regarded as sooner or later inevitable) with the backing of two great Christian Powers, and, judging that such a chance might never occur again, refused any compromise whatever.

Step by step the British Prime Minister, Lord Aberdeen, was driven into a war which he deplored and whose results he dreaded. Most of his Cabinet were men of peace like himself, but a small war group led by Palmerston and Russell and strongly aided by the British Ambassador to the Porte – Lord Stratford de Redcliffe – drove him ever further into a position from which there was no withdrawing. Public opinion, waking up to the fact that the country was being flouted by a notorious despot, suddenly became intensely bellicose. Aberdeen found it harder than ever to retreat. A guarantee to the Turk which had been intended as provisional was imperceptibly transformed by that wily oriental into a document whose execution lay in Turkish, not British hands.

Without having any clear idea of what the struggle was about except that it was against tyranny and without the Government having made any adequate preparations to conduct it, the British people in the spring of 1854 found themselves in alliance with France and Turkey and at war with Russia. The country, apparently so pacific a few years before, had completely changed its outlook: John Morley in his free-trading, radical Lancashire home, remembered hearing at his parental fireside heartfelt wishes that Cobden and Bright – still bravely advocating peace – should be flung together into the insanitary waters of the Irwell. What was even more surprising was the alignment of England beside the French 'usurper,' whose 'foul lips' – in contemporary radical parlance – actually kissed the cheeks of Queen Victoria during a royal war-time visit to France. A few far-seeing observers predicted that the war would be hard to wage and impossible to bring to a successful conclusion, and that the British people would soon be as heartily sick of it as they were now hot in its favour. They were an insignificant minority and no one took the least notice of them.

The difficulty was to find a scene of operations. Despite universal hatred of the Russians and intense detestation of the Czar, the first six months of the war passed without any hostilities worth mentioning. An Anglo-French naval expedition to the Baltic accomplished nothing. A military force sent to aid the Turk in the Balkans saw more of cholera than the enemy, and it was not till the late autumn of 1854 that British and French troops landed in the Crimea peninsula and set siege to the naval fortress of Sevastopol.

The battles that followed – Alma, Balaclava, Inkerman – and the long siege in the trenches proved that the English had lost nothing of their ancient valour. They also revealed their curious inability to plan adequately ahead. The army command, which had neither learnt nor endeavoured to learn anything since 1815, might have been ready for the battle of Waterloo but was certainly not for a winter campaign in the trenches of Russia. In the first few months of the campaign everything failed: transport, commissariat, supply and hospitals. The Government and public which had talked glibly of taking Sevastopol in a few weeks were faced by the prospect of a long and hazardous campaign thousands of miles from home against a superior and apparently inexhaustible enemy fighting on his own ground.

During that winter – even in England it was one of the coldest in human memory – the losses of the little professional army were appalling and the foolish boastings of the summer soon turned to mourning.

Tales of men fighting in the frozen trenches without greatcoats, or packed, filthy with dysentery and gangrenous wounds, into unequipped hospitals built over Scutari cesspits, aroused a wave of indignation which brought down the Government and temporarily disgraced and even imperilled the aristocratic system of the country. But the story of their courage and endurance also thrilled England: the charge of the Light Brigade in the valley of death was like Thermopylae. The national mood was reflected by Macaulay, who told a friend in a letter how anxious he was about the brave fellows in the Crimea, how proud for the country and how glad to think that the national spirit was so high and unconquerable. The annals of the tough simple soldiery who stuck to their hopeless task until the Muscovite, unable to endure longer, abandoned Sevastopol, were remembered in after years by one of them, a farm labourer who had enlisted at sixteen, as cold and starvation, unremitting duty for days at a stretch, and what to lesser men would have been almost indescribable suffering.

The Crimean War continued till 1856. It ended in a nominal gain for Britain and France, though there were no fruits of victory. But it produced at least three results: it gave time for the Balkan peoples to achieve independence from the Turk before the Russian could absorb them; at home it showed the new power of the press and led to a number of great administrative reforms. William Howard Russell's reports to *The Times* revealed the generals' ineptitude in the field and behind the lines, and ended the complacency of the politicians and bureaucrats at home who now had to share responsibility with the generals. For the first time a voice spoke, almost daily, directly from the battlefield to middle-class people in their homes about the suffering of the ordinary soldier – his death, wounds, hunger, distress and lack of simple shelter.

The soldiers had another friend in the candle-lit form of Florence Nightingale, whose presence and actions lightened their darkest moments, on the operating table and in the wards: her hard administrative discipline, heroic in its unyielding passion, achieved unprecedented levels of comfort and sanitation. It was these same unique qualities which she employed in the wider field of nursing and medical reform during the half century of work which lay ahead of her. Her astonishing achievements in nursing had even wider effects in making the women of Britain appreciate what they could do in other spheres, including the professions, if only the illogical barriers to their doing so were removed.

*   *   *

Within a year the country was fighting again. For several months, until the tide turned in favour of the little handful of red-coated columns moving under a burning sun across distant jungle and plain, England waited in suspense at the end of the electric cable for news of beleaguered Cawnpore, Delhi and Lucknow. Of the causes and significance of the Indian Mutiny the English had no notion. A few among them who had spent a working lifetime under the oriental sun among the 'drums and gaudy idols . . . the black faces, the long beards, the yellow streaks of sect, the turbans and the flowing robes, the spears and silver maces' of an alien continent, knew something of their country's Eastern destiny. But to the great mass of the respectable middle-class electors of Victorian England, India was only a name.

This philosophical indifference to, almost unawareness of, the origins and nature of their own empire was a source of recurring bewilderment to the English. An event like the Indian Mutiny always took them by surprise. The Scots, a proud race trained to poverty who had had to travel to live, and even the Protestant Irish who had the instinct for garrisoning in their blood, knew more of the empire than the English commercial classes whose wealth and power sustained it. It had come into being almost accidentally, not as a result of conscious national or governmental effort but as the by-product of the activity of innumerable private persons. Among the landed classes the law of primogeniture, by creating in every generation a surplus of portionless younger sons educated in a standard of comfort which they could only maintain by going out into the world to seek their fortunes, had had the effect of changing the status and allegiance of a quarter of the globe.

The process of expansion went on without either the initiative or the conscious will of an imperial Government which obstinately refused to recognize itself as imperial. Palmerston, himself the embodiment of the spirit that made the British Empire, pooh-poohed the idea that his country should annex Egypt in order to safeguard her communications with India: a gentleman with an estate in Scotland and another in southern England, he remarked, did not need to own the post-houses along the Great North Road. Initiative was left in this, as in all things else, to the individual: the state in its corporate capacity only existed to protect the individual in his just gains and lawful occasions. The continued growth of the Empire was forced on an ever reluctant government (which, having to consider the interests of taxpayers who were also voters, was always cautious) by the restless energy of its private citizens. For every Englishman who had courage, a strong body, willing hands and capital enough to buy a passage there was boundless opportunity and elbow room waiting in lands beyond the oceans. Two brothers, aged nineteen and seventeen, belonging to a family of twelve, left for New Zealand with £2,000 capital between them and a superabundance of animal spirits prepared for any risks and any labour. To 'build, fell trees, plough, reap, pasture cattle, shear sheep, all these with the hands!' was the task they cheerfully set themselves. Within a dozen years each looked forward to returning with a capital of at least £20,000 to seek a wife and found a family. And the interests represented by that new capital and its future returns would demand in due course the protection of the imperial government, whether these interests lay in the British dominions or, as often happened, in more populous lands under some other flag.

CHAPTER SEVEN

Palmerston's England

'With his hat o'er his eyes and his nose in the air,
So jaunty and genial and debonair.
Talk at him – to him – against him – none
Can take a rise out of Palmerston.'

Punch

THE UNIT OF British national life was the family – the sacred nursery of the individual. The wealth and power of the country and the English-speaking parts of its colonial empire grew in ratio to the size of this homely unit. The middle years of the nineteenth century saw the population increasing more rapidly than ever before, not only because more children were being born, but because, thanks to advances in hygiene and medical science, more survived, particularly among the better-housed and educated middle class. Between 1841 and 1861 the population of England, Scotland and Wales rose from 17 to 23 millions, while that of Ireland fell from 8 to 5 millions through starvation, sickness and emigration. Not only in working-class homes – where insanitary conditions in the industrial towns kept down the numbers of those who survived – but in those of the upper and middle-class large families were still the rule. The Queen herself had nine children and a judge of the High Court twenty-four. Strangers admitted to the sacred circle of the home would usually find their hostess in the family way and be greeted by the spectacle of a flock of little boys running off to hide and little girls running out to peep. Often the children would mount in unbroken yearly steps from the baby at the breast to the grown youth of nineteen.

Around that holy of holies centred a life of the strictest regularity and order. Paterfamilias, for all the love he bore his family, was an awe-inspiring figure, infallible in his judgments and irreproachable in

126

his whiskers and moral conduct: his wife – a few years before a slender and clear-complexioned girl – 'a housekeeper, a nurse, a sitting hen,' as a distinguished French critic saw her, 'broad, stiff and destitute of ideas, with red face, eyes the colour of blue china . . . spreading dresses . . . stout masculine boots . . . long, projecting teeth.'

In the more prosperous families the boys would start work early with a tutor and at eight or nine leave home for the rough republic of one of the great boarding schools which were constantly expanding and multiplying to train new rulers for a growing commercial empire. Here sensitive children from rich and sheltered homes would rise in the small hours of the morning to light fires and boil water for their majestic seniors, sweep rooms, run errands and do the meanest chars, endure flogging and bullying without a murmur, and sleep at night in noisy, crowded dormitories subject to influences which would have made their mothers and sisters swoon.

In contrast, the lives of girls in well-to-do families were often sheltered to an extent that cut them off from the roots of life. The men were trained to make wealth: the women to transmit and form part of it. They were regarded as the chief measure of a husband's or father's opulence and social dignity: their elegant accomplishments, their delicacy and chastity were sources of male pride and satisfaction. As girls they were taught to play the piano, draw, dance, make wax flowers and beadstands and do decorative gilding and crochet work. That a man's womenfolk should be able to devote themselves to occupations so materially useless was a tacit tribute to the labour and self-sacrifice that had gone to the making of the wealth which sustained it. 'Oh, yes, mum,' said the cook in *Punch* of the squire's bride, 'she's a perfect lady, mum. Don't know one j'int o' meat from another.'

The strong, imitative instinct and desire to excel of the English led to a constant approximation of the lower types of social life to the higher. On a simpler and more spartan scale the family life of the north country manufacturer followed that of the lawyer in Kensington and the banker in Bayswater. Often he still lived on the premises of his own works in the shade of the smoke and within earshot of the hammering that created his wealth. In other cases he had moved out to one of the suburbs of gardened, Gothic villas which were growing up on the outskirts of places like Manchester and Birmingham. His daily round and social habits were less leisured than those of the Londoner: he still went to the mill at six, dined in the middle of the day and went early to bed after a hot meat supper and family prayers.

Sometimes his working day would last sixteen or more hours. He sent his sons into the works in their early teens instead of to public school and college which, he held, unsettled the mind for commercial pursuits.

Though many of those engaged in trade were men of cultivation – buyers of pictures and founders of libraries and colleges – the bulk of the provincial merchants tended, like their richer Forsyte brethren in London, to be Philistines, valuing all worldly things by the sterling standard, ignoring and despising art and having little truck with intellect which they left to the leisured and endowed landed gentry. The spiritual side of their natures would have been stifled but for their feeling for religion. This was like themselves: downright, undiscriminating and practical. Its dominant note was a militant Protestantism, which comprised a great readiness to criticize, a strong sense of self-righteousness, a very real respect for integrity and sound moral conduct and an unreasoning distrust of the Pope and of all foreign fal-lals. It found vigorous expression in the busy black-coated, white-tied unction of Exeter Hall where middle-class opinion was ceaselessly mobilized in favour of missionary, pacifist and humanitarian ventures, all of a strongly Protestant trend. Its antithesis was the Puseyite movement which, spreading out from Oxford – still the home of lost causes – was filling long-neglected, sober Hanoverian parish churches with painted chancels, niches, candles, altars, Popish-looking rails to keep off the profane laity, and painted windows bearing the idolatrous image of the Virgin Mary.

There was no doubt about the genuine piety of the English middle-class home. Occasionally tyrannical and more than frequently oppressive – for the English seldom did things by halves – it was none the less the central core of life for a great body of men and women who represented between them the major portion of the wealth, power and activity of the world. It gave them regularity of habit, a rule of sober conduct that made them invincible in their narrow achievement, and a certain intensity of purpose which lent dignity and even beauty to their otherwise monotonous and ugly lives. Over the frieze of one of the chief London banks were written the words, 'Lord direct our labours': the very railway terminuses provided Bibles chained to reading-desks for the waiting business man to consult.

One saw the full intensity of that spirit of worship on the sabbath. The English kept this day holy and unspotted from the world: that is to say, they did no work on it, avoided travel, attended church or chapel and stayed at home. Sunday observance was one of the salient peaks of the mid-Victorian scene. On that day over a busy nation there fell an awful calm. Any attempt to relieve it was met by the full terrors of the canalized English forces of moral righteousness. In 1856 an effort was made by certain scholarly aristocrats to open the National Gallery and the British Museum on Sunday. The storm this aroused in a House of Commons assailed by all the propagandist powers of Exeter Hall caused them quickly to withdraw. A proposal in the same year to provide Sunday bands in the dreary Manchester and Salford parks met with a like repulse.

At midnight on Saturday – a noisy drunken evening in any working-class district – all movement and sound suddenly ceased. As Big Ben's new clock chimed its last stroke a solemn hush announced that the sabbath had begun. Next morning the food shops opened for a few hours, but at eleven, the time for divine service, every shutter went up. For those with large houses and affectionate families, the quiet scene had a familiar and reassuring air: to those who lived in tiny tenement rooms and had no playground but the drab streets it was less pleasing.

*　　*　　*

The virtuous middle class had the franchise: the working-class majority had not. It was the middle class, therefore, that enforced the new urban English sabbath in conformity with its own frugal virtues. But there was one point on which the rough majority insisted: sabbath or no, it would drink when it pleased. Beer and gin, and plenty of them, were the unspoken price with which the busy Gradgrinds and Bounderbys reconciled the proletariat to the social chaos and vacuum of *laissez-faire*. When, in 1856, an evangelical peer brought in a Bill to close the pubs on the Lord's Day, the church parade of high society in Hyde Park was interrupted for three successive Sundays by an angry multitude who booed every rider and carriage on the first Sunday, pelted them with showers of turf and stones on the second, and on the third made the few daring survivors ride for their lives till the police, in long lines, raining blows on rioters and spectators alike, cleared the park. After that the Bill was withdrawn and the pious aristocrat left the country.

At midnight on Sunday the sabbath gloom lightened. The respectable classes, replete from their devotional exercises and anticipating an early start to the new week of labour and lawful gain, slept the sleep of the just. But the dancing saloons and the all-night haunts of vice in the metropolis turned on their lights and began to revel again openly.

This was of a piece with the national taste. England kept its more austere moments with great solemnity and decorum, but it liked to do itself well and knew how. The rich carried their love of good living from the country to the town and, with their new wealth, were the better able to gratify it. They loved to take the summer steamer to Blackwall or Greenwich and dine in Lovegrove's great room or at the Ship or Trafalgar off piled plates of whitebait, salmon and India pickle, spitchcocked eels and stewed carp, followed by roast duck and haunch of mutton, tarts and custard, iced punch, hock, champagne and port, while the river shimmered in the rays of the setting sun and the white sails passed against the twilight. Toasts, pipes and good stories rounded off the feast, with singing in the train all the way home, and a draught of soda and a purge of pills before negotiating the stairs to join one's sleeping partner.

They did themselves as well at home. The merchantry and the semi-commercial professional classes were making money hand over fist and they disposed of it, partly in ever-growing investments but partly in comfortable living. They spent little on splendour, art and travel: they left these to the aristocracy and gentry. They concentrated on dinner parties. In this there was much competitive expenditure. A man and his wife measured their status by the weight of their table silver – vast épergnes, massive salvers, tureens and candlesticks – the fineness of their table damask, cut glass and china, above all on the quantity of dishes served. Vast saddles of mutton and sirloins of beef, whole salmons and turbots, interminable courses of potages, fishes, removes, entremets and removes of the roast, were helped out by vegetables boiled in water, pastries and enormous Stilton and Cheshire cheeses. The wines followed each other in equal profusion until the table was cleared for further orgies of dessert, preserved fruits, nuts, port, madeira and sherry. All this suggested to a foreigner that the race would soon eat itself to a standstill. Taine reckoned that to the one and a half sheep consumed in a year by a Frenchman, an Englishman ate four. In England, an American noticed, even the sparrows seemed fat.

The circumference took its standards from the centre. The larger industrial towns were beginning to evolve a social life for the well-to-do modelled on that of the metropolis, with their own clubs, assembly and ball-rooms. In Liverpool, the most aristocratic city of the industrial North, the merchant princes wore white cravats and evening dress coats on Change, and in Manchester's Athenaeum and at its world-famous Hallé concerts, first established in 1857, well-to-do Quakers could be seen soberly conversing in broad-brimmed hats, neat grey or mulberry-coloured coats, frilled shirts and knee breeches. The urban sporting world, familiar to the twentieth century, was beginning to take shape: the I. Zingari was instituted in 1845 and a regular All England cricket eleven began to play a few years later, travelling the country in billycock and checked shirt and arousing widespread enthusiasm for the game, soon to bear fruit in the first county matches. Rugby football was also evolving from a local into a national sport, with its own customs and rules: the Blackheath Club was founded by a little group of old Rugbeians and Blackheath boys in 1858.

For though England was turning urban and the old field sports could no longer suffice, the strong national love of pleasure reasserted itself as soon as the first rush for wealth was over. A new form of recreation, tentatively essayed at Weymouth, Scarborough and Brighton in the days of George III, found especial favour with the well-to-do merchant and professional classes. The annual seaside holiday had the advantage of catering for the whole family, and its healthful properties gave a fillip to business. Many London families emigrated for the summer to Margate, the breadwinner coming down the river for the week-end on Saturday night on the 'husbands' boat'. The place was already an institution before the middle of the century, with its trim houses and spired church, its famous pier and fishermen, arbours and seats, its old ladies in deck-chairs and gentlemen in straw hats and its rows of horse-drawn bathing-boxes and bottle-nosed bathing women wading through the water in great bonnets.

Though newer resorts of quality like Folkestone and Hastings were winning favour, Brighton was still the first seaside town in England with many survivals of its Regency heyday, including 'old, wicked-looking gentlemen with thin faces, long noses and quaint hats who had drunk Regent punch with King George IV at the Pavilion.' These mingled, a little incongruously but in the English mode, with demure young ladies in curls and bonnets, armies of children in jackets and knickerbockers, and fanatic-looking preachers in tall hats and white ties who attempted to hold prayer meetings on the beach. The normal costume of the seaside holiday-maker was a loose-fitting check suit and a bowler. It was fun, after days in counting-house and office, to stroll along the windy pier (where the French were periodically expected to land) and watch the gulls and fishing-boats and the old salts in jerseys and straw hats, to dine off turtle and strawberry ices at Mutton's, to drive in an open fly from one cliff to the other, eyeing the 'gals' as they passed to and fro in their crinolines and parasols before the rows of dazzling white houses with green blinds and sun-blistered verandas, to hear the fisherwomen hawking their prawns with shrill 'Yeo Ho's!' and, in the cool of the evening, to listen to the negro melodists singing 'I would I were in Old Virginny' and the band playing the Overture to Zampa or the March from Athalie.

Unlike the older territorial aristrocracy to which in its power and wealth it was already beginning to give moral tone, the new industrial English middle class was still only half civilized, and its advance in manners, rapid as it was, could not keep pace with its fortunes. The moment it relaxed its puritanical decorum, the rude native Adam, so full of rustic nature and vitality, emerged. In its pleasures, urban England still smacked of the earth. When it went on the spree, it left its prudery at home. It sat top-hatted, eating devilled kidneys, drinking *aqua vitae* and joining in the roaring choruses of the smoky Cider Cellar in Maiden Lane: it kicked up its flounces and heels and stamped them on the ground in the rhythmic surge of the polka. All the vulgarity and vitality of the nation burst out in such annual institutions as the Christmas pantomime, when even the family split its sides in uninhibited and unashamed laughter at the gargantuan jests and antics of the Dame and goggled its eyes at the tight-laced, broad-bosomed, ample-flanked Principal Boy.

To see Victorian England really enjoying itself, no spectacle compared with the Derby. With the growth of London it had become the chief sporting event of the year. On the way to Epsom all the world mingled, fours-in-hand with rakish young gentlemen smoking cigars and wearing check trousers and muslin shades on their top-hats; ladies with parasols in open carriages; crowded family brakes; pearl-buttoned costers in donkey carts; cabs, barouches, droskies. Every one was laughing, chaffing and shouting, with only a single thought and destination. The windows and balconies of the mellow, shaded Georgian houses along the road to the Downs were alive with smiling faces, the walls crowned with cheering schoolboys and on every village green stood groups of pretty girls with new ribbons and finery fluttering under the tender, sun-kissed leaves of the chestnut trees. Every girl who acknowledged the waving hands and kisses blown to her was greeted with a cheer. Among the sweet-williams and Canterbury bells sat old gentlemen at their cottage doors smoking long pipes and giving as good as they took from the wags on the passing brakes. At each successive turnpike there was a jam, and here and at the roadside pubs the noise was like all England speaking at once.

On the course itself the colours of the rainbow, and many more crude, mingled. Round the carriages and coaches barefooted, hungry-looking beggars, gipsies and children swarmed seeking food. The world of fashion and the workaday City rubbed shoulders with comic negro singers, hucksters selling trinkets and red-haired Scottish lassies dancing to the sound of bagpipes. On vehicles overlooking the course sat jolly old boys from Change or counter in top-hats with side whiskers, high stocks and massive gold chains suspended across monumental waistcoats, drinking champagne out of long glasses and eating game pie, sandwiches and melon. Behind them were painted booths and bookies' stands, and all the fun of the great day – boxers and banjos, thimble rigs and knock-em-downs, shooting and archery galleries, skittle alleys and dirty, bright-coloured, bawling vendors of every kind.

Towards evening, when the races were over and swarms of carrier pigeons had borne their news of triumph or disaster into every corner of England, the carnival entered on its final stage. Bacchus and the old Saxon gods of horn and mead seemed to have descended on to the packed, twilit downs.

A drunken land at times the old fighting England of the urban 'fifties was: the right to empty his can of beer whenever he pleased was the first clause of Magna Carta which the Englishman took with him from the country to the town. In 1850 Manchester, with its 400,000 inhabitants, had 475 'publics' and 1,143 beer houses. Every night the eternal revelry would begin outside their flare-lit doors: the tip-tapping of the wooden clogs, and tangled hair and dirty, sodden faces swaying, swinging, and leaping to the music of fiddle or seraphine. In the casinos or music saloons, where a man might pay 2d. or 3d. for admission, eat apples and oranges and afterwards sup on tripe and trotters, drink and harmony went hand in hand, as, amid a strong flavour of gin, corduroy and tobacco smoke, the rough audience joined in the chorus of the latest music-hall ditty. On Saturday night, after the workman's weekly pay had been taken, it was a revolting sight for a sensitive man to witness the ghastly scenes at the tavern doors. Drunken women by the hundred lay about higgledy-piggledy in the mud, hollow-eyed and purple-cheeked, their ragged clothing plastered with muck. Occasionally one would stagger up to fight or to beat off some whimpering wife come with her bedraggled babes to seek a drunken husband before the coming week's housekeeping money was all spent.

For though the worst days of hunger, destitution and low wages were over and the industrious, frugal artisan, like the resourceful manufacturer, was enjoying better times, the more the nation became industrialized, the more squalid became the background of the bulk of its people. The greater towns – several of them now nearing the half-million mark – were still organized on the parish model which had sufficed when they were half rural: that is to say they were without efficient local government, sanitation or communal amenity. Even the capital, seat of Parliament and the centre of national culture and fashion, was by modern standards indescribably filthy. Here, as everywhere else, the rate of expansion had outgrown the civic institutions and organization of the past, and the result was pandemonium. London was increasing at the rate of 2,000 houses a year. Efforts of public-spirited individuals to cleanse it were always defeated by the flow of fresh immigrants from Ireland and the country. Even the new fashionable districts of Belgravia and Pimlico were unpaved and almost without illumination. Footmen carried lanterns at night in front of their masters, and the highway down the centre of Eaton Square was a sea of ruts with islands, brickbats and rubbish.

For the new London as it grew outwards rose on the muck of the old. Its medical officer of health, in a report issued in 1849, described the subsoil of the City as '17 million cubic feet of decaying residuum.' Belgrave Square and Hyde Park Gardens rested on sewers abounding in the foulest deposits which blocked the house drains and emitted disgusting smells, spreading purulent throats, typhus, febrile influenza, typhoid and cholera among the well-to-do and their servants. As late as the middle of the century a summer's evening walk by the waters of the Serpentine sometimes ended in fever and death brought on by the morbid stench of the stream-borne drainage of Paddington. Even the Queen's apartments at Buckingham Palace were ventilated through the common sewer.

If these were the sanitary conditions among which the prosperous lived, those of the workers can be imagined. Off Orchard Street, Portman Square, a single court 22 feet wide, with a common sewer down its middle, housed nearly a thousand human beings in 26 three-storied houses. And the passer-by, pursuing the course of Oxford Street towards Holborn, was favoured by the sight and whiff of a narrow, winding, evil-smelling lane lined with hovels, through the open doors of which could be seen earthen floors below the level of the streets swarming with pallid, verminous, crawling human animals.

In Wapping the courtyards were deep with filth, in which incredibly ragged and often naked children crawled seeking for vegetable parings and offal among the refuse. In Bethnal Green there were 80,000 inhabitants living under almost completely primitive conditions. Until the first parliamentary Sewer Commissioners in the middle 'fifties laid down over fifty miles of underground arterial drainage and pumped out millions of cubic feet of nauseating sludge, almost every street was barricaded against overflowing sewers. London that had become a city such as the world had never before seen was still governed like a village.

As for the state of the river into which all this unmastered nastiness drained, it beggared description. In a famous cartoon England's leading comic journal apostrophied Father Thames as a filthy old man dragging up dead rats from a liquid, gaseous mass of black mud and dying fish. The water supply of three million people was polluted. But with the establishment in 1855 of the Metropolitan Board of Works – forerunner of the London County Council – the evil began to abate through the work of its chief engineer, Joseph Bazalgette. His main drainage scheme was constructed between 1858 and 1875 – an unseen revolution which improved the lives of all Londoners. He constructed also the Victoria Embankment, another great civil engineering feat, under which ran one of the main sewers.

Inertia and a certain spirit of muddle continued to keep mid-Victorian London dirty and unhealthy. Until 1851 anyone could open a slaughtering yard, which allowed private citizens with the stomach for the task to make fortunes out of the suburban dust-heaps which poisoned the atmosphere for miles around. In Smithfield itself half a million beasts were slaughtered annually, and the heaping of carcasses resisted the assaults of the sanitary reformers for ten years. Until 1852 some families claimed the right to be buried within the City walls, so breeding disease and unhealth. It was a good England for the healthy and successful; a fearful one for the weak and inefficient. Yet, for all the gloomy horrors of its growing towns, the nation still had enough of vigorous country blood in its veins to make light of its cancers. It stood four-square to the world with a confident smile on its good-humoured, pugnacious face, ready to take on all-comers. Its wealth was growing day by day, its ships sailed triumphant and unhindered on every sea, the beauty, order and peace of its countryside were the wonder and admiration of every foreigner who visited it. The loveliness of that Miltonian landscape, the prosperity of its rose and ivy-covered cottages, the strength and assurance of its thriving farms and lordly parks and mansions blinded the indulgent eye to its darker corners. There was so much to love in England – those wonderful oaks and green lawns, the sleek, lowing cattle, the smoke curling up from cottage chimneys in a mysterious and blended sea of tender verdure, the strong, kindly men and women who were so at home among its familiar scenes. One just took this strong-founded, dynamic island of contradictions for granted and accepted it as a whole.

It was fitting that the chosen leader of such a land should be Lord Palmerston. With his jaunty mien, his sturdy common sense, his straw between his lips and his sobriquet of Cupid, the game old man was the idol of mid-Victorian England and the embodiment of everything for which it stood. From 1855 until his death at the age of 81 in 1865, he was continuously Prime Minister, with one short break in 1858–9 when the discredited protectionists under Lord Derby and Disraeli had a brief spell of minority office.

The last of the aristocratic Whigs of the tradition of the 'Glorious Revolution,' 'Pam' represented the Liberals in his contempt for obscurantist mysticism and the Tories in his hatred of doctrinaire reform. For ten years he kept a fast-changing Britain in a political backwater and ruled, not by the magnetism of ideals nor the machinery of party organization – for he had neither – but by sheer personal popularity. Nothing could shake his hold on the British people. They loved him for his brisk contempt for foreign ways and threats, for his English balance, for his unshakeable individualism, for his courage and assurance – 'an old admiral cut out of oak, the figure-head of a 74-gun ship in a Biscay squall.' They delighted in his sporting tastes, his little jokes – 'it is impossible to give the Shah the garter: he deserves the halter!' – even his little scrapes: a rumoured affair at the age of 78 with a clergyman's wife on the eve of an election brought from the lips of his opponent, Disraeli, who understood his countrymen, a hollow, 'For God's sake don't let the people of England know, or he'll sweep the country!' That familiar figure – the tilted white hat, tight-buttoned coat, cane, dyed whiskers – riding down Piccadilly before breakfast or rising to jest or bluff away an awkward situation in the House, gave the English confidence. It was just so that they liked to think of themselves, boldly confronting a world of which they had somehow become lords.

The spirit and health of this old man sprang from the same sources as the nation for which he stood. Palmerston directed the course of a commercial empire from his house in Piccadilly. But when he needed recreation he rode in white trousers across the green fields to the wooded Harrow Hill of his schooldays or went down for the vacation to his native Broadlands in Hampshire. So it was with England. Since the 'forties John Bull had donned the sober civic wear of the towns, abjured horse for train, and settled down to work at lathe or ledger among the chimney pots. But his strength still derived from the countryside of his fathers in which, for all his new absorption in money-making, his heart lay. 'Home, sweet home,' the Englishman's favourite song, pictured not a tenement building but a country cottage. London was only an encampment from which all who could afford it fled so soon as the Season and parliamentary session were over, when the blinds were drawn, the hotels left empty and the clubs asleep.

'In France,' a French traveller wrote, 'we live in the towns and go to the country. The Englishman resides in the country, where his real home is. There he keeps his treasures, and pride of race and station is given full play.' Here the rural gentry, still untouched by commerce and living on the cultivation of the classical and leisured past, had its strong roots, sending out its shoots into the professional and administrative life of the nation and empire. At the back of the educated Englishman's consciousness in the 'fifties lay always the thought of the country house and the green shires: of slow talk of acres and timber, of bullocks and crops, of sport by covert-side and river, of sitting in the saddle among the blackthorn bushes, of the smell of the gun-room, meadow hay and hot leather, of dining out at the full moon, of archery parties and croquet on smooth lawns, of familiar names and faces and childhood's remembered scenes repeated in the churchyard on Sunday mornings after service, when countrymen met their neighbours among the mounds beneath which their fathers slept.

Somewhere in the 'fifties the urban population of England began to exceed the rural. But agriculture remained the great central productive industry of the country, excelling in importance and influence even cotton. The competition of the new wheat-growing lands overseas had still to be developed: free trade spelt cheap and abundant raw materials for the manufacturer but not yet unlimited imports. Despite the ceaseless rise in population, not more than a quarter of the country's wheat was imported and very little of her oats and barley. The urban worker had more in his pocket, and he spent it on the products of the English farmer. During the Crimean War wheat prices rose, averaging 74s. 8d. in 1855 – a figure not to be equalled till 1917 – and fluctuating for many years around 50s., or 10s. a quarter more than they had been in

THE SEARCH FOR JUSTICE

1850. The nemesis of Free Trade was not yet. The middle of Victoria's reign constituted a golden age for British agriculture, when capital was cheap and plentiful, markets expanding and improvements profitable for landlord and tenant farmer. Employing more than a million skilled workers and supporting the richest aristocracy the world had seen, it gave bread to 17 millions and meat to the whole population.

The age of the small man was almost done. But there were still nearly 100,000 men farming holdings of less than fifty acres without hired labour. The agricultural worker was ill-paid and without a real stake in the country, but his wages, which averaged well under 10s. a week in the South in 1850, touched 11s. in the early 'sixties and 13s. in the next decade. He had his garden, a wife who could bake his bread, and many small perquisites – harvest money, beer or cider in the field, occasional firewood and gleanings. So long as he was healthy – and his life kept him so – he was happy. Old Jas Dagley of Gawcott, Bucks, who with his low forehead, eagle eyes, powerful nose and jaw, and stern trap mouth, looked like Gladstone, paid £2 a year rent for his cottage, never wanted for good wholesome food in all his long life of thrift and labour – 'plenty a vegetables the whool yeeur roun and a flitch a beacon . . . alwiz hangin' up in the kitchen, and plenty a rabbuts round the meddurs' – worked on his allotment every night when his day's work was done and boasted that he had never missed a feast in any one of the villages about, and that he had once carried a nine-gallon cask of ale in a sack on his broad shoulders for three miles.

Strength and endurance were still the virtues which England, rustic or urban, prized above all others. In April, 1860, on a lovely spring morning, Tom Sayers, the English champion, met Heenan, the American, known to the fancy as the Benicia Boy, on the edge of a wood near Farnborough to fight for the championship of the world. For weeks in every town and village in the land men and women had canvassed the chances of the event, and the police, fearing a fatal casualty in those days of timeless contests and bare fists, had forbidden the fight and kept close watch on the would-be combatants. But where there was a will there was a way; old England was not to be disappointed. On the night before the great day every tavern and public-house in London remained open all night until the word went round where the trains to the secret ringside were to start.

Sayers was thirty-four, stood five foot eight, and weighed ten stone twelve. His American challenger was eight years younger, stood five inches taller and weighed thirteen stone. In the opening rounds the

Englishman was knocked down repeatedly, only to rise smiling for more. The blood poured down his brown, tanned face which shone in the morning sun as though it had been carved of old oak. For two hours after his right arm was broken by a terrific blow of Heenan's he fought on, and, when the police broke through the exultant crowd into the ring, the English champion, giving as good as he took, was still undefeated.

CHAPTER EIGHT

Men of Property

'I wander thro' each charter'd street,
Near where the charter'd Thames does flow,
And mark in every face I meet
Marks of weakness, marks of woe.

In every cry of every Man,
In every Infant's cry of fear,
In every voice, in every ban,
The mind-forg'd manacles I hear'.
William Blake

TO A FOREIGNER visiting England for the first time in the 'sixties and 'seventies, there seemed something terrifying about its energy and power. 'Every quarter of an hour,' wrote Taine of the entry to the Thames, 'the imprint and the presence of man, the power by which he has transformed nature, become more visible; dock, magazines, shipbuilding and caulking yards, stocks, habitable houses, prepared materials, accumulated merchandise . . . From Greenwich the river is nothing but a street a mile broad and upwards, where ships ascend and descend between two rows of buildings, interminable rows of a dull red, in brick or tiles bordered with great piles stuck in the mud for mooring vessels, which come here to unload or to load. Ever new magazines for copper, stone, coal, cordage and the rest; bales are always being piled up, sacks being hoisted, barrels being rolled, cranes are creaking, capstans sounding . . . To the west rises an inextricable forest of yards, of masts, of rigging: these are the vessels which arrive, depart or anchor, in the first place in groups, then in long rows, then in a continuous heap, crowded together, massed against the chimneys of houses and the pulleys of warehouses, with all the tackle of incessant, regular, gigantic labour. A foggy smoke penetrated with light envelopes them; the sun there sifts its golden rain, and the brackish tawny, half-green, half violet water balances in its undulations striking and strange reflections . . .'

For over this vast city had fallen a perpetual pall. The classical pillars and ornaments of the churches and the larger buildings were half hidden under soot: the naked Achilles in the park, tribute to the Iron Duke, was almost black. Even the dripping trees and foliage were grimy. It was like Homer's Hell – the land of the Cimmerians. 'The vast space which in the south stretches between the earth and sky cannot be discovered; . . . there is no air, there is nothing but liquid fog.' Tall chimneys cast a shroud of smoke between earth and sky; the Thames ran no longer blue and sparkling but rayless under the grimy bridges. The summer's trip to Greenwich – joy of many generations of Londoners – was no longer a thing of delight; the trees on the Isle of Dogs had begun to give way to ugly factories and mean houses, and the yachts and pleasure boats to belching steamers and strings of coal barges. Even the time-honoured ministerial Whitebait Dinner was soon to be abandoned: men had less leisure than before for the graces and amenities of life.

The complete absorption of the English urban middle classes in the pursuit of wealth was both impressive and terrifying. The old talkative, hail-fellow-well-met London was yielding place to one more sombre and self-contained. Men went silent and absorbed about their business: 'faces do not laugh, lips are dumb; not a cry, not a voice is heard in the crowd; every individual seems alone; the workman does not sing; passengers travelling to and fro gaze about them without curiosity, without uttering a word.' They were on the make, each man pitting his strength and cunning against his neighbour and seeking not to make things for the joy of making or to win the applause of his fellows, but to amass sufficient wealth to keep himself and his family in time of need. Their perpetual nightmare was the fear of poverty. Unredeemed by the neighbouring field sports of the countryside and cut off by the factory smoke and the high walls of the houses from the cheerful sun, the life of the streets was not to be borne without wealth. Those who had won it by their sweat and struggle dreaded to lose it: 'to have £20,000 in the funds or cut one's throat' was their unspoken thought. Those without it were driven back, as the fields receded, into a life ever more drab and uninviting. Taine noticed how many working-class faces wore a starved, thwarted look; hollow, blanched and spent with fatigue. In their patient inertia they reminded him of the old 'screws' in the cabs standing in the rain.

In the world of the new city, property was the breath of life: without it men and women shrivelled and died. Save for murder, offences against property were more severely punished than those against the person. A barman and a glazier for stealing 5s. 4d. were sentenced to five years penal servitude: a hideous assault on a woman with child was expiated with six weeks' imprisonment. Against the supreme right of commerce – duty as it came to be regarded – nothing was held to weigh: social amenity, happiness, beauty. Whatever did not contribute to this one great commercial object was neglected. In the British Museum in grimy Bloomsbury the greatest masterpieces of human sculpture stood covered with dust on filthy floors in a neglected yellow hall that looked like a warehouse.

No one protested, for the English townsman had come to accept such a state of affairs as the natural order. On the railways, the second-class carriages were without upholstery; in the third the windows were unglazed and the floors never swept. Men had no rights but those they paid for after process of free bargaining with their fellows; not even, it seemed, the right of life for, though accidents were frequent, the railways directors kept the doors of the carriages locked while trains were in transit lest any passengers should escape without paying for their tickets.

Business was business: wherever English commerce reigned the phrase was sufficient to explain and justify almost every terrestrial happening. A man must abide by the law: he must keep his bond: he must deliver the goods he had promised or pay the forfeit. From that, there could be no challenge: Shylock was entitled to his pound of flesh. He had earned it by his industry, skill and integrity. In the innumerable little grimy brick houses between the Tower and St Paul's, whose modest brass plates bore names famous throughout the world, the sons of millionaires arrived each morning with the punctuality of their own clerks to transact business and later bought their mutton chops and threepenny loaves in a Cheapside tavern for their Spartan midday meal. Only when they went home in the evening to Portland Place or Grosvenor Square did they indulge the princely tastes to which their hard-earned wealth entitled them.

Such men were resolute in purpose: iron when anyone crossed their strong intent. Taine on his visit observed their kind closely:

'When at eight o'clock in the morning, at the terminus of a
railway, one sees people arriving from the country for their daily
avocations, or when one walks in a business street, one is struck
with the number of faces which exhibit this type of cold and
determined will. They walk straight with a geometrical movement, without looking on either hand; without distraction,
wholly given up to their business, like automatons, each moved
by a spring; the large, bony face, the pale complexion, often
sallow or leaden-hued, the rigid look, all even to the tall, perpen-
dicular, black hat, even to the strong and large foot-covering,
even to the umbrella, rolled in its case and carried in a particular
style, display the man insensitive, dead to ideas of pleasure and
elegance, solely preoccupied in getting through much business
well and rapidly. Sometimes one detects the physiognomy of
Pitt – the slight face, impassive and imperious, the pale and
ardent eyes, the look which shines like the fixed gleam of a
sword; the man is then of finer mould yet his will is only the
more incisive and the stouter; it is iron transformed into steel.'

Under the pressure of the claims of money-making, the character of
the English middle class was changing. It was growing sterner, narrower
in sympathy since too much sensibility weakened the will. The new
kind of public school which Arnold of Rugby had made the model for
England catered for those who needed hardening: the virtues it bred
were reticence, regularity and rectitude, above all self-reliance. An
English boy of the mid-Victorian age if he was short-sighted was not
expected to wear spectacles. If he was cold he was not expected to wear
a great coat. His heart and senses were put on ice: from the first day
he was chucked into the lonely maelstrom of a great boarding school
he was taught to keep a stiff upper lip. For the highly sensitive or
affectionate child this stern schooling was hell: in self-defence boys
learnt to keep their emotions to themselves, if possible to eliminate
them. In France, Taine reflected, happiness depended on affection; in
England on having none.

Boys brought up in this way were like young bulldogs in their
teens: tough and tenacious, sometimes ferocious, unconquerable. Being
discouraged from excessive feeling, the average product of the public
school could feel little sympathy for the classical authors whose works
he laboriously and mechanically translated and parsed: he preferred
organized games. From this time dates the start of the decline in
English upper-class culture and classical learning. Save at a few schools
like Eton and Winchester, where much of the older and freer tradition

lingered, the scholar of an earlier age was to become the despised public-school 'swot', the solid lad of brawn and muscle the hero. This made little difference to the object of the new public school, which was the training of character for a competitive world, and was as well effected by the harsh discipline of the dormitory and the football ground as by the Greek syntax.

At the universities the early discipline of the public school was relaxed. Here the freer and more liberal model of the past was retained: a gentleman was encouraged to choose his own life and tastes and to be a scholar if he chose. But the harm as well as the good of the public school system was already done. The average lad from Harrow or Rugby when he came up to Oxford or Cambridge was what his school had made him. If, as still frequently happened, he came from a cultivated home or had an exceptionally brilliant teacher, he might have wide sympathies and genuine love for learning. More normally he cared for nothing but sport, which he pursued in the academic groves with the same zest as on the Sixth Form Ground or Old Big Side. He had character, integrity, energy – the qualities needed for worldly success. But his emotional and intellectual development was stunted. For that reason he fell the more readily into the unthinking worship of material attainment which was the fault of his age. The poor prizeman of the schools might still be the talk of the Upper Common Room; on the long benches of Hall the man acclaimed was the 'Blue' and the 'blood' with money to burn.

The commercial type created by the conditions of the urban middle-class homes and academies that had not yet attained public school status – the nursery of Matthew Arnold's 'Philistines' – has been drawn by John Galsworthy in *The Forsyte Saga*. It valued strength, order, above all things property: it despised weakness, subtlety, width of sympathy. It was redeemed by its native boyishness and by a certain inherent kindliness. But to a foreigner its superficial appearance was not congenial: these English merchants with their stiff, big-boned frames and repressed, self-contained faces looked stupid, frigid and unfeeling, caring for nothing but money and the animal pleasures of the chase and table. There seemed to be too much roast-beef in them. Sometimes they were lean, gaunt and awkward; more often they ran to fullness of flesh, brick-red faces and apoplectic tempers; Taine met such a one in the train going to the Derby – 'large ruddy features with flabby and pendant cheeks, large red whiskers, blue eyes without expression, an enormous trunk, noisy respiration.'

For those with gentle blood, with family traditions and connections, and the status afforded by a university degree, there was employment in the civil and military services of the Crown, in the empire and the learned professions. For the great majority commerce was the one sure road to the desired goal of private wealth, security and comfort. With the rapidly expanding population and with improved transport – supported by British sea-power and arms – opening ever new markets in lands overseas, the opportunities for growing rich were enormous. Between 1850 and 1872 the annual exports of Britain, almost doubling themselves every ten years, increased from £90,000,000 to £315,000,000.

A walk through the central districts of London revealed that wealth. A circumference of nearly a mile round the country-like parks of the West End was being filled by large six or seven-storey houses, mostly built in the Italianate style, for the residence of the upper middle merchants and professional classes. 'Paris', Taine reported, 'is mediocre compared with these squares, these crescents, these circles and rows of monumental buildings of massive stone, with porticoes, with sculptured fronts, these spacious streets . . . Sixty of them as vast as the Rue de la Paix; assuredly Napoleon III demolished and rebuilt Paris only because he had lived in London.' Such great houses needed establishments of seven or eight servants apiece and could not be supported by incomes of less than £2,000 or £3,000 a year: yet scarcely any were empty. They were the homes of 'carriage-folk' – of families who kept private carriages, whose numbers by 1856 ran into five figures.

The great summer afternoon parade in Hyde Park between four and six revealed Victorian society in all its glory: the long unbroken stream of brilliant equipages and lovely horses between Cumberland and Albert gates, the fine ladies with their glaring coloured silks, crinolines and parasols gossiping and quizzing under the chestnuts, the Dundreary-whiskered gentlemen with their white top-hats and silver-topped malacca canes, who leant over the iron railings of Rotten Row to chat with elegant, long-skirted, veiled equestrians or lolled on the fashionable grass slope by Lancaster Gate. To a poor man who had ventured into the park at such an hour amid all this splendour, the spectacle might well have seemed to represent the wealth of the entire world assembled in the persons of a few thousand fabulously favoured creatures in this little space of English earth. Taine recorded that if one took a cab from Sydenham where the re-created Crystal Palace stood, one could travel for five continuous miles past houses representing an annual outlay of £1,500. In this feast of property the professional as well as the commercial classes had their share. While a professor at the Sorbonne had to content himself with the equivalent of £500 a year, the head of an Oxford or Cambridge College could look for several thousands. The headmasters of Eton and Harrow, the poet Tennyson and the novelist Thackeray all enjoyed incomes of £5,000 or more. And successful lawyers and doctors made far more, in days when income tax stood at 7d. in the pound. Yet even their comfortable emoluments paled into insignificance when set against the princely incomes of the great industrial, manufacturing and engineering masters of the north. The Fairbairns, Hawthornes, Kitsons, Platts, Stephensons, Whitworths constituted a new millionaire aristocracy of effort whose title deeds of wealth and power were their own revolving wheels of iron.

Of course there were critics of the materialistic smugness and moral and religious self-satisfaction of the new business and industrial classes who did not, or could not, link the loving obligations of their religion to the pain so obviously suffered by the children they employed. But increasingly there were employers, nonconformist as well as Anglican, who organized Sunday schools for their worker children and were fierce in enforcing their attendance.

Matthew Arnold was the most notable of the critics. In his *Culture and Anarchy* he defined the Philistines as 'the people who believe most that our greatness and welfare are proved by our being very rich, and who most give their lives and thoughts to becoming rich . . .'

This commercial aristocracy looked far beyond the boundaries of the little misty island which their works and warehouses enriched. There was scarcely any place on earth capable of trade where their representatives were not established. In distant Shanghai and Hong Kong one met the English merchant princes of the China trade, men of almost fabulous wealth made out of tea, silk and opium. Every year the tea-clippers – the fastest sailing ships ever made – took part in the famous race from Foochow to London river to win the £600 bonus for the first cargo of the season to reach the English market. John Masefield in his *Bird of Dawning* has drawn the picture of one coming up the Channel, her three months' voyage done, and of the rough, simple men who manned her. Galsworthy's Jolyon Forsyte, the elder, is the counterpart of Captain Trewsbury: the City merchant of taste and flawless integrity with his great house in South Kensington and his fastidious ways, whose palate for tea was a byword.

Since the repeal of the Navigation Act in 1849, the lovely ships which carried the tribute of the world to the cliffs of England sailed under many flags. Yet most of them, including the best, were owned and built by Britons, for free trade, if it took privileges from the merchant marine with one hand, gave with another, since it stimulated interchange of sea-borne merchandise. With the absorption of her chief shipping rival, the United States, in its long and exhausting Civil War during the early 'sixties, Britain had things very much her own way at sea for three halcyon decades. The new iron ships, triumphs of the marine engineering works of the Clyde and Tyne, of Birkenhead and Belfast, were beginning to come into their own: the *Great Eastern*, the famous iron leviathan, 700 feet in length and 80 in beam, was launched at Millwall in 1858. Yet two years later not more than a tenth of the merchant service of the United Kingdom was steam driven. In that year the country's sailing tonnage reached its zenith. These proud masterpieces of timber and canvas, cleaving the ocean 'with mainyards backed and bows of cream and foam', were the key to Britain's commercial and industrial supremacy. They were recognized as the élite of the sea in every port of the earth.

This art and skill and the wealth that sprang from it rested in the last resort on the British command of the seas. During the late 'fifties and early 'sixties fear of the French Empire under Louis Napoleon had recalled an island race immersed in moneymaking to the necessity of looking to its moat. After the Crimean War a period of naval reorganization began which, quickened by a panic over the new French strength in ironclads, culminated in the launching in 1860 of the 9,000-ton iron frigate, *Warrior*, the fastest and most powerful ship in the world. It was the first of a new fleet of iron-hulled, armoured, screw-driven ships armed with muzzle-loaders, the latest product of Armstrong's, and capable of blowing the old three-decker navies of the past out of the water. This mighty force – the strongest single unit of ordered power in the nineteenth-century world – was supported by a secondary fleet of unarmoured wooden frigates and corvettes and by naval bases in all the seven seas – a standing terror to the slaver and pirate.

Soon after her launch a young lieutenant joined HMS *Warrior* as a gunnery specialist. He remained only a short time, as he was marked out for higher things, but Jacky Fisher's professionalism, uncommon for the age, was to ensure, half a century later, that the Royal Navy could fight and win the first great naval war of steam and high explosive. He was the living link between *Warrior* and *Dreadnought*.

Out of all this power sprang great comfort for the English possessing classes. Peasants toiled in distant China and Ceylon to fill the teapots of rich old ladies in Lancaster Gate, naked Malay boys laboured to draw up pearls from the bottom of shark-infested seas, and trappers fought with bears in the frozen snows of Hudson Bay to send home furs and hearthrugs. As they grew rich the hardy English surrounded themselves with costly comforts, the elder generation of the Forsytes because they valued the outward forms of the wealth for which they had laboured so hard, the younger because they were growing accustomed to them. Soft-pile Brussels carpets, thick padded settees and ottomans, elaborately-carved tables of polished mahogany and rosewood with marble tops, enormous gilt mirrors flowed in a never-ceasing flood out of the factories and warehouses and fashionable furniture emporiums into the spacious houses of Kensington and Bayswater, Edgbaston, Stockport and Everton, until even their great rooms seemed crowded out with these heavy symbols of tribute. A cultured foreigner staying in an English house in 1861 was amazed by the furniture of his bedroom – the entire floor carpeted, a strip of oilcloth in front of the wash-stand, matting along the walls; two dressing-tables, a swing looking-glass, a great bed covered with the whitest and softest of tissues, three pairs of candles, two of them in a writing-table, porcelain extinguishers, wax matches, paper spills in pretty holders, pin-cushions. The most intimate piece of furniture in the room was a miracle of elaborate ingenuity, made of the finest mahogany and marble: the washstand was furnished with a large and smaller jug for hot and cold water, two porcelain basins, a dish for toothbrushes, two soap-dishes, a water-bottle with a tumbler and a finger glass with another. In addition there was a large shallow zinc bath, and a towel-horse in the cupboard with several towels of different sizes. A servant visited the room four times a day to see that all was in order.

When an Englishman of the upper-middle order travelled, the same observer noted, he carried so many glasses, opera-glasses and telescopes, waterproofs and wrappers, dressing-cases, flasks, books and newspapers that it seemed astonishing that he should ever have set out under such a burden at all. Every year the English with their all-conquering Midas touch sank deeper under the weight of their own possessions. From the Queen on her throne, who in the course of her reign accumulated a vast museum of objects, each acquiring with usage attributes of an almost sacred kind and possessing its own hallowed and unalterable place in one or other of her palaces, to the thrifty and well-to-do artisan who filled every inch of wall-space in his cottage with engravings, keepsakes, mementoes, grandfather clocks, samplers and photographs, and kept apart a special air-tight compartment named the parlour for the display of more treasured pieces of furniture and *vertu*, the nation seemed to have gone mad on property. As ever with the English and the object of their heart's desire, it became invested with a semi-religious and mystical quality. Since the pursuit or retention of wealth was for the time being the first end of their single-hearted lives, that which wealth bought was worthy of worship. The drawing-room furniture, the silver and best china in the safe, the contents of the maternal jewel case, were the sacred vessels on the altar, and a visit to the banker or solicitor was conducted with a solemnity like going to church.

From this arose tragic consequences. Poverty in other lands was regarded, as it had been in England in the past, as part of the eternal human lot: to be pitied, to be avoided if possible, to be relieved or ignored according to a man's nature or temperament, but not to be despised. It was a share of humanity's bitter heritage, like sickness, tempest and death. But in London and urban England in which the making of wealth had been elevated into a moral duty, poverty hung its head for shame. It crept out of sight into that new phenomenon of industrialization – the working-class district in which no man of wealth or position lived. The new East End of London, with its miles of mean, squalid streets covering an area greater in extent than any continental city, was something of a portent in the world. It was not for nothing that the scholar Marx was studying economic phenomena in the British capital.

Here lived the poor – not merely the respectable artisans but the countless broken outcasts of the industrial system. They were pallid and gin-sodden; their ragged reeking clothes, which had passed through many phases of society in their long, declining history, were so vile that they left a stain wherever they rested: they stank. They herded together in bug-ridden lodging houses and rotting tenements; they slept under railway arches and on iron seats on the new Victoria Embankment. They were the 'submerged tenth', the skeleton at the rich Victorian feast, the squalid writing on the whitened wall.

They were not merely congregated in the 'darkest London' of Charles Booth's survey in the 1840s: they were to be found in every place where the untrammelled march for wealth had broken down the old world of status and social morality. They were living testimonies of that against which Coleridge had warned his country – trespasses on 'its own inalienable and untransferable property, the health, strength, honesty and filial love of its children.' Across the lives of the rich and comfortable, of all who inherited or had acquired established property they passed like a remote shadow: to the remainder of their countrymen, especially in the lower middle class and the skilled and respectable artisan, they were a terrible menace whose horrid existence it was almost impossible to shake from the mind. Their pale, degraded, beseeching faces and dripping rags were a reminder of what unemployment, sickness or any lapse from the straight and narrow path of social integrity might bring: like wraiths they rose out of a precipice into which every man without property might at any moment of his life fall. More than any other cause, they account for the almost fanatic desire of the Victorian of all classes to acquire and retain property.

In 1849 a young evangelist called William Booth left his native Nottingham to follow his calling in London, and in 1865 he set up, at first in a tent, his Christian Mission in Whitechapel where he and his friends lived alongside the degraded poor of the East End. They talked and listened to them, face to face, so they could help them in practical ways and, above all, show them that other human beings cared for them.

Booth was a revivalist intent on his Christian vocation, with a limited and uncompromising religious view. But he and his band of helpers recognized the absolute need to relieve the physical destitution of the homeless, the starving and the criminal. For Booth there was no conflict of priorities between the material and the spiritual. In 1878 his Mission became known as the Salvation Army, and thus was born the uniformed organization which has since brought comfort and succour, food and shelter, to millions of unfortunates, of any or no denomination, throughout the world.

However, in 1868, three years after William Booth pitched his mission tent in Whitechapel, the House of Commons was to pass the Executions Within Goals Act which ended public executions in England. To Michael Barrett, the author of the Clerkenwell Explosion, fell the distinction of being the last person to be hanged in England in public. In 1849 Charles Dickens wrote to *The Times* after witnessing the hanging of Mr and Mrs Manning outside Horsemonger Lane gaol in Southwark.

'I do not believe that any community can prosper where such a scene of horror as was enacted this morning outside Horsemonger Lane gaol is permitted. The horrors of the gibbet and of the crime which brought the wretched murderers to it faded in my mind before the atrocious bearing, looks and language of the assembled spectators.'

But nineteen years, which included the period of the Great Exhibition, were to elapse before the equally dreadful scenes outside Newgate in 1868 marked the end of a custom which was wrongly imagined for centuries to have strong deterrent value.

Despite Peel's improvements of the criminal law in 1827 it remained harsh. Transportation was still a punishment and was not abolished fully until 1864, mainly because the Australian territories no longer wanted the convicts to be sent to them. As early as 1813 the Quaker Elizabeth Fry had visited Newgate and then told the world of the horrors of, in particular, 300 women, with their children, convicted or not yet tried, all mixed together in two wards and two cells. Mrs Fry's efforts bore results but they were slow in coming. Nevertheless, her work and that of others testified to the power of the will and moral and physical courage of spirited individual reformers who, comfortably off themselves, could so easily not have bothered to dedicate their lives to the lot of the outcast, the inadequate and the helpless.

For most of the great industrial and commercial individualists who had made nineteenth-century Britain rich beyond the dreams of avarice had forgotten that man was part of an undying order. The price of a social crime – greed, slavery, the oppression of a subject people – is seldom paid by those immediately guilty of it. It is paid later – by their innocent descendants. The sins of the fathers are visited on the children and the children's children.

> 'Thro' midnight streets I hear
> How the youthful harlot's curse
> Blasts the new-born infant's tear,
> And blights with plagues the marriage hearse.'

Victorian Britain, for all her wealth, power and empire, was no exception. Her rulers, in their devotion to their creed of self-help and holding that through liberty good would grow naturally out of evil, allowed social injustice to be done on a vast and terrible scale. The progeny of those to whom that injustice was done were to become in the fullness of time sources of national weakness and division.

CHAPTER NINE

A Leap In The Dark

'Those who take "leaps in the dark", as we
are doing, may find themselves in unexpected
places before they recover the beaten tracks
again'   *James Anthony Froude*, Oceana, 15

'The life of a constitution is in the spirit
and disposition of those who work it'
                                    Walter Bagehot

'THE DEATH OF His Royal Highness Prince Albert, on Saturday last,'
said the *Illustrated London News* in December 1861, 'is the heaviest
national calamity which has befallen this country for many years. Our
gracious Queen! The hearts of her people bleed with hers. They share
her agony of grief. They are overwhelmed with the same sense of
desolation. Every family in the land is smitten with the awe and the
sorrow which Death excites when he breaks into the domestic circle
and snatches from it its chief pride and joy. For the moment there is
no consolation. Even faith is stunned . . .'

Although a foreigner, the Prince Consort was, thanks to his generally benevolent disposition and to his enthusiasm for the Great Exhibition of 1851, one of the most popular, if not fully understood,
members of the Royal family. Since the long insanity of George III,
the English monarchy had been in jeopardy. The dignity and good
sense of Queen Victoria had done something to redeem it from the
odium into which it had fallen through the scandalous lives of her royal
uncles. But in the 1860s it was far from being a popular institution.
The gloomy, interminable and teutonically exaggerated retirement into
which the royal widow fell after the Prince's death caused widespread
criticism. The tone of radical youth increasingly tended towards a
republic. To many thoughtful minds it appeared improbable that the
young Prince of Wales, who in his pleasures seemed to be reverting to

the less decorous traditions of his Hanoverian forebears, would ever succeed to the throne. The spirit of a progressive age demanded a republic.

But to Disraeli and those such as the great constitutionalist Walter Bagehot who thought like him, the hereditary throne, more than any other institution, represented the continuing community as opposed to the government of the hour. For it embodied his conception of perpetual trusteeship. His wise and delicate conduct towards his sovereign whom he encouraged to resume her traditional functions in the pageantry of state was part of his creed. It was not the least of his services to posterity that he laboured to revive popular sympathy and affection for the throne, and with the aid of his royal mistress to re-establish it on the firm foundation on which it had been the pride of the great Tudor monarchs to rest it – the hearts of the people.

Ten years after Albert's death, the narrow escape from a near-fatal illness of his son, the future Edward VII, marked the beginning of a change in the public enthusiasm for royalty. After his recovery his mother published a personal letter of thanks to her subjects and there was a service of thanksgiving in St Paul's Cathedral. In the next thirty years she was to become Empress of India and to enjoy Golden and Diamond Jubilees, each of which increased her own popularity.

Victoria's life combined in an extraordinary fashion the greatness of a queen with the ordinariness of a wife and a widow – even if an ordinary widow would not have been able to obtain such seclusion for so long. As husband and wife, Victoria and Albert enjoyed in their relatively short life together a truly domestic and genuinely happy marriage which, with stricter standards of conduct at court, helped to set a better example for all classes of her people. Had Albert not succumbed so early to the typhoid fever which took the lives of so many of his wife's subjects, the age might have been tempered even more by his political and social sensitivity.

*　　*　　*

In 1864 while the Commons were perfunctorily debating a private member's motion for reform of the franchise – a question which in the view of most people had been dead since 1832 – Mr Gladstone, then Chancellor of the Exchequer, electrified the House by declaring that every man who was not incapacitated by some consideration of personal unfitness or of political danger was morally entitled to come within the pale of the constitution. The declaration marked the beginning of a new phase in English history. Electoral power which thirty-two years before had passed from the aristocracy to the middle-class was now to shift by ordered stages to the masses. The workers by virtue of their numerical superiority were to become the dominating class of the future.

Hitherto no one but a few fanatic reformers had regarded such a development as within the sphere of practical politics. Pure democracy was an ultimate goal: an equal vote for every citizen a pious aspiration, widely honoured like the Beatitudes and acceded to by none. The rough type produced by the factory and the housing conditions of the factory town was not one to which the wealth, safety and honour of a rich and ancient kingdom could be entrusted, even by the most sanguine. Where in other European countries, like republican France, democracy had been tried, the result had been an orgy of blood, plunder and anarchy followed by a military despotism. A practical people like the British felt little drawn to such visionary courses.

Even in America where the experiment of eighty years back had so far escaped shipwreck – presumably through the smallness of the population and the immensity of the territory – pure democracy had seemed in the early 'sixties to be culminating in disaster. The educated classes in Britain believed that the war waged by the vulgar Yankees and their backwoodsman President against the aristocratic Southern cotton-planters and slave-owners, could only end in one way. Even the liberal-minded *Punch*, until the final magnanimous apology over the great democrat's murdered corpse, persistently depicted Lincoln as a crude demagogue, half clown and half dictator. His defeat by an army of gentlemen had been thought inevitable.

The triumph of the North, after three years of disaster, surprised the English ruling classes. It did not surprise the British factory hands who grasped from the first the real significance of the 'Slaveowners' War'. Their strong sympathy for Lincoln's cause helped to prevent the recognition of the South by the Government of Palmerston and Gladstone. During the cotton famine caused by the Confederate blockade in 1862-3, the patient fortitude of the cotton operatives impressed and shamed their betters. Gladstone's pronouncement that such men were entitled to a place in the constitution awoke an answering chord in thousands.

The movement towards electoral reform, stagnant since the collapse of the People's Charter in the 'forties, now took on a new complexion.

It coincided with the end of the Palmerstonian era and the succession of Gladstone to the Liberal leadership in the Commons. In 1866 a Liberal Government introduced a bill reducing the occupation franchise in the counties from £50 to £14 and in the boroughs from £10 to £7. By this it was hoped to add another 400,000 voters to the electorate.

The Bill's promoters regarded it as a logical step in the utilitarian process of advancing the happiness of the greatest number through the exercise of intelligent self-interest. It was assumed that the better class of working man was a rational being. In making him master of his destiny and the nation's, he could be trusted like his bourgeois betters to follow the law of his own advantage and so automatically serve the common weal.

But, though the Liberals were in a majority, their Whig supporters, led by Robert Lowe, regarded the measure as an uncalled for step towards the destruction of property and freedom. 'With our own rash and inconsiderate hands,' he declared, 'we are about to pluck down on our heads the venerable temple of our liberty and our glory.' Entering the lobbies with the reactionary Tories, the 'Adullamites,' as the old reformer Bright called them, defeated the Bill in committee. The Government resigned, and in 1866 the Conservatives, still in a minority, took office.

But Disraeli, their leader in the Commons, having nursed his Party for twenty years in the wilderness without enjoying a majority, had no intention of committing it in its hour of recovery to the same policy of obstinate resistance to the popular tide which had ruined it in 1830. The debates had re-awakened the country to an interest in reform. There were demonstrations in its favour in Hyde Park that July when, the gates being locked by the police, the mob tore up the railings of Park Lane. The Government opened the session of 1867 by introducing a reform measure of its own. *Punch* depicted the Prime Minister, Lord Derby, in bonnet and petticoats making off with the infant bill while its mother, Lord Russell, surveying the empty pram, cried out, 'Hi! help! ple-ae-ce-! She's a takin' away me cheild'.

The new Bill went farther than that of the Liberals. In the counties the basis proposed was household suffrage qualified by personal rating and two years' residence. In adopting what seemed to many a Liberal policy Disraeli was honouring an ideal which he had proclaimed at the outset of his career. For it had always been his contention that the first Reform Bill had impaired the English principle of representation. He had objected to it not, as many Tories had done, because it increased the electorate, but because it made the representation of opinion less effective. The object of a parliamentary system, he held, was not to count votes – a mere means to an end – but to weigh opinion. And if a nation was to pursue a responsible policy, it must be responsible opinion.

It was an English principle that the vote, like the exercise of any other form of authority, should be entrusted only to those fitted for responsibility. The Whigs, in their remedy for the electoral anomalies of five centuries, had forgotten English history. It was right that the manufacturers and shopkeepers of the new industrial towns, wrongly excluded from the pre-1832 constitution, should have been enfranchised. But, in Disraeli's view, it had been wrong to allow a single class, hitherto without political experience, to outvote every other national interest merely because of its numerical superiority.

Disraeli had therefore always contended that the defence of the settlement of 1832 was no concern of a Party which claimed to represent national, as opposed to sectional, interests. During a brief spell of minority office in 1859, he had proposed an extension of the franchise to important interests overlooked by the Whig reformers, and had advocated an additional vote for university graduates, ministers of religion, lawyers, doctors, certificated schoolmasters, Civil Service pensioners, fundholders and Post Office Savings Bank depositors. Opinions were not merely to be counted but weighed. The House of Commons, reverting to its older tradition, was to become a 'mirror of the mind as well as the material interests of England'.

This conception, which had received little support at the time either from Disraeli's own party or his opponents, was now revived in the proposals which he placed before Parliament. In addition to bringing the responsible artisan within the constitution by widening the borough qualification, he offered a dual vote to every direct taxpayer and extended the franchise to all with a certain standard of education or £50 in the Funds or Savings Bank.

In all this Disraeli challenged the whole utilitarian thesis of his age. If, as Bentham argued, the happiness of the greatest number was to be secured by giving every man the maximum power to pursue his own selfish good, the more electors admitted to the constitution the better. The Liberals accepted this in theory, but qualified it in practice by denying the vote to the majority. For their rough habits and lack of even the most rudimentary education unfitted the workers in middle-class eyes for the suffrage. An electorate of respectable shopkeepers and city merchants was poised uneasily on the horns of a dilemma. It had either to refuse to honour its Benthamite ideals or subject its security and property to the vote of a rude multitude of unlettered toughs – of garrotters, wife-beaters, drunkards, foot-pads, and ragged, lousy beggars.

Disraeli shared neither the practical fears nor the idealist hopes of the bourgeois. He had no illusions about the consequences of further extension of the franchise on a numerical basis. He was not less willing to trust his countrymen – he was more so – but he knew that in any State which based power purely on numbers the result must be 'the tyranny of one class and that one the least enlightened'. For against an unchanging popular majority, the individual has no appeal. However mildly exercised, such uniform despotism was bound to destroy diversity and wealth of type and character.

'I have no apprehension myself that, if you had manhood suffrage tomorrow, the honest, brave and good-natured people of England would resort to pillage, incendiarism, and massacre. Who expects that? But though I would do as much justice to the qualities of our countrymen as any gentleman in this House, though I may not indulge in high-flown and far-fetched expressions with respect to them like those we have listened to – for the people may have their parasites as well as monarchs and aristocrats – yet I have no doubt that, whatever may be their high qualities, our countrymen are subject to the same political laws that affect the condition of all other communities and nations. If you establish a democracy, you must in due season reap the fruits of a democracy. You will in due season have great impatience of the public burdens combined in due season with great increase of the public expenditure. You will . . . reap the fruits of such united influence. You will . . . have wars entered into from passion, and not from reason; and you will in due season submit to peace ignominiously sought and ignominiously obtained, which will diminish your authority and perhaps endanger your independence. You will, . . . with a democracy, find that your property is less valuable and that your freedom is less complete. I doubt not, when there has been realized a sufficient quantity of disaffection and dismay, the good sense of this country will come to the rally, and that you will obtain some remedy for your grievances, and some redress for wrongs, by the process through which alone it can be obtained – by that process which may render your property more secure, but which will not render your liberty more eminent . . .'

*　　*　　*

In the Reform Bill of 1867 Disraeli, with a minority Government, added a million voters to the electoral roll, roughly doubling it. By proposing a dual vote for education and property he had sought to make the franchise a reward rather than an undiscriminating right, 'to be gained by virtue, by intelligence, by industry, by integrity' and exercised for the common good. He wanted to see the working man a partner in the constitution rather than its arbiter. But his party held office on sufferance, and his device for restoring an older and more English basis of representation than a purely numerical one was sabotaged in committee. The Bill created a democracy of heads of houses, of men with some stake, however small, in the country, but its weakness in its author's eyes was that it gave too much ultimate power to mere numbers. It was in the Prime Minister, Lord Derby's, phrase a 'leap in the dark'. And the direction it took suggested further leaps into deeper darkness before long.

The first general election fought on the new register gave the Liberal party a six years' lease of power. But, as Disraeli had prophesied, the interests of artisans and middle-class utilitarians were not necessarily the same. The latter wanted to restrict the functions of Government and leave the ring clear for the individual with talent and industry. The workers on the other hand needed protection against the economic excesses of the individual. As soon as they realized the power which the vote had given them, they began to demand it. They leant not towards the classic liberalism of *laissez-faire* but towards that social reform which Disraeli had preached since his Young England days and which Shaftesbury and the factory reformers had fought for against the utilitarians. Gladstone's programme of civic emancipation, Irish Church disestablishment and administrative reform there made little appeal to them. After a few years of Liberal rule the country became surfeited with change. The sun of 'the People's William' waned: that of 'Dizzy', the inspired pragmatist who had 'climbed to the top of the greasy pole,' rose. In 1874 for the first time in 33 years the Conservatives obtained a parliamentary majority.

The date marked the dividing line between the utilitarian legislation of the middle half of the century and the collectivist or socialist legislation which thereafter increasingly took its place. Since the collapse of the Chartists the working-class movement had been silently gathering momentum. In every town where skilled workers were assembled, trade unions had made their appearance. The quiet years in the 'fifties and 'sixties of widening trade and employment helped their growth, giving them cohesion, tradition and financial reserves. Local consolidation was usually followed by amalgamation on a national scale. The first great national union, the Amalgamated Society of Engineers, was founded in 1851 with the fusion of over a hundred local trade societies. In the next fifteen years its membership of 12,000 more than doubled. With its many imitators it fought against piece-work, overtime, victimization and the employment of unapprenticed men, survived early attempts of impatient employers to destroy it by lock-outs and taught a hostile bourgeois world to tolerate and fear, if not to respect, it.

To the middle-class citizen in his top-hat and castellated home, the trade union was something of a bogey – a secret and treasonable society threatening mob violence and plotting confiscation and revolution. In popular repute its path was attended by a succession of outrages: explosions, stones and broken glass, striking mobs intimidating honest Britons out of their property and right to work as they pleased. None felt this more strongly than the progressive radicals of the North. 'Depend upon it,' wrote Cobden, 'nothing can be got by fraternizing with trade unions. They are founded upon principles of brutal tyranny and monopoly. I would rather live under a Bey of Algiers than a trades committee.'

The law, reflecting middle-class opinion, treated the Unions with suspicion. Judges, who still regarded them as combinations in restraint of trade, refused to protect their funds from the defalcations of dishonest officials. A trade union was an association to coerce individuals and limit their profits. It was therefore viewed by a generation educated in *laissez-faire* principles as injurious. It was only tolerated because it was impossible to prevent it.

Though those brought up in the principles of Bentham tried not to see it, everything that was happening in the crowded urban world which individual enterprise had created was minimizing the importance of the individual and raising the power of the herd. The sturdy pupil of self-help, who by his devotion to his individual interests had created a thriving industrial unit employing 5,000 workers where only fifty had worked before, had unconsciously called into being a community whose common hopes and interests must presently clash with his own. For though the more he prospered the more they multiplied, the more they did so the more certain became their ultimate triumph over himself. So soon as they realized that their opportunity of happiness lay not in their action as individuals, in which being poor and ill-educated they were powerless, but in their collective strength, their final victory was certain.

In his great work, *Capital*, first obscurely published in 1867 'amid carbuncles and the constant dunning of creditors', Karl Marx demonstrated the course events were taking. He saw that with its ever-increasing scale of operations capitalism was digging its grave. The evolution of a society which put its faith in figures was predestined. 'While there is thus a progressive diminution in the number of capitalist magnates . . . there occurs a corresponding increase in the mass of poverty, oppression, enslavement, degeneration and exploitation; but at the same time there is a steady intensification of the wrath of the working class – a class which grows ever more numerous and is disciplined, unified and organized by the very mechanism of the capitalist method of production. Capitalist monopoly becomes a fetter upon the method of production which has flourished with it and under it. The centralization of the means of production and the socialization of labour reach a point where they prove incompatible with their capitalist husk. This bursts asunder. The knell of capitalist private property sounds. The expropriators are expropriated.'

To Marx's logical, academic but violence-loving mind the inevitable end was revolution. Divorced by his circumstances and temperament from the contacts of normal life and society, this morose prophet never grasped the nature of the people whose commercial institutions he studied with such brilliant and prophetic insight. He failed to see that in an ancient country like England, with its strong social character and representative institutions, revolution would be deflected into smoother channels.

The change that Marx predicted happened. But it took place in so unexpected a way that nobody, not even Marx, realized that it was happening at all. The utilitarians' thesis, which supported *laissez-faire*, involved the extension of the vote to the poor man. He used it to obtain legislation to offset his disability in contractual power. In England the passage of the second Reform Bill, and not the shouting proletarian crowds and the blood-bath of the exploiters, marked the end of unlimited freedom of contract and therefore of *laissez-faire*.

The new direction was first set by Disraeli's Government in the later 'seventies. In the course of five years this administration of rich hereditary peers and landowners passed legislation which, though little noticed at the time, struck at the roots of the Benthamite thesis that the individual should be left free to enrich himself as he chose. Factory acts were extended and consolidated and the hours limited by an Act of 1874 to 56 hours a week, 10 on five weekdays and 6 on Saturdays and conditions of labour codified. The process of private enclosure was reversed – though too late to save more than a fragment of what once had been public property – and the conversion of common land forbidden unless it conferred a public as well as a private benefit. By the Public Health Act of 1876 the interests of the individual were first subordinated to the requirements of public sanitation. Defending a policy of 'sanitas sanitatum, omnia sanitas,' Disraeli replied to those who complained that he was reducing statecraft to an affair of sewerage that 'to one of the labouring multitude of England, who had found fever always to be one of the inmates of his household, who had, year after year, seen stricken down the children of his loins on whose sympathy and support he had looked with hope and confidence,' it was 'not a policy of sewerage but a question of life and death.'

The same Government introduced an Artisans' Dwelling Bill, empowering local authorities to demolish insanitary dwellings and replace them by houses built expressly for working men. The measure was not compulsory but only permissive. It was no more than a tentative beginning: a mere drop in the still rising ocean of slum. Yet its ultimate effect was revolutionary. For it revived, in however dim a form, the ancient ideal of the Crown as the guardian of the people's homes.

Behind all this legislation lay the silent voting power of the workers. In 1874 there were returned to the House of Commons two men who were to be the pioneers of a mighty army. Even at the time Alexander Macdonald and Thomas Burt, the first two working-class MPs, were something of a portent among the landed squires and thriving manufacturers at Westminster. Burt was Secretary of the Northumberland Miners' Association, which, by helping to establish that the occupants of colliery houses, though not paying rates direct, were entitled to voting rights like the compound householders in the towns, had secured a majority of pitmen in the constituency of Morpeth. These representatives of the sons of toil tended at first to vote with Disraeli's 'gentlemen of England' rather than with his opponents. Macdonald told his constituents in 1879 that the Conservative Party had 'done more for the working classes in five years than the Liberals in fifty.'

For the old man, now nearing his end, for all his absorption in duchesses and oriental splendour saw in the working man, with his native prejudices and conservative instincts, an ally against the levelling utilitarian forces he had fought all his life. By redressing injustices he sought to end the fatal gulf between the 'two Englands' which he had perceived in his youth and still – though it was almost thirty years too late – hoped to bridge. His administration's labour laws were an attempt to do so. The Common Law, dating from an age when status was fixed and the workman given security of tenure by the State, treated breach of contract by an employer as a civil offence and that of his workman as criminal. The application of *laissez-faire* to commercial relationships had long made this distinction grossly unjust. By an act of 1875 Disraeli ended it by placing the workman on the same legal footing as his employer. In the same year he righted a still greater grievance of industrial labour against the law. Though the ancient doctrine of 'conspiracy' had been modified by an Act of 1825, the Courts still refused to accord trade unions full legal status. Their funds were unprotected against breaches of trust by their own employees and their officers criminally liable for certain actions carried out in the course of their duties. By a new Act of 1875 trade unions were given the protection of the law. The mere fact of association to defeat an employer was freed from criminal taint. It could only be indicted as a conspiracy when it constituted what done by a single person would have been a crime.

By this change in the law 'peaceful' picketing became permissible if unaccompanied by violence or threat of violence – though, as the upshot proved, it still remained open to judges to take such a view of 'intimidation' as to constitute all picketing 'unpeaceful.' Not until the Trades Disputes Act of 1906, passed by a Liberal Government which had repudiated *laissez-faire* for full-blooded collectivism to win working-class support, did the trade unions establish the privileged position they sought. To a believer in great national institutions, preserving by their trusteeship undying liberties and rights, it was a position to which a trade union was entitled. To a middle-class lawyer, nursed in the tenets of Benthamism, it was not. For several decades after the second Reform Bill the struggle continued between *laissez-faire* and the new socialism of the great towns *laissez-faire* had created.

It was often for the early leaders of labour a cruelly hard one. They had to do their public work in their spare time and finance it out of their wages. The pioneers of the Dockers' union met 'like conspirators hatching a second Guy Fawkes plot in a gloomy cellar with only the flickering half-lights given by tallow candles thrust into the necks of pop bottles.' In the 'eighties the members of even the executive council of so famous a union as the Amalgamated Society of Engineers – at least two of whom in after years became cabinet ministers – used to receive one shilling and sixpence a night for their direction of the leading union of the time and think themselves lucky to get it. Trades union leadership in those days was less a career than a vocation. It was sometimes a martyrdom.

For this reason, and because of the wrongs from which their class had suffered and was still suffering, these pioneers of a still inconceivable future were often politically embittered. The good-humoured rank and file in pub and music hall, on the beach at Blackpool or the racecourse at Aintree, troubled their heads little about past history or future proletarian aspirations. But their leaders and the earnest young men studying under immense difficulties in public libraries and mechanics' institutes who were to be their leaders in the next generation, were painfully aware of the fact that they and their class had not had a square deal. The Working Men's College in London was founded by the Rev Frederick Denison Maurice in 1854, with a voluntary staff of middle-class 'Christian Socialist' sympathizers who included Ruskin, Tom Hughes – author of *Tom Brown's School Days* – Lowes Dickinson, Ford Madox Brown, Dante Gabriel Rossetti and Edward Burne Jones.

Yet, with the vote in the workmen's wallet, time was on their side. They felt that they had only to open the eyes of the wage slaves, teach them to combine and use their latent strength with discipline and loyalty to obtain their share of the kingdom. The prejudices against them – the malice and victimization of employers, the biased use of the civil arm and even the military in time of strikes, the snobbery and class treachery of the workers themselves – were not so strong as the social impulse of the exploited to combine or perish. Whenever times were hard the men the unions battled for, who were oblivious of their efforts when employment was regular and beer and bread plentiful, were reminded of how much still remained to be won before there could be any security for themselves and their dear ones. Without the trade union there could be only loss of hearth and home and starvation for the workman who lost his job, and worse for the family of the man crippled or killed by accident in the course of his employment. 'Life was cheap in those days. It was by no means an uncommon thing to see the maimed and sometimes the dead being brought up from the dock bottom,' wrote G. N. Barnes '. . . I remember two cases in our gang. George Washington, a smith's striker, fell into the dry dock one foggy night on his way home and was found at the bottom half dead in the morning. Jim Platt, a machinist, had his back nearly broken by the fall of a loose plank from the workshop roof. The result was the same in both cases – patched up in the hospital and then death after a year or two of lingering pain at work. But compensation was never thought of.'

Neither the error and human frailty of leaders nor the folly and shortsightedness of the rank and file could halt the steady march of organized labour. In 1880 the Trade Union Congress represented only 600,000 members: by 1892 the figure had doubled. It was not only for advances in wages that the older unions fought, but for recognition as the sole representatives of the workers in all negotiations with employers. They demanded a share in the direction of their labour. To the fury of the old-fashioned capitalist, to whom freedom of contract meant freedom of choice for the master and obedience for the man, the new trade unionism sought to abolish overtime and regulate piece-work. It went further. It used the worker's vote to appeal over the head of the employer to a Parliament now dependent on that vote, for legislation to enforce its demands. At its annual Congresses, begun in 1866, the TUC instructed its members to press parliamentary candidates for such reforms as an eight-hour day, compulsory compensation for injured workers, the limitation of shop hours, new factory regulations, further amendment of the law of conspiracy and the abolition of child labour. It also demanded free elementary education, land for allotments in country districts and the appointment of working men to the Bench.

Organized labour in these years sought more than the protection of the skilled worker. As Cobden had prophesied in the hungry 'forties, the triumph of *laissez-faire* had brought enhanced prosperity to many workers. The skilled artisan had taken his share, however small, in the increased prosperity of his country. He had enjoyed good wages, untaxed and plentiful food, long continued employment, cheap transport and amenities – municipal parks, libraries, galleries and concerts – such as his father in a grimmer age had never known. In many cases he had been able to put away money, insure against old age and sickness, even to buy his own home. The utilitarian State had given him opportunity and he had taken it.

But the skilled artisan in employment was only a part of labour. For if *laissez-faire* postulated the successful workman growing rich like his master through his own thrift and industry, it also necessitated a residue of unskilled labour to meet the fluctuating demands of a competitive world. This the capitalist used in good time and discarded in bad. Such a system multiplied the wastrel, the diseased and the ne'er-do-well. It multiplied their inefficient and unhappy posterity. The statistics of the economist showed the profits of unrestricted competition. The slums of the industrial cities revealed its wastage.

It was no part of *laissez-faire* that the successful should burden themselves by helping the failures. The only economic place for the weak was the rubbish heap. It was at this point that *laissez-faire* always clashed with the English temperament. The middle-class employer in the rarefied privacy of his sanctum might – in the interests of a higher wisdom – suppress his inherited feelings of charity and kindness. But the working man, who had never heard of *laissez-faire*, could not. He never even tried. For he was nothing if not sentimental, and under his corduroys beat a heart full of English instincts and prejudices. One of them was an incorrigible desire to help the underdog.

It was from such a motive, unreasoning and unscientific, that English socialism sprang. Abroad socialism followed more logical channels: the brand that Karl Marx was preaching to his fellow Germans and to embittered and excitable French and Russian comrades was of a severely practical kind. There was nothing that Marx despised so much as an underdog. He merely wished to use him and his misery to destroy the capitalist system. But it was precisely because they wished to help the underdog that the English socialists were socialists at all. Men like William Morris and Arnold Toynbee devoted their lives to the working-class movement because their sense of justice and kindliness was affronted by the sickening misery and cruelty of a great reserve of unskilled labour such as that in the East End of London. They did not wish merely to use the underdog but to tend and cherish him, just as they wished not to exterminate the bourgeois but to convert him. The university settlement, then first taking shape, was a characteristic product of both these wishes. And in their dreams for the future the early English socialists sought a gentle Christian paradise after their own kindly middle-class hearts. Morris's *News from Nowhere* published in 1890 is as far removed from Marx's *Capital* as the Gospel of St John from the Book of Judges. 'I know,' said its author of a working-men's procession, 'what these men want: employment which would foster their self-respect and win the praise and sympathy of their fellows, and dwellings which they would come to with pleasure, surroundings which would soothe and elevate them; reasonable labour, reasonable rest. There is only one thing that can give them this – Art.'

Haranguing in his gentle voice on Eelbrook Common and looking in his blue serge reefer jacket like a cross between a farmer and a sea captain, this lovable, and to the Marxist mind, incurably futile old poet, and his proletarian prototype, John Burns, were the life and soul of English socialism. Their object was to save the underdog from sweating and exploitation by organizing him like his comrades, the prosperous artisans of the skilled trade unions. During the recurrent trade depressions of the 'eighties they organized vast processions of unemployed – of the unwanted and starving army of *laissez-faire* capital. One of these, on 'Bloody Sunday,' November, 1887, became part of English history. Long drab companies of pallid ragged men, marching behind red banners and bands of antiquated instruments, converged in defiance of the police from the outer slums on Trafalgar Square; here they were repeatedly charged by massed constables with drawn batons until hundreds of skulls were cracked and bleeding. It was the first glimmer of the red light that threatened social explosion. 'No one who saw it will ever forget the strange and indeed terrible sight of that grey winter day, the vast, sombre-coloured crowd, the brief but fierce struggle at the corner of the Strand, and the river of steel and scarlet that moved slowly through the dusky swaying masses, when two squadrons of the Life Guards were summoned up from Whitehall.' Afterwards two of the leaders, John Burns and the chivalrous Cunninghame Graham, were taken into custody.

The red light was not unheeded. Two years later the selfless pioneers of the British socialist movement won a great triumph. In August, 1889, several thousand labourers in the London Docks struck work. Such men were the poorest of the poor – the flotsam and jetsam of the water-side. They were unorganized, despised even by their fellow workers, without hope or craft. They slept in the fo'c'sles of empty ships and subsisted on scraps of mouldy biscuits left over by their hard-bitten crews, were subjected by sub-contractors – often more brutes than men – to work with rotten plant and defective machinery and left to perish in crippled destitution and misery when their limbs had been mangled in some squalid accident on the dock-side. In the frantic competition for freights, they could scarcely ever look for more than two days' continuous employment. But stirred by the new spirit among their downtrodden kind, they now made the unheard of demand that their labour should be hired at not less than four hours at a time and at a uniform rate of 6*d*. an hour. It was rejected by dock-owners who relied on the poverty and stupidity of the poor derelicts they exploited to ensure their defeat. But the sullen resolve of the men, fanned to anger by the fiery eloquence of one of their number, Ben Tillett, and sustained by the growing sympathy of the public, proved stronger than the familiar weapon of starvation. For two months the docks remained closed. Then the dock-owners gave way. Not only was 'the docker's tanner' won, but a great union of 'unskilled' labour – the Dock, Wharf and Riverside Labourers' Union – had been founded.

Yet by itself trade unionism was not enough. In a society seeking profits through world trade and based on economic fluctuation, an army of surplus labour was inescapable. Under the existing system its periodic unemployment was attended by the extreme of destitution and degradation. This hard rock of unorganized poverty was a constant threat to the trade union movement. In the highly-skilled trades the aristocrat of labour could present a solid front to the capitalist aggressor. But elsewhere the employer could always count on the amorphous mass of starving poverty from which to draft non-union or 'free' labour into his factories and so break a strike. The bitterness of union feeling against the 'blackleg' – generally some poor down-and-out in need of a meal – and the sullen insistence on the rightfulness of peaceful picketing sprang from this.

Before labour could secure its full rights the working class as a whole needed to be redeemed from extreme poverty and given self-respect, knowledge and *esprit de corps* through better housing, education and, above all, some sort of living wage. Organized labour could not stand erect so long as it rested on the social morass of the submerged tenth. State action was necessary to give the workers' organizations – trade unions and co-operative societies – a secure field of operation. Otherwise the capitalist, with his constant recourse to new machinery which displaced skilled men by unskilled, might beat them in the end.

It was the recognition of this which inspired the foundation in 1884 of the Fabian Society. It began as a little group of youthful radicals – drawn mostly from the middle class – who had repudiated the *laissez-faire* tenets of utilitarianism but who retained the utilitarian's contempt for the inefficient and illogical. One of the members was a young, red-haired Irishman named Bernard Shaw who about this time electrified a conference of intellectuals and high-brow politicians by reading a paper to prove that the landlord, the capitalist and the burglar were equally the enemies of society. The Fabian thesis was that before social revolution could be achieved, the educated leaders of society must themselves be brought to see the necessity of revolution. In a law-abiding country like England mob oratory and emotional appeals to mass violence could never succeed. The capitalist state was not to be stormed but gradually occupied by a process of infiltration.

This was the policy of 'permeation.' The Fabians were encouraged to seek membership of every society – Liberal, Tory or Labour, Christian or atheist – that would admit them and there secure, by the arts of persuasion and lobbying, the adoption of socialist measures. Especially were they to seek to permeate the Opposition, since by its very nature parliamentary opposition is inclined to be revolutionary and always seeking to overturn the Government.

The Fabians pinned their faith to an extension of legislative action. They announced that 'the era of administration had come.' The State was to be socialized through its own machinery. Instead of concerning themselves with such questions as free trade, retrenchment, Church disestablishment and the abolition of the House of Lords, the Fabians were to concentrate on free education, municipal trading, the provision of state-aided houses and small holdings and the graduated taxation of incomes and estates. They were not to dictate but to throw out suggestions. Nothing could have been better adapted to the spirit of the time or the character of England.

Fabianism went with the tide of contemporary thought. The Benthamites had long emphasized the sanatory qualities of reforming legislation supported by an incorruptible and centralized bureaucracy and inspectorate. As a result of their teaching, Liberals had purged the Civil Service of corruption in the name of utility and reason. An efficient administration, subject to a Parliament increasingly taught to regard itself as a legislative rather than a debating assembly, was now to be applied for a purpose which its utilitarian sponsors would have viewed with horror – 'the practical extension of the activity of the State.' The weapon the utilitarians had forged was to destroy economic utilitarianism.

For only the State's intervention could now redress the State's neglect. The only remedy for the evils of *laissez-faire* seemed to be to repudiate *laissez-faire*. For many years past, great teachers like Ruskin and T. H. Green at Oxford had impressed on younger consciences the ideal of social responsibility. A new generation of educated men and women was growing up whose minds were contemplating the necessity of solving the problems created by a century of industrialism.

But it was too late to undo what *laissez-faire* had done. In fifty years its hold on English thought had transformed the face of society.

By 1881 seventeen and a half out of twenty-six millions were living in towns: by 1891 twenty-one millions out of twenty-nine millions. Eager Americans visiting Britain in the 'eighties and 'nineties looked in vain in the city streets for the hordes of rosy, golden-haired, blue-eyed children whom they had been led to expect in the Anglo-Saxon island. The national type, already affected in London by the constant influx of cheap foreign labour, was growing smaller and paler. Bad teeth, pasty complexions and weak chests were becoming British traits.

For the great mass of the population the traditionary, religious and rural England of the past had already passed out of memory. In its place had risen a new Britain of 'male employment, boy labour at relatively high wages, early marriages, over-worked mothers, high birth and death rates, high infant mortality, bad housing, a landscape scarred and smudged', wrote Thomas Jones. In the interests of capital the majority of the British people had assumed lives that bore little resemblance to those of their country forebears. The age-long birthright of man – pure air, fresh food, the sight and touch of growing nature, space for reflection – had ceased to be theirs. In its place they had been given the atmosphere of the smoke-stack and the pea-souper fog, the herd society of the streets, the gin palace and the halfpenny newspaper. After a generation they scarcely any longer missed what they had lost.

CHAPTER TEN

The Old Kent Road

'Knocked 'em in the Old Kent Road'
Albert Chevalier

CAPITALISM HAD CREATED the proletariat, and the proletariat was not a theory but a fact. It could not be destroyed or ignored: it could only be transformed by education and improved urban conditions. Education and municipal reform became the themes of the hour. 'We must educate our masters,' Robert Lowe had declared before the passing of Disraeli's Reform Bill. The older ideal of education based on religion and the teaching of hereditary crafts in the home had vanished with the migration to the towns. Only the most rudimentary instruction in reading, writing and arithmetic had as yet taken its place. The great mass of the nation was illiterate. In 1869 only one British child in two had been receiving any education at all. Of those, more than half were being taught in schools maintained by the Church of England, which together with other denominational and voluntary schools had for some time been in receipt of small Government grants-in-aid.

In 1870 William Edward Forster, a Quaker member of Gladstone's first Liberal administration had introduced an Education Bill, setting up compulsory local school boards to provide secular elementary education for all children between the ages of five and thirteen not already provided for by denominational schools. (The school-leaving age was raised to fourteen in 1900 by a Conservative government which in the previous year established a national Board of Education.) The cost was met partly out of State grants and rates and partly out of parents' fees. Owing to jealousy between the churches, the principle was laid down that all grant-aided education should be unsectarian. By this means religious teaching inspired by real conviction was virtually ruled out. It thus came about that the idealism of future generations, founded on a secular State education, differed from that of the old, which still derived from the Christian ethic.

Forster's Act affected little more than half the children in the country. It was unpopular with working-class parents who resented the limitation put on the family earning capacity by school attendance. Yet its underlying principle served the ends of organized labour, not only by bringing cheap education within reach of the workers but by its indirect check on the competition of juvenile labour and its tendency therefore to raise adult wages. A strong demand arose, therefore, to extend its scope. In 1876 a Conservative government tightened the obligations of parents and in 1880 a Liberal government made them universally compulsory. In 1891 another Conservative administration dispensed with fees and made elementary education free for all. Thus both parties acknowledged the collectivist principle that the rich should be compelled to contribute to the education of the poor.

The insignificance of the contribution could not alter the significance of the principle. Once established, the pressure of electoral numbers was bound in the end to do more. Because of the normal Anglo-Saxon indifference to the claims of intellect, the advance of State education was at first deliberate rather than rapid. But the figures speak for themselves. In 1870 the total grant out of revenue towards national education was £912,000. By 1888 it had risen to £4,168,000. By 1905 it was nearly £11,000,000 and the contribution from local rates another £7,000,000. At the turn of the century London alone was paying a million a year of £28 per child – almost the equivalent of a contemporary farm labourer's wage. After the Liberal triumph in 1906 school medical services were established and public funds afforded for feeding necessitous children. To an old Chartist, W. E. Adams, who fifty years before had paid 6d. a week for his fees at night school, the new policy appeared one of 'coddling.' 'It is well to educate the people,' he wrote, 'but the tendency of much of the school board policy of the day is to pauperize the people. Yet school boards ought, above all things, to beware of undermining the independence of the individual.'

These measures, together with the Balfour Act of 1900, had a beneficial effect in improving the lot of millions of humble individuals, even if they were at first limited to elementary education. Reading, writing and arithmetic were well, if mechanically, taught and most pupils left school with reasonable basic skills, and some went on to higher education. In *The Naval Treaty*, one of Conan Doyle's stories, published in 1894, Dr Watson and Sherlock Holmes are in a train whirling up to London. Holmes observes that it is very cheering to come into the city by train, to look down at the houses and see the Board schools rising up above the slates. 'Lighthouses, my boy! Beacons of the future! Capsules with hundreds of bright little seeds in each, out of which will spring the wiser, better England of the future'. Newspaper proprietors saw that the new literacy was creating an enormous market for the printed word and they developed powerful new printing technology to satisfy it. A list of the newspapers and periodicals established in the half century up to 1903 would contain the *News Chronicle, Daily Telegraph, Daily Mail, Daily Dispatch* and *Daily Mirror*, while in the provinces there were the *Liverpool Daily Post, Birmingham Mail*, and *Western Mail*. Periodicals were equally varied, ranging from the *Illustrated London News, Country Life* and *Boys' Own Paper* to *Titbits* and *Answers*. The new publications were, in time, to help in the search for justice by creating greater political and civic awareness among their readers, and platforms for their views.

In municipal administration the collectivist advance was even more striking. Within a generation a vast new vested interest, officially subordinated to the general will as expressed in local and parliamentary elections and controlled by salaried public servants, had sprung into existence in the island dedicated to the sanctity of private wealth. Parliamentary powers of collective control and ownership, and some-times of monopoly, were sought and obtained, at first by the greater cities, later by the counties and smaller urban areas. The Local Government Act of 1888 established elective county councils with control of local affairs and taxation. In that year London achieved its county council – presently to revolutionize the life of its poorer inhabitants. The services of communal life, which individual effort had failed to give to the vast urban agglomerations it had created, were supplied step by step by local authorities. They were paid for out of rates and loans charged on rates. The first successful flotation of municipal stock was made in 1880 by the Liverpool Corporation. By 1896 the local government debt of the country was already 200 million pounds. Only fourteen years later it was three times greater.

The first services performed by the new local authorities were lighting, paving, and cheap transport. By far the most important were education and housing. In nothing had *laissez-faire* achieved so much and so badly as in housing. It had built homes for millions of new factory workers, not to endure but to perish. The vital attribute of a home is that it should be permanent. The principle of the jerry builder was to make as quick a profit as possible on as large a turnover for as little expenditure of labour and money. The houses went up fast enough but they did not last. They were not meant to.

They were built in rows and usually back-to-back – poky, hideous, uncomfortable and insanitary. The last thing a builder thought of in making them was the convenience of the occupant. Except in the granite towns and villages of East Lancashire and the West Riding many were so flimsy that they swayed with the wind and their walls so thin that their inmates were traditionally reputed to be able to hear their neighbours making up their minds. Frequently such houses were erected by the companies which employed their occupants. This was particularly so in the iron and coal districts where there was little alternative employment. A man who lost his job lost his home. The rents were 'kept back' from the weekly wages. The feeling of security and the pride of ownership which home should foster in a free man were lacking.

It was due to the slowly-growing realization of at least some of this by the comfortable classes, many of whom were now encountering slum conditions at first hand in their 'settlement' work, as well as to the galloping deterioration which had by now begun in the earlier industrial dwellings, that a Royal Commission on the Housing of the Poor was set up by Gladstone in 1884. It was, most significantly, presided over by the Prince of Wales. Its interim report published a year later proposed a preliminary purchase at a statutory price of three old prison sites for housing estates. This, in itself, was a most important modification of utilitarian principle since it recurred – in however tentative a form – to the old medieval ideal not of a market, but of a 'fair', price. It was the first sign of recognition of a new, or rather a very old, ideal of government.

The Housing of the Working Classes Act of 1890 which embodied the main part of the recommendations of the Royal Commission stemmed if it did not reverse the rising tide of slum-dwelling. It created new powers of buying and demolishing insanitary houses, opening out congested alleys and *culs-de-sac* and building new dwellings on their sites. In practice, until tightened up by increased powers of government inspection and the growing force of organized working-class opinion, the Act was frequently evaded or perverted. Representation on local councils was usually confined to the smaller capitalists who alone had both the time and the inclination to give to municipal work: all too often they were prompted by the opportunities afforded of serving their own interests. Jerry builders were apt to pack Health and General Purposes Committees in order to frame – and what was worse supervise – the bye-laws about building and sanitation which Parliament had intended to control them. And the purchase of land for building purposes was often preceded by elaborate and shady manoeuvres by those who were – according to democratic notions – supposed to represent and protect the people but who used the machinery of democracy to exploit them further.

Yet, as the theory of social responsibility increasingly haunted the minds of the educated minority, a process characteristically English took place. The larger and better-established capitalists – and above all their sons – began to devote themselves to the service of the public they or their forebears had fleeced. They did so without hope of further profit and out of a sense of *noblesse oblige*, gained more often than not at the new public schools which, since Arnold of Rugby's days, had opened their gates and their ideology to the commercial classes. A new type of public man arose – provincial, aggressive and democratic in method and appeal – whose interest lay neither in foreign policy nor parliamentary debate but in the extension of municipal services. Living on the private wealth acquired or inherited under *laissez-faire*, they were able to throw their entire energies into the work of mitigating the evils wrought by *laissez-faire*. These new, and to their individualist fathers' way of thinking, heretical radicals were still iconoclastic towards the older notions of privilege and decorum. But though they resented the power of the landed aristocracy and lost no opportunity of humbling it, they were no enemies to the capitalist and manufacturer. The very inroads they made on *laissez-faire* practice helped to maintain the prestige and opportunities of their class by appeasing the social unrest of the masses. The most famous of these local radical reformers was Joseph Chamberlain, the dapper young hardware merchant with orchid, monocle and terrible republican sentiments who became mayor of Birmingham in 1873 at thirty-seven, and President of the Board of Trade in Mr Gladstone's second administration in 1880.

In all this the domestic history of Britain during the last two decades of the nineteenth and the first of the twentieth century constituted the first act of a great revolution. During these years a vigorous capitalist, and less vigorous but still powerful aristocratic, England were imperceptibly converted to an elementary socialism whose basis was that the weak and inefficient should constitute a first charge on the strong and able. The pioneer activities of a humane and intelligent minority of their own members contributed to that conversion. But the real driving force came from the superior votes of the urban workers which, by a third Reform Act in 1884, had been reinforced by those of the county householders.

The ruling classes did not consciously admit their conversion for they were unaware of it. And their struggle against it, like all English struggles, was grudging and tenacious. But, while denouncing the name of socialism which they believed to be synonymous with mob plunder and the bloody destruction of their homes and altars, they allowed socialist principles to inspire their laws and, in an illogical, piecemeal and incomplete way, they increasingly applied socialist practice. For the void in the great industrial towns which their fathers' search for wealth had created left them no alternative. The more the towns grew the more it clamoured to be filled.

*   *   *

The triumphs of science and invention hastened the triumph of the collectivist. Gas and electric lighting, steam and electric transport, the telegraph and the telephone made for a communal rather than an individualist organization of life. So did the course of capitalism itself. For the new collectivism that was imperceptibly destroying *laissez-faire* did not only spring from working-class discontent at *laissez-faire* conditions. It arose out of the very core of Benthamism. For the Benthamite, in his exaggerated tenderness for the individual, proclaimed his right to make any contract he liked in the pursuit of his own interests. It followed that two or more individuals were free to associate in any way they chose and in pursuit of their aggregate interests to agree to act as a single person.

With the extension of machinery and transport, industry perpetually tended to increase its scale of operations. For this it needed ever more capital. The individual trader was thus increasingly impelled to bind himself in association with others. The fictitious trading personages so created enjoyed the same legal rights as the individual of *laissez-faire* society. But the powers created by their joint wealth far exceeded those of a single person. Just as organized labour acquired rights against the individual, so organized capital assumed powers which left the private merchant a pygmy in a realm of giants.

Though the ordinary man was slow to perceive what was happening, his vaunted absolute economic freedom and significance were imperceptibly dwindling. Even by the 'seventies a handful of railway companies owned wealth equal in the aggregate to three-quarters of the National Debt. In the course of their business such corporations sought vast powers. Where these were denied them by the Common Law, recourse for legislation could be had to a House of Commons in which the successful business man and financier was beginning to succeed the country gentleman as the predominant type. Through new forms of investment the entire propertied class of the country was learning to delegate its wealth and responsibilities to corporate bodies. The historic justification of private property had been that it fostered responsibility and acted as a bulwark against tyranny. It was now unwittingly being used by the individual to purchase freedom from responsibility. It was putting despotic powers in the hands of mechanical corporations without personal conscience or sense of obligation.

A generation which had been taught to believe that the pursuit of profit was the one road to national prosperity made no attempt to secure the threatened birthright of its race. The freedom of the subject inherited from the great English patriots and martyrs was unconsciously bartered away for increased dividends. The later Victorians, for all the probity of their private and domestic lives, allowed the economic initiative of their posterity to pass to the soulless corporations which gave them their wealth and income.

Yet in all that they did as individuals the Victorians were guided by conscience: in this they were the inheritors of the English past. No generation ever had a higher record in this. The honesty and integrity of the Victorian merchant and manufacturer was a byword throughout the world. Again and again private charity, pity and a sense of duty and public service redeemed the consequences of a false economic philosophy.

None the less the conscience of the individual was betrayed in the end to the theory of the overriding sanctity of profit-making. In the late 'fifties and early 'sixties, to suit the convenience of the commercial community Liberal Governments passed legislation conferring on joint-stock companies the privilege of limited liability. Henceforward fictitious bodies, enjoying the legal rights of individuals, could incur unlimited financial obligations without their individual shareholders becoming fully responsible for them.

Up to this time a man's power to make money by transferring his credit and freedom of commercial action to others was restrained by his liability for the obligations they might incur. This check on irresponsible delegation was now removed. A man could grow and remain rich in security and even innocence from business practices which would have outraged his conscience as an individual. He could avoid both the risks and stigma of transactions done by others in pursuit of profits in which he shared.

At first the investing public was slow to avail itself of the opportunities afforded by the Companies Act of 1862. (By this Act it became possible for any one to found a limited liability company by obtaining signatures to a memorandum of registration and adding the word 'Limited' to its nomenclature.) For a generation the use of limited liability was chiefly confined to the professional commercial community. But after the failure of the City of Glasgow Bank in 1879, when private shareholders were called upon to meet obligations many times greater than the value of their shares, private investors increasingly entrusted their money to concerns carrying only limited liability. During the last eight years of the century more than thirty thousand limited companies were floated and ten thousand wound up. In 1899 there were 27,969 registered companies in the United Kingdom with a paid-up capital of £1,512,098,098: by 1914, 64,692 with £2,531,947,661. Ownership and enjoyment of the nation's wealth was thus increasingly separated from its control. And the conscience of the individual ceased to regulate its use directly.

The consequences of the Companies Act of 1862 completed the divorce between the Christian conscience and the economic practice of everyday life. Legally speaking it paganized the financial and commercial community. Henceforward an astute man by adherence to legal rules which had nothing to do with morality could grow rich by virtue of shuffling off his most elementary obligations to his fellows. He could not only grow rich by such means. He could grow immensely powerful.

The break-up of the medieval Church had transferred power from the Christian state, with its theoretic moral control over all human economic activities, to the landowner, who though he may have begun as an avaricious courtier and a plunderer of monastic lands, was gradually transmuted by the magic of the English countryside, and the personal responsibility attaching to his rustic form of wealth, into the country gentleman. In less than two centuries the hard, grasping usurer of Tudor times had grown into Sir Roger de Coverley. But by that time the pursuit of wealth was already taking new forms. The great fortunes of the eighteenth century were made by overseas trade. The Turkey merchant and the East India nabob were the pioneers of the new national economy. They also were absorbed by marriage and purchase into the ranks of the landed gentry until in the early nineteenth century their place was taken by still newer leaders – the bankers, industrialists and shipowners, the capitalists of coal, beer, cotton and iron.

The principle of limited liability now set up another arbiter of economic society. The company promoter – Sir Gorgias Midas of du Maurier's drawings and uncle Ponderevo of Wells's novel – was the social wonder of the last years of the old and the first of the new century. Before his glittering, if nebulous, throne all who had money to invest prostrated themselves, lured by his promise of quick and easy profits. His craft consisted in raising money on loan to float or purchase commercial concerns on favourable terms and in subsequently disposing of them at a profit, not necessarily by developing their productive capacity but by enhancing their financial market value. He raised the latter by the arts of display and suggestion as a stock breeder raises a fat pig. His journeymen were advertisers, publicity agents, stockbrokers and share pushers. If in the course of his over sanguine efforts to boost them, his concerns collapsed before they were ripe for selling – and in his early days they frequently did – he could escape under cover of limited liability, wind up the company and, with the full blessing of the law, start again. The burden was borne by the company's creditors and by such credulous investors as, allured by his arts, had bought their shares at an exaggerated price.

But the effects of these operations did not stop there. For by directing money into enterprises designed not so much for stable long-term production as for quick capital appreciation the new financier tended to make industrial employment even more precarious than before. The stimulus to joint stock manufacturing and trading afforded by the principle of limited liability had another fatal consequence on the life of the working man. Under *laissez-faire* individualism it at least paid to be efficient. The workman who by his skill and industry furthered the interests of his employer had a reasonable chance of promotion, for he was too valuable to lose. But when the control of business passed out of the hands of the private employer using his own capital into that of the financial company representing an intangible mass of absentee shareholders without active knowledge of its affairs, the industrious workman found it increasingly difficult to better himself. In any case he was less likely to be noticed by managers whose stake in the business was confined to salaries paid them by the shareholders and who were less personally interested in its success. Thus the conscientious workman was increasingly discouraged. The man with ambition and intelligence, instead of identifying himself with the industrial system of which he was part, was driven to rebel against it. Instead of becoming a small capitalist, he became a proletarian and socialist.

Adam Smith had always maintained that manufacturing by joint-stock companies must prove injurious to the public interest. He argued that efficiency and consequently wealth resulted from every man attending scrupulously to his own self-interest. Such attention could not be successfully delegated. A large joint-stock company, financed by distant and 'amateur' shareholders and managed by salaried nominees, tended to be less efficient than a small concern directed by the man who would be the sole beneficiary if it succeeded and the chief loser if it failed. With the growth of this kind of business, the control of commerce passed into less vigorous hands. The financial speculator with the talent for exploiting the shareholder and the man of routine who gave no trouble to the speculator took the place of the man of initiative and drive. Genius was discouraged: mediocrity preferred.

Had the world been governed by the purely mechanical and mathematical processes that so fascinated the pedants of *laissez-faire*, this would have mattered little, for it could not have endured. The joint-stock company would have cut its own throat and so perished. Its inefficiency would have promptly limited its capacity for harm. But what Adam Smith failed to see was that manufacturing by joint-stock companies might be financially successful though injurious to the public. For with the enormous concentration of capital secured through company promotion, success often turned upon ability to corner the market.

The growth of collectivism in finance widened the gulf between the man of property and the proletarian. The latter found it increasingly hard to rise out of his class. The former, if he invested his capital wisely, found it increasingly easy to live on its fruits without contact with the industrial processes in which it was employed. He became a *rentier*; a mere enjoyer of automatic wealth to whose making he contributed nothing in thought or effort. His responsibility towards those who did so became negligible.

All this strengthened the case for the state control of private wealth. The justification for privilege and power is the fulfilment of social duty. Possessions divorced from any personal sense of obligation seem a kind of theft on all who do not share them. They outrage the moral sense of mankind. Once the sanctity of *laissez-faire* itself was repudiated, the riches of the Forsytes and still more of their *rentier* children were harder to justify. They seemed to serve no other purpose but the private enjoyment of their owners. Even where, as often happened in kindly England, their possessors spent their fortunes in charitable deeds, their philanthropy had no visible connection with the processes, harsh and inhuman, by which they obtained their wealth.

The socialist attack that developed as the nineteenth century drew to its close was therefore levelled at the whole principle of private property. Because individual wealth was abused, it was argued that it should be abolished altogether. As a reaction against the maldistribution and inhuman conditions of capitalist production, the old demand was made – long unheard in Christian England – that production should be directly for use and not for profit. But those who voiced it, being either men without property or *rentiers* whose ownership was divorced from personal use, demanded not that the producer and craftsmen should resume their lost control over their own industry, but that the State should assume the functions of the capitalist. They were so accustomed to the despotism of absentee capital that their only remedy for its ill effects was to transfer its ownership from the individual to the community, and its control from the capitalist director to the state bureaucrat. They made no attempt to restore it to those who could make the best use of it – not the people in the abstract but the people as individual producers. The scale of modern machinery and the gargantuan organization of life to which it had given rise seemed to them to render such an attempt impracticable.

The intellectual socialist, who superseded the more sentimental Christian socialist of the past, appeared as the champion of an omnipotent State. He argued that the State should restrict the power of the rich and powerful by taxing and ultimately confiscating the wealth which was the source of their power. In 1893 the Fabian Society issued its famous manifesto demanding the ownership by the community of the means of production, distribution and exchange. In the same year the Independent Labour Party was founded, dedicated to the same end and seeking it by direct socialist representation in Parliament and on local authorities.

From this development arose a curious contradiction in the character of the British working-class movement. Its intellectual leaders set up the State as the *deus ex machina* which was to rescue society from the abuses of individualism. But the State is an abstraction and its supremacy can only be exercised through individuals. If the State is to be all powerful, the individuals who exercise its authority must be all powerful, too. To a Latin, German or Russian socialist, accustomed from birth to the ideal of an overriding centralized despotism, there was nothing repugnant in such a claim. But in England, the traditional home of individual liberty, a proposition which restored to a State official the power of the Stuart kings was disquieting. To argue that this omnipotent Whitehall would in turn be controlled by the elected representatives of the people was merely to say that uncontrolled power should rest in the hands of whoever could persuade the electorate into entrusting it to them. It might be a party caucus, it might be a popular dictator. It might even be the very capitalist whom the new state power was designed to suppress.

The early socialists in their enthusiasm for their thesis did not detect the weakness in their remedy. Their emotional appeal to the masses, and even more to their middle-class sympathizers, was to that love of liberty which the capitalist monopoly over the work and daily life of millions had outraged. Yet by attacking the private ownership of property they struck unconsciously at the foundation on which, in the historic polity of England, individual liberty had always rested. Because the privilege of ownership had ceased to be widespread as in the past and had become restricted to the few, they supposed that its destruction would extend the freedom of the many.

They forgot that, apart from economic liberty, political liberty has little meaning. Only so long as a man knows that he can defy superior power and still support himself and his loved ones is he a free man. Without that knowledge, whatever his standard of living or theoretical status, he can be a kind of slave. And when all power is vested in the State and the State is the owner both of the workers' homes and the means of production, private liberty becomes a rather nebulous thing. There was little enough liberty for the workers under the rule of the nineteenth-century joint-stock capitalist, except, of course, the liberty to starve. But in the Fabian paradise which was to take its place though there might be a great deal more comfort, there was to be no liberty at all. The State, or rather the State official, was to rule all things.

Such a paradise, at first sight, seemed to offer so many things of which the English worker stood in need. It offered better wages and conditions of labour, cleaner and more commodious homes, social services and public amenities in place of the drab negation of the utilitarian city, above all the end of the shameless exploitation of poverty by wealth which robbed men and women of their self-respect. Yet, when the promised land was examined more closely, it was seen to contain a presence which was not readily acceptable to an Englishman. For there in the midst of the garden stood Nosey Parker with the sword of the all-seeing State. And of all men none was more temperamentally likely to resent that presence than the rough and liberty-loving workman of England.

The socialist thinkers could see no problem in this. The dictatorship of the state would be exercised, they argued, on behalf of the working classes. Being for the most part men of the study, they failed to see how their republic would work out in practice. They never realized how heavily in an over-crowded country, in which the productive work and home life of the million had been centred in great towns, the tyranny of the official, if vested with absolute power to ordain, prohibit and tax, would press on the working man.

The English working man, even after a century of factory labour, did not take readily to aggregate conceptions of himself. He did not want liberty as a member of a class: he wanted it as a man. An official bossing him about was no less a tyrant in his eyes because he was vested with popular authority. The English proletarian was a contradiction in terms: economically a wage slave, he was still spiritually and in his own eyes a freeman. He was easily 'put upon', but did not readily brook interference. His fists and his tongue were always quick to assert his independence.

The love of liberty came out in his phrases, in his jokes, in his invincible, half-blasphemous, ironical commentary on the ups and downs of his harsh life. His ''Ere, who d'yre think y're a'getting at?' or his 'Tell us anuvor, guvnor,' like his jokes about mothers-in-law and old gentlemen slipping on banana skins, were part of his protests against interference and pompous power. He refused to part with his humour, his right to grumble, his right to what little liberty the wage struggle left him in which to go about his private business in his own way. Not clearly understanding how he had been cheated of his birthright – home, status and privilege – he was yet aware of the dignity of his descent. He knew himself to be as good as any man, and better.

Robbed by the machine of pride and pleasure in his work, he still kept inviolate his rights to take pleasure in his liberty. His most precious possession was his right to enjoy himself in his own way. On Hampstead Heath or Hackney Marshes on a bank holiday one saw him at his most uproarious, expressing himself in cockney carnival: costers in all their pride of pearls and feathers, frolicsome young women with tambourines singing and making unblushing advances to jolly strangers, old parties with bottles of stout and jests for every passer-by, side-shows and booths with giants and dwarfs, nigger minstrels and performing dogs. So in the trains from Stepney to Highbury one might in the course of half an hour's journey encounter a lad playing airs on a fiddle, an old man beguiling his journey with an accordion and a chorus of young workmen singing in unison. By being jolly and having a good time when the occasion offered, the English poor reminded themselves and the rich men they served that Jack was as good as his master and that freedom was his birthright.

One saw industrial England at its roughest and freest in any town where seamen congregated. In the Ratcliff Highway in the 'eighties and 'nineties almost every house was a tavern with a dance hall at the back where a steam organ kept up perpetual revelry. The whole place resounded with music, the shouting of drunken sailors and their bright-scarved girls, the clatter of the steam organs and the strumming of nigger minstrels. But any poor street on frequent occasion presented the same scene in miniature: a German band, a dancing bear, a visit from the Salvation Army or a band of morris dancers could bring the population of every crowded house into the street. Most poor districts had their quota of barrel-organs, whose owners, having finished their day's work in wealthier parts, could generally be prevailed upon to oblige with a tune to which the whole street stepped it on the flags. A wedding was always the occasion for the hire of a barrel-organ for the day and for continuous music from the time of the bridal couple's return to the adjournment of the company to the nearest 'boozer.' Only a fight – a common occurrence – could bring the harmony to a stop.

The supreme embodiment of the surviving character of the English working people was the music hall. Here art held up the mirror to nature. Springing spontaneously out of the sing-song of the upper tavern room and the old out-of-door gardens of the artisan of the pastoral past, it became for a space of time a British institution. Its morality was to make the best of a bad job: its purpose to make every one free and easy. Performers and audience, under the genial and Bacchanalian presidency of the chairman, with his buttonhole, his mesmeric eye and his town crier's voice, combined in expressing their own individuality. At the old South London, whenever there was a hitch in the programme, the chairman, 'Bob' Courtney, glittering with false diamonds and laying aside his glass and cigar, would rise to sing his traditional song, 'Britannia's Voice of Thunder,' while the whole audience kept time, drowning singing and even big drum with an equally traditional refrain of 'good old Bob! Bob! Bob! Bob!' Its songs, circulating in succession among the entire population – 'Champagne Charlie,' 'Lardi-da,' 'It's all done by kindness,' 'How's your poor feet,' 'What ho! she bumps,' 'Pretty Polly Perkins of Paddington Green,' 'Ask a policeman,' and 'Knocked 'em in the Old Kent Road' – were vernacular, irreverent, democratic, yet intensely individualistic, as of a nation of disinherited, cheery aristocrats, and arose from deeply felt experience: they were the English answer to the lot which had befallen the English worker. They told a man, in rousing chorus, to 'paddle his own canoe,' 'to cling to his old love like the ivy,' and to fill himself up with 'beer, beer, glorious beer,' bade Tommy make room for his uncle, and the nation put the foreigner in his place:

> 'I'd wake men from their torpor, and every foreign pauper,
> That helps to make the sweater rich and wages always low,
> I'd send aboard a ship, Sir, for an everlasting trip, Sir,
> And a chance give to the English if I only bossed the show.'

Such rough songs spoke of unchanging virtues: of courage and cheerfulness in adversity, of loyalty to old 'pals,' of constancy to home and wife. There is no ballad more English than that which Albert Chevalier wrote for his cockney impersonation of the old London workman philosophizing over his pipe on the faithful wife of his youth:

> 'We've been together now for forty years,
> And it don't seem a day too much,
> Oh, there ain't a lidy living in the land
> As I'd swop for my dear ole Dutch.'

Above all the music hall expressed the English passion for liberty: the English desire, so hard to translate into the life of the factory, to follow the current of one's own nature and be true to it by being free. What was, however bad it seemed, had to be and was therefore, in a humorous way, good, since man being free could turn his necessity to glorious gain. So the fat woman, the grace and opportunity of youth gone for ever as it was for most of her audience, would stand up, mountainous and undeterred, and, announced by the leering chairman as 'your old favourite, So-and-So,' send her steam-roundabout voice pulsating through the thick pipe and cigar smoke:

'I weigh sixteen stoney O!
I'm not all skin and boney O!'

So, in a more studied and perfect expression of the inner soul of a great
people who had lost everything but its cheerfulness and courage, Marie
Lloyd in a later age, when the old music hall was dying, would sing,
a vinous old female, moist-eyed, wandering but invincible:

'My old man said, Follow the van
And don't dilly dally on the way!
Off went the cart with the home packed in it,
I walked behind with my old cock linnet.
But I dillied and dallied, dallied and dillied,
Lost the van and don't know where to roam.
I stopped on the way to have the old half-quartern,
And I can't find my way home.'

It was to the people whose life this vulgar, proud and humane
art represented that the socialist offered his collectivist remedy. He
assumed, not without the justification of logic, that the English working
man was already a proletarian slave and that he would be only too
willing to band himself as a nameless comrade in the great army of
his class against the rich and privileged. But this was not so. The
downtrodden wage-slave did not think of himself as such. All the while
that the socialist propagandist was telling him of the proletarian heaven,
he was dreaming of the day when a rich unknown cousin would die in
Australia or the horses he so hopefully and religiously backed each
week would bring him a fortune and he would be able to have a house
and a garden of his own and go to race meetings and cricket matches
every day instead of working with his fellow proletarians in the factory.

Thus it came about that the first missionaries of the new socialist
religion were treated with derision by the rough, unbelieving multitude.
They were denounced as atheists, anarchists and republicans, as liars
and quacks who offered 'sum'at for nothing.' Their meetings were
frequently broken up amid rude noises. In those days it was the
socialists who were heckled by the local toughs and practical jokers,
not the Tories. England was so accustomed to being governed by well-
spoken gentlemen in top hats that the spectacle of an avowed socialist
going down to the House of Commons in a check cap with a brass band
blaring at his side profoundly shocked many humble men and women.
Working men were at first exceedingly suspicious of members of their
own class who sought to enter Parliament as if they were toffs and were
ready to listen to any malicious charge, however wild, of peculation or

self-seeking brought against them. Their creed was regarded, in pubs and other places, where sound men congregated as laughable if not lunatic. In the 1895 election – a Conservative triumph – only one working man held his seat, and every one of the twenty-seven candidates put up by the virgin independent Labour Party suffered defeat at the polls. (The Party Chest for the Election totalled only £400. Ardent supporters pawned their watches, Sunday suits, accordions and fiddles.) It was not till the great Conservative rout of January, 1906, when the rising tide of collectivism swept an almost revolutionary Liberal government into power that a Parliamentary Labour Party took its place as a permanent force in politics with a solid bloc of 51 seats and a strength sufficient to sway the course of legislation.

Even many of the trade union and Co-operative Society leaders – often stalwarts of the local Tory working men's club – regarded the new socialism with disfavour. It was too highbrow and foreign for their shrewd liking: too far removed from the familiar tastes and prejudices of the simple men they represented. Had those who represented the larger forces of organized capital been a little more sympathetic towards their Labour *vis-à-vis* instead of treating them, as they too often did, as impertinent inferiors who had forgotten their place, the intellectual socialist movement might well have died still-born. G. N. Barnes complained 'Much daring, I went one night to speak at the Battersea branch of the Social-Democratic Federation where I was so belaboured with words about exploitation, bourgeois and others of learned length and thundering sound just then imported from Germany that I . . . determined to go no more to Social-Democratic Federation Branches.'

Yet a new spirit was abroad. For just as the first translation of the scriptures spelt out by unlettered zealots lent wings to an earlier English revolution, so the education of the board school helped to carry a new conception of life into the homes of the people. To cater for the needs of this new class of reader, a halfpenny press made its appearance, jejune, snappy, sensational. The first in the field was the radical *Star* – the 'twinkle, twinkle little star' of the late 'eighties and 'nineties. It had many imitators. Those who controlled this revolutionary power might differ in politics and educational purpose, but the circulation of their papers and the advertisements from which they drew their profits depended on their giving to the million what the million wanted. Being obscure it wanted flattery and, being poor, a share of the pleasures of the rich. The cheap newspaper gave it the one and fed its appetite for the other. It promised that a time was coming when the hungry should be filled with good things.

For the intelligent young worker, to whom State education had given the key to the world of books and new ideas, and to whom the pub and the humorous philosophy of his class were insufficient solace, the background of life – even though it was already vastly improved – was dreary and uninspiring. As Joe Toole remembered, it was that of the street corner, the smell of the tripe-works, the clatter of clogs, the street brawls, short commons, the pawnshop and the cries of women giving birth to new citizens. The usual lot was to start selling papers after school hours at eleven, borrowing $4\frac{1}{2}d$. to purchase thirteen with a hope of making $2d$. profit for each bundle sold. Three years later the scholar left school to plunge into a battle for life which took the form of constantly changing casual labour – sweeping floors or streets, holding horses' heads for commercial travellers, laying tram tracks, storekeeping, running errands and monotonous machine-minding sometimes for ten hours at a stretch. All these occupations were 'blind alley'; the weaker brethren never climbed beyond them out of the ruck of the unskilled. Between jobs one stood at the corner of the street or scoured the shop windows for a notice of 'Boy Wanted.' In such a start to life there were constant temptations: the skylarking, chi'iking gang of boon companions who slipped imperceptibly from practical joking into petty larceny on sweet shops and battles with sticks and broken glass; the pubs to which a boy became accustomed from his earliest years, the racecourse and the bookie at the street corner. Later came the long losing battle with poverty, undernourishment and insecurity, the home with the verminous walls and broken window-sashes in the crowded dirty streets, the risk of accident and maiming, and the certainty sooner or later of 'slack times' and unemployment with the sickening tramp from factory gate to gate, the days of idle, hopeless hunger, the rot of body and soul and the dread of the workhouse at the end of that bitter road.

It was to those whom this dreary heritage inspired to bitter anger that the new socialism made its initial appeal. Behind the solid structure of trade unionism and the brittle façade of the intelligentsia fermented the spirit and fervour of a new religion. During the quarter of a century which preceded the first World War, socialism was preached through the crowded cities of Britain as Methodism had been preached in the eighteenth century and Puritanism in the seventeenth – as a salvationist crusade. Into the drab lives and starved minds of the industrial masses came a new message of hope and righteousness, uttered on evangelist platforms by ardent believers with red ties and flashing eyes: that poverty and injustice could be abolished by State action. The little handful of the elect who gathered in the north-country market square after some crushing electoral defeat to sing Carpenter's Labour hymn, 'England, arise! the long, long night is over,' were like the grain of seed which grew into a great tree.

Among the younger generation of the workers there were many who read more seriously. Henry George's *Progress and Poverty* sold in thousands, and Blatchford's *Merrie England*, published at 6*d*. in 1893, in tens of thousands. The latter's humble *Clarion*, issued under many difficulties, made proselytes wherever the factory chimneys and slated roofs marked the abode of the toiling masses. For humbler minds the new gospel was preached in its simplest and most appealing form. The bloated capitalist with his white top-hat, his gold watch-chain and his money-bags, was the Devil who sucked the blood of the workers. The upright young socialist with his union ticket and his Fabian pamphlet in his pocket was the pioneer of a new and better world, ready for martyrdom if need be but never for compromise with the evil spirit of greed which kept the virtuous proletariat in chains. In a more sophisticated way this point of view was broadly adopted by a whole generation of middle-class writers and artists who, appalled by the accumulating evils of *laissez-faire* industrialism, carried the message of socialism into their art. Generous youth at Oxford and Cambridge and newer centres of learning thrilled at the gospel of apocalyptic hope: the schoolmasters, journalists, clergymen and civil servants of the future went out to their labour consciously or unconsciously imbued with the teaching of socialists of genius like Shaw and Wells.

Yet the advance of socialism was nearly always anticipated by the premature retreat of the individualist. Before the vanguard of the red revolutionaries reached each successive barricade the capitalists were already receding. Many of the demands of organized Labour were granted by Liberal and Tory politicians – quick to sense the changing wind of electoral favour – long before its socialist representatives were in a position to enforce them. Successive Employers' Liability Acts limited and largely abrogated the old legal doctrine of common employment. Under pressure from the unions the scope of the Factory Acts was steadily extended. Within a few years of bringing the dockers within the scope of the acts, the number of dock accidents was halved. The Employers' Liability Act of 1897 made an employer theoretically liable for all the risks of his workers' employment. Charity, now invested with the prim pince-nez of the statistical bureaucrat, was restored to its former place as a civic obligation. The stigma of pauperism was removed and those in receipt of poor law relief were admitted to the franchise and small holdings were provided for agricultural labourers.

The socialist principle that the State as the ultimate owner of all property had the right to tax capital as well as income was admitted by the imposition of death duties in Sir William Harcourt's Liberal budget of 1893. Fourteen years later, Mr Asquith introduced the distinction between earned and unearned incomes and a new impost on very rich men called super-tax. In order to finance a nationwide scheme of old-age pensions and other 'rare and refreshing fruit for the parched lips of the multitude,' the new levy was extended to all incomes of more than £5,000 a year by a Liberal Chancellor of the Exchequer, David Lloyd George. To modern minds such modest measures of working-class amelioration, now taken for granted, may appear trifling. To a Liberal of the 'sixties they would have seemed a revolutionary inter-ference with the laws of supply and demand and a half-way step to wholesale confiscation and communism. To many old-fashioned per-sons like the Conservative die-hard peers, who sacrificed the powers of their own House in a last desperate attempt to stay the new electoral will, they seemed so even in 1910.

In the decade before 1915, the election of Liberal governments with their policies for social reform lightened the harsh burdens on the old, the poor, the sick and the unemployed. Old age pensions lifted the horror and despair of the workhouse which Crabbe had described as '. . . a prison, with a milder name/ Which few inhabit without dread or shame'. A contributions-based national insurance scheme began to provide medical assistance, and there was medical attention for children in school. Labour exchanges and benefit for the unemployed were established, while those in work were protected by legislation against sweated labour and for workmen's compensation.

For the underdog it was a far cry from the socialized industrial England of Lloyd George's budgets to the grim commonwealth of liberty to survive or perish of the mid-nineteenth century: from the omniscient government inspector, the statutorily enforced closing hours and half holidays, the working-class housing estate with its bathrooms and gardens to the 'young ladies' of Madame Elise's dressmaking establishment with their fifteen hours' working day and airless, fever-stricken dormitory, the filthy, ragged child crossing-sweepers sleeping under the Adelphi arches, and the days when W. E. Adams, tramping through Salford in search of work, found at Peel Park with its museum and free library an almost solitary example of municipal enlightenment.

Looking back in 1923, G. N. Barnes whose whole life had been passed in the service of the Labour movement which had raised him from a poor apprentice's bench to a Privy Councillorship and a seat in the Cabinet, attempted to sum it all up. 'I have seen many lands,' he wrote, 'but none as good as my own. I have mixed with many peoples but found none with so large measure of fellow feeling or sense of fair play. I have seen freedom broadening down to the class in which I was born and bred and which I have tried to serve. When I was young, working folk were uneducated and unenfranchised. They were poor and dependent and their working days were bounded by age and want without concern by the State which their labour had enriched. Now they have at least a modicum of education, they are politically as well as industrially organized, and although there is still unemployment and, in too many instances, fear of want, yet these grim problems are being tackled with greater knowledge and more humane feeling than ever before. I take the present signs and tokens as indications of better things to be.'

All this was true. The good man, looking back on his life of struggle and seemingly miraculous achievement, knew how much greater were the opportunities of the young workers of the new age than were those of the old. But the young who had never experienced the full fury of the storm of *laissez-faire* merely knew that they were born into a world of mean streets, monotonous labour, cramping poverty and narrowing uncertainty. They inherited from the past, not only elementary and secondary schools, labour exchanges, and council houses, but bad digestions, uninspiring surroundings and the instability of a commercial system based not on human welfare but on profits. They were better off than their parents, but they were not satisfied with their lot. For their instincts, as well as the professional preachers of discontent, told them that something was still lacking.

CHAPTER ELEVEN

Kith And Kin

'If you're planning for one year plant grain; if you're
planning for ten years plant trees; if you're planning for
a hundred years plant men.'

Old Chinese Proverb

THE SUMMER OF 1879 was the worst recorded in modern times. It
rained continuously. Everywhere the harvest blackened in the fields,
and farmers were faced with ruin, landlords with depleted rentals. In
England and Wales alone three million sheep died of rot. Meanwhile
industry struggled against one of those periodic slumps which seemed
inseparable from the capitalist system. It was a universal tale of woe;
of cataclysmic falls in prices and streets full of unemployed. The fog
which lay over London that winter – yellow, choking and foreboding
– seemed to symbolize something out of joint in the times. The pursuit
of wealth for its own sake was resulting in what? For a moment the
British vision seemed to have grown too narrow: the basis of a community which lived on an uncertain and uncontrollable export trade
too small.

Yet for industry the trade depression of the early 'eighties was only
a passing phase: a pause in the progress of expansion. It was followed
by recovery and renewed prosperity. Demand for industrial products
was still expanding faster than supply; rich veins of unexploited markets
remained to be developed by the capitalist. But for English agriculture
the blackened crops of 1879 and the years of continued rain and cold
that followed marked the end of an era. It never recovered.

It had enjoyed a glorious evening. The three decades between the
repeal of the Corn Laws and the fall of Disraeli's last administration in
1880 were the golden age of farming. The bumper harvests of the
'fifties and 'sixties had been accompanied by expanding home markets,
plentiful capital and cheap transport and labour. The landed estates of

Britain, employing more than a million skilled workers and supporting the richest aristocracy the world had seen, gave bread to 17,000,000 and meat to the whole population.

Those were the days when the Earl of Ladythorne sat at the covert side like a gentleman at his opera stall, thinking what a good thing it was to be a lord with a sound digestion and plenty of cash, when tenant farmers built conservatories and planted ornamental trees, and young ladies in flowing skirts and jackets and little feathered caps played croquet on ancient lawns or gossiped over 'hair brushings' in rooms once habited by Elizabethan statesmen and Carolean divines. The great parks with their noble trees slumbered in the sunlight of those distant summers; children born heirs to the securest and happiest lot humankind had ever known, rode and played in their shade never guessing that in their old age they would see the classic groves felled by the estate breaker and the stately halls pulled down or sold to make convalescent homes for miners or county asylums.

Yet all the while behind the dark curtain of time harvests were ripening on the virgin plains of other continents which were to put an end to all this prosperity. Year by year the railways crept farther into the prairies, while the freight of the iron ships increased and man's ingenuity found new ways to preserve meat and foodstuffs from decay.

When the trumpet sounded the walls of Jericho that had seemed so strong fell. They could not stand against the inrush of cheap foreign food. They lacked defenders. The urban voters had lost interest in the countryside. The rural workers were without votes and, since the enclosures of the past century, without a stake in the land. The social basis of British agriculture was too narrow: its ownership concentrated in too few hands. Some four thousand squires owned more than half the land of England and Wales. Seven hundred thousand cottagers between them only possessed 150,000 out of 39,000,000 cultivated acres. They could not defend an interest they did not enjoy.

Henceforward the foreigner was to feed Britain. Corn in bulk came from America: frozen mutton from Australia as early as 1872, and beef from the Argentine made the work of the English farmer superfluous. In the next two decades more than four million acres of arable land went out of cultivation, and more than half a million workers left the country for the town. Against the competition of the new lands the farmer was powerless; a bad season spelt ruin, for a diminished turnover could no longer be offset by a rise in price. Falling rents, mortgages and bank overdrafts broke the back of the smaller squires before death duties and rising taxes drove them in the next generation from their ancient homes and lands. Only the very rich who had urban estates to offset their rural ones, and the farm labourer, helped after 1884 by the vote and the rising tide of social conscience, prospered a little in the general tide of decay. But the heart was going out of British farming. Henceforward the old conception of home as a place permanently associated with man's life and labour to be inherited from his forebears and transmitted to his children was for most Englishmen a thing of the past. The utilitarians thought of home only as a shelter from the weather. They could not see the need for beauty and continuity in human life. Under their guidance and that of the manufacturers and changers of money to whose keeping they trustfully committed England more factory workers could be supported with cheap food than ever before. But from the plain man, on whose character, integrity and valour England in the last resort rested, something precious had been taken away. The home smoke rising from the valley, the call of the hours from the belfry, the field of rooks and elms, had given place to a tenement in the land of the coal truck and the slag heap. Here his life was cast and the earliest memories of his children formed.

Yet the dream remained in pathetic attempts to keep curtains white in grimy back rooms above East London railway yards or to grow flowers in window-boxes in Bolton and Oldham. And English history suggested that whenever for any reason Englishmen failed to find the elements of home, as they conceived them, in their own land, they tended to seek them overseas. Such had been the history of the colonization of the transatlantic virgin forests and deserts that had grown into the United States of America. Denied opportunity in their own country, a race of invincible romanticists had made new homes in the wilderness to meet their heart's desire.

The new English nations so formed had rebelled against the home government's claim to control them and had formed an independent polity of their own. Yet even in the hour of the English schism the age-long process continued. As the first Empire fell away a second grew in its place. The United Empire Loyalists, unable to fit their own conception of home into that of a rebel federation, tramped across the Canadian border to seek a new habitation in the wilderness. Here they mingled with conquered French settlers and British emigrants to form in the fullness of time the Dominion of Canada. During the next century others crossed the oceans to make homes under the British flag in Newfoundland, Cape Colony, in the islands of New Zealand and the virgin continent of Australia. Most of these emigrants were poor men who sought on a distant soil the happiness and freedom they had failed to find in their own country. The graveyards of Quebec and Montreal were piled high with British immigrants who died in the crowded holds of the immigrant ships in the terrible transatlantic passage against westerly gales. Few amid the hardship of their lot found the promised land for themselves. They left it for their children to create after them.

In this process the pioneers received small help from the imperial Government. The ruling classes at home were not interested in British settlers overseas. Their thoughts of them were coloured by the memories of the War of Independence and of the humiliations which had then befallen English statesmen. They wished to have nothing further to do with colonials. They regarded the Empire, apart from India, as a strategic network of trading factories, spice islands and naval bases in which squatters' settlements had no part. At the end of the eighteenth century they found a use for New South Wales and other territories as a dumping ground for convicts. But when this practice was eventually stopped in the 'sixties the interest of the English official classes in the colonies sank to zero.

The utilitarians had even less use for such troublesome appendages. For to their way of thinking their only function was to embroil the country in expensive foreign entanglements. The old view of the Empire as a profitable monopoly for native traders was outmoded, since it was a canon of free trade that a monopoly defeated its own ends. Even the preferential treatment of Empire producers, granted by Huskisson in 1823 in the course of a general reduction of tariffs to obtain reciprocal concessions in foreign markets, had since been discarded without regard to the interests of colonial traders. For the Benthamites held that the latter, like every one else in the utilitarian paradise, were best left to look after themselves.

This view of colonial possessions accorded with that held in official circles. 'I suppose I must take the thing myself,' Palmerston remarked to Sir Anthony Helps when he had some difficulty in filling the Colonial Office. 'Come upstairs with me, Helps, when the Council is over. We will look at the maps, and you shall show me where these places are.' Gladstone's opinion was that the Empire was too heavy a burden to be borne. Even Disraeli at one moment of his career so far fell into the fashion of the day as to refer to the colonies as millstones. They were an expense to the taxpayer, and, with their tiresome local politics, a constant source of annoyance to the official mind. For the exporter

their under-inhabited markets were valueless compared with those of
Europe, South America and the United States. Nor were they of any
use to the politician. For the colonists had no votes at home. They
even objected to the use of their chief official and magisterial appoint-
ments for uses of domestic patronage. The general view of the upper
classes was that the colonists were rough and uneducated provincials
unfit for refined company.

All that the rulers of England were prepared to do for them was to
give them their freedom. After the painful lesson of the American War
of Independence no obstacle was placed in the way of their political
development. They were given such constitutions as they desired and
quietly encouraged to go their own way. Whenever opportunity arose
they were reminded in frigid official language that the time of parting
was at hand. 'Colonies,' Turgot had written, 'are like fruits that cling
to the tree only till they ripen.' This was the view of Whitehall. A
policy of veiled but deliberate disintegration was adopted. 'It is no use
to speak about it any longer,' a Colonial Office official said to the
historian Froude. 'The thing is done. The great Colonies are gone. It
is but a question of a year or two.'

But the colonists themselves, though they had no love for Whitehall
and resented interference, wished to remain British. They wanted to
enjoy their lands of promise under the flag their fathers had known. In
other words, they were sentimental about patriotism. They refused to
view it like superior folk in England as an old-fashioned thing to smile
at. Few in numbers and without electoral influence, their protest would
have availed nothing but for one of those inexplicable movements that
occur in the lives of great nations.

It came not from the ruling classes but from the common people. For
those who thousands of miles away were building new and freer Englands
were their own kith and kin. They had left home in poverty and obscurity:
years later their success had gladdened the humble kinsmen they had left
behind. Fresh settlers were always following the old. There was formed
a link of sentiment and hope between working-class homes in Britain and
thriving townships and farms in Canada and Australia. The rich and
powerful might have no use for the self-governing colonies. To the poor
they seemed the promise of a happier future: an appeal from the black
chimneys, the herd life of the slum, the selfishness of the lords of rustic
England with their closed parks and game preserves.

It was only after 1867, when the artisan householder received the
vote, that this feeling became a political factor. Yet it was already a

rallying point for all not content to subscribe to the utilitarian thesis. The British middle-class were not all bagmen and cotton-spinners: there was Norse blood in their veins and an ineradicable love of adventure which kept cropping up under their maxims of shopkeeping prudence. Buying in the cheapest market and selling in the dearest was not everything. And as foreign tariffs rose against British manufacturers and the employment of the crowded city population became ever less secure, more and more questioned whether the utilitarian basis of the economists was not too narrow and whether the time had not come to call in a new world to redress the balance of the old.

One of the first to do so was Disraeli. At the moment when a new Europe was being born out of the national wars and uprisings of 1859, he predicted a course for his country diametrically opposed to that held in contemporary official circles:

'The day is coming, if it has not already come, when the question of the balance of power cannot be confined to Europe alone . . . England, though, she is bound to Europe by tradition, by affection, by great similarity of habits, and all those ties which time alone can create and consecrate, is not a mere Power of the Old World. Her geographical position, her laws, her language and religion, connect her as much with the New World as with the Old. And although she has occupied an eminent . . . position among European nations for ages, still, if ever Europe by her shortsightedness falls into an inferior and exhausted state, for England there will remain an illustrious future. We are bound to communities of the New World, and those great States which our own planting and colonizing energies have created, by ties and interests which will sustain our power and enable us to play as great a part in the times yet to come as we do in these days and we have done in the past. And therefore now that Europe is on the eve of war, I say it is for Europe not for England, that my heart sinks.'

Many people thought Disraeli's growing interest in the Empire an affectation. It was certainly politically prescient. Just as he was able to associate his party with the growing demand for social reform, so he was able to associate it with that other popular longing – for a new world of opportunity overseas. He understood the nature of the attempt the utilitarians were making on the unity of the Empire, and realized that working men could have little sympathy with it. Almost alone at this time – though his foresight was later equalled from the Liberal benches by that of Charles Dilke – Disraeli realized that in a fast

Above: 'The new iron ships, triumphs of the marine engineering works of the Clyde and Tyne, of Birkenhead and Belfast, were beginning to come into their own: The *Great Eastern*, the famous iron leviathan, 700 feet in length and 80 in beam, was launched at Millwall in 1858.' The *Great Eastern* leaves Southampton for New York on her first voyage, 1860.

Right: 'From Greenwich the river is nothing but a street a mile broad and upwards, where ships ascend and descend between two rows of buildings, interminable rows of a dull red . . . To the west rises an inextricable forest of yards, of masts, of rigging. These are the vessels which arrive, depart or anchor with all the tackle of incessant, regular, gigantic labour.' (Taine on the Thames.) An engraving by Gustave Doré, 1872.

'To see Victorian England really enjoying itself, no spectacle compared with the Derby.'
Derby Day by William P. Frith, 1856-58.

Above: 'On "Bloody Sunday", November 1887, long drab companies of pallid, rugged men, marching behind red banners and bands of antiquated instruments, converged in defiance of the police, from the outer slums, on Trafalgar Square; here they were repeatedly charged by massed constables with drawn batons until hundreds of skulls were cracked and bleeding. It was the first glimmer of the red light that threatened social explosion.'

Right: 'The principle of the jerry-builder was to make as quick a profit as possible on as large a turnover for as little expenditure of labour and money. The houses went up fast but they did not last. They were not meant to. They were built in rows and usually back-to-back – poky, hideous, uncomfortable and insanitary.' Back-to-back housing in Straithes, Yorkshire, late nineteenth century.

expanding Europe, an England that insisted for the sake of profit on remaining a small manufacturing island in the North Sea would presently find herself in danger from other and more despotic empires jealous of her wealth and resentful of the libertarian ideals she so light-heartedly and provocatively championed. It was this that made him the critic of those who, 'viewing everything in a financial aspect and totally passing by those moral and political considerations which make nations great,' granted self-government to the English-speaking colonies not 'as part of a great policy of imperial consolidation' but merely in order to get rid of them. His instinct of coming danger made him alive to the necessity of responding to their craving for unity before it was too late.

The wise old man saw that the world which Cobden and the great Liberals had known was yielding to a new and sterner. He knew how nearly it threatened England. In 1860, with the help of a French assault on Austria, Italy achieved unity and a place, however at first precarious, among the European Powers. In 1864, Prussia under the inspiration of a Junker squire of genius, defied the protests of a disarmed England and seized the southern provinces of Denmark with the ultimate object of building an ocean fleet. Two years later Bismarck struck at his ally, Austria, and in the course of a six weeks' *blitzkrieg* won the leadership of Germany. The formal union of a new Empire under the Prussian dynasty was completed on New Year's Day, 1871, in the Hall of Mirrors at Versailles while Moltke's shells burst on the ramparts of a besieged and starving Paris.

Of these dynamic events liberal England, dedicated to the rule of reason and the peaceful making of wealth, remained a spectator. The Europe she had helped to reshape after Waterloo crumbled before her eyes. The principle of militant nationality which she had defied so successfully in the first years of the century was triumphing in every country. With a little voluntary army of 200,000 she was left to face a continent of great conscript armies running into millions of men and actuated by motives far removed from Manchester's reckoning. Even the industrialization in which the continental nations now feverishly began to copy Britain was made to serve the ends of armed power, conceived in terms of strategic railways and gun foundries and protected by bristling tariffs. Essen was Middlesbrough in a nightmare.

Disraeli was sensitive to these mighty forces: his countrymen were not. He realized that England's present place in the world depended on the abandonment of the policy of 'meddle and muddle' so dear to liberal and humanitarian sentiment, and its replacement by her historic doctrine of balancing power against power. Still more clearly he realized that her future depended on her capacity to find an outlet for her swelling population beyond her own dangerously congested shores. Because of this he was the first statesman to grasp the significance of the great canal which French engineers built in the 'sixties across the eastern Egyptian desert to link the Red Sea with the Mediterranean. By securing for his country the bankrupt Khedive of Egypt's controlling shares in the Suez Canal Company, Disraeli during his final tenure of power placed the most vital artery in the British Empire beyond the control of an international financial power. By simultaneously opposing a renewed Russian advance on Constantinople and the Mediterranean he defended the same artery from the threat of what seemed at that time – though as many believe wrongly – the dominant European power of the future.

In doing so Disraeli was solicitous for interests still beyond the narrow ken of the average British voter and statesman. The tired imperial statesman who brought back 'peace with honour' in 1878 from the Berlin Congress unwittingly offended the humanitarian conscience of his country. It was his misfortune – many enthusiastic opponents regarded it as his fault – to have to maintain the independence of a Mohammedan despotism against an uprising of Christian peoples. To the kindly middle classes the inviolability of treaties, the balance of European power and England's strategic communications with India meant little or nothing. But the stories of the atrocities committed by Turkish irregulars in the Bulgarian provinces did. They aroused the country.

In the hands of Gladstone, the very incarnation of the English conscience, all this became a weapon to scourge a cynic in office. The north-country working man was swept off his feet by his appeal for moral righteousness. To humble minds the great Liberal's electoral campaign of 1880 seemed a crusade for the rights of small nations trampled under by the imperial aggressor, whether Turkish or English: for the sanctity of life in the hill villages of Afghanistan and in the veldt farms of the Transvaal. 'Amidst the din of preparation for warfare in the time of peace,' Gladstone declared in his final speech at Edinburgh, 'there is going on a profound mysterious movement that, whether we will or not, is bringing the nations of the civilized world, as well as the uncivilized, morally as well as physically nearer to one another; and making them more and more responsible before God for one another's welfare.'

The truth of this could not be resolved by statesmen. Its force lay in the fact that in his heart the ordinary Englishman believed it. The defeated and now dying Disraeli, whom the harsh experience of his race and a long life of struggle had made a realist, might have replied that there was no such instrument for bringing it about as the united and consistent policy of a world-wide commonwealth of peace-loving British nations.

*   *   *

Because Englishmen wished to exercise power not for its own sake but to further moral causes, Gladstone, on assuming office in 1880, found himself involved in remote imperial adventures. Having no imperial policy, he was at a loss in meeting them. Among the charges brought against Disraeli by his opponents had been that of scheming to occupy Egypt. Yet it was Gladstone who actually, and most reluctantly, did so.

Egypt was an independent tributary province of the Turkish Empire. In 1876, being unable to wring any more out of his over-taxed people or to raise further capital to pay the interest on his debts, its ruler, the spendthrift Khedive Ismail, agreed to the appointment of a British and a French Controller-General of Finance to safeguard the hundred million pounds he had borrowed from French and British capitalists. Three years later as Ismail, unable to break with his prodigal habits, intrigued against his financial advisers, Britain and France induced his overlord, the Sultan of Turkey, to depose him in favour of his son.

This measure of foreign financial control was enough to provoke the resentment of the Egyptian aristocracy and army. In 1882 a military adventurer named Arabi Pasha established a military dictatorship, and the Alexandria mob beat up and murdered foreigners. Save for remote outbreaks in China, the world was still unused to such popular jackboot reactions to the operations of international capital. The first 'fascist dictator' was dealt with by Gladstone's pacific government in the old vigorous John Bull manner. British tars bombarded Alexandria, and an expeditionary force under Sir Garnet Wolseley routed Arabi at Tel-el-Kebir. The French, fearful of another attack from Germany, preserved their freedom of action and left their British partners to act alone.

Having entered Egypt to restore order the latter were forced to stay to maintain it. For the only alternative was mob rule. The Khedive was restored to a nominal authority. Vague suzerainty continued to be vested in the Sultan of Turkey. But for the next quarter of a century the real ruler of Egypt was the British Agent and Consul General, Sir Evelyn Baring, later Lord Cromer. He was supported by British officials and soldiers.

Up to this point the Egyptian adventure had been prompted by financial interests. Capital, being free to operate where its owners chose, strayed outside the imperial field in its pursuit of profits. Its interest payments taking the form of imports on which the employment of British voters depended, any government which valued its existence was forced to use its diplomatic influence to maintain them. Where such influence provoked national reactions, military intervention became necessary to avert anarchy and punish outrages against British subjects.

Finance had led Britain into Egypt. Love of humanity and liberty impelled her next step. Almost immediately Gladstone was forced into further expansionist action by the moral forces from which he derived his authority. They sent Gordon to a martyr's death at Khartoum and Kitchener in the fullness of time to establish a new equatorial dominion in the heart of Africa.

The Sudan, stretching nearly 2000 miles south from Egypt along the Upper Nile, was an Egyptian province. The misrule of corrupt officials and the depredations of savage warriors and slave-traders had long been its lot. Shortly before the British occupation of Cairo the unhappy country was seized by a religious fanatic, the Mahdi. An Egyptian army, sent to restore order, was cut to pieces in the desert.

For this hell on earth Gladstone's government now found itself responsible. Feeling not unnaturally that a liberal Britain had no business there, it resolved on a policy of immediate evacuation. But, though nine out of ten Englishmen had never heard of the Sudan, many of the Government's most valued supporters were deeply interested in it. To the humanitarians of Exeter Hall it was a stronghold of the slave trade, a field for missionaries and the home of certain poor Christian converts.

In deference to their wishes Gladstone sent to the Sudan one who, while formerly its Governor General under Khedive Ismail, had won merit in their eyes by his Christian vigour in repressing the slave trade.

General Gordon was a strange soldier – half-crusader, half-adventurer – but he was also a genius. His instructions were to withdraw the Christians and all remaining British and Egyptian subjects. But he deliberately interpreted them in such a fashion as to secure his own martyrdom in the Sudanese capital and the tardy dispatch of an eleventh-hour expeditionary force to relieve him and the country to which he had given his heart. Gladstone's natural reluctance to rescue this unjust but heroic steward aroused a wave of moral and patriotic indignation. After the fall of Khartoum he found himself regarded almost as a murderer. He had tried to refrain from action in the Sudan because he wished to avoid extending the already vast empire of Britain. But the very humanitarians who applauded his dislike of imperialism could not refrain from using the national might to suppress wrong-doing and cruelty. They hated force. But when it came to the point they hated slavery more. They did the hating and the soldiers they deplored did the fighting. And the end of it was a still larger empire than before.

This contradiction lay at the root of Britain's imperial difficulties. It was not practicable for a democracy which both indulged strong moral feelings and allowed its wealth to be used in large-scale operations outside its own borders, to govern an empire without an imperial policy. The only result was to provoke confused and angry situations in which the pressure of popular opinion compelled more violent imperial action than any originally contemplated. The bounds of empire continued to expand because its energies, moral and commercial, were never canalized in any clearly defined channel. Sometimes the force that made for expansion was God, sometimes Mammon. But it was nearly always a confused force.

Nothing illustrated this so well as the history of South Africa. Britain had first appeared at the Cape during the war with the French Directory when her ally Holland, being overrun by the enemy, the Prince of Orange asked her to take the Dutch colony under her protection. Restored to Holland by the Treaty of Amiens, the Cape – the chief port of call on the ocean route to India – was reoccupied by British troops on the renewal of hostilities. This time the Dutch colonists resisted, but in vain. After the war the Cape was retained by Britain as one of her few territorial rewards for her long struggle against Napoleon.

The Cape Dutch would probably have accepted the situation and have become loyal British citizens like the French Canadians but for one circumstance. They incurred the enmity of those very elements in

England who might have been expected to defend their rights against over-zealous imperial administrators. For unhappily the Dutch attitude towards the South African native was different from that of the English humanitarian. The latter viewed him as a defenceless black brother whose welfare was a sacred trust. The Dutch farmer thought of him as a dangerous savage who could only be kept from vice and idleness by strong paternal discipline and a liberal use of the whip. Of the two views that of the Dutch was perhaps founded on the wearying closer knowledge of the Cape Hottentot. But if the Dutch farmer was the man on the spot, the English middle-class humanitarian was the man who had the vote. The British Government inevitably interpreted the views of the latter.

Sooner than suffer interference with their ancient rights and ways of life many Dutch left the Cape and trekked into the interior wilderness. Here they made new homes and founded two independent republics. But they were not allowed to enjoy peace, for they were represented by Exeter Hall as carrying fire and sword into the hereditary lands of the Kaffir, Basuto and Zulu. There was truth in both points of view.' But interpreted by the strong if reluctant arm of the imperial Government, that of the evangels of human equality and brotherhood usually prevailed in the end. The pity was that it did not always correspond with the facts as known to those on the spot. The British liberal voter genuinely cared for the welfare of the South African native. But he knew little of South Africa. Having no imperial principle or interest in the Empire he did not trouble to learn.

In this he and his rulers were to blame. For no aversion to imperial responsibility could alter the fact that they were morally responsible for the peace of South Africa. To interfere on behalf of their own ideological convictions and simultaneously to refuse to take any long view of imperial policy on the ground that imperialism was expensive and morally wrong was to light a fire on the veldt and leave it. Yet this was the habit of the English humanitarian left for more than a century.

This hiatus in the application of moral principle to the government of an Empire again and again vitiated the history of British South Africa. In 1852 an attempt was made by a treaty with the Boers to stabilize the situation. Britain agreed to 'meddle no more beyond the Orange River and to leave the Dutch and the natives to settle their differences among themselves.' Yet seventeen year later Gladstone's first administration, yielding to the pressure of humanitarian supporters, intervened in breach of treaty to protect the Basutos against the Boers of the Orange Free State. Two years later it broke faith with the Dutch again, annexing Griqualand to satisfy not missionaries but prospectors. The diamond diggings – the richest in the world – which had been discovered on a Dutch farm beside the Vaal river, were named after the Liberal Colonial Secretary, Lord Kimberley. But, despite the production of a highly dubious treaty with a native chief, the annexation was repudiated by the Dutch electors of the Cape. To complete the circle of ill-will, the natives in the new occupied territory were armed by the British against the local farmers.

Almost as imperfectly informed about the internal situation of South Africa as Gladstone's Government, but animated by a different ideal, Disraeli's Administration of 1874-80 applied imperial instead of humanitarian principles. The Colonial Secretary, Lord Carnarvon, satisfied that the union of Dutch and English was the only solution of the African problem, paid compensation to the Orange Free State for the loss of Griqualand and admitted the wrong done. But ill-advised as to the local facts and impatient to effect a federation of South Africa before the swing of the political pendulum should put a term to his office, he sent Sir Bartle Frere to the Cape with a premature mandate to unite the two races. Ignoring the accumulated animosities of generations and without waiting for the reviving trust of the Dutch to mature, he allowed its peril from Zulu tribes to be made an opportunity to annex the bankrupt Boer republic of the Transvaal. Shortly afterwards in 1879 Britain became involved in a costly war with the Zulus.

In the general election of 1880 the Liberals for the first time professed sympathy with the Dutch and promised to reverse the Transvaal annexation. This, however, they subsequently felt themselves unable to do. 'If Cyprus and Transvaal,' Gladstone had declared during the election, 'were as valuable as they are valueless, I would repudiate them because they are obtained by means dishonourable to the character of the country.' After the election, he explained that he meant the word 'repudiate' in the sense of dislike. The Boers, freed by British arms from the fear of Zulu massacre, rose in defence of their freedom. The Government, torn between its aversion to imperial conquest and its desire to pursue its own native policy in the former Boer territories, failed to give its commander-in-chief sufficient support. On February 27th, 1881, Sir George Colley with a small force was cut to pieces by the Boer farmers at Majuba. Gladstone, with great moral courage but at a serious sacrifice of prestige, thereupon agreed to grant virtual independence to the Transvaal. The British at the Cape were left smarting under a sense of humiliation and injured patriotism. The Dutch both in the Boer republic and the Cape Colony and Natal were left with an even more dangerous contempt for the courage and tenacity of the British.

*　　*　　*

The difficulty of ruling an empire while disbelieving in the virtues of imperial rule involved the Liberals in difficulties nearer home and for which they were not to blame. Ireland was the *damnosa hereditas* of British politics. Deep in the Irish heart, whether in Ireland itself or in England, America or the Colonies, survived the memory of ancient and terrible wrongs. Sir James Sexton, whose father was evicted from the Vale of Avoca in the 'forties by an absentee landlord and whose maternal grandparents had been driven out of Ireland into industrial Lancashire by the religious and political persecutions that followed the Rebellion of 1798 wrote in his autobiography. 'The story of those days of terror was handed on to the children of all who endured their agony; it spread all over the world, and engendered in the mind of every Irishman and Irishwoman who heard it hatred – bitter and boundless hatred – of everything connected with Britain and the British. That, so far as my mind was concerned, was my principal political and spiritual inheritance.' No kindly intentions or benevolent acts of English Liberals could wipe out this all too persistent past. The pig-nosed 'Paddies' in their high hats, tight breeches and ragged tail-coats who ambushed evicting landlords and chased their agents with shillelaghs and shot-guns across the stony fields of Kerry and Clare; the Fenians or Republican Brothers who took fearful oaths and plotted in every part of the world and even invaded Canada from the United States; the invisible dynamiters and 'Manchester martyrs' who swung from the English gallows tree for murder and arson were the terror and bugbear of the respectable English in the prosperous middle years of Queen Victoria's reign.

In vain did a just Gladstone sternly and righteously offer up the Irish Church to an ungrateful Irish priest and peasant. In vain did successive governments vote grants to Catholic colleges and pass land reform acts to protect the Irish tenant. Between the English humanitarian and the credulous, priest-led 'Paddy' whom he wished to befriend and civilize a great gulf was fixed. The former did his best to believe in the existence of a body of loyal, respectable and peace-loving Irish ready to enrol as special constables against the Fenians, whose bloody and senseless doings outraged the peace and fair name of their country. Such Irishmen did exist, but they were Orangemen: black, Protestant Ulstermen from the grim north – an object of detestation to every southern Irish patriot.

The Irish wished to avenge themselves on the English. The English wished to let bygones be bygones and, though they would never admit they were in the wrong, to make amends for the past by making the Irish comfortable. The Irish did not want to be comfortable. They wanted to make the English uncomfortable. Above all they wanted to be rid of the English and their benevolent, insulting ministrations: they wanted to be free. The English could not afford to let the Irish be free. Ireland lay across England's lifeline. An Ireland in the hands of a stranger might one day mean death for England.

All through the middle years of the century a new Ireland was waking. Among a little minority in Dublin it was an Ireland of poets and scholars fired by a passionate dream of their country's future. Celtic Ireland, the Poland of the Western world, would be a nation once more. For the great majority, the motive power was a dull and sullen hatred: an angry resolve that spread in aimless trickles of murder and outrage over a dark, haunted land. They could do nothing without a leader. And a nation born of a long time of degraded, landless, persecuted peasants – feckless, cynically jesting and despairing – bred rebels more readily than leaders.

Yet the leader was forthcoming. He was a Protestant, an aristocrat and a landowner: the last man in the world any one would have predicted as a lawgiver to poor, squalid, rebel Ireland. He despised the arts of the demagogue: loathed crowds and politicians, and had an icy pride and reserve which few even of his closest lieutenants could penetrate. But he had three supreme assets: brilliant intellectual power, unshakeable resolve and a cold burning passion which nothing could quench. That icy flame Charles Stewart Parnell applied for twenty years to a single task: the breaking of the link that bound Ireland to England.

His work began in the 'seventies when he first entered the House of Commons as member for County Meath. Until that time the Irish members had been an ineffective body, regarded by the desperate men who rode the stormy anarchy of Irish assassination and land agitation as helpless prisoners of England. Parnell realized from the first that the key to the Irish future lay at Westminster. If he could weld the four score or more members whom Catholic Ireland returned to the imperial Parliament into a single disciplined body, he might use the balanced rivalry of the English parties to wring legal concessions that would open the road to Irish independence.

In the new Parliament of 1880 Parnell began to make his power felt. He discovered that by taking advantage of the intricate rules of parliamentary procedure which had grown up in the course of centuries, he could trepan the conservative English with their own love of legality. His quick penetrating mind made him master of these, and he taught his followers how to use them. There ensued an extraordinary situation. Night after night the most dignified and orderly parliamentary assembly in the world was held up by an interminable succession of unnecessary speeches, questions and interruptions as Irish member after member rose to delay business. The administration of a great Empire was hamstrung because, through an irony of fate, a handful of resolute and alien obstructionists happened to be members of its sovereign assembly.

By his success Parnell achieved two things. He became the most hated man in England. He united the Irish nationalists. It became realized that the battle of wits that the Irish members were waging nightly at Westminster was a struggle for the rebirth of a nation. It was more. It was a gauntlet flung down to England and her age-long dominion. The eyes of the entire world turned towards that little, mighty arena.

The Nationalist Party in Parliament had its counterpart in Ireland. The Land League, though not founded by him, also marched at Parnell's orders. The one aimed at destroying the rule of Ireland by the English Parliament: the other her exploitation by the English landlord. The League was an association of Catholic tenant farmers and peasants against the Protestant landowning garrison which had given local rule to Ireland since the seventeenth century. It prescribed rents, banned or 'boycotted' all who paid more and made the taking of a farm from which a member had been evicted a social crime. 'When a man takes a farm from which another has been ejected,' Parnell told his followers in September, 1880, 'you must show him on the roadside, you must show him in the streets, you must show him at the shop counter, you must show him in the fair and in the market place, and even in the house of worship, by leaving him severely alone, by isolating him from his kind as if he were a leper of old – you must show him your detestation of the crime he has committed, and you may depend on it that there will be no man so full of avarice, so lost to shame, as to dare the public opinion of all right-thinking men, and to transgress your unwritten code of laws.' It was accompanied inevitably, though this was contrary to Parnell's wishes, by gang intimidation, cattle-maiming, rick-burning and murder.

The Liberal rulers of Britain were in a quandary. They wished well to Ireland. They hated coercion. But they were also men of peace and lovers of parliamentary government. They could not see law and order flouted and the democratic machinery of Parliament sabotaged. They were forced against their will to act. They tried suspending the Habeas Corpus Act and putting Parnell in Kilmainham Gaol. By doing so they made him a martyr and themselves tyrants. As soon as they released him he continued the struggle. They were driven to limit the freedom of parliamentary debate and to abandon part of the democratic practice of centuries. They only heightened Parnell's prestige. Ireland thrilled at the tale of his triumphs in the very temple of the Saxon tyrant. To aid his campaign thousands of pounds poured in from Irish sympathizers in America.

But the greatest of Parnell's conquests was Gladstone's conscience. Gladstone was a devout churchman and a man of splendid probity of life. Parnell was a concealed adulterer. Yet Parnell made Gladstone ashamed. And what Gladstone's conscience felt to-day, England's conscience would feel to-morrow. In 1882 the 73-year-old Prime Minister, appalled by the difficulty of governing Ireland and controlling the Irish members, wrote to his Irish Secretary that so long as there were no responsible bodies in Ireland with which a British Government could deal, every plan framed to help them came to Irishmen as an English plan. It was therefore probably condemned: at best regarded as a one-sided bargain which bound the English but not the Irish. Because of the miserable and almost total want of responsibility for public welfare and peace in Ireland, reform was impossible. Such a sense of responsibility could only be created through local self-government. 'If we say we must postpone the question till the state of the country is more fit for it, I should answer that the least danger is in going forward at once. It is liberty alone which fits men for liberty.' The faith of a Liberal was never more nobly expressed.

For Gladstone's mind, more sincerely wed to the conception of freedom than that of any of his followers, had grasped the logic of the Irish situation. Either England must rule the subject peoples of her Empire according to her own moral standards and through strong and consistent imperial policy, or she must make no attempt to impose her ways of life, however noble, on others and trust to liberty to teach its own lesson. Gladstone believed in liberty and was prepared to rely on it. He was even prepared to give it to the Irish.

To initiate a new departure in Irish policy, he therefore released Parnell from Kilmainham Gaol, and appointed Lord Frederick Cavendish, his beloved niece's husband and the most sympathetic figure among the younger members of the House, as Chief Secretary for Ireland. Four days after Parnell's release Lord Frederick was murdered by Fenian assassins as he walked home across Phoenix Park.

It was a mark of Gladstone's growing greatness that he allowed neither this terrible crime nor the crop of Irish dynamite outrages in England in the following year to deflect him from his purpose. Others, including Liberal elements in the Tory Party, who were influenced by the example of the self-governing colonies, were moving in the same direction. In 1885, when the balance between the major parties was sufficiently even to give the eighty-six Irish members under Parnell's leadership a deciding voice in a new Parliament, he let it be known that he proposed to introduce a scheme of Home Rule for Ireland.

Had the question only been political, Gladstone would probably have carried his measure. The religious issue split the Liberal majority. Though religion as a political factor was a dying force in England, there were many of Gladstone's followers who could not look unmoved on the subjection of a Protestant minority to a Catholic majority. In such a case the democratic formula was somehow inadequate. The little handful of Whig aristocrats who still provided leaders for the Liberal Party derived their lands and honours from the glorious day when a Protestant Prince delivered England from a Catholic King. From the conquests of that Prince the Orange patriots of Ulster still boasted their claim to be the ruling faction in Ireland.

If the right wing of the Liberal Party could not conscientiously drive Ulster out of a Protestant union into a Papist province, nor could the left. Nonconformity, with its strong local organization, was still a mighty power in the land. Though fast mellowing into humanitarianism, its historic inspiration had always been hatred of Popery. Its political leader was the uncrowned king of Birmingham, radical Joe Chamberlain. Though a man of wide sympathies who had looked with a lenient eye on Irish rebel aspirations – perhaps because he had so many himself – he now showed himself a true mirror of provincial middle-class England. Sooner than endorse Home Rule, he resigned from the Cabinet and joined hands with the Whig leader, Lord Hartington, to raise the fiery cross of Protestant and imperial unity.

When the Home Rule Bill came up for its second reading, more than a hundred Liberals voted against the Government or absented themselves. Defeated by thirty votes, Gladstone appealed to the country. Protestant scruples, patriotic pride and the fear and hatred engendered by the long Irish campaign of violence and intimidation were stronger even than his courage and magnetism. Three hundred and sixteen Conservatives and 78 Liberal 'Unionists' were returned, but only 191 Gladstonian Liberals.

The decision was vital. The English democracy had refused to allow the Irish the right to govern themselves. Though for a further nine years Gladstone laboured to reverse that decision, giving all his immense powers to this single task, fate was against him. In 1890 Parnell's divorce case shattered the unity of the Irish Nationalist Party. 'For five years I have rolled this stone patiently uphill,' Gladstone complained, 'and it is now rolled to the bottom again, and I am 81 years old.' Yet even then the old man would not give in. His venerable courage almost won over England in spite of itself. In the autumn of 1892 an election brought him back to office with a chance of carrying Home Rule with the help of Irish votes. But as the dreaded hour of separation drew near opposition in the country became intense. *Punch* depicted an aged and sworded pilgrim advancing along a narrow ridge called Home Rule with the bog of Irish Nationalism on one side and the last ditch of Orange resistance on the other. After scraping through the Commons, the Bill was rejected by an overwhelming majority in the Lords. An appeal to the country would certainly have endorsed their decision. Soon afterwards Gladstone, 84 years of age and almost blind, laid down his burden.

With him died the last hope of self-government for Ireland for a generation. In its place she received a course of strong Conservative 'repression' and of enlightened agrarian reform which, applied half a century earlier, might have made her a contented province like Wales. But the hopes aroused by Parnell's fire and Gladstone's intensity were not to be stilled by Balfour's elegant firmness or George Wyndham's squirearchal benevolence. The resolve of the Irish to be free persisted and grew acid for the waiting. Their hour came in 1910 when English internal divisions and an even electoral balance between the parties once more made the Irish Nationalist members arbiters at Westminster. Making Home Rule the price of their support, they assisted one English faction to make a fundamental change in the constitution to spite another. They then demanded their price. The guttering candle of English Protestantism was by that time too dim to light another religious crusade to save the Irish Protestants. Though Ulster swore to fight, Home Rule was granted. But it was too late. The Irish ulcer had become too inflamed to be cured by any minor operation. In 1916 the Irish took up arms against the age-long oppressor. In 1922, still fighting, they achieved their independence.

CHAPTER TWELVE

Lest We Forget!

'Far-called, our navies melt away;
On dune and headland sinks the fire:
Lo, all our pomp of yesterday
Is one with Nineveh and Tyre!'
Kipling

UNTIL THE FIRST REJECTION of Home Rule in the 'eighties, the British people had shown no consciousness of the necessity for an imperial policy. But during the two decades of Conservative supremacy which followed Gladstone's defeat, they had become increasingly aware of the Empire. For the big steamer, the electric telegraph, the inventions of Marconi, were making the world a smaller place. They even made a united commonwealth scattered haphazard over its surface seem a practical possibility.

A few scholars and dreamers began the fashion that made men think in a new way. In 1883, John Seeley, Regius Professor of Modern History at Cambridge, published his lectures on the Expansion of England. His theme was that the outward spread of the English race had been the main human trend of the past three centuries. If England was wise enough to recognize her chance, her future could be more glorious even than her past. If she neglected it she would decline like Rome and Spain and see her commercial wealth pass to younger rivals. For the potamic and thalassic ages had been succeeded by an oceanic, and the future of the world lay, not with the small nation states of the past, but with composite world states like the USA and Russia linked by the new forces of steam and electricity.

It was a question not of lust for power or empire, but of common sense and civic responsibility. If the race were to survive in a changing world, its leaders must secure the conditions necessary for it to do so. Already hundreds of thousands in Britain were hungry and in need of work and living space. Yet they could have both for the asking: their heritage was already made. 'It may be true that the mother country of this great Empire is crowded, but in order to relieve the pressure it is not necessary for us, as if we were Goths or Turcomans, to seize upon the territory of our neighbours . . . It is only necessary to take possession of boundless territories in Canada, South Africa and Australia where already our language is spoken, our religion professed, and our laws established. If there is pauperism in Wiltshire and Dorsetshire, this is but complementary to unowned wealth in Australia. On the one side there are men without property, on the other there is property waiting for men.'

Three years later Seeley's work, which ran through many editions, was followed by one even more widely read. The historian Froude's *Oceana* was named after the seventeenth-century Harrington's dream of an English 'commonwealth for increase . . . embraced in the arms of ocean.' It described a voyage to the Cape, Australia and New Zealand, and compared the freedom and opportunity of a young country like Australia – an England set free from limitations of space where he never met a hungry man or saw a discontented face – with the slums which every year were engulfing a larger part of the English race – 'miles upon miles of squalid lanes, each house the duplicate of its neighbour; the dirty street in front, the dirty yard behind, the fetid smell from the ill-made sewers, the public-house at the street corner.' Posing the age-long question that the utilitarians had ignored, he asked what sort of men and women urban England was breeding to succeed the generations who had made her great?

The British could not survive only as factory drudges forced by hunger to be eternally manufacturing shirts and coats, tools and engines for the happier part of mankind. Like a tree a nation had to breathe through its extremities. 'A mere manufacturing England, standing stripped and bare in the world's market-place and caring only to make wares for the world to buy,' was a pollard tree. The life was going out of it.

The colonists were already Britain's best customers, buying from her in proportion to their tiny population three times more than any stranger. They would not always be a mere ten and a half millions, weak and scattered. The Prime Minister of Victoria predicted in 1885 that in half a century at its present rate of development Australia alone would have a population of fifty millions. Should danger ever come to England, the colonists' response would be unquestioning and automatic.

Above: Gladstone by Sir John Millais, 1879. 'Gladstone was a devout churchman and a man of splendid probity of life. What Gladstone's conscience felt to-day, England's conscience would feel to-morrow.'

Above right: Benjamin Disraeli, 1st Earl of Beaconsfield, by Sir John Millais, 1881. 'He realized that England's present place in the world depended on the abandonment of the policy of "meddle and muddle" so dear to liberal and humanitarian sentiment, and its replacement by her historic doctrine of balancing power against power.'

Right: Charles Stewart Parnell: 'He was a Protestant, an aristocrat and a landowner: the last man in the world any one would have predicted as a lawgiver to poor, squalid, rebel Ireland. But he had three supreme assests: brilliant intellectual power, unshakable resolve, and a cold burning passion which nothing could quench.'

Above: Joseph Chamberlain in 1885. 'This dapper ex-radical and Brummagem hardware merchant with the frock-coat, monocle and orchid infused a new spirit into imperial administration. A businessman of initiative and energy, in the days when business still required both, he sought to make the Empire pay by making it efficient. But he took the long view of efficiency, looking to the interests not merely of the living but of the unborn.'

Above right: 'Rudyard Kipling did more than tell stories. He told his readers to think imperially. His message was not of opportunity but of duty and destiny.' A portrait by Sir Philip Burne Jones, 1899.

Right: This was Rhodes' favourite photograph of himself. He was only 49 when he died. 'So little done, so much to do.'

Froude did not advocate imperial federation. The time was not ripe for it. Nor was it needed. What mattered was that the patriotism of the colonies should be reciprocated. It was because they valued the imperial tie so much that they felt the sting in the suggestion of parting. Their attachment might not always be proof against contemptuous hints from frigid aristocrats and civil servants to take themselves away. Indifference might produce indifference.

Britain was refusing her destiny. There might be no second chance. 'Were Canada and South Africa and Australia and New Zealand members of one body with us,' Froude wrote, 'we might sit secure against shifts and changes.' Without them a little overcrowded island would not be able to support its people or assure them the kind of life that made free men. Already in her squalid mushroom cities multitudes were growing up pale and stunted or were leaving her shores in despair. For lack of an imperial policy four-fifths of those who emigrated went to the United States, frequently in association with British capital invested there. Other nations – Russia, Germany and United States – were seeking new territories to provide for their people's future. England alone, in her materialist absorption with the present, seemed indifferent to hers.

Yet in her splendid past she had unconsciously made provision for it, 'in the fairest spots upon the globe where there was still soil and sunshine; where the race might for ages renew its mighty youth, bring forth as many millions as it would and still have means to breed and rear them strong as the best which she produced in her early prime. The colonists might be paying no revenue but they were opening up the face of the earth. By and by, like the spreading branches of a forest tree, they would return the sap which they were gathering into the heart. England could pour out among them, in return, year after year, those poor children of hers now choking in fetid alleys, and, relieved of the strain, breathe again fresh air into her own smoke-encrusted lungs. With her colonies part of herself, she would be, as Harrington had foreshadowed, a commonwealth resting on the mightiest foundations which the world had ever seen. Queen among the nations, from without invulnerable, and at peace and at health within – this was the alternative future before Oceana.'

Froude was an old man with his historian's heart rooted in the past. He was no friend to democracy: he feared its destructive influences. But he ended his book with an appeal to the masses with whom future power lay to be wiser than the calico and hardware merchants they were supplanting. The other great Anglo-Saxon democracy sooner than forfeit its future had shed the blood of half a million of its sons to preserve the Union. The continuance of a commonwealth of freemen was worth some sacrifice.

That was in 1886. Four years later came the biggest literary sensation since the appearance of *Pickwick*. A young man of genius born in Bombay 'between the palms and the sea' and bred half in India, half in England, painted the life of the Anglo-Indian community for his countrymen: the colour, scent and sound of the East, the crowded bazaar opening for the sahib's horse, the contrast with the grey, suburban, northern island from which the characters of his witty, glittering, malicious stories hailed. Since the day when Lord Craven drew his interminable cocoa trees for Harriette Wilson, the English had been bored by tales of their own Empire. And here was a young journalist, still in his early twenties, who could cause a run on them in every circulating library in London.

But Rudyard Kipling did more than tell stories. He told his readers to think imperially. His message was not of opportunity but of duty and destiny. From its hallowed centre at Westminster – 'where the Abbey makes us we' – to the fringed palm and the snow-capped fort at the outer circumference, the Empire was a vast trust of humanity. 'The white man's burden' constituted the peculiar contribution to human progress of the Anglo-Saxon race. Despite its strident energy, Kipling's work was as moral in its purpose as Milton's or Bunyan's. A French critic André Chevrillon, realized this more clearly than Kipling's own countrymen. 'Kipling, of all the great living writers of his country, stands alone for the absolute in ethics, with a militant faith. A Wells, a Shaw, a Bennett, a Galsworthy, serve other gods, the gods of reason or sentiment. Kipling's work appeals to our will . . .; he is the teacher of conduct.' His aim was to remind Englishmen of their duty, by relating the vigour, courage and pathos of those who dedicated undemonstrative lives to a great ruling tradition. 'As to my notions of imperialism, I learned them from men who mostly cursed their work, but always carried it through to the end, under difficult surroundings, without help or acknowledgement.'

With Kipling as with all the great English moralists, duty was no mere negative virtue – a prudent, middle-class insurance against Hell. It was a mighty force, giving life, poetry and fire as it did to the Hebrew poets of old. His vision of the English was of a race finding its destiny in free surrender, self-training and self-dedication to a divine purpose.

In his hymn of the old Scots engineer McAndrew, published in 1893, he epitomized it as: 'Law, Order, Duty and Restraint, Obedience, Discipline.'

But the man who above all others turned the thoughts of his countrymen to the Empire they had neglected or taken for granted was not a writer. Cecil Rhodes was born on July 5th 1853, the fifth son of a Hertfordshire vicarage. He was one of a line of small gentry and yeomen farmers: his forebears, he loved to boast, kept cows at Islington.

Though his elder brothers went to Eton and Winchester, the family resources restricted Cecil to the local grammar school. When he was sixteen, having developed a tendency to consumption, he was sent to join an elder brother on a Natal cotton farm. On a summer's day in 1870 he landed at Durban – a shy, tall, fair-headed lad, as lonely as Robert Clive at his first coming to Madras.

After a year of unsuccessful farming he followed his brother across the high veld to the new diamond diggings at Kimberley. Here he spent the next two years in a crazy community of rough diggers from every corner of the earth, Jewish speculators and native labourers; mud holes, mud slides, refuse dumps and tin roofs. In this school he learnt to know mankind.

As the youthful Kipling was impressed by the alternate scenes of England and India – the little, crowded, fog-bound island and the vast glittering empire it ruled by force of character – so Rhodes responded to the mining camp of Dutoitspan. He came back to England to complete his education with a profound sense of the honesty, kindliness and courage of the ordinary Englishman. While at Oxford, paying his fees by periodic visits to the diggings, he conceived a burning desire to further the expansion of his race. It was at the time that Ruskin, as Slade Professor, was firing the imagination of a new generation of undergraduates by lectures on their country's destiny, telling them that they were still undegenerate in race and blood, not yet dissolute in temper, with the firmness to govern and the grace to obey. 'Will you youths of England,' he asked, 'make your country again a royal throne of kings, a sceptred isle, for all the world a source of light, a centre of peace; mistress of learning and of the arts, faithful guardian of time-tried principles, under temptation from fond experiments and licentious desires; and amidst the cruel and clamorous jealousies of the nations, worshipped in her strange valour of goodwill towards men? . . . This is what England must either do or perish. She must find colonies as fast and as far as she is able, formed of her most energetic and worthiest men; seizing any piece of fruitful waste ground she can set her foot on, and there teaching her colonists that their chief virtue is to be fidelity to their country . . . If we can get men, for little pay, to cast themselves against cannon mouths for love of England, we may find men also who will plough and sow for her, who will behave kindly and righteously for her, and who will bring up their children to love her . . .'

Rhodes did not doubt Ruskin's message. He linked it to his own experience, and to the healthy, empty uplands of the South African hinterland which he had seen on his travels – lands where Englishmen could live, labour and multiply without injury to others. To win those lands for England and to awaken the imagination of his countrymen to their possibilities was to be his life's work. He went further. Since the English at their best almost alone possessed the three attributes which seemed to him to express most nearly the divine will – a sense of justice, a respect for liberty and a love of peace – the next stage in human evolution could best be accomplished through the peaceful expansion of the Anglo-Saxon race. Like Milton, Rhodes held that if God wanted a thing done He sent for his Englishman.

With the crazy arrogance of youth he began to preach his creed while still at Oxford. With debts pouring in and the pump on his claim in the flooded diggings at Kimberley breaking down, he drew up a will – the first of many – in which he left a still non-existent fortune to found a secret society to spread the British rule into every unclaimed part of the earth where white men could live by their own labour. The whole Anglo-Saxon race was comprised in his grandiose dream; there was to be an end to the eighteenth-century 'schism,' a reunion, if necessary under the Stars and Stripes, complete freedom and self-government for every part of the vast commonwealth so formed, an imperial Parliament and internal free trade. This great achievement in human co-operation would guarantee the permanent peace of the world. 'I contend,' he wrote, 'that we are the first race in the world, and that the more of the world we inhabit, the better it is for the human race. I contend that every acre added to our territory provides for the birth of more of the English race who otherwise would not be brought into existence. Added to which the absorption of the greater portion of the world under our rule simply means the end of all wars.'

There was nothing unusual in a young man dreaming dreams. What was extraordinary was the speed and consistency with which Rhodes put them into practice. In an age when money had become power, he decided that nothing could be achieved without cash – 'the needful,' as he called it. He proceeded to make himself the richest man in the Empire. At 27 he founded the De Beers Mining Company with a capital of £200,000. Within eight years he was dictator of the South African diamond industry. Six years later, at the age of 41, he had achieved a similar position in the new gold-mining industry of the Johannesburg Rand.

His enormous wealth, and the power it gave him, Rhodes did not devote to personal or vulgar ends. Seeking, as he expressed it, to combine the commercial and the imaginative, he still pursued his dream. To his contemporaries there was something staggering, and to many even incredible, in the spectacle of a nineteenth-century specu-lator 'spending the profits of a mining company on the development of an empire.' Yet this was precisely what Rhodes did. 'And the fun is,' he loved to say, 'we make Beit pay!' But his friend Alfred Beit, hard-headed Hebrew and shrewd financier as he was, never grudged a penny. He knew Rhodes, honoured his vision and loved him; and his devoted service to Rhodes's ideal continued after death.

> 'The friend he loved he served through good and ill,
> The man struck down, he served his memory still,
> Nor toiling asked more recompense of fame
> Than to be coupled with another's name.'

As part of the task he had set himself Rhodes entered Cape politics. His success was as dazzling as in business: there seemed no resisting his energy and charm. At 36 he became Prime Minister of the Cape Colony. He had two objects: the expansion of British rule into the northern hinterland, and the union of British and Dutch in a federal South Africa.

To gain the first he had to fight against time. The early 'eighties saw the last scramble of the European powers, all fast industrializing themselves, for unclaimed lands of settlement which might afford them raw materials and new markets. The African interior, recently opened by the missionary explorations of men like Livingstone, offered the last unoccupied territories of size in the world. To the north-western deserts of South Africa came in 1884 the armed and bustling pioneers of Bismarck's Germany. Their annexation of Damara and Namaqua struck a blow at Rhodes's dream. For between the new German South-West Africa and the two straggling, ever-expanding Boer republics lay only a narrow corridor of disputed land linking Cape Colony with the uplands of the African hinterland which Rhodes coveted for the settlement of his race. If the British did not speedily secure the missionaries' road through Bechuanaland to the empty north, the intriguing, ambitious German and the stubborn, jealous Boer would join hands and shut them out for ever from their lands of promise.

It was the same situation which had confronted the American colonists in the eighteenth century when the French in Canada and Florida had sought to join hands along the Ohio valley and so cut off the Anglo-Saxon community from the interior. Had the French succeeded the future of the world would have been changed. Rhodes, a young man of 31 in the very thick of his struggle with fortune, saw himself at such a juncture of history. Neither his countrymen at the Cape nor in England shared his vision. He had to act before he could awaken them. With every ounce of his tremendous energy and will, he flung himself into the task of keeping the gateway open to the north. He got himself sent into Bechuanaland as Deputy Commissioner and played a leading part in the events that led to the establishment of a British Protectorate over the country. Here he made friends with his beaten opponents as was his way. 'I have never,' he said, 'met any one in my life whom it was not as easy to deal with as to fight.' In a letter he described how he came to terms with one Boer farmer, an angry giant who greeted him as he rode up to his door with the words, 'Blood must flow.' "No," said I, "give me my breakfast and then we can talk about blood." Well, I stayed with him a week, I became godfather of his children and we made a settlement.'

Having gained the corridor, Rhodes prepared to take the North. By devious ways he obtained concessions from the savage Matabele tribes who fought and hunted the vast empty hinterland. Then he turned to the imperial Government. By badgering all parties and politicians (he used to say that the story of the importunate widow was the best in the Bible) and using his wealth and powers of persuasion to win over opposition, he secured a Royal Charter for the company which was to create a new dominion. In 1890 he launched his pioneers along the northern road into the wilderness. In the next year, when he could escape from his official duties at the Cape, he followed them on a visit along the fifteen hundred mile trek to their primitive capital at Fort Salisbury.

In all that he had done Rhodes was animated by a single and unchanging ambition: to found homes – 'more homes' – for the race. His imagination never ceased to dwell on the future shade of the trees he planted. He loved to think that the road he made up Table Mountain would be used by men and women of his race in a hundred years' time. It was not chance that made him seek the friendship of General Booth and spend days with him in the crowded London slums: the contrast between the England of the utilitarians and the wider, freer England of Rhodes's dream was his constant spur. The province which he added to the Empire, and which later bore his name, was equal in extent to Germany, France and Spain together: a country where free men could work and breed and make a new English nation.

When Rhodes came back to England to seek for his projects the support of Conservative, Liberal and Irish politicians, of royal dukes and journalists, of speculators and social reformers, it was always with the same idea. Somehow he had got to save the English future from the blindness of the English – the greatest people the world has seen whose fault is that they do not know their strength, their greatness and their destiny.' 'Mr Gladstone,' he is reported to have said, 'the practical reason for the further acquisition of territory is that every power in the world, including our kinsmen the Americans, as soon as they take new territory, place hostile tariffs against British goods.' In his speeches to the shareholders of his Chartered Company, essays in imperial planning, he reverted again and again to the nightmare which haunted him: that the prohibitive tariffs of a hostile world would one day pauperise, and perhaps starve, an island people who could not feed themselves:

'The classes can spend their money under any flag, but the poor masses . . . can only look to other countries in connection with what they produce. Instead of the world going all right it is all wrong for them. Cobden had his idea of Free Trade for all the world, but that idea has not been realized. The whole world can see that we can make the best goods in this country, and the countries of the world therefore establish against us, not protective tariffs, but prohibitive tariffs . . .

'The question of the day is the tariff question and no one tells the people anything about it . . . These islands can only support six millions out of their thirty-six millions . . . We cannot afford to part with one inch of the world's surface which affords a free and open market to the manufactures of our countrymen.'

'When I came back to England the first time, I went up the Thames, and what did I find they were doing? . . . for whom were they making? They were making for the world. Of course, Cobdenism was a most beautiful theory, and it is right that you should look to the world; but the human beings in the world will not have that. They will want to make their own things; and if they find that England can make them best they will put on their protective duties; and if they keep on doing that they will beat you in the end.'

For a short while Rhodes made empire a fashion. It became the craze of society ladies and the theme of music-hall choruses. When Gladstone wished to evacuate Uganda in 1893 he was warned by his chief election agent that the price for doing so would be his own evacuation of Downing Street. The speeches which Rhodes made to his shareholders were listened to by breathless thousands and read by millions. Yet even he could not stir the sound, prosperous men who controlled the nation's trade and financial policy into constructive action or arouse the Westminster politicians from their dream of the parish pump and their eternal talk of municipal trams and three acres and a cow.

While Rhodes strove to expand South Africa he sought to unite her. His dream was of a single nation from the Block House at Table Mountain to the Great Lakes. He did not share the vulgar hope of the Cape patriots of subordinating the Dutch to the English. He liked the sturdy Dutch farmers and honoured the old Dutch culture of the Cape. 'The Dutch,' he said, 'are the coming race in South Africa and they must have their share in running the country.' He made friends with them, studied their interests and sought to find a solution of the native problem which had been the chief stumbling block between the two European races. His aim was their equal status in a South African union freed from the centralizing trammels of Whitehall (he supported Irish Home Rule as part of his policy of imperial self government) but linked with the rest of the Empire by the Crown, the flag and imperial preference.

Rhodes wanted that union, like the wider world commonwealth of self-governing nations he envisaged, to follow the English tradition of freedom, fair play and opportunity for all. He once said in a speech in the Cape Parliament that England had two cardinal and historic principles: that its word, once pledged, was never broken, and that when a man accepted citizenship of the British Empire there was no further distinction of races. He did not want the South Africa of his dream to be exclusive but open 'to all men who loved truth, freedom and the welfare of mankind.'

After a time Rhodes won the trust of the Dutch. Those in the British colonies of the Cape and Natal came to look on him as their leader – an unheard-of position for an Englishman. In the independent Orange Free State also he made friends. But he had one serious obstacle – the character of the primitive Dutch Transvaal and, above all, of its leader, Kruger. For the little republic of Boer farmers which lay in the centre of the new South Africa, bestriding its internal communications, had no sympathy with Rhodes's ideals. Its leader had no dream of the future nor belief in human progress: only a stubborn resolve to live the life of bygone generations and preserve their simple pastoral ways. To the old Dutch President, with his spittoon and his Bible, Rhodes's idea of 'equal rights for all civilized men, irrespective of race, south of the Zambesi,' made no appeal. His ideal was exclusion of all foreigners from the veld and if possible from South Africa. He excluded their goods by clapping on a 33 per cent tariff against all imports. He even tried to exclude their railways and telegraphs.

But mammon is a powerful dissolvent of conservative communities. The discovery of gold on the Witwatersrand in the 'eighties put President Kruger and his farmers in a dilemma. They could only secure the profit of that lucky find by admitting foreigners with capital and mining skill. And when they did so foreigners entered the country in such numbers that in a few years they not only paid the bulk of the country's taxation but outnumbered the Dutch burghers. Kruger could only maintain Dutch independence by denying them the franchise. If he granted them the rights of democratic citizenship, they would deliver his country and its ancient, primitive civilization to the enemy. For the uitlanders, most of whom were British, naturally preferred Rhodes's conception of South Africa to Kruger's.

Rhodes had only to be patient. Kruger was trying for the impossible: he was fighting against a majority and against time. But, though no one knew it but himself, so was Rhodes. In his early forties he learned that he was a dying man. He had accomplished only a tithe of his great dream. If he was to see it achieved, it must be achieved quickly. He could not trust others to complete it. Already the power that had come to him was impairing his character: he was growing arrogant and impatient of opposition. Discarding the virtues – tact, patience and conciliation – by which he had climbed, he staked all on a gamble. The gamble failed.

The armed Jameson Raid from Rhodesia into the Transvaal put a term to Rhodes's power as a politician. The Dutch felt he had betrayed them: the English liberals and humanitarians, who had been growing increasingly suspicious of his wealth, his dubious companions and his attitude to the native problem, felt their worst fears confirmed. Rhodes had shown the cloven hoof. His failure discredited his vision and made Little Englandism a permanent mood among idealists and progressives. It was even assumed that he had engineered the raid to improve the value of the Chartered Company's properties and shares. Henceforward he was a man tainted and cut off from the people he had sought to serve. Though there was much that was great in the final years of his life, the future of South Africa and the Empire passed into other hands. His legacy to his country was Rhodesia, the Rhodes Scholarships' Trust, and, when his mistake had been expiated by the Boer War, the Union of South Africa.

A few months before his death, at the bitterest moment of the war, when victory had become certain and foolish men were talking of revenge, Rhodes addressed the South African League at Cape Town. 'You think,' he said, 'you have beaten the Dutch! But it is not so. The Dutch are not beaten; what is beaten is Krugerism, a corrupt and evil government, no more Dutch in essence than English. No! The Dutch are as vigorous and unconquered to-day as they have ever been; the country is still as much theirs as it is yours, and you will have to live and work with them hereafter as in the past. Remember that when you go back to your homes in the towns or in the up-country farms and villages. Let there be no vaunting words, no vulgar triumph over your Dutch neighbours; make them feel that bitterness is past and that the need of co-operation is greater than ever. Teach your children to remember when they go to their village school that the little Dutch boys and girls they find sitting on the same benches with them are as much part of the South African nation as they are themselves, and that as they learn the same lessons together now, so hereafter they must work together as comrades for a common object – the good of South Africa.'

Rhodes's last recorded words were, 'So little done: so much to do.' He was only 49 when he died. Had he lived another twelve years, he might conceivably, by his strength and commanding influence in the Anglo-Saxon world, have made it clear in the summer of 1914 that the Empire would intervene against an aggressor and so have averted the Great War and all its incalculable consequences. Had he lived still longer, like his contemporary, Bernard Shaw, it is even possible that his full dream might have been realized, the 'Anglo-Saxon schism' be ended and the peace and economic unity of mankind permanently secured by the establishment of a pacific world power as omnipotent as Rome. The Fates willed it otherwise.

*   *   *

It was an English politician who took up Rhodes's work where he had left it half shattered at the end of 1895. In that year Joseph Chamberlain became Colonial Secretary. It was an office about which no one had troubled much before. For eight years Chamberlain made it the most important in the Empire. He reconquered the Sudan, which during the Mahdi's rule had lost three-quarters of its population, and established a British province twenty times the size of England in the heart of equatorial Africa. He transferred the rule of the vast country which is to-day called Nigeria from the Royal Niger Company to the imperial crown. He secured, by a war in which Australians, Canadians and New Zealanders fought side by side with Englishmen, British sovereignty over the whole of South Africa from the Cape to Lake Tanganyika. His policy of appeasement in the hour of victory was a first step towards a new and free South Africa without racial predominance. He helped to bring about the long-delayed federation of the Australian colonies.

These achievements were only part of Chamberlain's service to the Empire. This dapper ex-radical and Brummagem hardware merchant with the frock coat, monocle and orchid, the art of a demagogue and the vision of a Roman Emperor infused a new spirit into imperial administration. A business man of initiative and energy, in days when business still required both, he sought to make the Empire pay by making it efficient. But he took the long view of efficiency, looking to the interests not merely of the living but of the unborn. He regarded the Crown Colonies as undeveloped estates which could only be de-veloped with imperial assistance. Some of them, after a hundred years of British rule, were still in the same state as when they had been annexed. Britain's stewardship could only be justified if it conferred active benefits on their peoples and the greater populations comprised in the imperial union.

Chamberlain set up a Royal Commission to report on the West Indian sugar islands, derelict and half-ruined after half a century of *laissez-faire*, founded an Imperial Department of Agriculture in the islands to investigate the causes of insect pests and stimulate the planting of alternative crops, and granted loans for colonial transport development at low rates of interest. His Colonial Office fostered the study of tropical medicine and hygiene, established native colleges and trained a new school of scientific imperial administrators versed in the laborious arts of making the wilderness flower. In Africa in particular his policy produced remarkable results: provinces which for centuries had been savage areas of vice, fetishism, slavery, filth and pestilence became in the course of a single generation orderly and well-governed communities with schools, railways and hospitals and a most unfamiliar atmosphere of hope.

Hope was, indeed, the dominant imperial note while Joe Chamberlain remained at the Colonial Office. His forceful optimism brushed aside difficulties: distance, provincial jealousies, lack of population, non-existent markets, want of capital to develop and of trade to repay development. There was talk of imperial federation and of some grand, nebulous scheme of centralized government for the whole empire, for Chamberlain's mind ran on more bureaucratic lines than Rhodes's. A succession of Colonial Conferences discussed questions of imperial defence and federation and recommended the adoption of preferential trade within the Empire if ever Great Britain should feel able to modify her sacrosanct commercial policy of unrestricted imports. In the third Conference, in 1897, the Prime Ministers of the eleven self-governing colonies passed a resolution in favour of federation when geographically feasible. It was the year of the Diamond Jubilee: Empire and the pride of Empire were in the air. The aged Queen drove in an open carriage to St Paul's through streets lined by British troops from every continent, and Kipling, as the tumult and the shouting died away, recalled his countrymen to the age-long truth that sets a term to all empires:

'If, drunk with sight of power, we loose
Wild tongues that have not Thee in awe,
Such boastings as the Gentiles use,
Or lesser breeds without the Law –
Lord God of Hosts, be with us yet,
Lest we forget – lest we forget!'

That was the climax of the new imperialism. There was an inevitable reaction. For one thing there was the price of Empire. During the Boer War it was at times a heavy one. And to many people the new imperialism bore too much an air of swashbuckling and bullying: it was overloud and protested too much. Worse: it aroused too many financial hopes and offered too many opportunities for the speculator masking his sly operations under the folds of the Union Jack. For the new fashion of Empire attracted a rather miscellaneous crew of patriots: profiteering financiers, gold and diamond magnates of doubtful antecedents, shady adventurers from foreign capitals peddling concessions in African swamps and Australian mines to a public which, at first swept off its feet by the mingled appeal to patriotism and cupidity, became later increasingly suspicious of both.

In these ventures, some of which were animated by a genuine belief in the imperial future and some merely by a shrewd business desire to make hay while the imperial sun shone, much speculative capital was sunk in the Empire without any continuing return. A great deal of it was lost in inflated share values which could only have been justified by years of patient development. Such losses aroused deep-seated and subconscious distrusts. The imperial financial bubble of the 'nineties left a nasty taste in the mouths of men who might otherwise have wished well to a broad plan of social development for the ill-distributed populations who shared their allegiance.

But there was a deeper cause for the failure of the first attempt to use British capital to develop the imperial heritage. Backward and scantily populated territories can only be turned to profit by a far-sighted use of credit. Under a system of private enterprise such credit can not be afforded unless there is a reasonable certainty of an expanding and stable trade sufficient to repay initial expenditure. Except as a quick gamble in share values, investment in the British Empire seldom offered such certainty. For so long as Great Britain stuck to Free Trade, its Government could not, with the best will in the world, afford sheltered markets to young Empire industries. Other nations, wishing to foster the growth of national industries, were able to grant protective tariffs and bonuses. The economic faith of the British forbade their doing so.

In 1897 Joseph Chamberlain, trying to develop a long-neglected empire by parliamentary grants to agricultural institutes and schools of tropical medicine, received an offer from Canada of a tariff in favour of British goods. This was followed by a resolution of the Colonial Conference in favour of imperial preference. But without reciprocity in the home market to increase the colonial capacity to purchase British goods, such one-sided preference, however generous, could be no more than a gesture. All that the Colonial Secretary and his chief, Lord

Salisbury, could do was to exempt the British nations overseas from the operations of the 'most favoured' nation clause by which free-trading Britain regulated her commercial treaties. This ensured that if ever the British people should abandon the policy of free imports and be ready to offer tariff preferences to their imperial kinsfolk, they would not be forced to pass on such preferences to every other nation with which they had made a treaty.

This concession meant little at the time. There were no British duties to reduce in favour of the colonies. Least of all could Britain offer the colonies the sheltered markets they needed for their two most important articles of export – food and raw material. Absolute freedom from restriction in both was an article of faith of the Liberal Party. Since the day when Disraeli had taught his followers in the early 'fifties to seek electoral merit by discarding the *damnosa hereditas* of protection, it was scarcely less so with the Tory.

It said much, therefore, for Chamberlain's courage that, at the age of 67, with a reasonable chance of the reversion of the Conservative leadership and the premiership, he should have resigned his office in order to convince his countrymen of the necessity of an imperial tariff union. In 1903 this ambitious and vigorous man on his return from a tour in South Africa electrified England by going on the stump in a nationwide campaign of economic education.

The outcry was tremendous. The Liberals, now long out of favour, were jubilant. They raised the most popular of all electoral cries – the People's Food in Danger. The Conservative Party was terrified, and for a while split from top to bottom. Its leader, the aristocratic Arthur Balfour, saved its unity by temporizing. But when in 1905, refusing to follow his lieutenant's lead, he went to the country on a note of half-hearted interrogation, he was routed. Imperial preference was marked down for a generation.

It could hardly have been otherwise. For almost inevitably Chamberlain, in his Empire crusade, fell into a fatal error. He began by appealing to patriotism. He asked for tariffs against foreign imports in order to consolidate the imperial heritage of the unborn and to help the primary producers of the Empire who had fought for Britain in the Boer War and who were now voluntarily offering her traders preference. But having to win votes in a commercial age, he and his more worldly followers soon transferred the appeal to material self-interest. Ingenious and elaborately supported economic arguments were advanced to show that the British manufacturer and consumer would reap immediate rewards from a general tariff on foreign goods. The issue of imperial preference as a long-term patriotic investment became obscured by that of protection as an opportunity for quick profits. Great empire and little minds, as Burke saw, go ill together. The generous note first struck by Chamberlain became lost in a cacophony of log-rolling and auctioneering of rival figures.

Though the official Conservative Party refused to join open issue with them over protection, the general election of 1905 was won by the Liberals – largely on the cry of 'Hands Off the People's Bread.' Actually the addition to the price of the loaf involved in Chamberlain's original proposal of giving preference in the home market to imperial corn-growers would have been negligible. Owing to revolutionary changes in popular feeding habits, caused by new methods of ocean storage, bread was no longer the staple dietary of the masses. But in a conservative country the old parrot-cry sufficed.

The real strength of Free Trade lay not in its power to provision England cheaply but in the vested interests which in sixty years of commercial expansion had grown round its practice. A considered policy of imperial development might in the course of comparatively few years have afforded the British consumer and manufacturer adequate alternatives to most of the cheap food and raw materials bought from the foreigner. By guiding credit into the new area of preferential trade, and by adequately-financed facilities for migration, stable markets for British industrial exports could have been created in an expanding Empire. They would have involved some immediate sacrifice. But it would have been amply justified in, say, 1940.

But such a policy, however wise as a form of national insurance, would have involved a transfer of trade and investment from old-established into unproved channels. It scared cautious minds and threatened vested interests. In an old and rich country both were immensely powerful. With the extension of the franchise and the ever-growing cost of electoral organization, both the main political parties were becoming dependent on the financial support of the City. And the City, as opposed to the provincial manufacturers, was opposed to any change in the country's trade and financial policy.

Behind the City was the ordinary investor. Since the general adoption of the limited liability principle an ever-growing number of citizens had obtained a shareholder's interest in commerce. Their money was invested in British companies trading with foreign countries in every part of the world. Their dividends were paid by the imports with which those countries purchased British goods. A policy which transferred part of the British home market to Empire producers endangered their interests. They argued that Britain could not increase, say, its sugar imports from Jamaica without taking less from Cuba. And they had more money invested in Cuba than in Jamaica.

Such forces preserving the *status quo* in commerce and finance were cumulative. Every year, while its virtual monopoly of manufactures lasted, a free-trading Britain, after paying for its foreign food and raw materials with manufactured exports, had a favourable balance. This balance, which for many years averaged a hundred million pounds, was allowed to remain in the form of accumulating loans to the debtor countries. The interest could only be paid by still more of their goods. The richer British investors grew, the greater became the foreign debtors' share of the British market. A creditor inevitably tries to keep his debtor in employment. The young countries of the Empire not being so heavily indebted, could not look for such help from money-lending Britain. For, having been long under-developed and under-populated, they had only recently appeared as large-scale borrowers on the London money market.

Thus all attempts to unite the Empire economically were still-born, because the mother country had prior and more paying financial affiliations with the foreigner. The Dominions and Colonies, it was felt, must be left to develop as best they could by forming similar affiliations with other nations who were not so deeply committed to established channels of finance and trade. For though in political matters Britain had become conscious of her Empire, in those of finance and investment she still followed the teachings of *laissez-faire*. Scarcely any one seemed to see the contradiction in her doing so. The most ardent patriots, who glowed with pride at the thought of Australian bushmen fighting in a British cause in South Africa, invested their savings in Latin America and bought their beef from the Argentine without a qualm.

Such men could not foresee the future. They were ordinary, honest, unimaginative Englishmen who were enjoying a prosperity without parallel in human history but which they assumed to be eternal and took for granted. Though it was based largely on the purely accidental increase in national purchasing-power and credit due to the recent discoveries of gold on the South African Rand, the English never questioned their right to its individual enjoyment: for them it had nothing to do with England or Empire but was entirely their own affair.

That if called on to do so, they would die for their King and Country was not to be doubted. They sat, red-cheeked and clear-eyed, in Pall Mall clubs or the Pavilion at Lord's, shot, hunted and fished in the appropriate seasons and transacted business in boardroom or on 'change according to the unalterable laws of the Medes and Persians in which they had been trained. They paid their way with golden sovereigns and ruled the earth beneath tall silk hats in an aroma of lavender water and cigar smoke.

After the Boer War, with its early disasters and its long expensive litany of careless inefficiency, there were some misgivings. 'Let us admit it fairly,' wrote Kipling,

> 'as a business people should, We have had no end of a lesson: it will do us no end of good.'

But such frank admissions were only temporary. The poet's conclusion – 'we have had an imperial lesson; it may make us an Empire yet' – was not borne out by the course of events. A few months later he was writing savagely of 'the flannelled fools at the wicket and the muddied oafs at the goal' – of a people who in their wealth and ease grudged even the slightest sacrifice to arm against the coming day of reckoning:

> 'Ancient, effortless, ordered, cycle on cycle set,
> Life so long untroubled, that ye who inherit forget . . .
> But ye say "It will mar our comfort." Ye say "It will 'minish
>   our trade."
> Do ye wait for the spattered shrapnel 'ere ye learn how a gun
>   is laid?
> For the low, red glare to southward when the raided coast-
>   towns burn?'

But the only result of the poet's jeremiad was some loss of his own immense popularity. Everybody read him but nobody paid the least heed to his preaching.

For the English rich could not see what all the world but they could see: that their wealth created envy and jealousy, their empty empire greedy yearning, their all-pervading never-resting usury anger and resentment. They could not see that other nations impatiently seeking outlets for their rising manufactures and populations, and armed to the teeth, were watching amid their jealousies a rich, obese and luxury-loving Britain as jackals watch a dying lion. Night after night as the London seasons of the young century sped by, amid the decorous revelry of the great saloons of Mayfair and the new hotels – Ritz, Savoy and Claridges – the lords of the earth in their starched linen, pearls and diamonds enjoyed their goodly heritage unquestioning. To watchers there seemed to be something reckless in the feverish speculation and worship of wealth which had invaded the formerly exclusive society of the Imperial capital.

The little Englanders, and the radicals and socialists who accepted their kindly but narrow ideology, were no more aware of the dangers to their existence. To them the Empire seemed only a financiers' ramp for exploiting the backward races, or at best an invention of the Tories. That the cheap meat and bread which fed them came by grace of the foreigner, that others were toasting the day when the age-long security and Empire of the English should end, and that their own ways of life in the crowded cities might unfit them to stand in battle against the armies of young and jealous nations never troubled them for a moment. They went to their labours in the morning, perused their Sunday chronicle of murders and sensations, watched the gladiators of the football League battle in the arena for their favour, and cheered the cheapjack politicians of the hour who offered to plunder the rich and distribute the next year's seed-corn. And a despairing poet, feeling in his heart the imminence of doom, wrote:

'Now we can only wait till the day, wait and apportion our
　　shame.
These are the dykes our fathers left, but we would not look
　　to the same.
Time and again were we warned of the dykes, time and again
　　we delayed:
Now it may fall we have slain our sons as our fathers we have
　　betrayed.'

CHAPTER THIRTEEN

Battle In The Mire

'By all borne and left unsaid
By the soldier. By the mire
Closing o'er a comrade's head,
By the faces stripped by fire,
By daylight's dumb and crowded wire
By moonlight's lonely loathsome dead,
By the slow, the final dread
Slaying very heart's desire:
Englishman, whoe'er thou art,
That is theirs, and this thy part –
Constant hold the English heart!'
Robert Nichols

THE IMMEDIATE CAUSE of the Great War which burst on an apprehensive and excited Europe in 1914 was the arrogance of imperial Germany. Its people had been taught that war was the peculiar national instrument of the Teuton. Their philosophers had told them that in a German cause the end always justified the means. Nursed in the Prussian tradition and debauched by gross and ill-digested wealth, their statesmen had alternately alarmed and angered every neighbour. In the summer of 1914 they threatened and blustered once too often and then found themselves unable to stop what they had started.

The real causes of the war were deeper. Since her union in 1871 Germany, with all the thoroughness and vehemence native to her people, had embraced the industrial revolution. In forty years her population had increased by one half and her wealth, measured by industrial assets and profits, many times over. Her government, embodying the national passion to excel – which in the first flush of her new-found unity amounted almost to a mania – had extended unlimited credit to her manufacturers and traders. She was thus committed to a policy of unceasing industrial expansion, since without it her capitalists could not pay the interest on the loans advanced them by the community.

The pace set by this system of State usury was too furious to last. In the first fourteen years of the century Germany quadrupled her industrial output. Her whole economic structure – strong and flourishing to outward appearance – depended on her ability to secure rapidly expanding markets. The liabilities of her producers, ever accelerating their pace, pursued her: she could only keep ahead of bankruptcy by moving still faster. The nemesis of capitalism came to her more quickly than to any of her neighbours. It did so because she was more eager, impatient and efficient. She positively flung herself at the Gadarene precipice.

All the world was heading in the same direction. For following Britain's example and hoping to equal her success, the merchants of every larger nation in Europe had taken to manufacturing. Fostering their infant industries with State subsidies and artificial systems of credit, they struggled feverishly to undercut their rivals in foreign markets. The whole earth became a vast field of exploitation ranged by the agents of the more civilized peoples competing with one another for customers and raw materials to feed the wheels of their growing factories and the mouths of their fast-breeding factory populations. And after their agents came consuls, warships and expeditionary forces to establish spheres of influence. Envying Britain's vast empire, the industrial powers hastened to found empires of their own in still unexploited territories whence they could procure cheap raw materials and force their manufactures on natives subject to their exclusive control. During the latter half of the nineteenth century Germany, France, Italy and Belgium all pounced on large areas of unclaimed land in Africa and the Far East. Holland and Portugal already possessed colonial empires founded in an earlier age. Meanwhile the United States and Russia each pursued a policy of unceasing continental expansion. Austria, backed by Germany, turned towards the Balkans and the Middle East, and a new oriental manufacturing power, modelled on the most approved Western lines and sustained by modern fleets and armies, fought two victorious wars against China and Russia to establish a Japanese commercial sphere of influence in Manchuria.

But the unclaimed areas of the earth available were not enough to satisfy the cumulative and inexhaustible needs of the capitalist. The faster the usurer – state or private – supplied the more intelligent races with machinery, the vaster the territories and populations needed to pay the interest on his capital and the more important to him their political control became. The forces of diplomacy and those grimmer forces that give weight to diplomacy were inevitably marshalled in defence of the economic interests he created. There were successive crises which marked the clash of such forces, when one great power in search of markets for goods or loans encountered another in the same field: Fashoda, Venezuela, Agadir. At each of these there was ominous talk of war, and an unloosing of popular national and racial feelings which had nothing to do with economics but which, deep-rooted in human hearts, could only too easily be aroused by the instruments of mass-suggestion. And these, unconsciously but inevitably, tended to fall under the control of the contending financial interests.

For when there was no more unoccupied land to seize or spheres of financial interest to penetrate, the great powers began to covet each other's colonial possessions and economic fields. It was inevitable that those late starters in the twin race of colonial expansion and loan-mongering who had acquired the least should feel aggrieved. They thought of themselves as 'have-not' powers denied a 'proper place in the sun.' Germany, who, though second to none either in commercial or military pushfulness, had on account of her comparative newness obtained a rather bleak share of colonial plunder, made a special point of this.

The more ambitious of her people particularly resented the size of the British Empire. A young Englishman of education lacking an outlet in his overcrowded country could look for honourable and remunerative employment under his own flag and laws in one or other of his country's colonies. Germany, with half again Britain's population and apparently twice her energy and ambition, was less happily circumstanced: her hastily acquired colonies were confined mainly to tropical or semi-tropical deserts and forests in Africa and a few islands in the Pacific. She had nothing to offer the eager and pushing *alumni* of her overcrowded universities comparable in opportunity to the career afforded by the ICS or the Sudan Civil. And, as Germany was finding, one of the inevitable concomitants of capitalist enterprise is the creation of large numbers of bourgeois youth demanding university education and some outlet for their talents more remunerative than handiwork and more honourable than trade. They found it inevitably in a bureaucracy, and, in the nature of things, in an expanding bureaucracy.

For these and other reasons the Germans and the British were rivals. The British did not consciously think of the Germans as such: but the Germans did so think of the British. They envied them, they admired them and they hated them. For the Germans were seeking

233

what the British had long had and would not use for themselves – the hegemony of the world. Germany had her army. It was larger than any other army: it was better organized. It had the repute of being invincible. But the British, though they refused to concern themselves in Europe's untidy affairs, would not allow the German army to rule Europe. They would not let it march through Belgium in 1870: they refused to let it attack defeated France in 1875. The stronger it became, the more the British, true to the most unchanging point in their foreign policy, tended to tilt the scales against Germany. Though contempt for France and fear of Russia had long been second nature to them, their statesmen did not hesitate to lend their support to what the ingenuous Teuton regarded as a decadent France and a barbarous Russia in order to thwart the just and rightful ambitions of a virile central Europe. After the turn of the century and still more after Russia's defeat in the Far East, the British tendency was increasingly in this direction. Such spiteful interference in the affairs of the Continent could only be explained, Germans contended, by jealousy; the British, fearing their success, wished to encircle them.

There were psychological differences too. When the Germans, seeking the omnipotence they could never quite reach, gave themselves airs, the British laughed at them. They thought of them as conceited, slightly comical 'sausages' and enjoyed the name the discomfited but invincibly gay Viennese had invented for Berlin of 'Parvenuopopolis.' Their polite but occasionally ill-concealed contempt and their more normal indifference touched German vanity on the raw. There were always plenty of German statesmen, diplomats and merchants with a grudge against Britain which, fanned during war into a furnace of national hatred, was to astonish the British in 1914. In German regiments and in the ships of the High Seas Fleet toasts were drunk to *Der Tag* – the day that should not only be France's reckoning but Britain's.

But the most serious differences, apart from the invisible rivalry of commerce, was the blue ribbon of sea power. With an expansionist Russia preaching nationality to every Slav minority on one side of her and a France with no more ground to yield on the other, Germany had to look like Britain to the younger continents for her *lebensraum*. Her industrialists looked overseas also for their markets and raw materials and, accustomed to military victories at home, confidently demanded the protection of the imperial government. A deep sea fleet came to be regarded as a national necessity. Even as early as 1864 Bismarck's campaign against Denmark revealed the new trend of German policy. So did the purchase of Heligoland – unwisely sold by Lord Salisbury's government in 1890. After the succession of the young Emperor William II – Queen Victoria's grandson and in his own eyes heir-elect to Neptune's trident – the resolve to create a High Seas Fleet became a mania. The first German Navy Act of 1898 set a pace which within ten years had developed into a galloping race between Germany and a fast-awakening Britain for the command of the sea. 'There is no use in disguising the fact', Palmerston had said in the House in 1863, 'that what is at the bottom of the whole German design . . . is the dream of a German fleet and the wish to get Kiel as a German sea-port'.

At first the British had treated Teuton naval ambitions as an immense joke. To them there was something incongruous in the idea of fat Hans even trying to be a sailor. They had forgotten that in the Middle Ages the seamen of the Hanseatic League had sometimes given sea law to England and that in the seventeenth century the fleets, which under Tromp and de Ruyter had afforded her toughest naval encounters, had been largely recruited from the north German ports. But after the Boer War they began to wake up to the fact that a European power was challenging Trafalgar. In the closing years of King Edward's brief reign and the first of King George's, the attention of England was torn from internecine disputes about wages, national health insurance, votes for women and Home Rule for Ireland, by the disquieting spectacle of German dreadnought after dreadnought gliding down the slips of Kiel and Wilhelmshaven into the waters of the Baltic and North Sea. It was all very well for the Kaiser to assure an English statesman that it was *nonsensical and untrue* that the German Navy Bill was meant as a challenge to British naval supremacy and to state that 'the German Navy was built *against* nobody at all.' For what, then, was it built?

It was this challenge which made Britain's participation by France's side in a European War inevitable. The sea was Britain's lifeline. Though her people did not know it, her rulers – almost without realizing that they did so – were forced to commit her in advance. By an agreement to entrust the policing of the Mediterranean to France so as to concentrate the entire battle fleet in the North Sea, they made themselves morally responsible for the defence of the French Channel and the Atlantic coasts. Henceforward France and Britain had a common interest – resistance to Germany. For Germany threatened the existence of both.

Even then it was the educated minority rather than the majority who grasped the significance of what was happening. The unthinking multitude was still absorbed with its sports and its struggles for a happier existence. But in London *An Englishman's Home* played to packed houses, and young Winston Churchill, unconsciously turning towards the task that was to be his life's work, suddenly ceased to be the bitter opponent of Army and Navy estimates to become the Liberal First Lord who, defying Little Englanders and the Treasury, boldly laid down two keels to Germany's one and, in a turning-point of history, gave the order which kept the Grand Fleet at sea in the hour of Armageddon.

It was Churchill who recalled to service as First Sea Lord, at the outbreak of war, the redoubtable 'Jacky' Fisher. It had been the nation's good fortune to have had Admiral of the Fleet Sir John Fisher as First Sea Lord before, from 1904 to 1910, that same officer who, as a Lieutenant had served in the first ironclad, HMS *Warrior* in 1863. In the intervening years he had striven to face the reality of the German menace. First class ships, proficient officers, better weapons, efficient dockyards and proper planning all resulted from his driving genius. But his greatest achievement was the design and construction of the revolutionary HMS *Dreadnought* and her sister ships. He sought always the fleet's fighting efficiency and instant readiness for war.

* * *

It only remained to set a spark to all this explosive material. For this simple task the rulers of imperial Germany were more than equal. They were neurotic, they were voluble and they were vain. They were also intensely arrogant. They were so obsessed with their own point of view that they were constitutionally incapable of listening quietly to, let alone seeing, any one else's. At their head, though far from controlling them or the ruthless military machine they wielded, was the Kaiser – a clever, talkative, undisciplined, excitable egotist. His indiscretions were the terror of the European chancelleries. Add to this the fact that no German in authority, though quick enough to blunder and bluster, seemed able to apologize or withdraw, and that the jingo Press in all countries magnified every incident and hasty word, and it was obvious that an explosion could not be long delayed.

Everybody knew this except the islanders. In blind pursuit of new and urgently needed markets, and honouring a morality that placed her national *ego* above the law of nations Germany was set on expansion at all costs. On August 4th, 1914, the British people knew too. Throwing themselves at the eleventh hour on the side of an outnumbered France and an incalculable and distant Russia, they stood squarely in the way. An irresistible force had encountered an immovable body.

Thus it came about that the British people for the first time in sixty years found themselves involved in a European war. It was clear that Germany had made a brutal and unprovoked attack on Belgium and that Britain had long plighted her word – as Germany had also – to maintain Belgian integrity and neutrality. Beyond that only a small minority had any clear idea of what the war was about. Scarcely any one realized that it threatened the very existence of the country. Invasion had been a press bugbear for some years before the outbreak of war, and invasion scares continued to alarm the public mind until 1916. But the very fact indicated how little the English understood the real nature of their peril. For should the naval situation deteriorate sufficiently to make sustained invasion possible, no invasion would be needed to bring England to her knees. For three almost out of every four mouthfuls that sustained her, Britain was dependent on sea-borne food. And her rulers, in conformity with a national economy which left such matters to private capital, had omitted to lay in any reserves. An overcrowded and unprepared island that could not feed itself for more than a few weeks or escape bankruptcy without the maintenance of a vast and complex export trade had challenged the first military and the second greatest naval power in the world.

But the people of Britain only knew that the gauntlet had been thrown down and that their proud country was in the lists. After a century of security and of being taught by their rulers that the needs of the living were all that mattered, they were called upon to sacrifice themselves for the sake of the continuing community. Four generations of *laissez-faire* thinking and living had not robbed them of their patriotism. As one man they flung themselves into the fray.

> 'Comfort, content, delight,
> The ages slow-bought gain,
> They shrivelled in a night,
> Only ourselves remain
> To face the naked days
> In silent fortitude,
> Through perils and dismays
> Renewed and re-renewed.

No easy hope or lies
Shall bring us to our goal,
But iron sacrifice
Of body, will and soul.
There is but one task for all –
One life for each to give.
Who stands if Freedom fall?
Who dies if England live?'

It was as astonishing spectacle. On the continent of Europe patriotism was the peculiar concern of the State. It was taught in the schools: it was officially stamped on the mind and body of the individual citizen in his conscript years. There was not a Frenchman, a German, a Russian or even an Italian between the ages of 18 and 60 who was not trained and liable at a moment's notice to serve in his country's army. When war came, his place in a mobilized nation was awaiting him.

In Britain it was different. The State did not teach the citizen patriotism: it scrupulously ignored the subject. It did not teach him nor expect him to serve his country. The State existed to serve the individual, not the individual the State. It provided him with legal and police protection, street lighting and paving and, under recent socialist legislation, with – for those who wanted them – free education, municipal baths and health insurance. It asked nothing in return except obedience to the law and the payment of taxes. If the individual chose to be patriotic, that was his own affair – a kind of hobby like collecting stamps or big-game shooting. Thus there was a voluntary Navy League, supported by private subscriptions, for awakening public interest in the Navy, and quite a number of rival empire societies for persuading people to think imperially. But the State itself had nothing to do with them except to assess them for their share of taxation. It treated them in exactly the same way as it treated atheist or revolutionary societies. Even professional sailors and soldiers were only ordinary citizens without special privileges. Outside the close corporation of their ships and regiments they made no demonstration of their relation to the State: in England an officer when off duty did not swagger down the street in uniform, but punctiliously donned mufti and went about like an ordinary private citizen. It was what, in the eyes of the law, he was.

Continental observers – particularly German ones who loved to contrast their own strident patriotism with English casualness – assumed from this that English people had ceased to love their country and, under the influence of commerce and luxury, had become degenerate. They supposed them lacking in the fighting virtues of self-sacrifice, discipline and *esprit de corps*. They even thought them cravens. In the trenches before Ypres and La Bassée they received a rude awakening. For though in Britain the State had long disinterested itself in the private citizen's patriotism or capacity for war, the British with their long history retained a stronger national consciousness and underlying unity than probably any other people in the world. They took their love of country and their willingness to die for her for granted. For modern war they were out of date and out of practice. But, as the event proved, when once they set their minds to it, they caught up with the martial accomplishments of their militarist neighbours at an astonishing rate.

It was perhaps just because the State left the Englishman so free to serve the nation in his own way that he came to its aid in the hour of need with such enthusiasm. He valued the virtues of self-sacrifice, civic pride and comradeship the more because he had had to foster them himself. For doing so the English had unconsciously evolved a vast network of private organizations and associations which, though legally divorced from the State, kept alive the attributes on which the State depended. Theirs was a capacity for creating loved institutions which amounted to the highest political genius. Round these they wove a kind of affectionate mystery. The more venerable they were the more they loved them and the more sacred became every familiar and hallowed accompaniment. Nothing short of a life-work of close and loving scholarship could do justice to the lore that grew up in the course of a few decades round an institution like county cricket or foxhunting or an Oxford common room. Englishmen were almost ready to die sooner than pass the port to the right or omit a phrase of the customary chaff and larking that attended the August Bank Holiday on Hampstead Heath or at Blackpool.

This curious and apparently unconscious capacity for attaching individual effort to a corporate ideal embodied in group ritual informed almost every activity of the nation's life. Hospitals and charitable trusts like the City companies transmitted traditions as unchanging and proud as those of the Brigade of Guards. Money-making abstractions like the Stock Exchange and Lloyds and far humbler commercial concerns had their sacred laws of the Medes and Persians unenforced by law yet which no member would dream of breaking and which good men loved to honour. The very newspapers evolved their own individual pride and code of honour: *The Times* was as much a national insitution as Convocation or the House of Lords, and its staff regarded it with the same affection as a Pomeranian grenadier his regiment.

Even schoolboys shared the national aptitude. The ritual, increasingly hallowed by tradition, of a great public school was as intricate and finely woven as a Beethoven sonata and aroused in those who were subjected to it an affection which nothing but death could eradicate. When the school songs were sung in the Speech Room at Harrow grown and undemonstrative men – immersed in commerce or other individualistic pursuits – would let their eyes fill with tears in a surge of emotion which reason could not explain but which was an unconscious expression of their capacity for devotion to an undying ideal. In a humbler social sphere workmen's colleges and council schools began to gather traditions, and the ragged urchins of the street evolved their own rough loyalties and rules of honour. Playing for one's side was in the English blood. It needed the alchemy of war and national peril to harness these diverse enthusiasms and loyalties to the service of the community. For when the Kaiser with his mailed fist threatened England, he did not threaten England alone. He threatened the Fourth of June, and the May Day choir on Magdalen Tower, and the village bonfire on Guy Fawkes Night; the MCC and the Reform Club; the Amalgamated Society of Engineers and the Ancient Order of Buffaloes. Behind the easy façade of England there was something mightier than England: there was Hayward and Hobbs going in to bat, the Oddfellows' dinner and the Old Kent Road.

It was a people subject to such influences who created in the next few years, as though by a miracle, a military machine as vast and as efficient as Germany's. In the first eighteen months of the war Great Britain without compulsion raised two and three-quarter million men for the Services, and the self-governing Dominions close on another million. The miracle was achieved merely by asking for volunteers. They were told that their King and Country needed them, and it was enough. It was in the nature of things that the best went first and were the first killed. In the democracy of Britain there was no equality of sacrifice. The war graves of Gallipoli and the Somme are the memorials of a national aristocracy nobler than any Heralds' College could have conceived. That spontaneous and inspired loss – of her very finest – was the price Britain paid both for her voluntary system and her past neglect. It won her the war but it cost her the peace. For by their elected sacrifice she lost the leaders she was to need when the war was over.

A nation of amateur patriots was absorbed into the little professional peace-time Army, which itself suffered virtual annihilation while Britain buckled on her long-neglected armour. The traditions of that Army were perfectly adapted to the subconscious nature of the British. Men who a few weeks before had never seen a rifle handled or thought of soldiering with anything but contempt found themselves swelling with pride at regimental annals and titles won by remote forerunners, and boasted to their womenfolk that they were 'Pontius Pilate's Bodyguard,' or the 'Devil's Own' or the 'Diehards' or the 'Fighting Fifth.' For every unit in the Army had its own pride and its own privileges, won for it on the battlefield. To many men, long robbed by factory life of status and privilege, that return to the army – for all its harshness – was like a recall home.

There was little of ease or comfort about it, much of hardship; and men came to realize that the certain end of the road they trod was death and wounds. But nobody who lived in England in that first winter of the first Great War could ever forget the training battalions of 'Kitchener's Army,' marching in their ill-fitting blue tunics down muddy country lanes and singing as they marched:

'Why did we join the Army, boys?
Why did we join the Army?
Why did we come to Salisbury Plain?
We must have been ruddy well barmy!'

One young officer, C. H. Sorley, himself soon to fall in action, who shared the comradeship and common purpose of that great and gallant company, left behind him the picture of those wintry marches across the English countryside:

'All the hills and vales along
Earth is bursting into song,
And the singers are the chaps
Who are going to die perhaps.
O sing, marching men,
Till the valleys ring again.
Give your gladness to earth's keeping,
So be glad, when you are sleeping.'

Among those who in those early months of the war chose death for their bride were thousands of young men who had seemingly been born to the happiest lot ever enjoyed by man. Nursed in a traditional culture that had not yet quite lost its hold on the well-to-do classes, yet admitted to the greater freedom of a wider and more liberal educational ideal than the past had known, they inherited the best of both worlds.

Of this generation one man in particular became identified in the public mind. Rupert Brooke was in reality only one of many: he was not even wholly typical of those he came to embody. But the direct appeal of his poetry, the beauty of his appearance and the romance of his brief life caught the imagination of a wider circle than those who ordinarily read poetry. Even before the tempest burst and the publication of his 1914 sonnets took reading England by storm, he was known to many as the personification of a new kind of youth, careless of appearances, generous, out-spoken, almost Elizabethan in its uncalculating love of adventure, spiritual and physical. The dedication to death of one so much in love with life became momentarily the symbol of a whole generation's sacrifice. In the mood of 1914 he was youth going down with touched lips into the shadows as an earnest of a nobler and a happier life for all men in the years to come.

A greater poet than Brooke and a greater Englishman was Julian Grenfell. A fine scholar and a brilliant athlete, born to all the worldly gifts that any man could inherit, his sympathies – at a time when such sympathies were still unusual and regarded with disfavour – were always with the revolutionary, the crank and the under-dog. It was not that he rebelled against order but that he instinctively comprehended the causes of his age's discontent. A professional soldier before the war, he embraced the call to arms as a crusade – not so much against the German people or even their tiresome rulers as against the inertia and death that seemed to have fallen on the world. After enduring with astonishing happiness and cheerfulness the first harsh winter in the trenches, he fell in the spring of 1915. A few weeks before he died, looking over the April Flemish plain, he wrote one of the greatest lyrical poems in the language which, so long as English is read, will remain the epitaph of himself and his generation.

> 'The naked earth is warm with spring,
> And with green grass and bursting trees
> Leans to the sun's gaze glorying
> And quivers in the sunny breeze;
> And life is colour and warmth and light,
> And a striving evermore for these;
> And he is dead who will not fight;
> And who dies fighting has increase.

The fighting man shall from the sun
Take warmth, and life from the glowing earth;
Speed with the light-foot winds to run,
And with the trees to newer birth;
And find, when fighting shall be done,
Great rest, and fullness after dearth.

All the bright company of Heaven
Hold him in their high comradeship,
The Dog-Star and the Sisters Seven,
Orion's Belt and sworded hip.

*   *   *

The blackbird sings to him, "Brother, brother,
If this be the last song you shall sing,
Sing well, for you may not sing another:
Brother, sing"!'

*   *   *

The changing mood of the nation at war can be traced in the work of its poets. Almost at once there was a division between the professional poets at home and the combatant poets – amateurs in verse as in soldiering and astonishingly great in both. This division widened until in the end it became an unbridgeable gulf. It typified the greater gulf between the two Englands – the young living England which died and the old petrified England which lived. A quarter of a century later, when a second world war broke out, that gulf was still unbridged.

The early war poets were like the Britain that took up the challenge of the German war lords: passionate in their sacrifice, confident, uncalculating. They never doubted their victory or the rightness of their dedication. Theirs was an almost mystical exaltation: the war had been sent as guerdon of their manhood, to test them and by their testing to purify a world 'grown old and stale and weary.' They positively rejoiced in their unlooked-for, elected lot: it was for this, they felt, that they had been born.

'Better far to pass away
While the limbs are strong and young,
Ere the ending of the day,
Ere youth's lusty song be sung.

Hot blood pulsing through the veins,
Youth's high hope a burning fire,
Young men needs must break the chains
That hold them from their hearts' desire.'

But by 1916 the note had changed. With the commencement that July of the great slaughter on the Somme it could scarcely have done otherwise. On the first day of the battle alone, 60,000 casualties were sustained – the very flower of England. And week by week, as the brazen fury continued and a whole countryside was churned into a slimy mire of death, victory was realized to be an infinitely distant goal, far beyond the reach of most of those striving for it. Courage grew commonplace, strength faltered, vision faded. The poetry of fighting England became grimmer, often bitterly ironic, yet none the less, with the extraordinary capacity of her people for rejecting by ignoring calamity, soaring in moments of ecstasy above 'the smoke and stir of this dim spot which men call earth,' and seeing beauty above the horror of carnage.

> 'Music of whispering trees
> Hushed by the broad-winged breeze
> Where shaken water gleams;
> And evening radiance falling
> With reedy bird-notes calling.
> O bear me safe through dark, you low-voiced streams.
>
> I have no need to pray
> That fear may pass away;
> I scorn the growl and rumble of the fight
> That summons me from cool
> Silence of marsh and pool,
> And yellow lilies islanded in light,
> O river of stars and shadows, lead me through the night!'

In the last two years of the war, as poet after poet passed into the ghostly company of the mouthless dead, the lyrical note was drowned in the angry, unpitying clamour of a universe gone mad: the last snatches of a lost world of colour going down into a welter of mud and desolation:

> 'What passing bells for those who die as cattle?
> Only the monstrous anger of the guns,
> Only the stuttering rifles' rapid rattle
> Can patter out their hasty orisons.
> No mockeries for them from prayers or bells,
> Nor any voice of mourning save the choirs –
> The shrill, demented choirs of wailing shells;
> And bugles calling for them from sad shires.'

'What passing bells for those who die as cattle?' *Gassed* by John Singer Sargent.

'There is no sign of the defeat of the enemy's Air Force over southern England and the Channel area.' Grand-Admiral Raeder, September 10th, 1940. *The Battle of Britain, August-October 1940* by Paul Nash.

'He was an orator, a poet and a sage with a taste for splendour and good living, an aristocrat who possessed the common touch that the English like to see in their rulers. They liked his cigar, his glass of brandy, his bulldog face and figure, the twinkle in his eye. They loved his humour, his way of pronouncing foreign names, his indomitable courage. Above all, he had a power to touch chords in men's hearts that transcended politics. His sense of history never failed. He believed in a Providence that worked through human instruments and, like Elizabeth and Cromwell, he made the people he led believe in it too. He bade them be "unyeilding, persevering, indomitable, in the overthrow of another continental tyranny as in the olden times".' Sir Winston Churchill by Karsh of Ottawa.

It was a subconscious protest of the human spirit which common unlettered fighting men also echoed, but in blasphemies and grim jests which no one has recorded.

Yet this people, out of whose finest minds such poetry was rung, could not be deterred from its purpose. Their will was equal to their task. 'How to pull the English off?' wrote Walter Page, the American Ambassador in London, 'that's a hard thing to say, as it is a hard thing to say how to pull a bulldog off.' Watching day by day the never-ceasing procession of inquirers seeking news at the Embassy of missing sons and husbands, the Ambassador was struck by their stoicism. 'Not a tear have I seen yet,' he wrote. 'They take it as part of the price of greatness and of empire. You guess at their grief only by their reticence. They use as few words as possible and then courteously take themselves away. It isn't an accident that these people own a fifth of the world. Utterly un-warlike, they outlast everybody else when war comes. You don't get a sense of fighting here – only of endurance and of high resolve.' In another letter Page painted the same picture, set against the awful background of battle – of a nation 'sad, dead-earnest, resolute, united: not a dissenting voice – silent. It will spend all its treasure and give all its men, if need be. I have never seen such grim resolution.'

It was needed before the English came to their journey's end. There were disasters in distant places of the earth; allies – broken by the storm – fell away, and, as offensive after offensive with all their high delusive hopes failed, the angel of death beat his wings against the panes of innumerable homes. In the spring of 1917 the German submarine campaign, before it was brought under control, was sinking half a million tons of shipping a month. For a few weeks – though the hideous truth was hidden from the multitude – it seemed as though the price of uncultivated farms and a neglected empire would be famine and defeat. New agricultural methods, long obstinately rejected by leaders nursed in old ways, and the aid of American destroyers turned the tide at the eleventh hour.

The full magnitude of what the soldiers were called upon to endure was reached in the great offensive in the Flemish mud, sometimes called the third battle of Ypres and sometimes Passchendaele, which went on without a break for two drenching months in the autumn of 1917. The battle, long planned by the General Staff, was partly undertaken in the hope of driving the German submarine bases from the Belgian coast. But it was also fought in pursuance of a definite philosophy of war which, after the failure of successive attempts to break the ugly deadlock of trench warfare, had taken firm hold of the British military mind. It had already been pursued, it was argued, with considerable success, though at the price of half a million British casualties, in the four months' battle of the Somme. The dominating idea was that as the total population of the Allied powers was higher than that of their foes, the process of scaling down both fighting populations, man for man, as rapidly as possible must end in the ultimate survival of the larger. The quicker the rate of mutual destruction, the military statisticians argued, the sooner the war would be over.

For many weeks the Passchendaele offensive, begun on July 31st, was regarded as the prelude to victory. Every day brought its black lettering of triumph in the popular press: the autumn, as in the *annus mirabilis*, 1759, gentlemen abed in England woke to ask what new victory had been won. An advance of a thousand yards over Flemish mud so churned up and battered that even the oldest denizen could not have recognized it, and won with a loss of British life heavier than which it had cost a century and a half earlier to conquer India and Canada together, was hailed in *The Times* with headlines of 'German Defence Broken!' 'We had broken,' the Special Correspondent of that paper wrote, 'and broken at a single blow in the course of some three or four hours, the German system of defence.' Next day it was broken again, and the next and the next.

Night after night watchers of the bombardment that preceded each day's attack saw 'the flame of shell-fire . . . stretching away round a great horizon,' and heard 'from near and far the ceaseless hammer-stroke of great guns making the sky red and restless with tongues of leaping fire and bringing unseen, unimaginable destruction to the masses of men hidden in the dark woods and trenches.' Over such a landscape, if landscape it can be called, denuded by tornadoes of shells of all vestiges of vegetation or human habitation, men heavily laden with arms and military equipment were expected to advance against a pitiless rain of machine-gun fire. Whichever way they turned in pursuit of their orders, they floundered in oceans of knee-deep mud: even on the rare dry days of that ghastly autumn the solidest-looking earth proved as thin as half-cooked porridge into which a fully-equipped man sank until face, hands and tunic were soaked with black mire, foetid with the obscene and decomposing remains of dead comrades. 'Cold and paddling through a sea of slime' to reach objectives whose value seemed as worthless as their own water-logged shell-holes and whose cost must be probably their own lives or mutilation, men yet endured and kept their pride and manhood. Many were drowned as they went forward or dragged their mangled bodies towards the rear.

Looking down from a slight eminence on that vast battlefield in the swamps between Ypres and the Passchendaele ridge, 'the long bare slope down to St Julien, the valley of the Steenbeek, choked with wreckage, churned into swamp and dotted with derelict tanks; the rising ground to Poelcapelle, and in the far distance fields and pastures new, green trees and a church spire,' a young officer – no weakling but a hardened veteran – was reminded of a child's picture of *The Pilgrim's Progress*, unread since nursery days. 'Here was Christian descending into the Valley of Humiliation and seeing in the distance the Delectable Mountains "beautified with woods, vineyards, fruits of all sorts, flowers, also with springs and fountains" very delectable to behold, but in the path there lay "a wilderness, a land of deserts and pits; a land of drought and of the shadow of death!" There was "also in that valley a continual howling and yelling, as of people under unutterable misery who there sat bound in afflictions and irons; over that valley hang the discouraging clouds of confusion; death also doth always spread his wings over it. In a word it is every whit dreadful, being utterly without order; . . . at the other end of this valley lay blood, bones, ashes and mangled bodies of men, even of pilgrims that had gone this way formerly". In that place, though only the strongest and most faithful were gathered there, even the strongest and most faithful were near breaking-point.

Far from the blood-stained swamp, in the Olympian calm of GHQ, Haig, with his handsome head thrown back and his quiet, confident smile, would make a dramatic sweep with his hands over his maps to show visiting politicians how he was driving the Germans back to their frontiers. Mr F. S. Oliver, the historian, contemplating the deluge which poured continually from the skies, admired the serene way the commander-in-chief ignored the elements and persisted in his attacks. Presently the distant ridge would be captured and the plain of Belgium would open up before his victorious troops. Or so it seemed, looking out through the tall, rain-spattered windows of the chateau of Montreuil. The German generals pursued similar visions of early victory; that autumn Russia, rent by revolution and anarchy, collapsed before their advancing armies, and in October the Austrians, believed to be at the last gasp, struck back with German aid at their Italian assailants and sent them in headlong rout with a loss of more than half a million men towards the Piave. These disasters, like those which had befallen

Belgium, Serbia and Romania in the earlier years of the war, were attended by a mass flight of non-combatants – of whole nations on the trek leaving behind a vast, untidy trail of dying women, old men and children and the skeletons of starved animals. The sum total of human misery was past calculation. Men, crueller than the beasts, grew indifferent to it. German civilians sang specially composed hymns of hate against England and, in the most civilized country in the world, quiet, inoffensive English gentlemen and ladies who had never seen a blow struck in anger scouted the very mention of peace and spoke of the whole German race as they would of a pack of wild beasts. Only in the battleline itself was there no hatred: only suffering and endurance, death and infinite waste.

Through the autumn months the 'triumphal crawl through the mud proceeded.' Flemish villages, whose names had never been heard of before in Britain, fell amid national jubilations and at the cost of nearly 400,000 casualties – a loss equal to the entire population of Bristol. On the German side another 250,000 fell. For each of these casualties, somebody in some town or village far from the fighting line suffered anxiety, heart-ache indescribable, or irretrievable loss. It was a time when women all over the world wore set faces, knowing their dear ones were in danger.

When nearly half a million men had fallen, the battle was called off. For the time being there were no more men to send to the slaughter, and there was nothing for it for those who remained but to dig themselves into the mud and wait until the still undrained man-power of the new world beyond the Atlantic should arise to redress the exhaustion of the old. Then 'the bovine and brutal game of attrition could begin again.' Amid the stench of thousands of unburied corpses the victorious survivors consolidated their watery gains. These unfortunately were nearly all lost in the next German offensive.

Yet there was no surrender, for on both sides of the line congregated all that was most heroic and constant in the manhood of the most virile nations of the old world. These fighters, hidden from one another in the slime, subjected day and night to a ceaseless tornado of screeching death out of the darkened sky, tortured by every foul breath and sight that can appal the sensitive mind, were in that place and hour because they had chosen to be. There were many roads out of the battle-line; they were necessary since none but the strong could stand the test. No unit wished to keep the weak. Behind the lines were all those fulfilling a thousand lesser tasks, who could or would not fight it out. The stalwarts remained. Along either rim of the rat-haunted, corpse-strewn limbo of no-man's land the philosopher seeking virtue in 1917 would have found the elect of the earth.

The men who formed the rank and file of the army of Britain did not only retain their courage. Under a cloak of ironical and often blasphemous jargon they preserved their native good humour. Even cheerfulness was constantly breaking through – in a world of thunder and screeching, mangled bodies, foul miasmas and ceaseless terror they laughed and joked. Bruce Bairnsfather's cartoon of the old veteran with his grim, ugly, resolute face and his walrus moustache, telling the grumbling youngsters in his mud-bath of a shell-hole – 'If yer know of a better 'ole, go to it' – was the epitome of an invincible army. Whenever the nerves of the strongest were at breaking-point the British soldier fell back on an inner fortress of his soul. It was buttressed with a kind of stubborn laughter. He jested at fate because he did not wholly believe in it. For he knew it was too bad to be true.

Sometimes that defiant cheerfulness arose above the mire and squalor in some communal expression like the great shout which would spring from masses of men at the most unlikely moments of '*Are we downhearted – No!*' or the impossible songs with which troops beguiled the march, few of them printable.

> 'Send for the boys of the Old Brigade
> To keep old England free!
> Send for me' father and me' mother and me' brother,
> But for Gawd's sake don't send me!'

More often in the latter stages of the war the regiments marched in silence under their steel helmets with a certain monotonous, almost brute-like grimness. But the humour and cheerfulness found expression in an undertone of individual facetiousness: the ' 'Ave a 'eart, Fritz, we broke our bloody gun!' which accompanied an intensive German bombardment unreplied to; the time-honoured, 'There goes the —— receipt!' when the British response came at last.

Sergeant Tozer, Little Martlow, Shem, Weeper Smart, Madeley – the common soldiers of that great and forgotten epic of England in trial, *Her Privates We* – were drawn from life against a background of unimaginable nightmare which their incorrigible valour alone kept from being more than nightmare. 'These apparently rude and brutal natures comforted, encouraged and reconciled each other to fate, with a tenderness and tact which was more moving than anything in life.

They had nothing, not even their own bodies, which had become mere implements of warfare. They turned from the wreckage and misery of life to an empty heaven, and from an empty heaven to the silence of their own hearts. They had been brought to the last extremity of hope, and yet they put their hands on each other's shoulders and said with a passionate conviction that it would be all right, though they had faith in nothing but in themselves and each other.' They never broke, never gave way, never despaired; they only jested, stuck it out and died.

It was not numbers nor efficiency nor even courage that did Britain's business, though in all these, learning the art of modern war by harsh experience, she came to excel. In the last resort victory went to the nation with the greatest capacity for endurance. During the final terrible year of the war Germany, released from all danger on her long eastern front by the collapse of Russia and temporarily relieved of any fear of the Italian action, concentrated her entire armament for a decisive blow in the west. On the misty morning of March 21st 1918, 62 German divisions, attacking on a front of 25 miles, broke through the British Fifth Army. For the next four months the German attacks scarcely ever ceased; at one moment, driving a wedge between the British and French, they almost reached the vital junction of Amiens: at another there seemed to be nothing but one shattered, invincible battalion of Grenadiers between the grey-coated hordes and the Channel coast. The gains of the Somme, Cambrai, Passchendaele, the Aisne, even the Marne melted away in a few days.

Yet somehow Britain and her failing ally, France, stuck fast. The line held. American reinforcements were beginning to cross the Atlantic in large numbers; in Palestine, Allenby of Jerusalem and Lawrence of Arabia with shrewd hard blows brought down the Turkish Empire, leaving an open door in the German rear. By the beginning of August the Army of Britain, decimated and tired as it was, gathered its strength for a new spring. When it came on August 8th it proved, contrary to all expectations, the beginning of the end. The German Army had met its match. It struggled bravely, wavered and finally broke. On November 11th, still falling back across the French and Belgian soil it had conquered it surrendered unconditionally.

*   *   *

Behind the Army lay another force without which its efforts would have availed nothing. During the four and a quarter years of the war the Army absorbed nearly six million Britons, the Navy only half a million. But those five hundred thousand men and their Admiral could have lost the war in an hour. By their mere existence hundreds of miles away from the struggling armies and smoking towns that fed the battlefield, the strength of Germany was slowly sapped. The terrible purpose of Britain beset by foes was expressed in its final form in remote silence: among the islands of the North the Fleet was in being. It was enough. The only half-hearted attempt to challenge it had ended in June 1916 in the thunder of Jutland; but when the mists and smoke of that confused cannonade lifted, the seas remained as they were – England's forbidden waterway. The people of central Europe tried every way to avert and postpone the hungry negation of that invisible siege. Even while their armies, out-gunned, outmanoeuvred and out-fought, were falling back before the advancing surge of victorious khaki and blue, hunger was gnawing at the vitals of the German workers and housewives at home. Revolution and surrender went hand in hand. And at the end of all, the Kaiser's tall ships of war, manned by hungry and mutinous men, tailed in mournful submission to Scapa Flow.

Victory, eagerly hoped for in 1914, struggled for in vain and in the face of repeated disappointments and defeats in the long middle years, almost despaired of in the spring and summer of 1918, had come at last. Never a military nation, when it came to testing the martial virtues, Britain had outlasted all others. That was why she won. In after years successful men of peace were to argue that her financial resources had given her victory just as the defeated Germans, forgetting their sores, were to contend that there had been no victory at all. But in the grim days of March, 1918, and during the fierce, terrible advance against the struggling German lines of that September and October, the fate of the world rested on the stubborn shoulders of the British soldier. He and the superb fighters that the British nations overseas sent from their lands of snow and sun to stand by England's side, were the ultimate arbiters of that iron time. Had they failed the world would have failed, and the German ideal of rule by power would have triumphed while Adolf Hitler was still a corporal. Not Britain's wealth but her character was the deciding factor in that hour of destiny.

Though the exhausted French, the broken Russians and the still mainly untried legions of the United States all contributed to victory, the dominating force in the world on November 11th, 1918, were the five million fighting men – the greater part of them volunteers and amateur soldiers – drawn from a scattered community of thirty-five million English, four and a half million Scots, two million Welsh, perhaps two and a half million loyal Irish, eight million Canadians, six and a half million Australians and New Zealanders, and one and a half million South Africans – in all rather less than sixty million free people, of whom more than three-quarters were English or of English descent. Contrary to all expectation, they had given the German army the thrashing it needed and taught a would-be despot the lesson that, though imperial Britain herself would not give rule to Europe, no one else should.

CHAPTER FOURTEEN

Crumbling Heritage

'If England was what England seems,
An' not the England of our dreams,
But only putty, brass an' paint,
'Ow quick we'd chuck 'er! *But she ain't!*'
Rudyard Kipling

WHEN THE WAR ENDED the simple fighting men who had won it thought that a new world was about to be built on the ruins of the old. They looked across a desolate landscape of charred ruins and ghostly tree trunks – the very field of Golgotha and dead men's skulls. Between them and the life they had known before the war was an unbridgeable gulf of scalding tears and the blood of dead comrades and of incommunicable agony.

They had no clear idea of the exact form the world they felt they had earned should take. It was a romantic rather than a concrete conception, and one that, unspoken, had sometimes floated through the smoky air of battalion concerts when some prosaic enough looking singer regaled his comrades with 'A Long Long Trail' or 'Roses are blooming in Picardy,' homely tunes which no one who heard them in that setting ever heard again without a forewarning of tears. But being an English dream, it was curious how it reverted to ideas of roses round the door and nightingales singing and the sound of the rooster

'– the one that used 'ter
Wake me up at four a.m.'

For most of the rough, hard-tried men who listened approvingly and in the choruses sent their very souls humming into the rafters, hailed from scenes far removed from the rustic paraphernalia of their imaginary heaven. In the remote days of 1914 before they joined up, they would certainly not have thanked any utopian visionary who had shifted them from the crowded, noisy life of the street corner and planted them down in a country cottage or woodland glade. But somehow after four years of war they were far nearer, though they did not know it, to the vanished England of 1840 or even 1740 than to the *laissez-faire* industrial society of 1914. The encrustations of a hundred years of urban development had fallen from them, shed on the dusty, bullet-swept downs above Contalmaison or in the blood and mud of the Salient, leaving their souls naked as they had inherited them from their remote forebears. Bereft by the pitiless tempest of war of almost everything they had known in their brief, stunted city lives, their desires and needs were unconsciously dictated by their country's forgotten tradition. Put to the test the slum boy, made man by ordeal of battle, had acquired an atavistic memory of the things he had lost.

He wanted a home he could call his own, with perhaps a garden for vegetables and flowers, a regular job of work in which he could take pleasure and pride, security in his livelihood and the self-respect that comes from status and a fixed place in society. It was not a very exacting ambition, and by the universal acclamation of the nation he had deserved it. He had even been promised it by the politicians. There was nobody who wanted to deny it him.

Amid a wild delirium of hooters, squeakers, and flag-wagging men and girls on car-roofs, the nation shut off steam. No more digging potatoes for victory in dreary allotments beside the gas-works, no more going out on special constable's duty on cold winter nights: good-bye, reflected business England, to all that. The hour had come for every man to help himself and in his leisure to enjoy the good time to which his patriotic efforts had entitled him. For the British were not merely a profit-seeking people: they were an enjoying people. Golf, cricket, seaside holidays, sunny June afternoons on the river or at the wheel were the prizes which those able to awarded themselves.

Even in the armies overseas, after a slight pause, the same thing happened. The war was over: the goal was reached. There was no point in men who were not professional soldiers remaining soldiers any longer. The only thing to do was to get absorbed in civilian employment as quickly as possible. Self-sacrifice, devotion to the corporate idea, *esprit de corps*, were no longer needed: dreams must wait. Within a few weeks the amateur soldier had only one thought: to get 'demobbed' and back to clean sheets – if he had them – warm wife and the familiar sights of Blighty. A few old soldiers, cynical about politicians' promises and reckoning that they were in a tolerably snug hole and in a harsh world would find no better, made no hurry to doff their khaki and stayed where they were – so long as an indulgent Treasury would let them. The remainder evaporated. For four years they had placed duty and fidelity to comrades above self: now, the bugles having sounded armistice, there was a not unnatural reaction. Number One came first.

So the fighting man received the thanks of his country, a suit of civilian clothes, a pair of medals and a small cash gratuity. In the case of a private soldier it amounted to the equivalent of a few weeks' wages. In the case of an officer it was more liberal and was often sufficient to purchase a small chicken farm or a wayside garage and car.

Unless he had a disability pension – which carried with it the inconvenience of a disability – that was all. Like the Pied Piper, the man who, a little while before, had been acclaimed the saviour of his country, was given a matter of something to put in his poke and told by the mayor and corporation that any more was out of the question. The sacrifice of the past belonged to the past. It was already history.

The soldiers who came back to the land they had defended greeted the peace in the mood of their dream. They supposed that they were going to devote the lives so miraculously spared them to the rebuilding of a better Britain, worthy of the men who had died for it. But they and the civilian majority to whom they returned – who, lacking their revolutionary spiritual experience, had never shared their vision – were almost at once overwhelmed by the necessity of forcing a living out of the economic system in which they found themselves. Few of them had any time or opportunity for political or philosophical reflection, let alone action. They had more than enough to do to earn their daily bread and, so far as they were able, a decent life for themselves and their dear ones. Beyond voting in masses at set intervals for two or more organized groups of politicians offering stereotyped legislative programmes of a general kind, whose practical purport was never very clear, they could not shape the course of events. They merely lived through them, reacting to them as their native feelings and their limited knowledge – mostly acquired through the newspapers – dictated. For the rest, they looked for jobs, worked hard to hold them when they had them – though seldom for the joy of working since few available jobs offered any scope for this – and, Englishwise, took whatever pleasure their confined lives afforded: in the bosom of their families, listening to the wireless, watching League football or the flicks, and holiday-making in cheap cars or charabancs.

What followed in the world of public affairs bore small relation to their desire. The emphasis at first was almost wholly domestic. It seemed attended by a great deal of bitterness and strife. There were constant strikes and lock-outs, and violent speeches in which Britons in the public eye called each other tyrants, bloodsuckers, murderers, firebrands, and red revolutionaries. These industrial upheavals involved much recurrent inconvenience to the ordinary man: clerks had to make their way to the office without trains or trams, housewives to cook without coal or gas, shareholders to forgo their wonted dividends, and strikers their wages, and often, as a result of prolonged economic dislocation and the loss of foreign customers, their employment. There was a general atmosphere of uncertainty and among the industrial masses who, though the ostensible beneficiaries, were the worst sufferers from these acrimonious efforts to better conditions, a great deal of very real bitterness against the social system in general and their more fortunate countrymen in particular. The paradise of Blighty as seen in wistful anticipation from the trenches proved, on closer acquaintance, to be somewhat precarious, even for those who had had the luck of the economic roulette. For the less fortunate there were times when it seemed, what with slum housing, tightened belts, hungry, querulous womenfolk and pinched children, almost as grim as the trenches and far less friendly.

Seen through the medium of the daily papers the first years of the great Peace that succeeded the war to end war were disconcertingly unrestful. Anger and strife were not confined to the factory and soapbox. Ireland, India and Egypt were all in more or less open rebellion. At Amritsar General Dyer gave the order to fire on an Indian Nationalist crowd: in a few minutes 400 were killed and nearly 1000 wounded. Some said that the general had averted a second Mutiny, others that he had disgraced his uniform and behaved like a Prussian. In Ireland British officers were dragged from their beds by masked assassins and butchered in front of their wives, an imprisoned lord mayor starved himself to death to shame the Saxon despot, and Sinn Fein gunmen maintained a rival and forbidden administration with their own parliament, army, police and courts of justice defying those of the imperial government with whom they waged ceaseless, secret, and bloody war. The campaign was even carried into England, where a field-marshal of Orange views was shot by Sinn Feiners on the steps of his house in Eaton Place.

But when the Coalition Government responded in kind to lawlessness by abandoning law and recruiting a force of dare-devil, ex-service misfits – nicknamed 'black and tans' – to 'raise hell' in Irish villages, the tired British dream for a moment reasserted itself. The British did not like the Irish, who, as represented by the newspapers and their own actions, were a manifest nuisance, but they had a sense of justice and an invincible love of decent and legalized dealing. 'Authorized reprisals' against innocent householders and women and children were too much for them. Public opinion, for once rendered articulate by unanimity, made itself felt, and the government, with an election before it in the not distant future, changed its policy. In the latter part of 1921, assisted by a timely speech from the King, the more imaginative members of the Coalition made contact with the less intransigent of the Irish leaders. In the strained negotiations that preceded the Treaty which gave Dominion Status to Ireland, one great Englishman, Lord Birkenhead, long lost in the post-war moral confusion and welter, took his solitary chance to prove his own wasted genius for statesmanship and the enduring tolerance, common sense and humanity of British policy.

After 1921 imperial, like foreign problems, faded into the background. In that year the full force of the economic anarchy which scourged the post-war world struck commercial Britain. The orders for urgent reconstruction after the devastation of the war dried up: instead the European nations, struggling back into the industrial battle-line, began to manufacture for themselves. Their very ruin helped them: with their prior charges wiped out by inflation and their workers rendered servile by long famine, they were easily able to undercut British rivals. Prices, and with them wages, came tumbling down. So did employment. In June 1920 there were 67,000 unemployed in Britain. By July 1921 there were two and a half million.

The shock of this new adversity sobered the nation. It brought a temporary end to strikes and lock-outs and a drastic reduction in unnecessary spending. It also brought Lloyd George's grandiose coalition to a slightly premature end. An unknown Worcestershire iron-master named Stanley Baldwin, with an honest face and a penchant for pipes and pigs, led an unexpected Tory backbench rebellion against the Welsh wizard, and enthroned a Conservative government dedicated to tranquillity. The country, feeling by this time that tranquillity was about the best it could hope for, gave it a comfortable mandate; and its modest leader, Bonar Law, quickly falling mortally ill, the premiership passed unexpectedly to the unknown Baldwin. The new dispensation proved a success, certainly with the business community.

'Why all this fuss about the servant problem?' asked Mrs Britannia in *Punch*. 'There's my Baldwin – can turn her hand to anything, keeps the House in order, checks the accounts, doesn't want any evenings off, very tactful with visitors, especially foreigners, in fact a perfect treasure.' In the circumstances of the time it was an advantage that the new government seemed rather humdrum.

*   *   *

But if the business world was contented, the industrial workers were not. The terrible figures of unemployment were a cancer at the country's heart, retarding all recovery and embittering relations between Englishmen. For the commercial predominance of the past had vanished. The competition of younger rivals, most of them with inferior standards of living, was increasing. So was the urban population which Britain had built up behind her former manufacturing ascendancy and which could only be employed and fed by the sale of manufactured goods abroad. And the accumulated investments of the Victorian era which had helped to bridge the gulf between what Britain bought with her exports and what she was able to produce in foodstuffs and raw materials were dwindling. More than half her pre-war capital invested in foreign countries outside the Empire had already been lost or was soon to vanish in default and depreciation.

The uncertainty of an anarchical Europe increased her difficulties. Though her own social fabric remained unbroken, Britain was dependent on the custom of foreign nations whose ability or readiness to pay for their purchases was constantly in doubt. She had to trade to live. Trading with uncertain customers in uncertain currencies, she could only live uncertainly. Fluctuation in foreign prices and markets meant fluctuation in domestic employment and social standards. A revolutionary situation abroad threatened a revolutionary situation at home.

The City, Britishwise refusing to admit reverse, put a brave face on things. It still continued to base the economic life of the country on the time-honoured assumption that every man who was industrious and prudent could make profits. The absence of prosperity was explained away by the assurance that a good time was sure to arrive as soon as the depression was over. The unemployed man standing in the rain outside the labour exchange, and the small manufacturer vainly waiting for the return of lost orders, were told that their sufferings would be compensated for by the magnitude of the coming recovery.

It never came. True, there were ups and downs, periods of slump and boom. But the booms were mostly confined to the fluctuating values of Stock Exchange shares and a few new luxury trades due to redistribution of national wealth and changes of social habit. At no time was there any steady expansion of British exports: throughout the greater part of the period there was steady decline. In little more than a decade those to foreign countries fell by nearly a third.

Because of these things unemployment remained a millstone round the neck of every post-war government. In the twenty years between the two wars every third working-class family in the land suffered at some time the despair and indignity of the dole. Every statesman promised or tried to find a remedy. Within six months of taking office Baldwin, himself a manufacturer, seeing Britain's manufacturers undercut by foreign rivals with lower social standards and wage costs, sought a mandate for a modification of her policy of free imports to enable him to bargain for reciprocal advantages for her traders abroad. But a conservative people, brought up to regard free trade and prosperity as synonymous and to suspect all would-be protectionists of log-rolling, was still not ready for the hour of economic retrogression and repentance which Disraeli had foreseen as inevitable. The Conservatives, themselves far from unanimous about their untried chief's impetuous lead, were defeated at the polls, and the Labour Party, now the second largest party, took office for the first time in December, 1923.

The newcomers, still in a minority, did not remain in power for long. Their foreign policy was unpopular, and their domestic reforms did nothing to solve the problem of unemployment. After nine months their Liberal allies withdrew their hesitant support. An appeal to the country did not help the socialists. Despite their hold on the distressed areas and mining districts, they went down heavily. In November, 1924, Baldwin again took office.

During the next four years there was a slight improvement in trade, unemployment fell by nearly half a million and there was a reduction of 6d. in the £ in income tax. An attempt at a general strike, which for a dramatic week in the spring of 1926 created a revolutionary situation, was defeated by the refusal of the ordinary Englishmen – most of whom sympathized with the miners on whose behalf the strike was ordered – to permit an outside body to dictate to an elected and lawful government. The coal strike was subsequently allowed to drag on for six miserable months to its dismal, inevitable end; thereafter industrial conditions became temporarily more normal. There was a good deal of slum clearance carried out by the joint efforts of private enterprise and local authorities with the aid of government grants: in the four and a half years of the administration 8,000,000 houses were built. Workmen's savings increased by £170,000,000, and there was a steady, if unspectacular, improvement in the extent and quality of the social services, whose cost, only £63,000,000 in 1911, rose by 1929 to £341,000,000. The general achievement was not inspiring and fell far short of the soldiers' dream. Yet it was the nearest post-war Britain ever came to prosperity.

But there still remained over 1,000,000 unemployed. There were still millions of English men and women living ugly, undernourished, uncertain lives, in cramped, mean, verminous dwellings, and bringing up their children in dirt and degradation. When the Baldwin government, in the summer of 1929, relying on the unimaginative slogan of Safety First, asked for a renewal of its mandate, it was found it had forfeited the confidence of the country. The change of rulers was not based on reason so much as on the human feeling that there was more suffering in Britain than flesh and blood should be asked to bear.

Yet the socialists, who again took office with unofficial Liberal support, could do no more than the Conservatives to alleviate that suffering. In fact, through no fault of their own, they were able to do far less. In the autumn of 1929 a series of crashes on the New York Stock Exchange was followed by a failure of credit from one end of Europe to the other. The great world economic crisis or trade blizzard began. It was grimmer and bigger than any that had ever happened. By the autumn of 1931, unemployment in Britain was approaching 3,000,000. In the same month, the government's unbalanced borrowings to meet the deficit on the Unemployment Insurance Fund precipitated a panic among foreign depositors and an incipient flight from the pound. Amid much confused bandying of figures and waving of depreciated pound notes, and a wholly irrational but rather moving recrudescence of patriotic feeling, a hastily-formed coalition government appealed to the country for a 'doctor's mandate' to solve the economic ills under which its people were suffering. It received it with a majority unprecedented in British electoral history. The socialist and former pacifist Prime Minister Ramsay Macdonald, who had abandoned his party at the dictates of his conscience and the Bank of England, was returned to power with a following of 556 members, 472 of whom were Tories.

The new government made little impression on the unemployment figures at first, which, true to the uncontrollable laws which seemed to govern world trade, continued to rise gently until 1933. Thereafter they fell substantially for three years, and then with the 'National' government still in power, showed unmistakable signs of rising again. Yet it would be unfair to say that the administration's efforts, which were painstaking if uninspired, had no effect on them at all. Comprised in the doctor's mandate, though the purer and less accommodating Liberal free traders who supported the coalition subsequently denied it, was a *carte blanche* to adopt some form of protection for native and imperial industry. In the cumulative distress and anxiety of 1931, Britain, after close on a century, was ready at last to repudiate free trade. For men had cried to their totem, and their totem had failed them.

Not that any very vigorous protective policy was adopted. The worst abuses of dumping by state subsidized foreign importers, who had long regarded the unprotected British urban market as a happy hunting ground, were checked. And in 1932 a British Delegation, led by the Lord Privy Seal, Baldwin, agreed at the Imperial Conference at Ottawa to afford to the Dominions, in return for reciprocal advantages for British exporters, that preferential treatment which had been refused by Lord Salisbury's government at the Diamond Jubilee thirty-five years before. But the extent of such preference was strictly limited because the National government felt itself unable to reserve more than a moderate fraction of the home market in foodstuffs for imperial producers. Its reluctance was dictated not so much by the old fear of raising the price of food to the British consumer as by its deference to the vested financial, commercial and shipping interests which had grown up round the imports of foreign agricultural products. For it was plainly impossible for Britain to take her beef simultaneously from British farms and from the Argentine: if she sacrificed the latter for the former, it would become difficult and perhaps impossible to transmit the interest on the British capital invested in that country. And as the vast and costly party machines necessary to a country with a democratic franchise inevitably received more support from bankers and shipowners than farmers, it was only natural that the former's interests should prevail.

So imperial preference, though popularly approved, was but tentatively encouraged instead of boldly applied. It was not possible to create a new economic order for the British Empire as the public wished without breaking financial eggs. In 1938, the Anglo-American Trade Agreement, without any mandate from the electorate, actually whittled down the modest concessions granted to Dominion producers in 1932. As for protection, this was virtually never possible without the repudiation of a complicated system of foreign commercial treaties which had been built up during the free trade years, and of which the public knew nothing. The whole economic structure raised in a century of titanic capitalist enterprise was too intricate and interdependent for any one to be able to produce, let alone execute, a plan capable of mending any one of its defective parts without injuring, perhaps irreparably, some other. However delicately one stepped, the floor of the commercial edifice was alive with vested interests, every one of which was apparently sacred and defended by a whole chorus of jealous hierophants. The utter fiasco of the much-advertized World Economic Conference in London, in the summer of 1933, was an illustration, if any was needed, of the omnipresence of the disintegrating forces in contemporary human society. It was poor Ramsay Macdonald's last attempt to view the world as a unified whole. Despite his oratory and good intentions the task was beyond his or apparently any other man's comprehension.

*　　*　　*

Before the Conference broke up in cynical despair the emphasis was already passing from internal ills, still uncured, to still graver external ones. Adolf Hitler, rising to stormy political victory on a surge of angry oratory and the bitter despair of six million unemployed and thirty million underfed, became the ruler of Germany. His aims, shrilly enunciated for fourteen passionate years, were the repudiation of the peace treaties and the establishment of a greater Reich that should dominate the Europe which had humiliated her. He was a man of hate, who hated the French, hated the Jews, hated his own rivals and predecessors in hatred, the Bolshevists. He hated everything which opposed the interests and destiny of Germany and, as he always identified himself with Germany, by implication every one who barred his path.

Apart from an instinctive dislike for the man's manners and methods, the British people were not at first interested in Hitler. That they might themselves be among the causes, though as yet not amongst the immediate objects, of his vituperative fury never struck them. At the time of the Armistice, when almost every family in the land was mourning some relative and when many harsh and bitter things had long been said and done, they had not unnaturally responded to a hasty request from their politicians for a mandate to rebuild Europe by telling them to hang the Kaiser and squeeze the German lemon till the pips squeaked. After that, being heartily tired of foreigners and their problems, they had turned their backs on the Continent and, immersing themselves in their own affairs, left their politicians and publicists to reshape Europe as they chose.

Their brief spasm of ill-humour had soon passed. With temperamental British inability to nurse a grudge, they wished Germany nothing but well. The anxious efforts of the French to keep their ancient and terrible enemy prostrate only increased British sympathies for her. Moreover, an island state dependent on foreign trade found that she could ill afford so disturbing an economic factor as a ruined central Europe. When the French premier pointed to his country's devastated areas as a reason for tightening the screw, Lloyd George retorted by pointing to the export districts on industrial South Wales and northern England with an unanswerable 'These are *our* devastated areas.'

But of the treaties still standing in their name – their content, the extent of their enforcement, their effects on the conquered – the British people, except for a small minority of intellectual socialists and Liberals who had always opposed the peace treaties as politically inexpedient and economically suicidal, were almost totally ignorant. They were unaware that Germany had been ruined economically before a single mark of reparations had been paid or even demanded. They did not know – or had forgotten if they had ever known – that for several years the peoples of central Europe had starved, that the entire middle class of Germany had lost its savings in the inflation, that hundreds of thousands of German civilians had been driven at a few hours' notice from their homes by French soldiers. Because in the latter 1920s Germany thrived for a while on the reckless loans with which British and American financiers tried to resuscitate and exploit her industries, they never realized that millions of Germans were secretly nursing bitter grievances and irrational hatreds. They knew nothing of the dry timber which the orator Hitler was seeking to ignite.

According to their lights such grievances as existed had been allayed. The Locarno Pact, concluded in 1925 between Austen Chamberlain, Stresemann, and Briand, which, in effect, merely congealed the *status quo*, they enthusiastically acclaimed in the belief that it consecrated the policy of let bygones be bygones, and restored equality between victors and vanquished. That it had not done so they learned with perplexity when, in their successive attempts to achieve disarmament – historic British practice after all wars – the Germans insisted on parity with the French and the French on an overwhelming superiority in every weapon as their only security against Germany. Wanting nothing but peace – the one positive gain from the wastage, cruelty and misery of the war – the British people assumed in their insular, hopeful way that every one else felt the same. Through their voluntary associations and parliamentary institutions they affirmed over and over again their sense of its necessity and their faith in the League of Nations and the machinery of international law. They even succeeded in the help of their Anglo-Saxon kinsmen in the United States in persuading the statesmen of the world to affix their signatures to a document called the Kellog Pact, repudiating war as an instrument of policy. For, having suffered so much from the tidal flood of war, they supposed, like King Canute, that an edict against tides would protect them from further inundation. Their courtiers, the democratic newspapers and politicians, loudly assured them that it would.

Yet, everywhere, the old national jealousies and fears barred the way to that rule of perpetual peace and international law that was the Englishman's ideal. Italy wanted naval parity with France, and the USA with Britain, who in turn depended for her very existence on the freedom of her sea routes. Japan wanted hegemony in eastern waters; Soviet Russia, in order to secure and further the proletarian revolutionary experiment, wanted the largest air force in the world; Poland wanted a big army, preferably mounted, to defend herself against Russia; and Czechoslovakia and Belgium wanted the continued profits from the sale of the armaments they so industriously manufactured. Every disarmament conference failed. For no formula could resolve these eternal discordancies.

Into this imbroglio of rival expedients, figures and formulas, like a bull entering a china shop, burst Hitler. Even before the easy-going, preoccupied British public had become conscious of his strident rancour, their pacific hopes had been dashed. In 1931, Japan, seeking preferential markets for the expanding industrial population of her overcrowded island, marched into an anarchic China to seize Manchuria. British peace-lovers protested, the more logical of them even clamouring to go to war to vindicate the decencies of international law and the rules of the League of Nations. But neither their fellow members of the League, nor Japan's great rival, the United States, was prepared to go to such an extreme and desperate course. Nor were the British – then in the throes of a financial crisis – in any position, after ten years of disarmament, to impose single-handed the rule of righteousness on a great naval Power at the far end of the world. The only result of Anglo-Saxon disapproval for aggression was Japan's exit from the League, taking her conquest with her.

Two years after Hitler's irruption on the European scene, a still more brazen aggression occurred. A noisy Fascist Italy, seeking preferential markets, raw materials and an outlet for her expanding population – now shut out from the Americas by restrictive emigration acts – revived a long dormant claim on Abyssinia.

At the instance of Italy herself, Abyssinia had been admitted to the League, and was therefore recognized by the British public as an equal and sovereign fellow nation. What complicated the outrage was that Italy was still a kind of tacit ally of Britain and France. Mussolini, who, as western Europe's first dictator, was believed to have no love for his upstart Teuton imitator, had only recently declared from the stronghold of the Brenner Pass that Fascist Italy would not allow Austria to be absorbed in the Reich. With Germany rearming in open violation of the peace treaties, the loyal alignment of the three victor powers against the reviving barbarian seemed vital to the safety of them all.

The French, always more sensitive than the British to the peril beyond the Rhine, were painfully aware of this. When Italy, true to her boasts and warlike preparations, marched into Abyssinia in the autumn of 1935, they did their best to restrain the pacific enthusiasm of the British for vindicating the violated principles of international law. But the British were not to be restrained. Their politicians had repeatedly told them that the Great War had been fought to end war for ever. The heroic and loved dead had died and the millions had suffered for the sake of that great consummation. And the League of Nations, honoured in Britain as nowhere else, was the guarantee that peace should endure. Its Covenant was the British people's war gain. They would not allow it to be flouted.

But their dilemma was tragic. For they could not protect the integrity of League principles without waging another war – that which they had hoped above all things to avert – and so destroying the one achievement of the war to end war. Reluctant to ignore the Italian challenge, equally reluctant to embark on hostilities in which, as it became painfully clear, they could not count on the help of the nations associated with them in the Covenant, they tried the expedient of commercial sanctions. Even to these the associated nations, loath to dislocate their trade, gave only tepid support. Ineffectual for any purpose save to irritate Italy against what seemed British sanctimony – for who were the British to cavil at imperial conquest? – sanctions not only failed to stop her triumphal march into Addis Ababa but drove her out of the League into the arms of her hereditary enemy. Henceforward the two dictators marched together on one brazen axis, with the other aggressor of the Far East in uneasy co-operation. Their declared aim was a New Order constructed on falsehood, menace and violence.

Hitler snatched at his opportunity. While the Italo-Abyssinian war was still waging, he reoccupied the demilitarized Rhineland, relying on pacifist opinion in a disarmed Britain to prevent more than verbal protests at this breach of the Peace Treaties and Locarno. France, suffering from internal dissension and industrial unrest, dared not act alone. The door of Europe was slammed in her face. Henceforward she could only come to the assistance of her eastern allies by breaking through a fortified German frontier. It was the end of Versailles. It was virtually, though scarcely any one yet knew it, the end of peace. There were formalities to be performed – a guarantee given and an ultimatum ignored – and then 'the monstrous anger of the guns' would be heard once more.

*   *   *

Such was the fate of the dream which the soldiers brought back from the trenches. On September 3rd 1939, it seemed as if the dead had died in vain. The veterans of the Great War had seen their homely ideals of a decent life constantly frustrated by economic factors beyond their control or even that of their politicians. The home of their own with a garden, the job in which they could take pride, the security for themselves and their dear ones, had had to wait. In their patient English way they had accepted the fact, hoping that gradual amelioration of social conditions might one day ensure the promised land for their children and children's children. In that hope they had passively adopted the Baldwinian thesis, put aside bitterness, and worked for the slow realization of a more just and happier society in the days after their death. But even for this limited realization, peace was essential. A repetition of the terrible struggle of 1914–18 would put the clock of progress back fifty, a hundred, perhaps a thousand years. War marked the end of all their dreams, and war had come.

Yet there was nothing left for the British but to fight and beat the enemy, cost them what it might. They had at least done their best to keep the peace. Their cause, however tragic, was a noble one: they were fighting against evil things and a cruel, unappeasable aggressor who tortured racial minorities, who tore up treaties, who ranted and shouted and bullied and, when he was thwarted, would rain death and desolation on peaceful millions.

CHAPTER FIFTEEN

The Monstrous Anger Of The Guns

'Do not let us speak of darker days; let us rather speak of sterner days. These are not our dark days: these are great days – the greatest days our country has ever lived; and we must all thank God that we have been allowed, each of us according to our stations, to play a part in making these days memorable in the history of our race.'

Winston Churchill in 1941

WHEN ON SEPTEMBER 3RD, 1939, Britain, carrying with her a deeply-divided and hesitant France, met Hitler's invasion of Poland by war, the bulk of her battle-fleet had been re-armed against air attack and the first of the great ships laid down in 1936 was within a year of completion. And, having grown in four years from 500 to nearly 1500 first-line aircraft and from 30,000 to 120,000 men, her Metropolitan Air Force, though still only a third of the size of the Luftwaffe, offered, in its small but superlatively trained Fighter Command, some answer to the trump card of unopposed bombing with which for the past eighteen months Hitler had blackmailed Europe. For the first time, too, as a result of the rapid build-up of Anti-Aircraft Command, London and the principal ports and factory towns had some rudimentary ground defence against day bombardment from the air.

Yet on land, despite the past decade's immense technical changes, Britain's Regular Army was equipped only for colonial warfare and was far less ready for a Continental war than in 1914, when it had sent seven magnificently trained divisions to France. When partial rearmament began in the mid-1930s, absolute priority had been given to the needs of the Navy and Air Force, and the Army had been left almost in the same state of neglect into which it had fallen in the pacifist 1920s, when, with an armaments expenditure of less than two and a half millions compared with the Navy's thirteen millions and the RAF's seven and a half millions, its personnel had shrunk to under 150,000 men. Its artillery had little more than half the range of the latest German guns, it was without any but the lightest armour, and its men had had to do their training with flags instead of batteries and wooden dummies and hired tradesmen's vans instead of tanks and bren-guns.

Not until the anxious summer of 1938 – and then only on the spur of the moment and to reassure the French – had the possibility of sending two of its five divisions to the Continent in the event of a German war been considered. Even then, with the urgent needs of the other Services, little was done for the Army except to strengthen its anti-aircraft units for purposes of home defence. But in the spring of 1939, after the Chamberlain administration had met Hitler's treacherous invasion of Czechoslovakia with a guarantee of Poland's western frontiers and the threat to Germany of a European war on two fronts, conscription had been suddenly introduced. With the knowledge that the Army's training depots could be now filled and oblivious of its almost complete lack of modern arms, the Government had promised the French to increase the initial Expeditionary Force from two to four divisions – almost the entire Regular home-strength of the country – and to reinforce it as soon as possible after the outbreak of war by a further five or six Territorial divisions. Ultimately, it intimated, thirty or more divisions would be raised.

Yet, though there was now no lack of potential man-power, the utmost the Ministry of Supply could hope to arm and equip for France even by 1942 were five Regular and fourteen Territorial divisions. On the outbreak of war in September 1939, only two of these were approaching readiness. The Regular Army had only just received its peacetime complement of wheeled transport and barely half its tracked vehicles. The new National Service Army existed only on paper.

On the day after the declaration of war, however, the first detachment of the Expeditionary Force sailed for France. Two further divisions, constituting a hastily formed II Corps, though not yet trained or equipped and with nearly half its men reservists, followed at the end of September in accordance with the Government's promise to France. Together with its maintenance, supply and communications services in the rear areas, the Expeditionary Force constituted an initial reinforcement to the French Army of some 160,000 men and 24,000 vehicles. It was transported across the Channel, despite the threat from Luftwaffe and U-boat, without the loss of a man or weapon.

Before the end of September Poland had been driven out of the war and her territory divided between Germany and Soviet Russia. There then followed the months during which the campaign in the West was regarded by the authorities as the 'Phoney War', a continuation of the old, comforting peace-time delusion that Hitler was bluffing. Many ordinary people, too, were sure that 'it' would be all over by Christmas. But in September the aircraft carrier HMS *Courageous* was sunk; in October the battleship HMS *Royal Oak* was torpedoed in the protected Fleet anchorage of Scapa Flow; in November the armed merchant cruiser HMS *Rawalpindi* was sunk by the *Scharnhorst*; and in December the *Graf Spee* was pursued and damaged by British cruisers and then scuttled off Montevideo harbour. There was, from the first day, nothing phoney about the war at sea.

In April Denmark and Norway were invaded by the Germans and this, the first phase of their invasion of Western Europe, was completed with the virtual fall of Norway and, in early May, the forced departure of British forces from South Trondheim, though fighting continued in northern Norway.

In the House of Commons on May 8th a violent attack was made on Neville Chamberlain and his conduct of the war. The most damaging speech of all was made by one of his own followers, many of whom voted against him in the subsequent vote of censure. On May 10th, feeling he had lost the confidence of the House, the Prime Minister resigned, and on his advice the King entrusted Winston Churchill with the task of forming a National Government. On the same day the German Panzer attack in the West began. It was a lightning campaign, which resulted in the fall of France, Holland and Belgium and the near destruction of the British army at Dunkirk. From now on, until the might of the United States came to be exerted in Europe, the British people had to stand alone and fight their own battles while the world looked on.

The days between May 29th and June 4th, 1940, were a turning point in the history of mankind. For they marked the first check in Germany's triumphant march towards world dominion. In those few days the British Navy, with the help of the RAF, saved a British Army – at that moment virtually the only British Army – from what seemed certain destruction.

It was a deliverance so unexpected and unaccountable as to constitute a kind of miracle. And it was generally regarded as such at that time. Dunkirk, like Corunna, was a kind of British victory, and as such has tended to obscure the events that preceded it. But the occasion of Dunkirk was the greatest military disaster in British history. An army of nearly a quarter of a million men – a force far larger than any commanded by Wellington or Marlborough – with practically the entire available field equipment of Britain, was surrounded and penned in between the marshes and the sea with no apparent choice but immediate surrender or death.

The fault was not primarily the fault of that army, but of its allies who had been defeated on either flank. But in a larger sense the great disaster of May 1940, was as much the responsibility of Britain as of any other nation. It marked the apparent collapse of all values which an easy-going parliamentary democracy had stood for in the years between the two wars.

It marked equally the apparent triumph and material vindication of Hitler's barbaric revolution and of the cruel and ancient tyrannies he had enthroned. Right based on mere good intentions, it was proved, could not stand in the field against evil based on might.

At that moment the miracle occurred. It did not reverse the verdict of the disastrous battle beforehand; it redeemed it. It was like a sudden rainbow at the climax of some terrible storm. In the midst of it long columns of men, tormented, utterly weary, and in deadly peril were seen going down unperturbed to the water's edge.

Their only means of escape were the mole, blasted by enemy bombs and shells, and a line of exposed beaches with shelving shores from which evacuation would have been impossible in anything but a dead calm. They stood there in long, patient queues as though waiting for the last bus home, or sheltered in impromptu holes excavated in the sand, while overhead dive-bombers roared and screamed and fantastic air battles were fought out in the midst of immense pillars of drifting smoke and fountains of water.

After the traditional fashion of their race in the hour of crisis, the waiting men showed no sign of panic or despair, nor – it would seem – of any visible emotion at all. They merely waited, with a kind of dogged faith. And presently their faith was justified. The lean, crowded destroyers, now helped by hundreds of little boats – many of them last used for shilling trips on peacetime seaside holidays and just come out of England – provided the rescue.

By some strange magic of courage and improvization nearly 340,000

British, French and Belgian soldiers were taken on board and borne out of the reach of the enemy's closing jaws. For five days and nights the miracle continued until no one remained on the beaches save the dead. The living came back out of the delirium of modern war to the quiet and ordinariness of England, to neat railway carriages and smiling policemen and girls holding up cups of tea. And there they lived to fight another day – on the sands of Alamein, the beaches of Italy and the jungles of Burma. Among the soldiers who embarked were the generals Alexander, Brooke and Montgomery.

For a few days the nation breathed again and the free world with it. Then the terrible surge of German victory was renewed. For those who were not Germans, the world was being taught that there was only one virtue – instant and unconditional surrender: for those who delayed, only one fate – certain and imminent destruction. Under that knowledge France crumpled, broke, and yielded. The world prepared itself for the inevitable.

But the voice which came out of England at that moment was neither repentant nor submissive. It was not the voice of the hypocrite saying acceptable things before sacrifice, nor of the humbug temporizing to save his face. It was the voice of a man angry, defiant, and utterly resolved, or rather, of forty-seven millions looking in a single direction, and that direction seawards, and intoning in their hearts the words which one man spoke for all:

'We shall defend our island whatever the cost may be. We shall fight on the beaches, we shall fight on the landing-grounds, we shall fight in the fields and in the streets; we shall fight in the hills, and we shall never surrender.'

No one who lived in England through that wonderful summer of 1940 was ever likely to forget it. The light that beat down on her green meadows, shining with emerald loveliness, was scarcely of this world; the streets of her cities, soon to be torn and shattered, were bathed in a calm, serene sunshine, and in forge and factory, field and mine her people, with a fierce, unresting, yet quiet intensity, worked as they had never worked before in her whole history.

Never in all her history had victory seemed more remote or improbable than in 1940. Yet at the very hour when in the midst of unparalleled disasters he offered his colleagues blood, toil, tears and sweat, Winston Churchill defined his country's goal.

'You ask,' he said, 'what is our aim? I can answer in one word: Victory – victory at all costs, victory in spite of all terrors; victory, however long and hard the road may be; for without victory there is no survival.'

*   *   *

The miracle of Dunkirk was closely followed by another – the defence of the homeland by the Royal Air Force – which began in July. Already on the Kentish aerodromes, as the sirens began their low wail over the London streets, the few who were to save the many were preparing for battle and the Spitfires and Hurricanes were warming up. Already in the cities tens of thousands of men and women calmly awaited the hour when hell would descend out of the skies to blast their homes and pulp and tear their bodies.

The RAF had to be destroyed before Operation *Sealion*, the invasion of Britain, could begin. In Holland, Belgium and France the barges were ready. Throughout July and August the air battle raged, but on September 10th Grand-Admiral Raeder reported, 'There is no sign of the defeat of the enemy's Air Force over southern England and in the Channel area.' Next day Hitler, who had already postponed the invasion date from the 15th to the 21st, postponed it again until the 24th. Then, on September 15th, Goering, confident that Fighter Command was down to its last few hundred aircraft, launched on London the most concentrated attack of the whole battle. More than a thousand sorties were made against the capital and the proportion of fighters to bombers sent over was five to one. But to the Germans the defenders seemed more, not fewer, and their attack on the bombers more devastating than ever. The RAF's last reserves were thrown in but no German formation was able to destroy its target, and nearly 60 raiders, including 34 heavily guarded bombers, were shot down for a loss of 26.

Next day, unknown to the British, Hitler postponed the invasion *sine die*; his casualties had become too great. But the threat of invasion remained and his daylight raids continued until October 5th. The night bombing of London and other cities began on September 7th and went on throughout the autumn and well into 1941. Henceforth, with their will unbroken, civilians too were in the very front of the line.

In that late summer of 1940 the fate of the world had depended on the deeds of 1500 young pilots, of whom nearly a third were killed. Fighting with the British were Australians, New Zealanders, South

Africans, Canadians, Rhodesians, Czechs, Poles, Free Frenchmen and Belgians, and supporting them were the RAF ground staff and Anti-Aircraft Command gunners. In human annals there has been no single combat more dramatic or vital.

Operation *Sealion* would have proved costly for the German invaders but the test never came. Of the 700 tanks which had been sent to France by Britain only 25 came back with the retreating Army; when in June Churchill had inspected coastal defences at St Margaret's Bay there were only three anti-tank guns covering five miles of the most threatened beach in England. Such was the background against which he said in the House of Commons that August, 'Never in the field of human conflict was so much owed by so many to so few'.

* * *

Nor was Britain threatened only with invasion. Her sea communications were at the enemy's mercy. An over-populated, heavily industrialized island, dependent on ocean transport for two-thirds of her food and most of her raw materials, she could now only import by running the gauntlet of enemy U-boats, surface warships and aircraft established, as a result of Hitler's victories, in every harbour and on every airfield of Europe's western seaboard. Her life-lines were threatened at their home-water terminals, not only, as in 1914–18, from the east, but from north, south and even west. The blockader of the Continent had become the blockaded. And the vital sea-route that bound her to her eastern dependencies and dominions – to Egypt, the Persian and Iraq oil-wells, India, Malaya and Australasia – was outflanked for nearly four thousand miles of its course by a hostile shore: in the Biscay bay, in the Mediterranean, in the Red Sea. With the French fleet and French North Africa at best neutral and at worst aligned against her, with Italy possessing on both shores of the central Mediterranean a geographical position that virtually cut the sea in half, and with that ambitious power's large air force and navy of six battleships, twenty-three cruisers and more than two hundred destroyers and submarines, Britain's historic naval dominance seemed as threatened in Europe's southern waters as in its northern.

Meanwhile, in the Nile Valley 55,000 British and Imperial troops with some two hundred obsolescent aircraft were left, through the defection of the French armies of Syria, Tunisia and Morocco, to face the attack of 415,000 Italian troops (Italy having declared war on

Britain and France on June 16), based on Libya to the west and Abyssinia and Eritrea to the south of them, supported by an Italian air force of seventeen hundred first-line aircraft – nearly five hundred of them already in Africa. With the Mediterranean Fleet withdrawn to Alexandria, Malta was left an isolated outpost, only sixty miles from the Sicilian coast and eight hundred from the nearest British base. Even Gibraltar was dominated by the guns of Franco's Spain. It was scarcely surprising that most of the American Service chiefs regarded Britain at this time as a bad risk. The French high command, conscious of how quickly its own Army had collapsed, predicted that within three weeks her neck would be 'wrung like a chicken's.'

After the fall of France and the loss of nearly all Britain's military equipment there was only one country which could help to fill the gap between what she needed in her immediate plight and what her own factories were making. Not the least of Churchill's services in 1940 was to awaken in the American President the conviction that weapons sent to England would not be wasted. Despite the belief of many of his Service chiefs that, as she was doomed, to sell her weapons from America's scanty armoury would be to compromise the safety of the western hemisphere, Franklin Roosevelt responded to a faith and courage that matched his own. Under pressure from the White House the American army released from its First World War reserves half a million rifles, 80,000 machine and tommy-guns, 900 75-mm field-guns, and enough ammunition for them to meet a few weeks' fighting. They were hurried to the eastern seaboard, loaded on to waiting British ships and reached England during July.

In December 1940 the British forces in North Africa under General Wavell made their first offensive against the Italians, and captured Bardia, Derna and Tobruk and 100,000 prisoners. But a German invasion of Yugoslavia and Greece in April was successful and forced the evacuation of the Allied Expeditionary Force which had been generously sent by Wavell in March in anticipation of an invasion. In February Hitler, annoyed by the Allied successes in the Desert, sent Rommel to take command. 'The Desert Fox' wrought an almost immediate transformation, with the Afrika Korps and the Italians attacking and recapturing all the ground only recently won by Wavell. From then on retreat, advance and retreat ensued during the rest of 1941 and well into 1942.

Yet Britain's actions in the eastern Mediterranean that spring had consequences that, even if unintended, damaged Germany more than herself. For Hitler had by now resolved to attack Russia, and the diversion of armoured and airborne troops to smash the Jugoslav and Greek resistance and drive the British out of Greece and Crete, delayed the start of his Russian offensive, though the forces involved were only a minute fraction of the immense German and satellite armies assembling on the fifteen-hundred-mile western frontier of the USSR. And the very daring of Britain's offensive operations in the Middle East caused the German leaders to think her stronger in that theatre than she was and deterred them from attacking Turkey and so securing the Middle East oil-wells and a dominating position on Russia's southern flank. On June 22nd the impatient German dictator launched his armies in a frontal assault on the USSR. Barred by the tenuous ring of British sea-power from breaking out of Europe into southern Asia and Africa, he struck eastwards, like Napoleon, across the boundless plains of Russia.

After his failure in the autumn of 1940 Hitler was faced by a dilemma. If he attempted to invade England and failed, he would lose not only much prestige and the whole of Germany's available shipping, but, by depriving himself of the means of making another attempt, release the growing British Army and Air Force for operations elsewhere. As he put it, he was 'in the position of a man with only one round left in his rifle; if he missed, the situation would be worse than before.' If, on the other hand, he left the islanders alone, with the support of their backers in the United States they would grow steadily stronger, particularly in the air, and ultimately confront him with that major war on two fronts it had been his object to avoid.

For to the east of the Reich, incorporating the plains of eastern Poland and the Ukraine and the Caucasian oilfields he had resolved to conquer, lay the communist empire of Russia, with its vast resources and population and its Ten Years' Plan of industrialization, threatening Hitler with a mechanized military power that would presently surpass his own. Sooner or later, if he delayed his eastward march, he knew he would have to face a Russian attack – a possibility of which he had been unpleasantly reminded during his summer campaign in the West when the USSR had annexed the Baltic States and Rumanian Bessarabia. For all their fear of his victorious army and professions of friendship, the Soviet leaders were only playing for time. It seemed, therefore, essential for the German leader, if he could not induce Britain to make peace, either to rid himself of her by sudden invasion, or, alternatively, to keep her growing air and land forces tied down by the threat of it until the Soviet colossus had been dealt with.

Although Hitler's attention was now inevitably drawn to the east there was no lessening of Britain's troubles as she struggled on alone. The Atlantic war against the U-boats became ever more menacing as their numbers and their successes increased. The bombing of London and other cities reached the first of its climaxes, with many thousands dead, injured and homeless. Between May and December 1941 the Royal Navy lost two battleships, two battlecruisers, one aircraft carrier and numerous cruisers, destroyers and other warships. Unceasing help had to be given to keeping Malta alive, the brave heart of the Mediterranean war, where, in December 1941, except for the island's defiant guns, nothing remained in the 2000 miles between Gibraltar and Alexandria but three cruisers and a handful of destroyers and submarines.

There was, too, pressure on Churchill to give direct military assistance to Russia as, by October, with the Wehrmacht advancing deep into her territory, her situation was becoming desperate. He faced strong demands for a 'Second Front Now' in the west.

But on December 7th 1941 Japan struck without warning at the United States fleet in Pearl Harbor. Almost simultaneously their far-flung forces moved outwards in a vast arc attacking the American Philippines, British Malaya and Hong Kong. The United States declared war on Japan on the 8th, and her eventual involvement in the European conflict was assured when Germany and Italy declared war on her on the 11th.

Yet, though America's entry into the war had immeasurably increased the possibilities of an ultimate Allied victory, the manner in which it had been brought about had greatly increased the chances of immediate and perhaps irretrievable disaster. Churchill's vision was on the horizon rather than on the shambles at his feet. On that December morning Japan had struck simultaneously at the United States' advance-base in the Philippines and at its Pacific Fleet five thousand miles away. While General MacArthur's bombers were being mown down on Clark Field, seven out of America's nine battleships in Pearl Harbor – or nearly half her capital ships – were sunk or put out of action. All hope of the American Fleet advancing to the relief of Malaya and the East Indies had gone. On the same day part of the small RAF and RAAF contingent in Malaya was destroyed on its airfields, and Japanese troops landed in southern Thailand near the Malayan frontier. Next

277

day an enemy detachment, crossing the narrow Kra isthmus, reached the shores of the Indian Ocean, seized the British landing-ground at Point Victoria and cut the air-route by which reinforcements from India and Europe were flown to Singapore.

The whole balance in the Pacific was upset and the Japanese would be masters of the ocean until new forces were assembled there. The British Chiefs of Staff, two days after Pearl Harbor, examined possibilities of sending British battleships to restore the situation. But the next morning, December 10th, brought the worst news of the War since the fall of France. The battleship *Prince of Wales* and the battlecruiser *Repulse* had been sunk by torpedo-carrying aircraft while trying, without adequate air cover, to intercept a fleet of transports off the Malayan coast. Churchill's bold gamble to save Singapore had gone the way of Narvik, Greece and Crete. From Africa eastwards to America through the Indian Ocean and Pacific the Allies had lost command of the sea. Britain was to lose Malaya, Singapore and Hong Kong by Christmas and Burma by the middle of May, when the bulk of her troops there crossed into India.

Until the end of 1941 Britain could scarcely be said to have had a strategy for winning the war except to fight back with all she had and hold her European foes in a ring of salt water and desert. Beyond that she could only, as Churchill had taught her, hope for some change in the tide of world affairs that might weaken her enemies. She lived by the faith he gave her, and from hand-to-mouth, for she had no other choice. Her seamen sought to keep open her trade routes, her soldiers to guard the British Isles and Nile Delta, her airmen to build up a force that, by subjecting the Reich to growing air bombardment, might one day engulf it in a pyre of flame and rubble. America's entry into the war, and the unexpected toughness of Russia's resistance, offered new vistas of opportunity if only the German and Japanese drives could be held. With a victorious naval power to fight in the vast spaces of the Pacific, the American admirals naturally wished to concentrate the United States' war potential against Japan. Her soldiers, with the support of her President, favoured the nearer and more easily attainable objective of Germany first. But their experience of modern warfare was very small, and they at first grossly underestimated the difficulties both of transporting troops and supplies to Europe and of fighting inside Hitler's continental fortress. When the American Army Chief-of-Staff General Marshall declared his belief that the quickest way to end the war was to invade France in 1942 or 1943, Brooke, the Chairman of the British Joint Chiefs of Staff Committee replied, 'Yes, but not the way we want to end it!'

Brooke's strategy, like that of all Britain's greatest commanders, depended on salt-water. With his grasp of essentials, he saw that sea transport was the key to the offensive. Without it nothing could be done to take the pressure off Russia or deprive the enemy, with his central land position, of the initiative. In the early months of 1942 the Allies were losing vast quantities of shipping to the U-boats. There was only one way in which such losses could be made good and only one way to relieve the Red Army. That was not, as the Russians and Americans argued, by premature and inadequately supplied offensives against Hitler's Western Wall, but by striking at the Axis in the one theatre where, because of salt water and geography, logistics could enable the still comparatively minute land-forces of the Allies to exert an influence out of all proportion to their size. By expelling the Germans and Italians from North Africa, Britain and America could reopen the Mediterranean and, shortening their supply route to India and the Middle East, release at least a million tons of shipping for immediate offensive operations. Then by threatening the enemy across that sea and forcing him to man hundreds of miles of hitherto secure coastline, they could strike, through Sicily and Italy, at the point of his continental fortress where his communications were most strained. Having knocked Italy out of the war and made Germany deploy her reserves in the one area from which, owing to poor and mountainous communications, they would be hardest to extricate, they could thereafter assail Hitler's Western Wall across the Channel without having to face too powerful a counter-attack and maintain their thrust till it had reached her heart, while the Russians, similarly relieved from the threat of a central reserve using Germany's fast west-to-east communications – the cause of their defeat in 1914 – could safely advance on the frontiers of the Reich from the opposite direction.

Such was the policy that, after long and sometimes fierce argument, Britain and America adopted and, in spite of many differences of opinion, systematically carried out until, first Italy, and then Germany were destroyed, and the whole weight of the Allies could be turned against the surviving Axis partner in the Pacific.

On October 23rd 1942 the Eighth Army's concentrated artillery barrage began the battle of El Alamein, the first of the actions which were to sweep the Axis armies off the north coast of Africa. Only eleven days later Rommel was forced to give the order for a general withdrawal.

By the evening of November 6th, 30,000 prisoners, 350 tanks and 400 guns had been taken in the Western Desert. Rommel and the remnants of the Afrika Korps were in full retreat, four German and eight Italian divisions had ceased to exist, and General Alexander was able to cable the Prime Minister, 'Ring out the bells!' But that night rain started to fall and continued to fall all next day, turning the crowded desert tracks to the Libyan frontier into rivers of mud and making it impossible for the British armoured divisions to outdistance and cut off the flying remnants of German armour. By sundown on the 7th Rommel's rearguard was nearly two hundred miles from the battlefield and the main stream of his transport was starting to cross the Libyan frontier.

Yet, though the Desert Fox made good his escape, fifteen hundred miles in his rear the Allies were preparing to stop his earth. As the rain fell steadily in Egypt all that Saturday, a great armada in the western Mediterranean was steaming eastwards, while far ahead the battleships *Duke of York, Rodney* and *Renown* and the aircraft-carriers, *Victorious, Formidable* and *Furious*, trailed their coat to draw the enemy's fire. And as night fell, while the Germans and Italians scanned the sea approaches to Sardinia, Sicily and Malta, the transports turned south-wards on their true course, dividing into two streams, the one for Oran and the other for Algiers. Only a single American transport suffered any damage, being torpedoed a hundred miles from her destination by a stray U-boat.

These were the great transports of Operation *Torch*, which landed in North Africa on November 8th. Within three days the Vichy French authorities had signed an armistice. But there was to be long hard fighting against the Germans until the Allied forces, from the west and the east, met in Tunisia. On May 12th General von Arnim, Rommel's successor, surrendered a quarter of a million German and Italian soldiers, 1000 guns and several hundred tanks. At a speech made in London in November just three days after the *Torch* landings, the Prime Minister, referring to the good news from North Africa, could at last say, 'This is not the end. It is not even the beginning of the end. But it is perhaps the end of the beginning.'

Thus it was that the British people, quietly and in keeping with their character, realized that after all their sacrifice the initiative was now with them and their allies. By its capture the Allies had taken the pounce and fire out of Axis strategy. Even the Führer had lost his old resilience, and, brooding, pallid and twitching in his gloomy underground headquarters in the East Prussian forest, relaxed only when, in the company of old Party comrades, he speculated on the fine things he would do after the war. In March he had still been peddling dreams and talking of sending Rommel back to Africa to capture Casablanca, but before April was out he knew that the troops and supplies he had flown into Tunisia during the past six months had been wasted. He talked now only of a limited offensive on the Eastern Front, was pessimistic, though indignant, about the air-war, and saw no present means of victory but to hold on stubbornly to every inch of conquered ground and use the submarine 'to cut the arteries of the enemy's war of movement.' So defensive-minded had he become that in January he resolved to lay up his fleet of powerful surface-raiders and rely solely on submarines. Only with the utmost difficulty had he been persuaded by his new naval chief, Dönitz, to retain the *Tirpitz, Scharnhorst* and *Lützow* for use against the Murmansk convoys and the defence of Norway. As for his fellow dictator, Mussolini, he was now a mere shadow of his old bombastic self; when he visited Hitler at the beginning of April, the latter found him a broken man, sick, frail and tired.

In his memoirs Churchill declared that, 'The only thing that really frightened me in the war was the U-boat peril.' In one battle, lasting from March 16th to 20th, 40 U-boats sank 22 out of the 90 ships in two convoys. Only one U-boat was sunk.

But that spring the tide turned at last in the battle that Churchill and his colleagues always knew must be won before Europe could be invaded. A fortnight before the *Torch* landings and in the month that saw the worst shipping losses of the war, the most famous of all British submarine officers, Max Horton, had been appointed to the chief naval command against the U-boat. From the headquarters of Western Approaches at Liverpool, acting in the closest co-operation with RAF Coastal Command, this great seaman, during the long stormy winter of 1942–3, prepared his plans for taking the offensive. Applying to undersea warfare the Nelsonian adage that the best defence of the country was to lay his ships alongside the enemy, he assembled, in the teeth of acute shortages, enough escort-vessels and escort-carriers to form six roving Support Groups, whose crews and pilots had been trained as teams with one object – the hunting and destruction of U-boats. By the end of March the Admiral was ready. Concentrating

281

them in the mid-ocean gap – the 'black pit' as the Germans called it – where long-range aircraft from Britain and Canada were still unable to shadow Dönitz's submarines, he loosed them on the wolf-packs as they dogged the convoys of slow-moving merchantmen. The hunters suddenly became the hunted.

Horton's dramatic switch from the defensive to the offensive was only made possible by the substitution of a unified North Atlantic authority for the divided control that had hitherto kept that ocean in separate British and American zones. With the British and Canadian Admiralties now solely responsible for the North Atlantic convoys and the American Admiralty for the US convoys to the Mediterranean and North Africa, a great change came over the U-boat battle. Shortly afterwards the gap of unpatrolled ocean in the centre of the Atlantic was closed by very long-range aircraft operating from Newfoundland and Iceland and able to afford daylight air-cover for the convoys in the area where the U-boats were not only most dangerous but also, by reason of their concentration, most vulnerable.

The effect on the overall strategic situation was as spectacular as it was on the morale of the till now triumphant U-boat crews. During April the Allied losses in the North Atlantic fell by fifty per cent while those of the U-boats rose more than fivefold. In May Horton decided to press home his advantage and ordered the convoys to steam straight through waters where the enemy's concentration was known to be greatest. The effect was a knock-out blow. One support group, aided by long-range RAF Liberators, sank half a dozen U-boats without losing a ship from the convoy they were shadowing. With forty submarines lost in two months – or nearly half his normal operational strength in the Atlantic–Dönitz withdrew his hunted packs to less dangerous waters. As he did so Coastal Command intensified its attack with the submarine's deadliest enemy, shore-based aircraft, on the transit lanes in the Bay of Biscay through which the submarines had to pass on their way from their French bases to their Atlantic killing grounds. In June the aircraft sank seven U-boats in the Bay alone, and the Allied losses in the Atlantic dropped to a twentieth of the March figure.

Another crucial factor was that in December 1941 the relevant German code had been broken and could now be read instantly. Furthermore, the British code, which the Germans had broken, was changed and a machine cypher was used, thus ensuring greater safety. For the moment, until new methods could be found to outwit their attackers, the U-boats had ceased to be a menace. Just as Trafalgar created the conditions for an invasion of Napoleon's Europe, so the victory of the British and Canadian Navies and of RAF Coastal Command in the battles of 'the Gap' and Bay of Biscay created conditions for an invasion of Hitler's. The Führer had lost his first line of defence.

* * *

Yet the Axis still possessed immense strength. It controlled all Europe and everything in it on wheels, from Biscay to the Donetz and from the North Cape to Sicily, the whole eastern littoral of Asia and every Pacific island from the Kuriles to the Central Solomons. Its hold on this vast territory could only be broken by fierce, concentrated, sustained attack by the sea powers. Because of this the hopes of mankind in the spring of 1943 turned, apart from Russian resistance, on two factors: the training and equipment of invasion armies and their supporting air-arms and the provision of shipping and assault-craft to deploy and maintain them. Where and when they should be deployed and how that shipping, still desperately restricted by the U-boats, should be used, was the responsibility of the President and Prime Minister and a half a dozen British and American professional soldiers, sailors and airmen. And in the last resort it was the two soldiers, Brooke and Marshall, who had to shoulder the responsibility of solving the hardest problem of all. For, though securing the passage of the seas and winning control of the air were the responsibility of their naval and air colleagues, the direction and supply of the invading armies were theirs.

At that moment the Chiefs of Staff were having to plan four invasions and their supply and reinforcement. Three of these – Sicily, Italy and Burma – had to be launched before the winter; the fourth, the most ambitious amphibious expedition ever attempted, within little more than a year.

Just two months after the Axis surrender in Tunis the invasion of Europe began, when the Allied armies landed in Sicily on July 10th; on September 3rd, the fourth anniversary of the outbreak of the war, Montgomery's Eighth Army came ashore on the Italian coast, while the American General Mark Clark and the Fifth Army landed at Salerno, just south of Naples, on September 9th. For Britain in particular the day before was one for subdued triumph as Italy surrendered, the first of the Axis powers to fall.

283

Sicily had taken only thirty-eight days to conquer, with a loss to the enemy of nearly 250,000 troops, a quarter of them German. The Allies had lost 31,000 men, most of them wounded and therefore able to fight again. But heavier, bloodier fighting lay ahead, in battles of Salerno, Anzio and Cassino. The Germans under Kesselring were not surrendering.

Events were moving rapidly nearly everywhere. In Russia the Germans, to shorten their lines and release troops for Italy and the Balkans, were still withdrawing along the entire southern front; on September 23rd the great city of Kharkov was retaken by the Russians; Smolensk followed on the 25th and Taganrog on the 30th.

In 1943 the German homeland began to endure massive bombardment from the Allied air forces – from the RAF at night and the US Army Air Force in the day. Berlin, Essen, Bremen, Hamburg, Dortmund, Dusseldorf, Schweinfurt and Regensburg were struck hard. In some raids the Allied loss of life was very high.

*   *   *

The rising tide of American war-production and the loss of Germany's superiority in arms and equipment caused Hitler to react vigorously. A month after the January Casablanca conference, as the implications of the Allies' Mediterranean campaign became clear, he had called to the total direction of his war industry a thirty-six-year-old architect named Albert Speer whom a year earlier he had made Minister of Munitions. To Speer, an organizer of genius, was given the task of overcoming the crisis by rapidly multiplying German and European arms production, by building a new U-boat fleet of revolutionary design and by the development of secret aerial weapons of shattering power. With these, and the measures he was taking to strengthen the Channel defences and build a central reserve, Hitler believed he would be able to throw the Allies into the sea as soon as they landed and inflict on them a defeat so calamitous that all further danger of invasion from the West would be at an end. With the advantage of interior lines, he would then be able to concentrate the whole, instead of only two-thirds of his army, against Russia and achieve in the east the decisive result he had been vainly seeking for the past two years.

As a result the summer and autumn of 1943 saw an immense increase in German arms production. Despite the mounting weight of the air offensive against the Ruhr and Rhineland, the output of field, anti-tank and anti-aircraft guns rose during the year from 12,000, to 27,000, of tanks and self-propelled guns from 6000 to 12,000, and of aircraft from 13,000 to 22,000. Had it not been for Bomber Command's sacrificial efforts these increases would have been even greater and their deployment far more rapid. A particularly serious threat to the Allies' coming offensive was the building of giant submarines able to travel at high speeds underwater and to attack convoys without exposing themselves to watching aircraft. Just as six months earlier the Combined Chiefs of Staff had accepted Brooke's thesis that no decisive attack on Europe was possible until the submarine threat had been mastered, so Hitler had resolved to stake everything on breaking the conveyor-belt between America and Europe. On July 8th, after a conference with Admiral Dönitz, he ordered production of the new U-boats to be given absolute priority.

Two days later the Führer gave Speer a more momentous order. Following successful experimental flights in Poland of pilotless, guided, jet-propelled flying-bombs and of long-range rockets projected through the stratosphere, instructions were given for the immediate large-scale production of both these weapons for launching against London and the southern English ports. On June 10th, following an ecstatic visit to the secret rocket-research station on the Baltic island of Peenemünde, Hitler informed his generals that they had only to hold out till Christmas for the British capital to be razed to the ground. Rumours of these developments had reached London through the Polish underground movement during the spring, and RAF reconnaissance planes had brought back photographs from Peenemünde of large mysterious cigar-shaped objects. The Chiefs of Staff had first considered the matter in April, and at their request a committee had been set up under the chairmanship of the Prime Minister's son-in-law, Duncan Sandys, to investigate the facts. It concluded that a definite threat existed and that Peenemünde experimental station should be bombed at the earliest possible date.

Thus, by the beginning of 1944, Hitler reckoned, London and the embarkation ports would be under a continuous bombardment from thousands of flying-bombs and rockets – both impossible to stop – the convoys bringing American reinforcements and supplies to Europe would be at the mercy of his new submarines, and a striking reserve of twenty mobile divisions, in addition to the forty or fifty already stationed behind the Atlantic Wall, would be waiting to throw the western invaders into the sea. Yet at this moment, impervious to the fact that the Führer, with his three hundred million subjects and serfs and magnificent east-to-west communications, was certain to be planning counter-measures against their impending blow at his heart, the Americans – to whom all things now seemed possible – were allocating ever more men, ships, planes and assault-craft to Pacific campaigns whose logistics necessitated ocean supply lines far longer even than those with which the Germans were struggling in Russia. And, once launched, these were bound to absorb men and resources needed to ensure success in Europe. Already, despite the decision that Germany should be attacked first, there were thirteen American divisions in the Pacific to ten in the United Kingdom and Mediterranean, while only three or, at the outside, four of these could be deployed against Italy owing to shortages of assault-craft and shipping.

The first week of June 1944 marked the culmination of the Allied powers' strategy in Europe. On June 4th their victorious armies entered Rome and, two days before, the first American heavy bombers flying from Italy, landed on Russian soil on a shuttle-bombing mission that was to bring every corner of the Reich within reach of Allied air attack.

The Allied armies were about to strike at Normandy in the most ambitious action of the war, Operation *Overlord*, when they would try to break through Hitler's Atlantic Wall. Everything depended on whether the forces waiting in England to take advantage of this moment could force a landing in the teeth of the tremendous obstacles facing them, consolidate their bridgehead and break out before the winter. A few months earlier, in Brooke's view, none of these things had been possible. There had not been enough assault-craft to land on a front sufficiently wide to be held; the railway system between France and Germany had still to be smashed; the Luftwaffe had not been driven from the skies; and the means were almost totally lacking for building up the invaders' resources fast enough to contain the enemy's counter-attack. The first indispensable step had been to win the Battle of the Atlantic and remove the U-boat threat to the Allies' sea-lanes. The second had been to gain unchallenged command of the air, not only over the Channel and landing-beaches but over the rail and road communications of Northern France. During April and May the great Allied air sweep against the French railways for which Portal, Tedder, and Leigh-Mallory had contended so stubbornly succeeded beyond all expectation. Fifteen hundred of the two thousand engines of the *Région Nord* were immobilized and all but four of the eighty selected transport targets wrecked or destroyed. In a few weeks the whole of Northern

France was made a 'railway desert'. And it was done with such skill that no indication was given of the direction of the impending attack, which the German Command, fearing for the Belgian plain and the Ruhr, believed would fall on the Pas de Calais, where it continued to keep its best divisions. During May and the first days of June the Allies turned their attention to the Seine bridges, destroying eighteen of the twenty-four between Paris and the sea and damaging three more, so ensuring that there should be no quick reinforcement of the German forces west of that river. During the same period the enemy's radar warning system was almost completely paralysed. By June 5th only one in six of the coastal installations between Calais and Brittany was working.

While this great air victory was being won, the concentration of men, ships and material in England's ports was protected from German air observation. 'No one,' wrote an American officer serving in the Liberation armies, 'who had had a dose of enemy air action against one of our ports in the Mediterranean could believe that the invasion fleet would ever put to sea intact . . . We saw the tiny harbours along the south coast and the big sprawling harbour of Southampton packed like miniature Pearl Harbors, with ships stacked gunwale to gunwale. They had to crawl so close to one another that it did not seem as if a bomber could drop a pea and miss one.' All this assembly of maritime and military strength – so long planned and debated – had taken shape since December and the appointment of the Supreme Commander General Eisenhower and his operational Commanders-in-Chief. At the beginning of the year there had not been enough ships to meet even the requirements of the narrow front, three-division landing allowed for by the planners. By June the thousand craft allocated to the operation by the United States had risen to nearly two thousand five hundred, manned by more than 100,000 seamen, including three battleships and three cruisers which at the eleventh hour a reluctant Admiral King had released to join the four British battleships and twenty-one cruisers scheduled for the preliminary bombardment. In all more than five thousand ships and fourteen thousand aircraft were engaged and over a million picked troops, organized in 37 divisions, half of them American and half British and Canadian.

Yet the assembly, training and equipment of this vast force had been only the beginning. The Allies had now to do what no one had done since William the Conqueror, and what Philip of Spain, Louis XIV, Napoleon and Hitler had all attempted in vain. In two days they had to transport across the stormy tidal waters of the Channel, without hurt from U-boat, mine, E-boat or Luftwaffe, nearly 200,000 armed men and land them with 20,000 mechanical vehicles on open beaches along a fifty-mile stretch of fortified coast, negotiating a complex network of undersea obstacles and immobilizing shore defences of immense strength. Ever since November, when Germany's most original-minded commander, Field-Marshal Rommel, had been sent to organize the Channel defences under von Rundstedt, Supreme Commander in the West, half a million troops and conscript workers had been toiling to strengthen the 'Atlantic Wall'. The tidal stretches before the beaches had been strewn with steel and concrete wrecking devices, the sands and roads into the interior had been mined and barred by fortifications and tank traps, while every accessible landing-place was enfiladed by the fire of hidden batteries and the level spaces behind the coastline studded with wooden posts to prevent airborne landings. And though, thanks to Alexander's persistent attacks in the south, the Germans had been unable to transfer troops from Italy to the Channel coast and had even been forced to send half-a-dozen more divisions to that country, since the halting of the Russian winter offensive by the spring thaw they had been steadily reinforcing Northern France. In January twenty-four of their thirty-two Panzer divisions had been in Russia and only eight on other fronts; by June there were only eighteen facing the Red Army, while twelve were either in France or on their way there, three of them within striking distance of the Normandy coast and three more just beyond the Seine and Loire.

With so much to achieve and at stake it was inevitable that those responsible should have fears for the issue. Even the Americans, who two years earlier had wished to embark on it before their forces had been trained and equipped and before almost any of the logistical wherewithal to make it possible were available, were now assailed by doubts. Three weeks before the convoys were due to sail, Eisenhower's naval ADC was told by Bedell Smith that the chances of being able to hold the bridgehead were no more than fifty-fifty. 'Will the Channel run red with blood?' he asked in his diary. During those tense days of spring he noted how his chief, whose cheerful confidence sustained everyone, looked increasingly worn and tired.

The boldest of the Allied leaders – the apostle of attack and victory – had always believed that a cross-Channel invasion would be attended by appalling casualties. 'The possibility of Hitler's gaining a victory in France cannot be excluded,' the Prime Minister had written at the beginning of the year; 'the hazards of battle are very great.' Haunted by the massacres of the great frontal attacks of the First World War, he had never ceased to hope that their repetition could be avoided by a less costly approach through southern Europe, unlike Brooke, who, for all his insistence on a Mediterranean strategy as the indispensable preliminary to *Overlord*, believed that only through the latter could the fighting power of the Wehrmacht be broken. As late as May 3rd, only a month before D-Day, Churchill had confided to the assembled Dominions' Prime Ministers that, if he had had his own way, the lay-out of the war would have been different and he would have rolled up Europe from the south-east to join hands with the Russians. Yet, as always he accepted, and rose to, the challenge. At the first presentation of invasion plans on April 7th, General de Guingand noticed that when he spoke he at first appeared grave and tired but that 'he finished with great strength.' Five days later the Prime Minister wrote to Dill in Washington that he had 'hardened very much upon *Overlord* and was further fortified by the evident confidence of Eisenhower, Brooke and Montgomery.' 'I am in this thing with you to the end,' he told Eisenhower on May 8th, his eyes filling with tears, 'and, if it fails, we will go down together.'

Bad weather had caused the sailing of the invasion craft to be postponed from the 5th to the 6th of June. From all along the south-east, south and south-west coast they came, from those same ports to which the Dunkirk survivors had sailed four years before – from Fowey and Falmouth, Portland and Poole, Southampton and Shoreham – to gather at Area Z (nicknamed 'Piccadilly Circus') on their charts and then to make for the beaches. In that gigantic fleet off Normandy were battleships, including *Warspite* and *Ramillies*, sturdy veterans of the First World War, whose guns were to be of immense value bombarding the Wehrmacht up to twenty miles inland. Joining the fleet later was another group of warships, looking melancholy in their stripped, gunless state, whose last nautical service was to act as half-sunk break-waters in an artificial harbour.

While the main attackers sailed through the night to the five beaches, US and British airborne divisions were dropped successfully over the battle zone. A major deception plan in the east to attract German attention to the Pas de Calais area was brilliantly effective.

At around 6.30 am the first troops were coming ashore from their landing-craft; the operation on which the fate of the war depended had started. In England, the Chief of the Imperial General Staff, Field-Marshal Sir Alan Brooke, was to record in his diary:

> *June 6th.* By 7.30 am, I began to receive first news of the invasion. The airborne landings had been successful, the first waves were reported as going in, opposition not too serious, batteries firing from flanks, etc.
>
> 'Throughout the day information has come in. On the British front the landing has gone well and the whole of three divisions are ashore. On the American front the western landing was a success, but the eastern Corps has failed practically along its whole front. They are now asking to land on our western beaches. This will probably have to be done, but must inevitably lead to confusion on the beaches.
>
> It has been very hard to realize all day that whilst London went on calmly with its job, a fierce conflict was being fought at a close distance on the French coast.

At the end of that first critical day the news was better than had seemed possible when the weather closed in on the Channel at the week-end, though it was less good than had been hoped. Complete surprise had been achieved, partly because the gale that had postponed the landing had given the German Command a false sense of security. The preliminary sea and air bombardment and the specialized armour and swimming tanks that had landed with the infantry had been brilliantly successful, while the Luftwaffe had been swept from the skies, and at sea enemy interference had been negligible. The British had made firm lodgements in all their three sectors, penetrating inland at some points for five or six miles. Their airborne division had achieved nearly all its objectives, including the capture of the Orne bridges and of a precarious bridgehead beyond, thus giving protection to the vulnerable eastern flank where the German armoured counter-attack was expected. But it had still to be relieved by the seaborne infantry and had had to fight grimly all day to hold its positions, while an attempt to seize Caen – the all-important road centre through which the Panzers would have to move in for the kill – and the airfields beyond had failed. And though, despite delays, the British had taken most of their D-Day objectives, the Americans on the western flank had been less fortunate. One of their two landings had nearly ended in disaster, and for several hours the troops had been pinned down on the beaches. At the end of the day the beachhead here was still little more than a thousand yards deep and cut off both from the British to the east and the rest of the Americans to the west. With unloading everywhere from eight to twelve hours behind schedule because of the weather, everything turned on the speed and strength of the enemy's counter-attack and the weight of armour he could throw against the still confused forces in the isolated bridgeheads.

> *June 7th.* The invasion is a day older. I am not very happy about it. The American V Corps seems to be stuck. We are not gaining enough ground and German forces are assembling fast. I do wish to Heaven that we were landing on a wider front.

Although the bridgehead was strengthened and made safe it was to be seven weeks before a break out could be achieved which would free France and the Low Countries and also bring relief to the people of southern England from Hitler's terror weapons.

The invasion of Normandy coincided almost exactly with the arrival of the first of these weapons – the V1 flying bombs. This was on June 13th and until the Pas de Calais launching sites were overrun at the end of August the inhabitants of southern England, especially Londoners, endured their second great blitz, with 2,400 bombs falling on the London region alone, by day and night.

About two weeks after the V1s ceased, the first V2 rocket fell on Chiswick in West London on September 8th. These ballistic missiles, with the noise of their coming not heard until after they had landed, were to prove an even more terrifying weapon than the V1. Launched mainly from Holland, they continued to fall throughout the winter until March 29th, when the last one landed on Orpington in Kent. With 9,000 civilians killed and 25,000 injured, and fifty per cent of the British air effort devoted at one time to trying to stop them, Hitler's newest weapons exacted a disturbingly high toll of death, injury and destruction.

While these great events had been taking place in Europe, the British Fourteenth Army led by General Slim in Burma was fighting a lonely war to make India safe from Japanese invasion. The government had decided reluctantly to postpone a landing to recapture Rangoon, which had been planned to follow those of Sicily and Italy in 1943, until after the end of the war in Europe. Slim was now left to reconquer Burma, if he could, by driving the enemy with such troops as he already possessed out of the mountains and jungles across which he had retreated in 1942.

In March 1944 the Japanese Fifteenth Army attacked with the

intention of forcing Slim to retreat into India. By skilful infiltration it succeeded in advancing and then surrounding the key points of Imphal and Kohima. But Slim's British and Indian troops broke the sieges and by the end of June had begun their long advance into central Burma, which resulted in the destruction of the Fifteenth Army, the capture of Mandalay in March 1945 and of Rangoon in the following May.

The Fourteenth Army had fought and won the biggest land campaign of the war against the Japanese, a cunning, resourceful and barbarous enemy, and in alien conditions; its achievements were among the most brilliant and heroic in British military history. But Burma was far away and out of the limelight and the men of the Fourteenth Army were largely forgotten, except by their families at home.

After the break out from Normandy the British, Canadian and United States forces advanced steadily across France and into Belgium. On August 15th the Allies landed in the South of France, an invasion which for months had been a subject of dissent among the planners because of concern about its likely effect on the campaigns in northern France and northern Italy. But the northern forces liberated Paris on August 25th, followed by Brussels on September 3rd and Antwerp on the 4th. There were expectations among some leaders that the enemy could not last another winter.

Yet throughout the autumn and early winter there was stalemate in France and the Low Countries, and it was clear that the war would continue into 1945. There had been failure to strike at the Ruhr in early September, which was accompanied by a simultaneous failure to free the mouth of the Scheldt and make use of Antwerp. This great port was not in fact working until the end of November, though its earlier use would have had a profound effect on the speed of the Allies' efforts.

This loss of initiative, even if temporary, had allowed Hitler to husband a new army of young fanatics and to plan a second blitzkrieg, using them and his Panzer and Parachute units. On December 16th, in the dead of winter and with complete surprise, his chosen point of attack was the same hilly and wooded Ardennes across which the first blitzkrieg had been launched in 1940 and where he now judged the Allies to be at their weakest. He would aim for Brussels and Antwerp, turn and encircle the British and destroy them, and then deal with the Americans, as he had dealt with the French after Dunkirk.

It was his last throw and it nearly succeeded, but, thanks to the American fighting man's tenacity and the British Commander-in-

Chief's prescience, the Panzers never reached the Allied petrol dumps where they were to have refuelled for the final drive across the Belgian plain. By December 26th the advance was at an end and by mid-January their salient, the 'Bulge', was eliminated. There was no doubt that the Americans had had a severe shock. Their commanders had chosen to ignore the two most elementary rules of war – concentration and the possession of a reserve to counter the enemy's moves and keep the initiative. As a result, though Germany was all but broken, it had been able, like a wounded tiger, to inflict on them grave injuries. Their casualties had amounted to over 75,000 men, of whom 19,000 were dead.

But the British, who had so repeatedly warned them, had had a worse shock. And they took longer to recover from it. With their man-power and resources all but exhausted after five years of war and with no possibility of making good further losses, they had staked everything on an early victory in the West and had seen it, as they felt, thrown away by the inexperience of the American High Command. The war, instead of ending in 1944, had been prolonged into another year and, unless a very different method of conducting it was now to be adopted, seemed likely to continue until, not only their own position, but that of Europe was desperate. Eisenhower's statement at his meeting with the British Chiefs of Staff on December 12th that he did not expect to cross the Rhine before May had been almost as grave a blow to Churchill and to them as the German offensive that had followed.

There seemed only one remedy: to induce the American High Command, while shaken by its reverse, to concentrate at last on a single decisive blow and to prevent Eisenhower and Bradley from again indulging their preference for attacking everywhere at once. And this, as Brooke was aware, could only be achieved by persuasion; with more than fifty American divisions already in France to the Commonwealth's fifteen, it was not in Britain's power to dictate. Her ally had had a lesson, and it was possible that, having seen the consequences of their strategy, the American leaders might now take advice. Yet unless it was tactfully tendered, such advice was more likely to offend than persuade.

There was now a serious difference of opinion between the Allies about the pace and direction of their advance into Germany. Politically, too, there were other matters which caused the British concern.

During the Warsaw rising in August, the Kremlin had behaved with gross inhumanity, not only making no attempt to use its armies –

then only a few miles away – to aid the Polish insurgents but flatly refusing to allow the British and American air forces landing-fields from which to drop supplies on the city. As a result the rising had been crushed with the slaughter of 200,000 Poles, including the flower of those who might have re-created an independent Poland after the war, while a number of British and American airmen had needlessly lost their lives. Stalin's contemptuous excuse – so far as he deigned to give any – was that the Polish Home Army was worthless and led by irresponsible 'criminals' and 'adventurers'.

A few days before the Warsaw rising the Red Army had captured the Polish city of Lublin and had at once set up there, in opposition to the exiled Polish Government in London, a 'National Committee of Liberation' of Moscow-trained Communists. Behind this façade the Kremlin now proposed to re-draw Poland's frontiers so as to incorporate nearly half its pre-war territory in Russia while it denounced the Polish Ministers in London as fascists and traitors. As Great Britain had gone to war to preserve the independence of Poland and had given shelter to its Government and Army in exile, Churchill was faced by a grave moral challenge.

He met it with his habitual courage, proposing an immediate visit to Moscow and using his powers of persuasion to induce the Polish Prime Minister, Mikolajczyk, a man of moderation and goodwill, to meet the Russians half-way and collaborate with the hated Lublin Committee. In this he received small encouragement from Roosevelt, who was determined to do nothing that might injure the prospects of an American-Russian working understanding which was his recipe for the future governance of mankind.

At the end of March 1945 the Supreme Commander sent a telegram direct to Stalin to try to coordinate his offensive with the Russians'. The British considered that he had no business to do so and that the implications of its contents represented a change from what had previously been agreed on.

For the British, Eisenhower's telegram was one more disappointment and source of disillusion. Having gone to war in defence of Poland and the liberties of Europe at a time when Russia was in league with the aggressor and America concerned only with her own neutrality, they were now, with six years of struggle crowned by victory, forced to witness at the dictate of one of their principal allies the needless subjection of the whole of Eastern Europe to the totalitarian tyranny of the other. On March 28th, four days after Montgomery had crossed the Rhine and while strong German forces still barred the Russians' road to Berlin and Vienna, the Western Allies were confronted only by spasmodic resistance from a disintegrating, defeated Army whose mobility had been broken by their overwhelming air power and whose morale by the battle of the Rhineland and Westphalia in which it had lost, since the beginning of the month, 300,000 prisoners. On that day Montgomery's bridgehead was 35 miles wide and 25 miles deep, with twenty divisions and 1500 tanks already across the river, while the Americans had taken Frankfurt and Mannheim and Hodges's and Patton's armour was sweeping north-eastwards to encircle the Ruhr and join Simpson's Ninth Army in the rear of Model's routed forces. The green lights, it seemed, were clear for the long-awaited drive across the Hanover plains to the Elbe and Berlin – the goal of every Allied soldier since the start of the Western counter-attack at Alamein two and a half years before. 'My intention,' Montgomery had telegraphed the CIGS, on March 27th, 'is to drive hard for the line of the Elbe . . . I have ordered Ninth and Second Armies to move armoured and mobile forces at once and to get through to the Elbe with utmost speed and drive. The situation looks good and events should begin to move rapidly in a few days . . . My tactical HQ moves will be Wesel-Munster-Herford-Hanover – thence via the *autobahn* to Berlin, I hope.'

Yet on that very day, without reference to the Combined Chiefs of Staff or a word to the Commander-in-Chief of the British forces which still constituted nearly a third of his army, Eisenhower despatched a telegram to Stalin informing him that he proposed, after encircling the Ruhr, to concentrate in central Germany for an advance, on an Erfurt-Leipzig axis, towards the Upper Elbe, there to await the arrival of the Russians. His object, he explained, was to cut Germany in half, separate its northern defenders from its southern and thereafter concentrate his main forces against the supposed 'National Redoubt' in the Austrian Alps, in which, it was rumoured, Hitler and the Nazi fanatics intended to hold out until new secret weapons or a split in the Grand Alliance came to their aid.

In April the German armies throughout the Fatherland began to collapse. As Hitler took personal command of the Berlin defences, sixteen-year-old boys were being conscripted, Himmler was offering a general surrender to the Western Allies only, and the Russians drew nearer to the capital.

Although American and Russian soldiers met on April 25th at Torgau on the Elbe, some 50 miles south of Berlin, this was the nearest the Western Allied forces came to Berlin before the final surrender. This arose from Eisenhower's decision to halt the armies under his command without attempting to capture Berlin and Prague, which lay within their grasp. With Hitler dead by his own hand, the Russians in Berlin, and the German forces in Holland, Denmark and north-west Germany having surrendered to Montgomery on May 5th, the new Führer, Grand-Admiral Dönitz, ordered the surrender of all the German forces. On May 7th the surrender was signed at Rheims, thus ending the war in Europe.

But the ferocious war in the Far East continued until it was ended by the atomic bombs which fell on Hiroshima and Nagasaki in August. The conflict in that theatre had been calamitous for Britain, except for the magnificent successes and fighting qualities of Slim's Fourteenth Army and the fortitude in their prison hell of the men, women and children captured in Hong Kong, Malaya and Singapore and held by the Japanese for nearly four years.

*   *   *

The Second World War had begun with cavalry actions in Poland and ended with nuclear fission above Japan. It had brought to an end the unspeakable infamy of Belsen and Dachau and had showed mankind at its noblest in the bravery of the Resistance. It had indeed been total war, as much a civilian as a military conflict. Now the British people could at last be jubilant and, as Churchill told them on VE-Day, 'This is your victory'.

Soon they would be demobilized from the Services or end their civilian war work and turn to rebuilding their homes and their lives. For many the injustice which had afflicted them and had disgraced the nation before 1939 was still evident, but it was for justice in its various roles that they had fought, endured and triumphed. Accompanying the resolution that the dictators had to be defeated was a general will that sought to create sound social structures for employment, education, health and insurance, a will which Churchill and his coalition government encouraged when they inspired the Beveridge and other reports and the Butler 1944 Education Act. As well as breaking bodies and lives this war had, unlike that of 1914–18, broken the harshness of English social attitudes and encouraged the function of democracy.

*   *   *

To win this, the greatest war in their history, the people had been led by a parliamentary leader of genius.

No statesman save Alfred has done England such service as Church-ill. In the summer of 1940 his courage made her the hope of the world. His whole career had been an essay in fighting back from disaster. 'You ask,' as he had said when the German armies were driving through the broken lines of France, 'what is our aim? I can answer in one word: Victory – victory at all costs, victory in spite of all terrors, victory, however long and hard the road may be.' His resolve to attack the colossus dominating Europe at any point within reach was then the only policy. So long as the Navy held the narrow seas and the RAF the air above, the enemy, for all his immense strength, could bring Britain no lower than she already was. Every attack on her mighty adversary, however daring, could serve only to revive and rouse her people's courage and offensive spirit.

The Prime Minister's virtues as a war leader were immense. The higher the tide of trouble rose, the higher rose his courage. His nerves never failed, and the worst of disasters left his sleep and appetite unimpaired. He had the imagination to foresee dangers and opportunit-ies that others would have missed and the drive to ensure that neither took the country unawares. He would never take No for an answer. For five years he was a spur in the flanks of every military and civil commander in the land.

He was an orator, a poet and a sage with a taste for splendour and good living, an aristocrat who possessed the common touch that the English like to see in their rulers. For all his eighteenth-century eloquence and Victorian imperialism, he was the ideal champion for a people whose favourite song was 'The Lambeth Walk' and whose pet hobby a daily flutter on a horse. They liked his cigar, his glass of brandy, his bulldog face and figure, the twinkle in his eye. They loved his humour, his way of pronouncing foreign names, his indomitable courage. Above all, he had the power to touch chords in men's hearts that transcended politics. His sense of history never failed. He believed in a Providence that worked through human instruments and, like Elizabeth and Cromwell, he made the people he led believe in it too. He bade them be 'unyielding, persevering, indomitable, in the overthrow of another continental tyranny as in the olden times.'

His failings as a leader were impatience and impetuosity. The qualities that made him so great in adversity – the insistence on fighting back at all points, the obsession with attack, the tireless energy, the soaring imagination – sometimes made him essay enterprises which, had he not been dissuaded, would have ended in disaster. Nor, since he always threw the whole of his heart and head at the nearest fence, was he good at choosing between conflicting objectives – a choice which became increasingly important as Britain's resources and those of her allies began to offer a chance of wresting the initiative from the enemy. After 1941 any needless dispersal of force, any commitment that could drain away resources that might be needed at the decisive point at the decisive moment, might have deferred victory for a long time and, perhaps, for ever. Churchill's eloquence and persistence then became something of a problem to his military advisers. It was hard for them to concentrate and build up reserves and a striking-force for the future when he was always seeking, and with such intensity, to use them at once against the nearest foe.

The wartime dictatorship entrusted by Parliament to Churchill was the answer for which Britain and the free world had been waiting. After the braggarts and appeasers had failed to stem the tide of tyranny, it met Hitler's resolve and daring with a resolve and daring as ruthless as his own. Yet all dictatorships carry the defects of their qualities, creating deserts around the wielder of power. And, as Napoleon's fate proved, no single man, whatever his genius, can wage war without sooner or later making fatal mistakes unless he submits himself to the correction of facts and of others who know facts which he cannot know himself. Perhaps the greatest of all Churchill's claims to the gratitude of his country is that, though he had the power to be a dictator in the day-to-day conduct of the war, he refused to be one. That a leader so interested in strategy and the most detailed military matters, should for four years have endured the restraint of an official adviser, Brooke, so often in disagreement with himself and whom he could have dismissed at any time he chose, and that he should never once have overruled him and the Chiefs of Staff in a major military decision, is a tribute not only to his magnanimity, but to the genius of the nation's parliamentary system and Churchill's profound respect for it. Throughout those years of strain and trial, he remained true to England's tradition of consultation and ordered freedom. He constantly helped to form military decisions yet never dictated them. Had Hitler, also a man of intuitive genius, shown the same restraint and wisdom, the war might have ended very differently.

In the 1945 election, however, the people dismissed him from office. The brave old man had had his day and the world seemed a less troubled and safer place by all he had achieved. His passing from Downing Street in the hour of victory was almost as great a portent as the atomic bomb, and as astonishing. But for Churchill himself he took his defeat as might have been expected, with good humour and magnanimity, characteristics which had always shown his warm humanity. In 1945 the people no longer needed the man of 1940. It may have seemed ungrateful to dismiss him so peremptorily but they no longer had occasion for a Chatham at 10 Downing Street; they sought statesmen of a more domestic and homely kind. They quickly obtained them.

SUBJECT INDEX

Battles, treaties, etc., denoted by place names will be found in the Persons and Places index.

Afrika Korps, 275, 280
agriculture: post-Napoleonic wars, 19–23, 42–3, 46, 54, 74; golden age, 105, 137–8, 191–2; depression (1880s), 191–3; 1st WW and after, 245, 261; West Indies, 223–4; *see also* food; landowners; wages
Air Force, British *see* Royal Air Force
Air Force, German *see* Luftwaffe
Air Force, Italian, 274, 275
Air Force, United States (Army), 284, 286, 294
Amalgamated Society of Engineers, 159, 162–3
American Civil War, 74, 147, 154, 214
American War of Independence, 45, 68, 194, 195
Anglo-American Trade Agreement (1938), 262
Answers, 172
Anti-Corn Law League, 100, 101, 102
armaments industry, 43–4, 264; 2nd WW, 268–72, 284–5
Army, British: post-Napoleonic wars, 43, 45–6, 52; civil aid (19th C.), 56, 61–2, 64, 71, 88, 89, 110; at Great Exhibition, 113–14; uniforms, 119; Crimea, 122–3; size c. 1871, 197; 1st WW, 240–51; 2nd WW (Europe), 268–72, 276, 289–91, 292–3, 295; Far East, 277–8, 291–2

Army, Canadian, 292
Army, French: 2nd WW, 272, 274, 275
Army, German: 1st WW, 234, 240, 245–9, 250, 252; 2nd WW (Europe), 270, 277, 284, 288–91, 292–3, 295–6; North Africa, 275, 279–81
Army, Italian: 2nd WW, 274–5, 280, 284
Army, Japanese: 2nd WW, 277–8, 291–2
Army, Russian *see* Red Army
Army, United States: 2nd WW, 275, 286, 287–8, 289–91, 292–3, 295–6
Artisans' Dwelling Bill (1875), 161
Atlantic Wall, 285, 288
atomic bombs, 296

Balfour Act (1900), 171
banks: 19th C., 47, 51, 53, 54, 177; Bank Act (1844), 108; Bank of England, 46, 48, 260
Battle of Britain (1940), 273–4
Benthamism *see* Bentham, Jeremy
Berlin Congress (1878), 198
Bible, the, 7
Birmingham Mail, 172
'black and tans', 257
'Bloody Sunday' (1887), 166
Boers and Boer War, 202–4, 217–18, 220–2, 223, 224, 226, 229

Housing of the Working Classes Act (1890), 173
Hussars, 113

I. Zingari cricket club, 131
Illustrated London News, 93, 152, 172
Imperial Conference (1932), 261
Independent Labour Party *see* Labour Party
Indian Civil Service (ICS), 23
industry: early growth *see* Industrial revolution; factory regulation *see* Factory Acts; recession and recovery (19th C.), 43–4, 48–9, 59, 90, 108–9, 191; Victorian expansion, 108–9, 175–6; continental expansion, 197, 231–3; post-WW1 decline, 258–60; *see also* coal; iron; textile industries; trade and commerce
Industrial Revolution: growth of industry, 27–8, 58, 75–6, 80; effects on society, 17, 31–5, 40–1, 50, 58–9, 77–81, 83–90
inflation, 37–8, 47, 50
institutions: British, 239–40
Irish Nationalist Party, 205–6, 209
iron industry, 27, 44, 55, 75, 98, 173, *see also* ships
Italo-Abyssinian war (1935–6), 265–6

Jacobin revolution, 60–1, 64
Jameson Raid (1896), 222

Kellog Pact (1929), 264

labour exchanges, 189
Labour Party, 180, 186, 259, 260
laissez-faire see trade and commerce
Lancers, 114
Land League, 206
landowners and gentry: traditional role, 4–6, 22, 66–7, 73, 124, 137; new outlook (19th C.), 35–40, 42–3, 90, 95, 99, 100, 160, 177–8; careers, 145; private ownership question, 180–1; farming depression (1880s), 191–3
League of Nations, 264, 265

Liberal Party (from c. 1832): before 1832 *see* Whig Party; under Palmerston, 136; and franchise, 155, 156; under Gladstone, 158, 198; Trade Disputes Act, 162; and Civil Service, 168; education reform, 170, 171; fiscal measures, 176, 189; social reform, 189; foreign policies, 196, 198; Irish question, 204, 207, 208, 209; under Campbell-Bannerman, 186; free trade, 226, 227, 261; support for Labour, 259, 260, 261, 263
Liberator aircraft, 282
Life Guards, 4, 56, 166
Light Brigade, 123
Liverpool Daily Post, 172
Lloyds of London, 239
local government, 134, 172–5; *see also* municipal reform
Local Government Act (1888), 172
Locarno Pact (1925), 263–4, 266
Lords, House of, 2, 21, 65, 73, 189
Lublin Committee, 294
Luftwaffe, 268, 273–4, 286, 290
Lützow, 281

mail-coaches, 11, 30, 58, 94
Marxism, 35, *see also* Marx, Karl
Mechanic's Magazine, 98
medical care *see* health
Merrie England, 188
Methodism, 187
Metropolitan Board of Works, 135
Militia Bill (1852), 119–20
Monarchy, the: 19th C., 2, 63–4, 65, 106, 111, 152–3
Municipal Corporation Act (1835), 74
municipal reform and services, 74, 161, 170–8, 189, 220, 238, 260; *see also* State, the
music: English love of, 16–17; at Great Exhibition, 114; Hallé concerts, 131; wartime songs, 249, 253
music halls and pantomime, 132, 183–5, 220

National Debt, 46–8, 54, 70, 176

PERSONS AND PLACES INDEX

1st WW indicates the First World War; equally 2nd WW indicates the Second World War

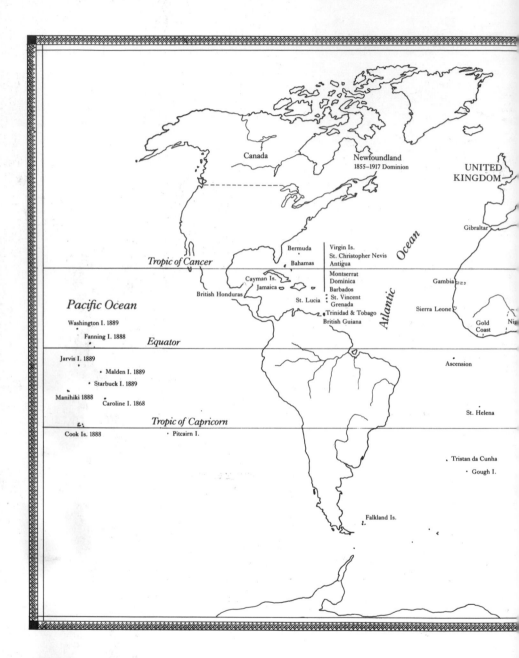

Canada

Newfoundland
1855–1917 Dominion

UNITED
KINGDOM

Gibraltar

Tropic of Cancer

Bermuda

Bahamas

Virgin Is.
St. Christopher Nevis
Antigua

Cayman Is.

Jamaica

British Honduras

St. Lucia

Montserrat
Dominica
Barbados
St. Vincent
Grenada
Trinidad & Tobago
British Guiana

Gambia

Sierra Leone

Gold
Coast

Nig

Atlantic Ocean

Pacific Ocean

Washington I. 1889

Fanning I. 1888

Equator

Jarvis I. 1889

Malden I. 1889

Starbuck I. 1889

Manihiki 1888

Caroline I. 1868

Tropic of Capricorn

Cook Is. 1888

Pitcairn I.

Ascension

St. Helena

Tristan da Cunha

Gough I.

Falkland Is.